The Prince
of
Castle Nowhere

Crayon drawing of Sam Hill by Gabrielle D. Clements, dated 1889. (Courtesy of Mrs. John Cabot.)

SAM HILL

The Prince of Castle Nowhere

John E. Tuhy

TIMBER PRESS
Portland, Oregon
1983

To Ellen Welsh, without whose tireless work in cataloguing Sam Hill's papers I would never have started this biography, and to Mildred, for ever so many reasons.

© 1983 by Timber Press
All rights reserved.
Printed in the United States of America
ISBN 0-917304-77-2

TIMBER PRESS
P.O. Box 1631
Beaverton, Oregon 97075

Contents

Preface

Biographies may variously be scholarly, "official," "muckraking," or re-habilitative (applied to a subject who has slipped undeservedly into oblivion, or near to it). This story is intended to be in the last class: to rekindle interest in a most unusual personality.

Most biographies lend themselves well to a chronological approach: not so with Sam Hill. Especially in the latter half of his long life, his pursuits, peculiarities, travels, feuds and friendships, accomplishments and failures, raced side by side. A year-by-year account would surely leave the reader more confused than the method the author has chosen.

If Sam Hill had never existed, it would not have been necessary to invent him: in fact, it would have been next to impossible. By definition, a self-made man must learn on the job, and he does not necessarily get better at it as years go by. Sam did not; he was his own complicated invention which eventually exploded. The sparks have long since faded and most of the witnesses are gone. One can only tell of the forgotten, spectacular, and flawed display with wonder and pity, or with disapproval perhaps mingled with a touch of envy.

Goodnight sweet prince, plagued not by doubt but by venturing too much. Shall we ever see your like again?

J.E.T.

Acknowledgements

Sternly repressing the secret conviction that no one reads an author's acknowledgements except those who expect and/or deserve to see their names there, I hasten to express my appreciation to the many people who helped in some way with this biography, often giving aid so essential that the work would have faltered or foundered without it.

My wife and daughters rallied 'round loyally in reading and commenting on the text, sometimes with disconcerting candor. Mildred photostated Sam's correspondence and helped in many other ways. Daughter Kathleen Nelson, abetted by Jean Eggenschweiler, made many corrections and suggestions for improvements in the text. Daughter Eileen did the translations from the French and was the legal consultant.

Ellen Welsh catalogued more than 5,000 letters and other papers at Maryhill Museum and in her home. She made copies of these available to me, often adding memos about important and interesting details of Sam Hill's life.

Patty Krier and I agreed in 1978 to collaborate on this book. She later decided to pursue graduate work in history at the Universty of Oregon, but generously contributed her notes and ideas on the chapters on good roads.

Jeffrey Grass, managing editor of the Oregon State University Press, gave much appreciated advice. To Dick Abel, editor and publisher, belongs the credit for the final shortened form of the book and elimination of thickets of verbosity, not to mention, lamentably, certain puns and passages of rich beautiful prose. In the rendering of the text, which the lard made a mite too long, only occasionally did my intransigence stand me in good stet.

Nicky Tom, then a member of the board of Maryhill Museum, persuaded me to undertake the biography and introduced me to Hisako Yoshinari, whose assistance with the chapter on Japan was most welcome.

Lois David Plotts met with me several times to discuss the project. Her booklet, *Sam Hill, Maryhill, and Me* was a valuable resource, especially for the chapter, "The Promised Land." Pete May, former editor of the *Goldendale Sentinel,* contributed to that and other chapters, and took time to show me landmarks of Maryhill Ranch. Edgar Babcock assisted with preparation of maps of the Maryhill area and identification of photographs, as well as furnishing personal recollections of Sam Hill and Edgar's father, Charles Babcock.

A Bibliography is given at the end of the book. References to Albro Martin's authoritative biography of James J. Hill are found throughout this volume, as are quotations from the two volumes of reminiscences of Clar-

8

ence Barron. The *Oregon Journal* columns of Fred Lockley, extending from 1915 to 1952, proved an essential source for Sam's early history, philosophy, and travels. Harcourt Brace Jovanovich, Inc. gave me permission to use excerpts from *In the Fullness of Time — The Memoirs of Paul D. Douglas.* Page by page references to newspapers, periodicals, and personal communications are to be found in the original unabridged manuscript. The author decided not to include them in the book in the interest of brevity and to avoid distracting the reader, who might otherwise be led to believe that this is a scholarly thesis.

However, some of the more helpful references, apart from books, and cooperation by various individuals are listed by chapter numbers:

Chapter 2:

The author is indebted to the following for data on Randolph County and Sam's genealogy and youth: James Bellarts, compiler of *Hill Heritage,* 1979; Treva Mathis, Curator, the Quaker Collection, Guilford College, Greensboro, N.C.; Carolyn Ann Hager, Randolph County Historical Society; *Friends' Review,* 1875; and Delores Davis, Recorder, Haverford College.

Chapter 3:

The information on the Minneapolis Athenaeum is from an article by Betty Engebretson in *Minnsota History,* March 1957.

Chapter 5:

Mrs. Ellen Welsh obtained the information on Sam's business activities in his Twin Cities days from the Minnesota Historical Society.

Chapter 7:

Elizabeth Crownhart-Vaughan corrected the spelling of place names and gave other help for the first draft of the chapter on Russia. Unfortunately, Sam's account of his travels had to be greatly shortened for this book.

Chapter 9:

The opinion about the handwriting in Mary Mendenhall's letters was rendered by J. Selig, Handwriting Consultants of Oregon.

Chapter 10:

Lawrence Coolidge of Boston sent a copy of the last will of James Nathan Hill. A photograph and information about Pearrygin State Park were furnished by the Washington State Parks Department. Elizabeth Nelson, Margaret Lehman, and Marjorie Martin corresponded with the author about Sam's ranch in the Methow Valley.

Chapter 11:

Mrs. Pauline Pierce kindly sent clippings from the *Berkshire Evening Eagle* about the estate at Stockbridge, and the paper's editor sent a photo.

Ruth Nuendorffer, librarian of the Historical Society of the Tarrytowns, and Nicholas Mazzio, volunteer, sent the author photos of Mamie's large estate with its imposing townhouse and carriage house, but could find no information about her last years.

Chapter 14:

Information about the Willamette and Cascade Mountain Wagon Road Co. was obtained from Carroll J. Amundson's master's thesis at the University of Oregon, 1928.

Chapter 15:

The author is indebted to Nell Conley, Editorial Associate of the Public Relations Dept. of Pacific Northwest Bell, Portland, for access to scrapbooks on the company's history. Other information came from E. D. Smith's article, "Communication Pioneering in Oregon" in the Dec. 1938 issue of *Oregon Historical Quarterly*.

Chapter 16:

References for this chapter include an address by A. E. Todd, "The Pacific Highway," before the British Columbia Road Superintendents convention at Victoria, 2/12, 1913; and articles in the *Oregon Motorist* (August 1925 and March 1931) and in the *Washington Motorist* (November 1923). The help of the Automobile Club of Oregon, the California State Highway Association, and Margarita Spivack of *Westways* magazine is also acknowledged.

Sam's address to the U.S. Senate in 1900 was reprinted from the *Congressional Record* by the Washington State Good Roads Association. Other references for this chapter include Fred Lockley's article on Sam Hill in *Pacific Northwest*, July 1928; Frederick L. Paxson's "The Highway Movement, 1916-1935" in the *American Historical Review*, 1946; *Pacific Builder and Engineer*, July 1909; *Colliers*, 10/2, 1909; *The Town Crier* (Seattle), October 1911; *Sunset*, September 1913; and "Casual and Factual Glimpses of the Beginning and Development of Oregon's Roads and Highways," compiled by Ralph Watson of the Oregon Highway Dept. The last named article was furnished by John J. Earley of the Oregon Division of Transportation.

Chapter 17:

Two articles from the *Oregon Historical Quarterly* were most helpful in the preparation of this chapter: "Oregon's Columbia River Highway," by C. Lester Horn (Sept. 1965) and "C. C. Lancaster and the Columbia River Highway: Engineer as Conservationist," by Ronald J. Fahl (June 1973). Other references include articles by Henry L. Bowlby in *American Forestry*, August 1916; George C. Warren and A. A. Rosenthal in *Contracting*, May and June, respectively, 1916; and Betty H. Huntress, *Highway Magazine*, January 1952. Chester Moore's 1915 scrapbook of *The Oregonian* clippings on motoring was loaned by the Multnomah County Public Library.

Chapter 19:

References for this chapter include *The Golden Jubilee History of the N.Y.K.,1885-1935;* Gary D. West's "James J. Hill's Lost Opportunity in the Pacific" in *Pacific Northwest Quarterly,* January 1973; and from Maryhill Museum files, articles from *The Japan Advertiser, Tokyo Times, Trans-Pacific, The Japan Times and Mail.* and *Far East Commercial and World Salesman.* Hikado Yoshinari kindly translated articles from Japanese newspapers and identified Sam's prominent guests at the Imperial Hotel dinner in 1920. She enlisted the help of Jean Pearce and Mr. Kiyoaki Murata, editor of the *Japan Times,* in identification of photographs.

Chapter 20:

Thanks are due to Thomas T. Thalken, Director of the Herbert Hoover Presidential Library, for checking for mention of Sam; to Marion Raines, Librarian of William Penn College; and to George Hutton of Vancouver, Washington for the information about Sam in Rumania.

Chapter 21:

Information about these memorials was obtained in part from the books by Maynard C. Drawson and Margaret Lang (see bibliography); a leaflet on the Peace Portal from the Washington State Dept. of Education; and an article by Dorys C. Grover in *Western Engines,* August 1965.

Chapter 22:

Information for this chapter was drawn in part from an article in *Klickitat Heritage,* Summer 1979, by Pete May. The story about Sam and the Jewetts comes from a *True West* article by Florence Bartholomew, Sept.-Oct. 1965.

Chapter 24:

The author thanks Margaret Hale Harris for corresponding about Loie. Patricia Failing's article about her (*The Oregonian,* January 22, 1978) was also helpful. Sam's gift of Rodin sculptures is cited in the *Maryhill Quarterly* (Spring 1982). Some of the information about Prof. Edmond Meany was obtained from articles by George A. Frykman in the *Pacific Northwest Quarterly* (October 1960 and July 1979).

Chapter 25:

Henry Gray's accounts of Queen Marie's tour are found in his privately printed booklet, *The Famous Ride of Queen Marie* and in an article in *Frontier Times,* January 1967. Other authors consulted include Ellerby, Douglas, Bolitho, May, Drawson (see bibliograpy) and Jack Pement (*Oregon Journal,* 9/15, 1978). The story of the royal flush comes from Stan Federman of *The Oregonian.*

Chapter 26:

A booklet by Ed Hanna, *Fifty Years from Ye Olde English Restaurants, Ltd. (1928) to Peace Portal Golf Course (1978),* was a helpful source for information about Sam's Semiahmoo resort.

Chapter 27:

Comments on the phrase, "What the Sam Hill!" are from various dictionaries of slang and contemporary usage. Thelma Kimmel wrote the booklet, *Who the Sam Hill is Sam Hill?* (Optimist Printers, The Dalles, Oregon, 1972). Catherine M. Troeh furnished the note about Sam's last hospital stay. Ellen Ewing's series of articles, "Sam the Magnificent" are from *The Oregonian,* 6/23, 6/30, and 7/7, 1940.

Chapter 28:

Copies of Sam's will and the court decrees were obtained from the clerk of the Probate Court, King County, Washington.

Two of Sam's three children born out of wedlock were most cooperative: Elizabeth Wade and Sam B. Hill. Another son, who lives in British Columbia, chose not to participate.

Epilogue:

The author is indebted to John S. Moore, attorney for Maryhill Museum, Capt. Leppaluoto, and Nicky Tom for reviewing the point of view of the museum's trustees on the recent history of the museum. Robert Campbell responded with his side of the controversy. Thanks to Mrs. Charles Munn (Alma Spreckels' daughter) and Phyllis Paulson (Mrs. Munn's secretary) for permission to copy a portion of the correspondence between Alma Spreckels and Clifford Dolph.

I wish to thank the staffs of several libraries for their courteous help, especially the Multnomah County Public Library; the Oregon Historical Society and its director, Tom Vaughan; Mrs. K. L. Winn of the University of Washington Library; Harold D. Wilson of the Seattle Public Library; Frank L. Green of the Washington State Historical Society; W. R. Pope, Beth Williams, and Ruby Shields of the Minnesota Historical Society, and Bonnie Palmquist, an independent resercher working there; and R. D. Swerczek of the National Archives and Records Service. Maggie Hanson of the Minneapolis Public Library arranged for its valuable ($30 an hour, to be exact) INFORM service for retrieval of newspaper items. The British Columbia contingent included Zane H. Lewis of the Provincial Museum; Ann Yandle, Special Collections, University of British Columbia Library; Paul Yee, Archivist, City of Vancouver, and Roger Wheelock, manager, Butchart Gardens, Victoria. William Whalen, Harvard University Library Archivist, provided invaluable information from the reports of the secretaries of the classes of 1879 and 1915, and copies of correspondence concerning Sam's term as a Harvard overseer. Paul Wittkopf and Robert W. Frame III of the James Jerome Hill Reference Library sent Sam's accounts of the railroad strikes of 1894 and forwarded letters from the Hill papers when these were opened to the public in 1982. In a letter to the author, Albro Martin noted that "much personal information" had been removed from the Hill files by

Sam's sister-in-law, Gertrude Hill Gavin: thanks a lot, Gertrude!

Mrs. John Cabot and her son Lewis deserve special thanks for sending photographs of the portrait and crayon sketch of Sam in their collection. Mr. Louis W. Hill, Jr. kindly wrote about sources and furnished a photo of the equestrienne portrait of Mamie Hill by Jan Chelminski. Mrs. G. Slade Reny sent the group picture of the Hill clan in Chapter 3.

Most of the photographs in this book are the property of Maryhill Museum, many taken from the large glass projection slides owned by Sam himself. The trustees generously have permitted use of these photos. Dorothy Brokaw and Harvey Freer assisted in making them available for reproduction. David Coomler kindly projected Sam's movies for the author at the museum. The photographs were prepared expertly by Tom Ethen, in spite of the not very reassuring name of his studio, "Sometimes the Magic Works." Sam Mallicoat made the schema for the photo of the site of Maryhill. The maps are by Alan Cardwell of "Geo-Graphics," Portland. The late Clarence Dolph furnished photostats of the *New York Times* coverage of Queen Marie's visit. Richard Meeker, himself engaged in writing a biograpy of S. I. Newhouse, gave helpful advice on several chapters, as did Patricia Garlan. The typing was done by several stenographers, of whom Virginia Weiner and Shirley Crow merit special thanks.

Possibly because of limitations of space, one rarely finds a negative note in authors' acknowledgements, i.e., a list of people or institutions not responding to requests for help or information. Bowing to tradition, I will make only one exception; the National Endowment for the Humanities, which turned down my request for a $2,000 grant. In charity, it must be said that the decision was no doubt based on the sheer magnitude of the request, rather than on any defect in the quality of the project.

I must add the usual disclaimer that any errors of fact or omission must be laid at my door, not at those of the vigilant supervisory personnel.

Sam Hill Chronology

1857 Born May 13 in Deep River, North Carolina.
1865 Family moved to Minneapolis.
1874 Worked on a railroad survey crew.
1875 Became a protégé of A. J. Cassatt of the Pennsylvania Railroad.
1878 earned B.A. at Haverford College, Pennslvania; head of Republican party in Minnesota.
1879 Spent a year at Harvard and received another B.A., the beginning of lifelong interest and support of Harvard. Organized Minnesota Harvard Club. Became clerk in a law office.
1880 Admitted to bar in Minnesota.
1881 Harvard Law School (probably briefly). Began practice in Min-

neapolis. Took the first of many trips to Europe. Active in Minneapolis Athenaeum and politics.

1886   Chosen by J. J. Hill for legal department, Great Northern Railway.

1888   Married Mary Frances Hill, J. J.'s oldest daughter. President of Minneapolis Trust Co.

1889   Daughter, Mary Mendenhall Hill, born.   In the next decade, was president or director of various busineses, including a dozen component railroads of the Great Northern.

1893   Son, James Nathan B. Hill, born. Sam went to Europe to promote investment in Great Northern Railway by Leopold of Belgium and other royalty; met Marie of Rumania.

1894   Involved in two railroad strikes.

1895   Minneapolis Trust Co. bought control of Seattle Gas and Electric Co.; Sam made president.

1897   First trip to Japan, on behalf of Great Northern. Met Prof. Edmond Meany, historian, enkindling Sam's interest in Indians of the Northwest.

1898   Beginning of long friendship with Albert of Belgium.

1899   First trip to Russia. Became first president of the Washington State Good Roads Association.

1900   Elected Harvard overseer. Resigned from railroad posts; announced intention to live in Seattle. Appeared before U.S. Senate committee to promote road building.

1901   Second trip to Russia; crossed Siberia and wrote an interesting account of his travels. Wife and children joined him in Seattle.

1902   Bought land for Seattle house. "Gas war" began. Started to order custom-made world globes for friends and institutions.

1903   Wife and children left Seattle to live in the East; Sam visited them at intervals for the next ten years. Began active and successful stock market speculations, the basis for his fortune.

1904   Sold out Seattle gas business. Advocated road laws in Washington State.

1905   Bought large estate at Stockbridge, Massachusetts and a ranch (Chewil-o-kap) in north central Washington.

1906   Son James visited Sam at ranch and in Seattle; performed poorly at prep. schools. Sam had site for Seattle house prepared.

1907   Influential in obtaining model road laws for Washington. Started U.S. Trust Co., Seattle, a personal holding company. Embarked on establishing a new town and farming community on 7,000 acres on the Columbia River (Maryhill, "The Promised Land").

1908   Construction of buildings at Maryhill and a large house in Seattle. Endowed chair of road building at University of Washington. Took engineers Lancaster and Thomson to study European roads.

1909   Meeting of first American Congress of Road Builders at the Good Roads Building at Alaska-Pacific-Yukon Exposition. Sam started construction of experimental roads at Maryhill. Negotiated unsuccessfully to buy vast land grant in central Oregon. Took over Home Telephone Co., Portland, and started long losing battle with the Bell System.

1910   President of the new Pacific Highway Association. Promoted convict labor on roads. Took daughter, Mary M., west, where she stayed intermittently through 1916.

1911   Efforts to build a highway on the north bank of the Columbia thwarted by Washington's governor.

1912   Turned attention to Oregon's highways, notably the planning of the Columbia River Highway.

1913   Took Oregon's governor and legislators to Maryhill to demonstrate experimental roads. Dream of town of Maryhill fades: project converted to cattle ranch. James entered Harvard.

1914   Construction of chateau at Maryhill begun. Daughter Elizabeth born.

1915   Columbia River Highway completed. Sam meets Loie Fuller and Alma Spreckels.

1916   Adventurous trips to Europe and Russia to aid in expediting shipments of war materiel to Russia through Vladivostok. Established chair of Russian language at University of Washington. Mary Mendenhall psychotic, hospitalized.

1917   Home Telephone Co. in receivership. Work on Maryhill "castle" stopped: Sam promises Loie Fuller it will become a museum.

1918   First good roads meeting in Japan. Siting of Stonehenge Memorial and dedication of altar stone.

1919   Forced sale of Home Telephone Co. Trip to Rumania. Awarded Order of Commander of the Crown (Belgium).

1920   Began construction of Peace Arch; returned to Japan to publicize it and continued promotion of improved roads there. Gave dinner for the most prominent Japanese businessmen and politicians.

1921   Dedication of completed Peace Arch. Sponsorship of movie, "The Sacred Faith of a Scrap of Paper."

1922   Trip around the world with Marshal Joffre and party. Awarded Order of the Sacred Treasure in Japan.

1923   Burst of letter and book writing and other projects, a manifestation of a manic state. Sam president of an Alabama coal mine; formed "Ye Olde English Restaurants, Ltd." near Peace Arch. Articles of incorporation for Maryhill Museum filed.

1925   Given honorary LL.D. by Penn College. Made proposal for building replicas of Solomon's temple.

1926   Queen Marie's famous trip to dedicate Sam's unfinished house at Maryhill as a museum.

1927   Loie Fuller urges Sam to build a museum-apartment house in Paris. Proposal for "Memory Gardens" to beautify Pacific Highway.

1928   Built house at Bonneville for mistress, Mona Bell. Son, Sam B. Hill, born.

1929   Continued advocacy of a highway on the north bank of the Columbia:

lack of success led him to leave his museum unfinished.

1930   Stonehenge Memorial completed and rededicated.

1931   Campaigned for regulation of trucks on highways; invited to address Oregon Senate and House on that subject, but developed acute abdominal condition. Died Feb. 26. Ashes placed in crypt below Stonehenge Memorial.

Prologue

The Road to the Castle

Twenty miles east of Portland along Interstate 84, the fields and wooded hills on either side of the Columbia River abruptly give way to cliffs and steeper slopes covered with fir trees. Rooster Rock on the left and Crown Point high on a rocky cliff to the right are the sentinels at the entrance to the Columbia Gorge and to one of the most dramatic scenic drives in America. One passes a dozen waterfalls on the Oregon side and the great monolith, Beacon Rock, on the opposite bank. Next, Bonneville Dam, with its great locks and hydroelectric power plant, sprawls across the river. Above the graceful span of the Bridge of the Gods, the river widens and its current slows. The waters of the great pool above the dam have engulfed the lower cascades of the Columbia, just as the water impounded by The Dalles Dam farther east has covered the once perilous Celilo Falls, traditional fishing grounds of Indian tribes for centuries.

Beyond the town of Hood River and its orchards, palisades of basalt slope more gradually to the river and the trees are fewer. East of the city of The Dalles, the hills become barren hogbacks, traversed by gullies with outcroppings of rock spilling obliquely downward to the broad river. Electric power lines on the hills march in file to the horizon. Then, high on a bench of land on the Washington side, there appears a large sand-colored building surrounded by trees and lawn, a strange oasis in this otherwise desolate landscape. The building is "Maryhill Castle," now the Maryhill Museum of Art. Three miles east, at the hamlet of Biggs, Oregon, there is a highway bridge to Washington. A vigilant driver will see on the bridge approach a bronze plaque, partially obscured by a highway marker, identifying the Sam Hill Memorial Bridge. An attendant at the service station 200 yards away did not know its name. "We just call it the Maryhill bridge," he said.

On the narrow lowlands of the river on the Washington side are Maryhill State Park and a dozen small farms and orchards. The road ascends some 400 feet to the upper benchland. Half a mile to the east a strange, rounded, columned, roofless, concrete structure broods over the river valley. It was evidently inspired by Stonehenge of England and is appropriately set in this primordial scene.

About three miles west on Washington State Highway 14, past a few scattered ranch houses and grazing cattle, is the entrance to the three-storied museum. Its great ramps on the east and west sides and barred windows are surrounded by a pleasant park, filled now and then with the cries of wandering peacocks.

At the east entrance to the building, a plaque bears the likeness of an old man, identified as Sam Hill, road builder, 1857-1931. Another indicates that the museum was dedicated by Queen Marie of Rumania in 1926. But questions arise which the plaques cannot answer. Why this great Flemish-style chateau here in the middle of nowhere? Why Stonehenge? Was the builder eccentric or mad?

There are more mysteries inside the building. Many museums set out to display examples of the arts of all ages, with emphasis on a particular century, artist or school. Some institutions reveal the taste of their wealthy founders and benefactors, just as the book titles in a private library may. But one would be hard put to divine Sam Hill's taste from the collections at Maryhill: a Rumanian throne and robes; portraits of Balkan royalty; pictures and Art Nouveau sculptures of dancer Loie Fuller; a fine collection of Rodin drawings, bronzes, and plaster casts; paintings of rather uneven equality; a group of French mannequin dolls dressed in costumes of the mid-1940's; icons and chalices; a large assortment of chessmen; and a great collection of baskets and other Indian artifacts. How did these wildly eclectic objects come together in what, at its opening, *Time* called the "loneliest museum in the world"?

The search for answers to these questions takes us on a road beyond Sam Hill's castle, a road which leads around the world, for he was an inveterate globetrotter. There have been other eccentric millionaires, many of them philanthropists, dreamers of great dreams, and proponents of good causes. Some have bequeathed their great houses to found art museums. Some have entertained royalty, the great, the famous, and have basked in their glory. Others have been entrepreneurs for disparate enterprises or world travelers and adventurers. Sam Hill was all of these, and yet his name, if known at all, is merely a footnote to American history.

What made Sam run, sometimes frenetically, the long road with many bypaths which ended for him 50 years ago? This biography does not contain all the answers. The story of Sam and his museum, to change the figure, resembles a jigsaw puzzle with the easy parts completed. But it is soon evident that some of the necessary pieces are missing. Some seem to have been altered, perhaps by the subject himself; others may never be found. The picture that emerges depends on the beholder. To some, Sam Hill was a Don Quixote trying to realize a private dream; to others, he was a windbag tilting at windmills. A dreamer and doer, he was shrewd and impulsive, hard-headed and kind. In his life of 74 years were packed more satisfying and frustrating experiences than are usually encountered in a dozen lifetimes of "interesting people."

Now let us set out at dawn on the road that will bring us back at sunset to the castle on the Columbia.

PART I
THE RISING STAR

1

Young Sam

An American Quaker will usually have no difficulty in finding his roots, at least those in the topsoil of America. Quakers have been careful record keepers, making things easy for genealogists. The Hill Family Historical and Genealogical Society, for example, had its own quarterly publication in 1979.

Sam Hill had strong Quaker roots. His mother, Eliza L. Mendenhall, was a descendant of Thomas Pearson, who came to America with William Penn in 1688. One of Pearson's daughters married Aaron Mendenhall in 1715. Their son James moved his family to North Carolina in 1754, to a land grant obtained from the earl of Granville along Deep River, not far from Greensboro. James Mendenhall established a Quaker meeting house near the town of Jamestown, named in his honor. The meeting dissolved during the Civil War when many Quakers moved west because of persecution for their antiwar and abolitionist views. Sam's mother, Eliza, born in 1823, was the daughter of Richard (a descendant of James) and Mary Mendenhall. Eliza married a country doctor, Nathan Bronson Hill, in 1845. Sam, the fourth of their six children, was born in the settlement of Deep River on the Uwharrie River on May 13, 1857, his father's 39th birthday.

Randolph County, with its large proportion of Quakers, had a " . . .century-long tradition of pacifism and antislavery sentiment . . . and an abolitionist tradition that went back at least to 1848." In fact, Sam wrote to a cousin about encountering " . . . a descendant of Benjamin Lundy, who held the first meeting ever held in the history of the world for the liberation of slaves at Deep River meeting house, North Carolina, in 1824. . . . " Sam Hill had at least half a dozen first cousins in Guilford County with whom he corresponded and visited through the years.

Sam was very close to his older brother, Dr. Richard Hill (1853-1923), who practiced for many years in Minneapolis. Richard, like his father, became president of the Minnesota State Medical Society. Their sister, Anna (b. 1860), was in a tuberculosis sanatorium near Milwaukee for some years. She wrote Sam in 1884, "I should like for thee to take charge of any share of father's property . . . I leave college in June, 1885." Sam managed her financial affairs, eventually through a trust set up in the Minneapolis Trust Co. He had two other sisters, Mary (b. 1846) and Maria (b. 1849), and another brother, William (b. 1863), to whom he does not refer, and who probably died young.

Late in his life, Sam Hill gave this account of his forebears and youth to Fred Lockley, a columnist for the *Oregon Journal:*

One of my early ancestors, whose name, like mine, was Sam Hill, was treasurer for Oliver Cromwell. When King Charles II came back to the throne, in 1660, Sam Hill came to America. In reading his diary, I ran across this quaint statement. He did not like to say that if he stayed in England he would lose his head, so he wrote: "I find the climate of England very unwholesome, so I am going to seek a change of climate." He came to North Carolina. He had had his fill of fighting, with Cromwell, so he joined the Quaker church. If you will look up the history of North Carolina you will find that Sam Hill was arrested for refusing to bear arms or to turn out on muster day.

Father attended Haverford College in Pennsylvania. Haverford is about nine miles from Philadelphia. [He] took his doctor's degree there in 1846. From there father went to Jefferson Medical College at Philadelphia and later to the Ohio Medical College at Cincinnati where he graduated. [He] became one of the strong men of North Carolina. Quakers are accustomed to persecution, and the more they are persecuted the stronger are their convictions and the more loyal they are to them. My father was a strong believer in the Union and he was unutterably opposed to slavery, so you can imagine that, living in North Carolina, his views were not always popular. In spite of his views, he was a leader in the state. He built the first cotton factory south of the Mason and Dixon line. He was vice-president of the Bank of North Carolina and to improve the conditions of the farmers and to make the country more prosperous, he agitated for the construction of better roads and he himself was instrumental in the building of 44 miles of plank roads. My father was the head of the "underground railroad" in North Carolina. Charles Coffin had charge of the other end of the railroad, at Indianapolis, and Mr. Harris was head of the Canadian end, at Guelph, Ontario, which, by the way, was the home of my father-in-law, James J. Hill.

So great was my father's reputation for integrity and business sagacity that many wealthy planters made him executor of their wills, knowing he would not allow their own flesh and blood, their sons and daughters by octoroon slaves, to go on the auction block. When a planter's estate was being settled and his slaves sold, father often bought [these] sons and daughters of the planter, and shipped them north. On one occasion father bought three young men who were put up at auction, as he knew they were the sons of a neighboring planter, a friend of father's. One of these slaves bore a striking resemblance to the planter, had blue eyes and fair hair, and from his appearance no one would believe he had any Negro blood. Father sent these three slaves north. The one who looked so much like a white man settled in Boston. He became the owner of three ships plying between Boston and New York. At the time when it meant a prison term to teach Negroes to read or write, father bought books in the North and brought them South, furnishing them to the Negroes, so they could learn to read and write.

As vice-president of the Bank of North Carolina, my father was instrumental in loaning money not only in North Carolina but all through the North and along the frontier. He made a trip to St. Paul and Fort Snelling to pass upon loans there. When it was evident that there was to be war between the North and the South, the directors of the Bank of North Carolina met to decide what they should do about their loans in the North. They had $15,000.00 on deposit in New York City. Fort Sumpter had been fired upon, and they were afraid they were going to lose the money. Father gave his personal check for $15,000.00 and took a draft on the New York bank. He mailed this to his brother in St. Louis, telling him to go to New York City, draw the money in gold, and hold it for him. When we escaped from North Carolina that $15,000.00 in gold came in very handy.

My father was away from home attending to a medical case shortly after the breaking out of the Civil War. [He] was so much loved and respected by our neighbors that none of them would have allowed us to suffer any harm, but some men from another community, hearing that my father was a strong Union man, came to our house to kill [him]. Naturally, they did not announce their intention, but Jim Brown, one of our Negro servants, who was devoted to my father and mother, heard by the Negro grapevine telegraph they were coming. "Uncle Jim" was not only devoted to us but he was very courageous and intelligent. We happened to have a lot of schoolbooks in the house father had sent North for to give to Negro slaves. We also had some books which were known as "abolition books." Mother invited the men in and said, "I regret that my husband is not here to receive you, but if you will come in and wait for him, I will get supper for you." While the men were waiting in the parlor, mother gathered every schoolbook and "abolition book" and burned them in the kitchen stove.

She sent one of the servants to call Uncle Jim Brown. When the strangers had come she had told Uncle Jim to take father's saddle horse, Gray Laurel, out of its box stall, to make room for the saddle horses of our visitors. Gray Laurel was the fleetest mare in that part of the country. My father was fond of fast horses. [He] never allowed anyone but himself to ride Gray Laurel. Mother told Uncle Jim to watch his chance and lead Gray Laurel back of the barn, where he could not be seen, and to mount her and ride to the crossroads and wait there till her husband came and to say to him, "Your wife is worried about her mother; she is sick. Will you ride there at once and see if she is all right?" She said to Uncle Jim, "Don't tell my husband that there are some men at the house here waiting for him, for if you do he will come home to protect me, and the men will kill him." Uncle Jim rode to the crossroads and when my father came he gave him the message and father changed his saddle to Gray Laurel and started off for the home of my mother's mother, while Uncle Jim rode back on the saddle horse my father had been riding. The men waited till after 10 o'clock, and then told my mother they would have to search the house for "abolition books." They searched, but did not succeed in finding any. They waited till nearly midnight for father, and finally rode away.

Mother had Uncle Jim get out the wagon, and in the bottom of it she put a trunk filled with clothing for us children. Uncle Jim put hay over the trunk, and mother sent one of our servants, with this load of hay, to drive to her mother's. Meanwhile, she put a few necessary articles into a couple of carpetsacks and we started, apparently, for town.

When we reached my grandmother's house we found father there, very much upset at having been sent on a wild goose chase, for he found that no one was sick and his services were not required. Mother told father what had happened, and he agreed that they would have to abandon their home and everything in it and try to make their way north.

To have started north would have been fatal, for we would have been made prisoners. We went to the station and father bought tickets for Georgia. In Georgia he bought tickets for Alabama, and from there we went to Tennessee and thence to Kentucky. We were now among strangers, who would not be so suspicious of us. Mother told all of us children to say, "We are going to visit our Aunt Nancy," when people asked us where we are going. We didn't know where Aunt Nancy lived, so we were perfectly safe not to give our destination away. We crossed the river at Indianapolis, Indiana. I was only 4½ years old, but I remember very distinctly seing men wearing narrow caps and dressed in blue uniforms, who were cooking meals in the street. I thought it was very unusual. I also remember seeing their guns stacked, and wondering why they had guns in town. From Indianapolis we went to my Aunt Nancy's at Carthage, Indiana. We stayed there several months. My father's brother turned over the $15,000.00 in gold to father. Father gave $5,000.00 each to two of his brothers and with the other $5,000.00 we went to Minnesota.

Another thing I remember very distinctly is our trip up the river to St. Paul. We went on a boat called the "War Eagle." Father had $5,000.00 in gold. He was afraid that if he took it in the stateroom it would be stolen, so he put it in his saddlebags and threw the saddlebags on the deck of the "War Eagle." He told us children to pay no attention to the saddlebags but to let him know if anybody started to take them or open them. We went by stage from St. Paul to Minneapolis. The actual distance is probably not over eight miles, but in those days we followed the river, and on account of poor roads it took us more than half a day to make the twenty miles. I remember very distinctly seeing the Falls of St. Anthony on the east side of the river. We stayed that night at the home of William Wales, a Quaker, and the next crossed the river to Minneapolis, where we arrived in September, 1861, and where I lived for the next forty years.

Carolyn Hager of the Randolph County Historical Society does not think that Sam's father was as prominent as made out, and she questions some other portions of Sam's story. It was his paternal grandfather, Samuel Hill, who owned shares in a cotton mill, the Union Manufacturing Company of Randleman, North Carolina. The first cotton mill in the state had been started at Greensboro in 1830. Nathan B. Hill is not listed as an officer of the State Bank of North Carolina. There was no bank near Deep River at the time, the citizenry depending chiefly on a barter economy. There were no slave auctions in Randolph County, the nearest such auction being fifty miles away. The flight of the Hill family did not occur until after the Civil War. According to Quaker records, Sam's father practiced medicine in Randolph County until 1865. He and his family were granted a certificate of membership to the Minneapolis Meeting in July 1865, and the war had ended in April. Finally, the trains in Georgia had been destroyed late in the war, so the Hill family's journey was probably by a different route.

Dr. Nathan Hill's 1875 obituary in the *Friend's Review* states that he was " . . . reared in the South, yet he was an ardent advocate of anti-slavery sentiments and he spent his time and means in aiding the oppressed — often at the risk of professional reputation and even of life. He went south in the winter of 1865-6 under the direction of the Society of Friends to aid in establishing schools among the freedmen."

Any errors in Sam's account cannot be charged to Lockley. In old age, Sam probably recalled the oft-told tales of childhood with romantic embellishments. He very likely unconsciously felt the need to dramatize the events of his childhood and Horatio Alger-style youth to fit in with the public (and his personal) perception of himself as a self made man, larger than life, but requiring affection and admiration. The author is not about to impeach his chief witness, but must admit that this will not be the last disputed chapter in the Sam Hill story. With these corrections, let the minutes stand as recorded.

Sam continued his account to journalist Lockley:

Mother went to a yearly meeting of the Friends in Iowa. In crossing the river the ice broke and mother got wet. She died as a result of this accident. I was only ten years old at the time. After my father died in Minneapolis in

February 1875, my oldest sister kept house for us. We had lost practically all our property when we left our home in North Carolina, so it was a case of having to work if we wanted to eat.

I got a job piling millwood at ten cents a load. I was paid fifteen cents a load for piling slabwood. I had to work hard all day to earn as much as a dollar. Later I got a job wiping joints for a plumber. I got lead poisoning and had to quit that work, so I went to Oseo, Minnesota, where I got a job as a farmhand with Isaac Potter, a North Carolina Quaker. On his farm I learned to milk cows, swing a cradle, and do other farm work. Later, I came back to Minneapolis and got a job with Nate Roberts, a carpenter and house builder. When I was about eighteen, I got a job on the geological survey of Pennsylvania under J. P. Lesley, a noted authority on geology.

I then came into contact with A. J. Cassatt. He was one of the men who helped make the Pennsylvania Railroad what it is. I was one of a group of six young men that Mr. Cassatt took under his wing. He discussed with us roadbuilding and railroad problems. This was in 1875. [In 1874, at age 17, Sam first worked for a railroad as a rodman for a surveying crew on the Lake Superior and Mississippi Road, later called the St. Paul and Duluth Railway.] From that day to this, I have had a keen interest in the building of roads.

I saved my money and went to Cornell University at Ithaca, New York. I took a cold which turned into pneumonia so I had to drop out. Later I went to Haverford College in Pennsylvania, where father took his degree in 1846. I took my degree there in 1878. Later I went to Amherst College and still later to Harvard. I worked during summer vacations on the geological survey.

Haverford College records show that he entered in 1875. There he took Latin, Greek, French, and German; courses in mathematics and science; and classes in English literature and history, logic, rhetoric, and political science. Evidently, there were few "pipe" courses in those days. There were fifteen other seniors in the graduating class of 1878.

In September of 1878, he entered Harvard as a member of the senior class, earning another AB degree. His curriculum was no less strenuous than at Haverford. His courses included advanced Latin, forensics, and two in the philosophy department, one entitled "German Philosophy of the Present Day," and the other "Advanced Political Economy," in which his grade was an embarrassing 64%. Dr. Henry Cabot Lodge taught his class in "Colonial History of America to the Year 1789." His grades were in the 85 percent range at Harvard and he placed 64th among 192 seniors, an undistinguished ranking, considering his later career.

We know little of his year at Harvard, except that he was a member of the Finance Club and the Philosophical Society. He mentioned knowing Theodore Roosevelt, not one of his heroes, " . . . whose principal reputation at that time was as a middle-weight boxer." That year evidently made a lasting and favorable impression upon him, because he was active in Harvard alumni affairs for the rest of his life (Chapter 18).

When he returned to Minneapolis to work in a law office, Sam lived with the William Krech family for about eight years before his marriage in 1888. Only German was spoken, which explains Sam's familiarity with the language on his subsequent travels. Alvin Krech, one of the sons, eventually organized the Equitable Trust Company of New York, with which

Sam did business later.

As a tall, handsome young man, the rising young attorney was doubt-less one of the most eligible bachelors of Minneapolis. Sam was, in fact, president of the Bachelors' Club. Some of the letters which he kept from that era are intriguing and enigmatic. Take the following, in which the unan-swered question is, was Sam the guardian of one of his relatives or of someone else?

Sam Hill Esq.   Wyzata* November, 1886

Dear Sir:

Your letter received. I hardly know what to suggest, unless that if she was taken to some new place and care taken as to the acquaintances she made, it might have the proper influence upon her. . . . As she has no respect for our wishes but adds falsehood when questioned by us, it is only our respect for you, her guardian, that we have tolerated her at all these past few weeks.

Very respectfully yours,

J. I. Tibbets, M.D.

In that era of role-playing, the pursuer was not always the male. Sam probably received more than one letter along the lines of the following, written the same year:

Dear Mr. Hill:

I had determined if you had returned, to make you have such a delight-ful time that you would forget the little unpleasantness of the last few days you spent at The Point, but you did not give me the chance; think of what you missed! . . . I would like to have [your photo] as a little memento of the pleasant hours by the sad sea waves. . . . When you come to Philadelphia, you have one friend who will always be glad to see you.

Yours very truly,

Marcelene Hurluk

Next, a note from Mary Pope McKay, complete with misspellings, written to Sam on a calling card in July 1887: "So sorry not to have seen you last night. I waited until half past ten. Come to the Frontinac. I will give you such a welcome! . . .Pardon writing with gloves on." A year later, the gloves were off: "Must I say I was glad I got an invitation to your wedding reception? Well I was. . . . Some time in the future I trust I will meet your wife. Let me welcome you to Louisville sometime. I may be in St. Paul a week or so this winter, but I have no plans. . . . "

Sam knew Anstice Abbot as a teacher from his school days in Min-neapolis and corresponded with her occasionally for nearly twenty years. He wrote her in 1904, "My mind goes back to the time when I was a boy in the public schools when you were always kind to me. . . . You are one of the oases in the desert, and I have always been grateful for the way in which

---

*The citizens of this hapless Minnesota town incurred the wrath of J. J. Hill when they complained of the nightly noise of switching engines. J. J. simply had the station torn down, moved two miles east, and renamed Holdridge.

you encouraged me and understood me." She was very fond of Sam and followed his career even after 1902, when she went to work in a "Christian Home for Widows" in India, where she contracted tuberculosis.

In cataloguing Sam's letters at Maryhill Museum, Ellen Welsh found a faded, fragile letter from which the name of the addressee, date, and a few words had been deleted, probably by Sam himself:

Minneapolis, Minn.
188?

Your letter pains and grieves me very much. The kindly directness of it, no less than the generous trust you show that you still have in me, affects me deeply. And all the more since I cannot write what you ask, and what I think is more than due.

Daily it seems clearer to me that my decision course is right. Events have so shaped themselves and circumstances beyond all human control have rendered any other course impossible. Great as my _____ are it is better surely to be thought capable of doing a wrong rather than to do one.

_____ has always done what she believed _____ and I thoroughly respect and admire her character. She is courageous, womanly, and truthful and I ask you as I did her when our paths separated, as I believe to cross no more — to judge with charity.

Truly yours,
Sam Hill

Was he sincerely conscience-stricken over some broken promise or simply determined to jilt someone, kindly but firmly?

Dr. Harry L. Taylor, a Haverford classmate, who later figures in the story of Sam's daughter (Chapter 9), wrote in 1887 that he had heard Sam had " . . . recently purchased a handsome residence — another spec. or does this portend marriage?" The speculation was true in the social, not financial, sense. By this time, Sam had met Mary Hill, his future wife.

At first reading, the following, dated December 3, 1886, is the most intriguing of the few letters about Sam's bachelor days:

My Dear Mr. Hill:

It is with considerable hesitation that I give you the slightest information concerning the Queen's health, as I realize it is impossible as well as questionable, to give you satisfactory news. If I could talk to you I could say many things I do not feel willing to write. She talked quite freely with me after knowing that I was intelligent on the subject. Among other things she said, "I am glad he told you."

She regards you as insincere, not much in love, if I have not misunderstood her, and I am not surprised, from some of the remarks she made, as coming from you. At the present time I do not think she cares for you in the least — entire devotion and a slight yielding to her views *occasionally* might do something for you. I am sure I cannot tell. . . . I pity the Queen as she seems unsettled and I do not wonder — she is a very sweet girl, but a very sad one. . . .

Sincerely your friend,
Beatrice M. Lowry

"My God! What queen?" may be the reader's first reaction to this. But Mrs. Lois D. Plotts who, as a girl, knew Sam, sensibly suggests that "the Queen" was a nickname for Mary Hill, applied behind her back, because of her remote and haughty manner. At any rate, one wonders if Sam ever contrasted these heady missives with the cold mashed potatoes dished up by his wife in the only two letters she wrote to him preserved from their engagement? (Chapter 3.) Let us turn from moonlight and roses to Sam's rising star in the firmament of law and the orbit of business.

2

The Law and the Profits

After graduation from Harvard in 1879, Sam began the practice of law in Minneapolis. In 1886 he became associated with James J. Hill's burgeoning railroad empire, first on the legal staff, then in its upper echelon. Within two years he had become president of the newly organized Minneapolis Trust Company and had married the boss's daughter. Nine years thus had seen a meteoric rise in his profession, in business, and in social position, a rise which was to continue until the turn of the century.

Let us return to Sam's account of his early years in the law as he told it to Fred Lockley:

> After finishing college, I went back to Minneapolis and got a job in a law office. There were six ahead of me. I had to get the ice, sweep the office and fag for the other law clerks, because I was boy No. 7. In those days all briefs and other legal documents were written in longhand. The firm I was with was Shaw, Levi and Cray. Judge Shaw, seeing some of my work, told me I would be his personal secretary, so that within two months I had graduated from boy No. 7 to boy No. 1. One day Charles H. Woods came to our office and said, 'I am going to Europe, and I want one of your law clerks to help my partner, Babcock, while I am gone.' Judge Shaw pointed to me and said: 'Hill can do the work for you.' I refused the job as I wanted to stay where I was. After Woods had gone I said to Judge Shaw, 'Why did you suggest me? Isn't my work satisfactory here?' He said, 'Your work is very satisfactory; that's why I recommended you. I want to see you advance. Babcock is lazy. You will soon be doing all the work. It would be good practice for you. What you ought to do is to be admitted to the bar and take the job.' I took his advice. I took the bar examination, was admitted to the bar [December 1880] and went to Woods & Babcock as a law clerk. Mr. Babcock began putting more and more work on me, and within a month I tried and won my first case. Meanwhile, real estate was moving actively and I had been making some pretty good commissions in

Oil portrait of Sam Hill by Gabrielle D. Clements, dated 1889. (Courtesy of Mrs. John Cabot.)

selling real estate. Upon the return from Europe of Judge Woods, I resigned [May 1881] and went to Harvard Law School. [This is not mentioned in the records of the Harvard Class of 1879, and while Sam does not say how long he was at Harvard Law School, he did not get a degree there. He spent the summer of 1881 in Europe before returning to practice.]

I knew that young lawyers had pretty hard sledding so I decided to be an exception to the general rule, if possible. At that time there were 35 volumes of the decisions of the Supreme Court of Minnesota. I committed volume 35 to memory. I then took volume 34, and continued till I had got to volume 1. I annotated all the cases. I decided that when I went into a courtroom I would not have to lug a lot of books but would be able to quote, accurately, the book and page of any case I referred to. I made a contract with the owner of the Vanderburgh block in Minneapolis whereby I would attend to his legal work, draw all leases, collect the rents, etc., in exchange for the use of four rooms on the second floor.

One of the four rooms I used for a file room. I subscribed for almost every newspaper in Minnesota. I cleaned up $1500 in cash on real estate deals, so I bought a safe and a library. I hired a law clerk, and, by the way, he worked for me for the next 48 years. [This was Charles Babcock, no relation to the firm's partner. Charles later joined Sam at the Great Northern Ry. and then at Maryhill (Chapter 22).] When a client came Babcock would get from him his name and address, which he would bring in to me. Babcock would tell him I would be at leisure in about 15 minutes. I put in this 15 minutes looking over the files of the newspaper from this man's home town, so that when he came in I was thoroughly conversant with the affairs of his town. It certainly made an impression on him for he took it for granted I was equally familiar with every other small town in Minnesota. I worked from 8 A.M. to 11 P.M., familiarizing myself with the history of Minnesota and the local affairs of the small towns. Saturday night, I would get on the train and drop off at some small town and its people. My boast in those days was that if I met a man once I would remember his name, his town and where we had met. As a matter of fact, I did have an unusually good memory. There is hardly any asset more valuable than a good memory. It will carry you far in law or in politics and in most other relations in life. My visits to the small towns resulted in my being asked to prepare the charters for many of the smaller towns.

I made it a rule never to take a case that I didn't believe in. I wasn't going to fight on the wrong side. This meant that I often passed up profitable cases, but in the long run it paid, for the juries got to believing that if I appeared in the case, right and justice were on the side of my client. I often heard men in the courtroom whisper, 'No, he doesn't have to carry any books; he's got the law in his head.' I took lots of damage cases against the railroad. The railroad attorneys would say to a prospective juror, 'Do you know Sam Hill?' If they did, they would excuse this juror. The railroad attorneys would usually use all of their preemptory challenges. I never used mine. I would look at the jury and say, 'I do not have to challenge any of the jurors, because I know they want to see justice done and I can trust to their sense of honesty and fair play.' The result was I had mighty good luck with my cases.

I won case after case of personal damages against the Hill railroads. Finally [in 1886, when Sam was 29 years old], James J. Hill sent for me and said, 'We would rather have you with us than against us. [Sam was involved in prolonged litigation against the St. Paul, Minneapolis and Manitoba Ry., J. J. Hill's first railway acquisition. The St. Louis and the Northern Pacific Railroads contested the right of the St. P., M. and M. Ry. to depress its tracks at a point in North Minneapolis. Sam won the case after nearly ten years, whereupon, with the consent, if not the blessing, of his former clients, he became assistant counsel for J. J.'s St. Paul and Pacific Railroad.] On what terms will you come with me?' I said, 'I do not care to be your hired man, Mr. Hill. I doubt if you would care to pay me as much as I am making. The only proposition that would interest me is to be allowed to come here without pay and learn railroading.' Mr. Hill finally accepted my proposition, and, as you know, he made me president of the Montana Central and a number of other railroads. James J. Hill was one of the greatest railroad men, one of the shrewdest, most farseeing, most public spirited men with whom I have ever been associated. I learned more from him than in all the college courses I ever took.

When Sam became J. J.'s son-in-law, it was surely a leg up on the giant step to becoming one of the country's top railroad executives. But the step would never have been invited had not J.J. recognized Sam's unusual qualities, among which were unlimited loyalty and determination.

There were other things than business matters on Sam's restless mind and crowded agenda in the 1880's. He became an inveterate joiner of social and political organizations in the Twin Cities. As he wrote of himself to the secretary of the Harvard class of 1879, "During the presidential campaign he was president of the Young Men's Garfield and Arthur Club of Minneapolis, and became president of the Young Men's Club and Union League Club, both organizations of a somewhat political nature." He helped to form the Minnesota Harvard Club, a step which led to his being elected a Harvard Overseer in 1900. In the presidential campaign of 1884 he wrote the secretary, "I was a 'mugwump'* and spent about three months in 1884 in an attempt to promulgate 'doctrines of opposition among the faithful.'"

He went abroad again in 1886, spending the winter in Munich and Vienna. His sister Annie, who had tuberculosis, accompanied him to Florence in 1887. The next year brought more responsibilities: presidency of the Minneapolis Trust Company and marriage to J.J. Hill's daughter, Mary.

3

The Limited Partnership: Mamie Hill

To paraphrase Mark the Evangelist, "What shall it profit a man if he shall gain the whole world and not find happiness in marriage?" For that matter, what doth it profit a biographer to have reams of letters about a man's business and buildings, and not know the secrets of his heart? There is no embarrassment of riches in our knowledge of Sam's courtship, married life, and separation; a small stack of curiously noncommittal letters and telegrams must suffice.

Mary Frances Hill, whom her family called "Mamie," was born in St. Paul in 1868, a year after the marriage of her father, James J. and Mary Theresa Mehegan. Mamie's mother was a Catholic and her father a convert to Catholicism, so she was educated by the sisters at Visitation Academy at St. Paul. She had three younger brothers and six sisters, one of whom, Katie, died in infancy.

The J. J. Hill family spent their summers at North Oaks, Minnesota. As an associate of J. J. Hill, Sam was no doubt invited to the house at Ninth and Canada in St. Paul. It is easy to imagine the attraction of a girl not yet 20 for

*Mugwumps were Republicans who refused to support James G. Blaine, the party nominee for President in 1884.

The Hill family (except for Walter Hill), following the wedding reception of Charlotte and George Slade, *center*, in October 1901. Others, *left to right*: Louis and Maud Hill; Clara; James Nathan B. Hill, age 8; George Slade's father; James N. Hill, J.J.'s oldest son; Mrs. J. J. Hill; Gertrude, Rachel, and Ruth Hill; Mary Mendenhall, standing in front of Sam; Mamie (Mary Hill Hill); and J. J. Hill. (Photo courtesy of Mrs. G. S. Reny.)

the tall, good looking, successful attorney, now 31 years old. He had "fluttered the dovecotes" of the nubile young ladies of the Twin Cities, and must have been considered the catch of the season. Mamie was handsome and rich, and the omens appeared right for a happy marriage.

The date of their engagement is not recorded. Years later, long after they had separated, Sam sent her 26 roses, specifying to the florist in Washington, D.C. that they arrive on the morning of April 26. Another time, his wire read simply, "1888-1912." In 1915, Sam sent her a telegram with only the dates "August 13, 1887-1915." Perhaps two of these were sentimental recollections of the dates of their first meeting and their engagement; 1888 was the year of their marriage.

Only two long letters written by Mamie to Sam during their courtship survive; there are none from Sam to her. Though he nearly always kept copies of his correspondence to others, no one but a biographer would expect a swain to make copies of his love letters!

Her two letters are chatty, impersonal, and for the most part, banal. In the first twelve-page missive written in March 1888 from the Hotel Albermarle to Sam, who was in Europe, she wrote about commonplace things; the weather, her family, friends, flowers in the shops and social calls. In something of a non sequitur for a Catholic, she wrote, "This being Good Friday, I went over to Delmonico's for lunch. . . . " She had gone for dinner to the home of Dr. Wier Mitchell, a surgeon famous for his reports on the phantom limb syndrome in amputees in Civil War days. He had called on Mamie and her mother several times when she was out, and pretended not to believe in her existence when he finally greeted her, saying, "This, I believe, is Myth Hill." Once when " . . . asked if his wife had any faults, 'Yes' he replied after some consideration, 'She saves old string.'" She thought Dr. Mitchell "clever and altogether agreeable," probably on the basis of other evidence.

She closed her letter with the following: "Hoping that you are all well and prepared for the ocean voyage, which I trust may be taken comfortably and 'sans Juifs,'* I am faithfully your friend,

Mary Hill"

In a letter written soon afterward, she said she had received two letters from Sam, one from Paris and one from London. She was returning that night to Minnesota where there was high water. "Did you bring a gondola, after all?" she asked. She spoke of a Dr. Metcalf, who " . . . sighed when he told me this morning that while his wife lives, we must make the best of it — he is a rare old man full of wit and humor."**

Albro Martin notes that Mary, with the help of her mother, sisters, and friends, " . . . spent an exciting summer assembling the trousseau, most of which came from Mannheimer Brothers dry-goods store in St. Paul. It had a value of $1,400 by the wedding day."

"A Wedding at St. Paul" was the lead for a brief *New York Times* account datelined September 6, 1888. "The social event that has been the absorbing topic of conversation in society circles of St. Paul and Minneapolis for the past week or two, the wedding of Miss Mary Hill, daughter of J. J. Hill, president of the Manitoba Railway Company, of St. Paul, to Mr. Samuel Hill of Minneapolis, took place this afternoon at Mr. Hill's house on 9th street. The wedding had been arranged as a private affair, and was witnessed only by about 100 guests, all of them relatives or intimate friends. The marriage service was read by the Rev. Father Caillette in the library, which was tastefully ornamented with flowers and vines. After the ceremony congratulations were in order. A reception was held at the house from 5:00 to 7:00 o'clock, for which 1,000 invitations had been sent out. Old friends gave the bride some of the most useful and ornamental gifts that a St. Paul bride has ever received. Upon their return, Mr. an Mrs. Hill will be at home in Minneapolis."

The Twin City newspapers devoted much more space to the wedding, listing the guests and describing in detail the floral decorations and the dresses of the wedding party, including the compulsory "bevy of little girls dressed in white." "The bride's presents, by request, came only from immediate friends. They included handsome jewels, plate, and between $3,000 and $4,000 of cut glass from the bride's parents alone . . . Mrs. Hill

---

*Perhaps she thought it more genteel to express anti-Semitism in French.
**Or at least a candidate for the Raised Eyebrows Department.

gave her one of the ropes of pearls that are claimed to be the finest in America . . . It is no doubt Mrs. Hill's intention to divide this necklace among her daughters, giving them each a rope* as they marry." The senior Hills also provided $70 in $5 gold pieces for the servants.

The *N.Y. Times* story continued, "This morning before Mr. Hill left Minneapolis, he was driving with his law partner, Mr. Atwater, discussing business matters, when the horse took fright, became unmanageable, and dashed down the street at break-neck speed. The buggy, a light one, swayed from side to side and suddenly struck an obstruction. Both occupants were thrown out. Mr. Atwater's leg was broken, but Mr. Hill escaped with a few light bruises. He was dragged a short distance, but fortunately succeeded in untangling himself. The buggy was wrecked." With this inauspicious prelude, "The bridal couple postponed their intended immediate departure for the East."

Mary was a Catholic and Sam a Quaker, so a wedding in the Catholic Church was not permissible. There is no record that the differences in religion gave the young couple any qualms, and they could scarcely have had any financial fears. J. J.'s presents, among the useful, if not ornamental, gifts, were one thousand shares in the Manitoba Railroad, with a par value of $100,000, and $100,000 in bonds. The dividends from this handsome nest egg played a large part in the lifestyle of the young couple after they returned to a house of their own in St. Paul. Their card announced that they would be "at home" Mondays in November 1888 at 314 South Seventh Street in Minneapolis. They traveled in Europe during the winter of 1888-9, visiting Munich, Vienna, and Italy.

Their first child, Mary Mendenhall Hill, was born on July 3, 1889. Sam diplomatically suggested that the girl be named Ann after J. J. Hill's mother, but J. J. preferred the name Mary. Her middle name was Sam's mother's maiden name. There was a confusing number of Marys about, including J. J.'s sister, Mary Elizabeth; his wife, Mary Theresa; his daughter, Mary Frances; and his first grandchild, Mary Mendenhall. Sam Hill called them Mary I, II, III, and IV as a family joke.

A second child, James Nathan Branson Hill, was born on August 23, 1893. He was named after his maternal grandfather, and his other names honored his paternal grandfather, Dr. Nathan Branson Hill.

Mamie and her little daughter accompanied Mamie's sister Rachel and their mother to Santa Barbara for the winter of 1892. Although Sam visited them there, one wonders if this early separation was significant. The change of climate was for the benefit of Mrs. James Hill, who had troublesome "bronchitis," eventually identified as pulmonary tuberculosis.

Sam could not have been home much while the children were growing up. His prodigious involvement with a dozen railroads and other companies and with various clubs and societies did not leave much time for his

---

* As in the adage, give a girl enough rope and she'll hang it on herself, or at least scatter pearls before the swain.

Mary Hill Hill ("Mamie"). Undated photograph, probably about 1895.
(Maryhill Museum files.)

family. But on occasion, Sam took his family with him on trips. Late in 1894,
he wrote to the Shoreham Hotel in Washington, D.C., inquiring about
prices for four rooms and a bath for his family and a nurse, and about the
monthly rate for " . . . horses, carriage, and driver set apart for our exclusive use."

Sam often communicated with the J. J. Hills, usually by telegram, to
report Mamie's health, appetite, and spirits. There were wires in November
and December 1891, for example, the first to report her arrival in New York
with her friend Mrs. Porter, and others from Asheville, N.C., where Sam
had joined her.

The busy years in Minneapolis from his marriage in 1888 through 1900
gave full scope to Sam's talents. Business must have occupied most of his

waking hours. There were diversions, however. He went to Europe with his wife for several months in 1890; visited St. Petersburg in 1899, leaving his family at Aix-les-Bains and Paris; stayed in France and Italy in the fall of 1900 with his wife and daughter; and in 1901, crossed Siberia alone as part of a round-the-world trip.

He wrote the Harvard Class Secretary, "I have occasionally dipped into poetry and rarely into prose, but have succeeded thus far in concealing my identity, and the Class of '79 has had no public disgrace on that account. My reading for the past four years has been of China and Japan. The Chinese language I studied during the winter of 1892. I find it difficult." A place on the executive committee of the Indianapolis Monetary Convention occupied some of his time in 1897-98, and his election to the Board of Overseers of Harvard in 1900 was the beginning of a six year term of service which greatly interested him.

Another interest was the Minneapolis Athenaeum, of which he became vice-president. Founded in 1859 as a private library, mainly by New Englanders bent on establishing an institution for advanced education in the pioneer settlement, the Athenaeum engaged lecturers, including Ralph W. Emerson and Thomas Nast, and made its books available to the public. In 1889, its collection of more than 20,000 volumes was moved into the new Minneapolis Public Library.

Sam was responsible for recruiting the distinguished librarian, George Putnam, for the Athenaeum in 1884. Years later, he told Fred Lockley of meeting Putnam " . . . back in the 70's . . . I persuaded him to go to Harvard. When he had been graduated, I told him he must be librarian of the Minneapolis Athenaeum Library. He protested that he knew nothing about this line of work, but I insisted that he should try. . . . He made good in splendid shape. Later he married and went to Boston. In talking with the directors of the Boston Library, I told them that their theory was to get a vast mass of knowledge, put it in their basement, and put a man with a gun in charge of it to keep any of it from getting away — that the real theory of a library was to get as much information to as many people as possible and make it as get-at-able as possible. [Putnam] revolutionized Boston's public library system and his work there led to his becoming the Librarian of Congress . . . The right man and the right job came together."

Sam gave a collection of Chinese prints to the Athenaeum in 1907. He remained a board member after leaving Minneapolis, and later acquired all of the stock in the Athenaeum Company. By donating the stock to the Minneapolis Foundation, in effect he eventually bequeathed to it the assets, about 100,000 volumes of scientific books valued at $300,000 and one-half block on Washington Avenue between Third and Fourth.

During the last twelve years of the 19th Century, Sam managed two demanding and parallel careers; one as legal counsel and executive for his father-in-law's railroads, the other as president of a trust company in Minneapolis. Though interwoven, they will be discussed separately in the next two chapters.

4

Money in Trust

In 1888, the year the Sam Hills were married, the Minneapolis Trust Company was organized by " . . . one hundred of the leading citizens of Minneapolis." Of the company's original capital of $500,000, J. J. Hill subscribed $100,000 and Sam $25,000. Sam was its first president and Clarkson Lindley secretary-treasurer. E. C. Cooke and Robert Webb, with whom Sam often corresponded, succeeded to these offices. William Dunwoody, later a substantial investor in Sam's gas business in Seattle, was an early stockholder, as was Charles Pillsbury, the miller. The trust company acted as executor of wills, manager of estates, and adviser for investments.

The Minneapolis Trust Company weathered the financial panic of 1893 and the depression which followed, whereas a number of banks in the Twin Cities went under. Sam's experience in stock and bond investments, including those in railroad and utility companies, provided a basis for the later success of his own investments and helped him obtain partners for his venture into the gas business in Seattle.

There are few items of interest to be gleaned from Sam's day-to-day business of wills, mortgages, and investments. An exception is a letter to Sam from John Ireland, Archbishop of Minneapolis, concerning a suit between a friend of Ireland's and an insolvent Minneapolis company in which the Minneapolis Trust Company, as assignee, was contesting the friend's claim. Ireland wrote, "I will take it as a personal favor if you will communicate with me, telling me what I may write Mr. Graham . . . , for I am quite certain that neither . . . yourself not any other officer of your company would place an unnecessary obstacle in the way of any rightful claim which it may be in your power to settle."

Ireland (1838-1918) was the Archbishop of St. Paul from 1888 until his death. He was considered a spokesman for the rights of the working classes but he had a foot in the other camp, as well. Sam helped him out once after Ireland had invested $75,000 of church funds in Twin Cities land, intending to sell it for the benefit of settlers. J. J. Hill gave Ireland the money to repay church funds. Unwittingly, Ireland paid the money without receiving a clear title to the property. It seems that Russell Sage, the financier, had bought a railroad having a land grant which included this property, and thereupon sold the railroad and kept most of the land. Sam advised Ireland to get President McKinley to put through a law protecting settlers when there was a conflicting claim to the title of their property. There was a brief interval between the time the Great Northern Land Company's claim lapsed before Sage's claim became good. The law was made to date from this hiatus so that Ireland could obtain a clear title. Sam then sold the land for him and turned over $450,000 to the Archdiocese. Not, perhaps, strict adherence to the separation of church and state, but there seemed to be no outcry, except perhaps from Mr. Sage.

Sam did not always find trust in his clients rewarding. If he had any convictions about the essential goodness of man, they must soon have been dispelled. He felt he had to make good on a couple of Minneapolis Trust Company transactions in which he had a moral, rather than a legal, responsibility. One involved the bonds of the Minnesota Sandstone Company, purchased, he said, "with a desire to aid that company to build up the town . . . not as an investment." He soon added, "It looks very much as if I were at my usual occupation of holding the bag. However, as I have started out in the role of the man who makes good, I shall have to continue, I suppose, to do so. I wonder how many men would make good on bonds payable to bearer? I would like to suggest that Mr. [J. P.] Morgan would hardly do this."

Another souring experience occurred the same year, 1902. He had helped W. J. Murphy place $30,000 worth of stock in the Minneapolis Tribune Company, which Murphy was to pay for with City Bank stock, then at 80 percent of par. Instead of selling the bank stock, Murphy held it, hoping for par. "To my grief and sorrow, I found out that he had never had it transferred to his name and when the bank's stockholders were sued, I had to make good," Sam wrote.

Much more trying was the seven year litigation involving the defunct Northwestern Guaranty Loan Co., for which the Minneapolis Trust Company had been appointed receiver in December 1894. In settling the loan company's affairs, the Trust Company sold $295,000 in bonds for ten cents on the dollar in a transaction authorized by a judge of the district court. Banks and other creditors of the loan company claimed the bonds should have brought 60 cents on the dollar. The *Minneapolis Times* took up the editorial cudgels with a vengeance in favor of this claim. Sam's company sued for criminal libel, but lost after a seven week trial in 1898. The Great Falls *Leader* congratulated the *Times* on " . . . winning a most signal victory against the Jim Hill outfit . . . [the *Times*] declared that the Trust Company was corrupt in its management, and that Sam Hill, as its moving spirit, was a swindler . . . Jim Hill is reported to have told his respected son-in-law that if he lost this case, he had better go to the Klondike or some other distant country, as his usefulness where he was known would be gone . . . but it is questionable if Sam will follow [this advice]. He has been so long associated with men who have overridden the law and public opinion, that he is likely to regard this as a mere passing annoyance." Hardball was evidently in vogue in those days, and libel a difficult thing to prove.

In April 1902, the State Supreme Court finally upheld the propriety of the Trust Company's original sale of the bonds. The *Minneapolis Tribune* chided the *Times*, and was pleased that " . . . the Minneapolis Trust Company has been completely vindicated from all charges. The worst of it is that innocent creditors must bear the heavy expense of defending their trustee against this piratical assault."

After the Guaranty Loan matter was settled, Sam wrote Cooke in March 1903: "Mr. [J. J.] Hill is anxious to have the Trust Company liquidated, and I must say I am getting to share this view very strongly . . . I am still thinking how foolish I was ever to consent to the appointment of the executive committee, for I hold that committee responsible for the condition in which the Minneapolis Trust Company got. If my views had been carried out and the proceeds of the property had been invested in the Manitoba [Railway] stock as I indicated, the company would have had about two millions of dollars besides its original capital; but we went into real estate mortgages, and the folly was in giving these men a vote when they in no sense shared the responsibility. . . . I begin to feel that I am like Frankenstein, that created a devil and the devil got too big for him. In fact, I am about ready to do anything to get rid of the executive committee — to cease to hear of them. Individually I think they are my friends; collectively, I won't say what I think of them, but I think."

The property Sam referred to in this outburst was the electrical side of the assets of the Seattle Gas and Electric Company. He had asked the Trust Company to release this part of the property from a consolidated mortgage, so it could be sold. Dunwoody wired approval of the sale in September 1902, but later put restrictions on the investment of the proceeds. Furthermore, he was disposing of his gas company bonds without notifying Sam. Sam wrote Cooke, acidly, " . . . From what you write me, he has probably transferred some of them to his wife or some of his friends."

Sam decided to quit the Trust Company some months before he formally resigned early in 1903. On the last day of 1902, he wrote a friend at the Chase Bank who was leaving for another bank, "I think you must feel as I did when I severed my relations in Minneapolis. However, it is one consolation [that] those of us who were together during the eventful ten years, '90-1900, have learned to measure each other, and in whatever field we may engage in labor, nothing can ever take away the feeling of mutual confidence which was established during that trying period." Sam obviously was not including in that sentiment all of his associates and clients.

About the time of his resignation, there was a flurry of correspondence from Sam about selling off several parcels of real estate he owned in Minneapolis, as well as the house on Stevens Avenue which belonged to his wife. He wrote offering to buy his old desk and chair and asking to have his law books sent to Seattle (at no expense to him because of his convenient Great Northern Express frank). As a modest notice of his prominence, he said, "Simply address them, 'Sam Hill, Seattle, Washington.'"

The aggravations Sam experienced as president of the Minneapolis Trust Company, as well as distate for Populism in Minnesota politics, did not endear him to the state. As he wrote Anstice Abbott in 1904, "I . . . rarely visit Minnesota, except for a few hours at a time, and usually go around the state, for while I have many friends there, I have no sympathy with those who have guided and led opinion. I have not yet begun to write my history . . . entitled, 'The History of Minneapolis, or Forty Years in the Wilderness.'"

5

Working on the Railroads

The early financial affairs of the vast Hill enterprises are tangled and do not lend themselves readily to summary. In 1878, J.J. Hill and his associates, starting with the proverbial shoestring, bought the troubled St. Paul and Pacific Railroad. They organized the St. Paul, Minneapolis, and Manitoba Railroad and sold most of its land holdings for nearly double the purchase price. They lost no time in expanding northward through the rich farmlands of the Red River Valley to connect with the Canadian Pacific, and then westward through Dakota Territory and Montana to Puget Sound at Everett, Washington in 1893. The Montana Central Railroad, with Sam Hill as its president, was built in 1886-87 and integrated with the Manitoba road. The Great Northern Railway, combining a dozen constituent roads, was organized in September 1889. Unlike other transcontinental railroads, it did not receive land grants or government financial aid.

The simplest way to report Sam's business activities in his Minneapolis days is in tabular form:

President:

Minneapolis Trust Company	Eastern Railway Company of Minn.
St. Paul, Minneapolis & Manitoba Ry.	Great Falls Water Power & Townsite Co.
Montana Central Ry.	Minneapolis Western Ry.
Duluth Terminal Ry.	Minneapolis Union Railway Co.
Red River-Lake of the Woods Ry.	Sand Coulee Coal Co.
Kettle River Ry. Co.	

Director:

Great Northern Railway

Great Northern Land Co.

Great Northern Express Co.

Willmar & Sioux Falls Ry.

Duluth, Watertown &
Pacific Ry.

Northern Steamship Co.

St. Paul & Pacific Ry. Co.

Lakewood Cemetery Assoc.

The directorship in the cemetery association might mean either that he was a compulsively thorough planner or that his mind, even then, was on last things. Some railway companies of which he was an officer were small outfits, such as the Minneapolis Union Railway Company, which did not own an engine but furnished terminals for the Minneapolis Union Depot. Others, like the St. P.M. & M. and Montana Central Railways, became important segments of the Great Northern system. It may be that Sam was designated by J.J. Hill as his legal representative on these various boards so that Sam's duties were not necessarily always burdensome. Still, one has to marvel at the organization and energy involved in wearing so many hats. The eyes glaze over at the thought of all those meetings and correspondence!

Through his railroad connections, Sam met people who later were to figure in the dealings of his Seattle gas company. In 1893, Judge Thomas Burke of Seattle sent Sam a carload of cedar shingles, specially packed in order to save space, and asked him to call J. J.'s attention to the method and the potential for increased freight revenue.

Sam gave his father-in-law credit for extensive reclamation of marshy lands in northern Minnesota and North Dakota. J. J. accomplished this by promoting " . . . drainage ditches which turned the water into the river flowing north to Hudson's Bay . . . Now instead of land being worth less than a dollar and a quarter an acre it is $200 an acre . . . This is the work of Hill which nobody seems to know." Sam did not add that Montana was another story; many homesteaders, encouraged to raise wheat there, abandoned their farms in the second decade of the 20th century when wind and erosion led to loss of topsoil and to disaster.

Another J. J. Hill coup was purchasing the Duluth and Winnipeg Railroad from the Canadian Pacific in 1897, and linking it to the Great Northern at the Red River. This railroad owned extensive properties in the Mesabi Range, fabulously rich in iron ore. During a trans-Atlantic crossing in 1921, Sam told Clarence Barron, the Pepys of Wall Street, "I reported on the value of the Mesabi range and sold it to J. J. Hill, but he would not believe us until he had seen the range himself personally. When the lawyers told him the railroad could not invest in the Mesabi range he bought the ore lands himself for $3,000,000*, and when the earnings had paid out the cost,

*Sam was probably in error on this figure, which Albro Martin gives as $4,000,000, terming it "one of the bargains of the century." In 1904, in what was not quite a characteristic gesture, J. J. sold the land at cost to a trust formed for the benefit of Great Northern stockholders. By then the land was worth perhaps 100 times what he had paid for it.

he presented the shares to the Great Northern shareholders. He never permitted any side deals or speculations. Everything had to go to the shareholders. He considered them all as partners. If a woman or small shareholder was unable to take his rights, which were what gave value to Great Northern shares, the rights were sold and a check for the rights sent them."

An odd sidelight on the Mesabi properties was the interest of Bishop James McGolnick of Duluth in recommending to Sam construction of a branch line to the mines. Two years later, the bishop, who apparently kept a close eye on secular matters, recommended land purchases along the railroad to Bemidji, Minnesota. He may not have been aware that the Hill interests had these matters well in hand.

Sam told Barron a story, without giving the date, about Jay Gould and J. J. Hill:

> Jay Gould was in charge of the Union Pacific and the Oregon Short Line* when James J. Hill started to build his Great Northern. Gould soon found out. There was a meeting at Gould's house which young George Gould and I attended. While the old men talked, we looked out of the window, but kept our ears open. Gould told Hill it was not necessary for him to build the Great Northern and he would arrange everything through the Union Pacific and Oregon Short Line. Gould offered also to build and issue securities at $30,000 a mile on roads costing $15,000 a mile.
>
> Hill replied, 'Our one desire is to build up the country and share in the prosperity that must follow. A railroad is a tax on the community. It has no reason for going there unless to perform a service not now provided . . . We should build our railroad through and capitalize it for exactly what it costs, not a dollar more nor a dollar less, and hope to share in the prosperity that will follow. I will not join with you in a real estate speculation, for a real estate speculation is not a railroad.'
>
> Jay Gould said, 'Will you take me in as a partner?'
>
> Hill said, 'All our stockholders are partners. There is no inside deal. Our stock is on the Exchange and we shall be glad to have you as a partner.'"

Sam did not hold Jay Gould in high regard. Many years later, he wrote his friend Edward Tuck in Paris, "I feel that I am on the outside of everything, and that the railroads are like the Missouri Pacific was when George Gould met the yard foreman at Kansas City and said, 'You don't know who I am, do you?'

"'Ah, yes, Mr. Gould, shure I do. You are Mr. Gould, the president of the road. Shure, I knew your father before you . . . he was president of the road and he will be president again.'

"'Oh, no.' George Gould said, 'my father is dead.'

"The Irishman said, 'Shure, I know that, and the road is going to hell as fast as it can.'"

Sam introduced Weyerhaeuser, the lumber man, to J. J. and was much chagrined to have them fight within five minutes. Hill said he would not

---

*The Oregon Short Line, completed in 1884, ran from Granger, Wyoming northwestward through Idaho to join the U.P.'s Oregon, Washington Ry. and Navigation Co.'s line at Pendleton, Oregon.

give a special freight rate on logs to Weyerhaeuser. Later they became close friends and neighbors in St. Paul.

To return to railroad matters in the 1890's, it was not always nose to the grindstone for Sam. He told Paul Douglas that he had gone to Europe to raise money during the severe depression of 1893, when the Great Northern had had to stop construction westward. Sam " . . . decided that the royal families were the only ones who were depression-proof." After studying the *Almanach de Gotha*, he concluded that King Leopold of Belgium was the key to his acquaintance with royalty. Leopold, with his swarm of feminine favorites, then held summer court at Ostend. By judicious flattery, Sam gained entrance to the court there, and not only sold a big block of Great Northern bonds, but obtained a letter to Queen Victoria, who also became a purchaser. She passed him on to Marie,* the Crown Princess of Rumania. After journeying to the Balkans, he made a big sale to the Rumanian royal house. "We built the line to the Pacific . . . while I became the intimate of royalty. Not bad for a North Carolina Quaker."

In a letter to President Harding in 1922, Sam recalled:

> When I was president of Montana Central Railway, ten million dollars was deposited to be given as a bonus if that road were extended to San Francisco. Mr. Hill and I went to San Francisco to examine conditions. He said to me, 'This is not the point to best develop the Oriental trade; we must go to Puget Sound.' Neither of us had been there prior to that time. He worked out the plan for the union of the Northern Pacific, Great Northern and Burlington roads with the idea that through Puget Sound the Oriental trade could be secured. He built the steamships *Minnesota* and *Dakota*, believing that the merchant marine under the United States flag would succeed. But for adverse legislation, this belief would have blossomed into reality, because, at that time, he sent me to the Orient and arrangements were made to supply cotton direct via the Burlington Lines; later, the Colorado Southern, reaching to the Gulf, was used for that purpose, and he made Seattle that year the second largest cotton port in the world. He could do this because he had the return haul on the lumber and shingles. He said to me, 'I will capitalize the cedar stumps in Oregon and Washington.' He did this, and with one stroke of his pen added enough to the wealth of the United States to pay the entire national debt as it then existed.

Sam did not say who had offered the bonus to construct a railroad to San Francisco, nor when the proposition was made. J. J. did not start to build toward California until 1910, when he and Harriman of the Union Pacific built parallel railroads into central Oregon. Both gave up on developing shipping trade across the Pacific when they were compelled to publish domestic freight rates, thus exposing the favorable differential they had been giving to Southern cotton shippers. This was the "adverse legislation" Sam refers to above.

The letters from Sam to J. J. Hill about railway affairs often relate to minute details of operation of the various roads. For example, Sam discusses dropping out two stations on the Minnetonka line and dispensing with one telegraph operator. He was concerned about delays in getting ten cars

---

*Marie, then age seventeen, was a granddaughter of Queen Victoria.

of stone a day to keep the workmen busy on the Minneapolis Western Stone Arch Bridge over the Mississippi. In his business letters to his father-in-law Sam usually reported conscientiously on the state of health of his family.

There must have been many opportunities for investment for a man in Sam's position, especially through inside information about the ups and downs of Great Northern and Northern Pacific Railway stocks. There were advantages, too, in knowing in advance the locations of proposed railway lines, stations, and terminals. In spite of foreknowledge, however, not all such ventures proved profitable for Sam. One was an investment in the Great Falls (Montana) Waterpower and Townsite Company. Construction of Jim Hill's railroad had reached the vicinity of Great Falls in 1887. Nearby Fort Benton had rejected Hill's request for a free right-of-way through the town. Hill redirected his tracks a mile or more away from Fort Benton. Great Falls got the message and decided to give the railway a strip of land through the middle of its city park. The waterpower company, however, was not a moneymaker.

Sam kept a close eye on legislation affecting the Great Northern, especially that of the Minnesota state government, where the Populist movement was strong in the 1880's. He wrote J. J. in February 1891, "Today, a majority of the entire legislature went to Duluth on the regular Eastern Minnesota train — four coaches were added. . . . They will be banqueted* there tonight. . . . " He was pleased to report, "The usual number of vicious bills had been introduced into the legislature and had been hung up or beaten. . . . " For vicious, read "anti-railroad."

One of the prominent legislators was Ignatius Donnelly, politician, editor of *The Representative,* orator, and novelist, who was not above accepting favors from the Hill camp. He wrote Sam in 1897 thanking him for a thousand mile ticket for his assistant editor. "One good turn deserves another," he said, "which I interpret to mean that if a man does you a good turn you are justified in asking him for another." The turn he had in mind was to ask Sam to put in a good word with the Northern Pacific, which was then trying to sell lands, to take advertising space in Donnelly's publication.

Though he did not hold with Donnelly politically, Sam admired his gifts as an orator and writer. As a boy, he had heard Donnelly speak, and contended that, " . . . to my mind, in my day, no man has ever lived in the United States who, as a stump speaker, was Donnelly's equal."

Two strikes affecting the Great Northern Railway occurred in the spring of 1894. Sam recalled these in accounts he dictated from memory in 1930. The first was the Pullman strike, brought about by the harsh measures imposed by George Pullman after the panic of 1893. House rents and store prices were kept high in the company town of Pullman, near Chicago. He fired one third of his workers and reduced the pay of the others by 25 percent, without reducing their living costs. The workers struck, supported by the American Railway Union, which refused to move Pullman cars. In

---

*Perhaps they were more likely to vote properly on a full stomach.

44

the ensuing violence, President Cleveland sent army troops, ostensibly to keep the U.S. mails going, but in reality to break the strike and discredit the unions.

Sam was president of the Minneapolis Union Railway, a small outfit with 53 employees, which did not own an engine and operated less than a mile of track. It was strategically important because it furnished terminals for the railroads using the Minneapolis depot and crossing the Stone Arch Bridge across the Mississippi. The superintendent told Sam his men would not handle Pullman cars, whereupon Sam gave him three minutes to change his mind and then fired him. The railroad commissioners of North Dakota and Minnesota were concerned that the wheat crop would be lost for lack of shipments of farm machinery and binding twine. Sam asured them his men would not strike. J. J. Hill hurried to Minneapolis and when Sam told him triumphantly, "There is no strike," J. J. smiled and said, "That was a good way, Samuel!"

The second strike of 1894 began on April 13, when Eugene Debs, president of the American Railway Union, demanded an increase in pay for his men. The basic wage had been $4 per ten hour day. Train crews received $4.50 per day, but could often earn more because a one hundred mile run was considered a day's work. Sam suggested that Minnesota Governor Knute Nelson appoint an arbitration committee consisting of Minneapolis capitalists, with J. J. Hill presiding. Debs and his men appeared before this committee and a new wage scale for every type of railroad worker was agreed upon with J. J., who did not find it necessary to consult his books. By introducing the per day rate instead of the one hundred mile run schedule for train crews, the Great Northern saved four and one half percent on its total payroll. When the union's committee returned later to inquire about pay raises, J. J. told them that he also had responsibilties to his investors and the general public, and they " . . . would have to look to Mr. Debs for [their] increase in pay."

Reflecting on these high handed ways, one can conclude that if the establishment wanted to teach Labor a lesson, Labor learned it very well in the twentieth century. Two strikes for the unions, two hits for the Hill interests: but history also keeps track of the errors.

Soon after the American Railway Union strike, Sam sent a long handwritten letter to H. W. Cannon, president of the Chase National bank, in response to Cannon's request for an analysis of conditions on the Great Northern. It was in good health, Sam said. "Physically, the railroad is planned and put on the ground as no other line is or has ever been between Chicago and the Pacific." Sam was optimistic about the future. He hoped "to see Congress pass laws affecting interstate railways which will make strikes seem impossible" — wishful thinking which no doubt seemed more of a possibility then than in years to come.

Of himself, Sam wrote, "I am well, happy, cheerful and have sand . . . Of course I am very tired and a little grayer than a year ago and I am just past 37." During the strike, he said, "My Minneapolis Western men stayed with me. . . . I passed several hours per day . . . in the shop with my old clothes on, helping put locomotives together and when I told Mr. Hill I felt competent to take a train out, he was somewhat surprised. I believe I have in a small degree the faculty of getting along with men such as Mr. Hill has to a large degree. . . . I was reelected during the strike president of the alumni of all high schools in Minneapolis." Even Ignatius Donnelly, he said, " . . . was with me during the war, so you see I am conceited enough to think I haven't yet lost my grip."

Sam's duties included being legal counsel for the land department of the Great Northern Railway until late 1900. His long-time friend and law associate, Charles Babcock, wrote him in 1901, "It seems as though you had withdrawn from the land department so that I might be advanced." Sam, now living in Seattle, was kept informed by Babcock of changes in personnel and gossip at Great Northern headquarters. Babcock, a friend of Debs and other labor union leaders, patiently argued with Sam in favor of the rights of labor unions. There is no evidence he made a convert.

At the turn of the century, we come to an enigma, not the first or the last in Sam's career. Abruptly and without fanfare, he resigned from his association with the Great Northern Railroad in November 1900, but he does not tell us why. At forty-four, he was to all appearances enviably placed in the catbird seat in Minneapolis. December 1901 found him in Seattle prepared to take over direction of the Seattle Gas and Electric Company. Some possible reasons for this midlife change, not merely of occupation and interests but of the whole direction of his life, are examined in the next chapter.

By many of those people who recognize his name at all, Sam Hill tends to be identified as a railroad man; some add, "Oh, yes, J. J. Hill's son," an error Sam would have regarded with mixed emotions. He did not express regret or bitterness, at least in correspondence, for the curious truncation of his career with the Great Northern. In fact, he was uncharacteristically silent. But in a letter to Arthur Hill, his former law partner, he once wrote wistfully of an earlier time. "Sometimes the longing comes back to see those kindred spirits whom I knew when I was Sam Hill, and before I went to work for the railroads and before I lost, in a measure, my identity."

6

Derailment Near the Summit

If any of the lieutenants of the great railroad barons of the 1880's and 1890's had an inside track to wealth and power, it was Sam Hill. After joining J. J. Hill's legal staff in 1886, he soon moved up to become president or director of most of the dozen subsidiary roads which eventually made up the Great Northern system. Though he appeared, with J. J.'s sons, to be in line to rule the empire after J. J.'s death, Sam abruptly resigned from the various railroad enterprises in November 1900. Why did he vacate that choice spot near the summit of one of the great enterprises of American business? It was surely not because there were no new worlds to conquer in railroading. Did he jump from the train or was he pushed?

The most intriguing of Sam's stories to Barron was the one about the organization of the Great Northern in September 1889. Sam said, "Lord Mount Stephen [George Stephen, head of the Bank of Montreal], Lord Strathcona [Donald Smith of the Hudson's Bay Company], J. Kennedy Todd, James J. Hill, and one other [he may have meant Norman Kittson, also of the Bay Company], controlled the Great Northern and it was agreed that Sam Hill should be J. J. Hill's successor. They first scaled the stock of St. Paul, Minneapolis, and Manitoba by $8,000,000. They then built it up as the Great Northern. At Hill's death, he had only seven percent of the Great Northern."

Note the throw-away line, "It was agreed that Sam Hill should be J. J. Hill's successor." When J. J. resigned as president of the Great Northern in June 1907, it was Louis, his second son, who succeeded him.

Did J. J. back out on a verbal promise to Sam in order to permit his sons to rule the empire after his death? Or did Sam grandly and falsely magnify his role and his prospects to Barron? Judging from the official histories of the Great Northern, one would have to conclude that he did do so. Sam's name is not even in the index of J. J. Pyle's authorized biography of J. J. Hill, nor in J. J.'s book, *Highways of Progress*. Sam plays a very small part in Albro Martin's definitive biography of J. J. A suspicious mind might even imagine that his father-in-law managed to make a non-person out of Sam for some family reason.

The *Minneapolis Journal* in its "Railroad Rumbles" column of September 2, 1901, noted, "Word comes from Tacoma that Samuel Hill . . . is to make Seattle his home, and to be general western representative of Great Northern interests . . . He is president of the Seattle Gas and Electric Company. James J. Hill is spending more and more of his time in New York. Vice-President Miller and Mr. Hill's sons will be left to control affairs at the Twin City headquarters if the plan is carried out."

Sam had been interviewed in Seattle and was quoted as saying he intended to move there permanently with his family, but when he returned to Minneapolis on Sept. 5, he declined " . . . either to deny or affirm the story, saying that he did not want to discuss the matter. However, it is more than likely that the published statement of the intended removal is correct . . . His duties [as president of the utility company] require his presence in Seattle much of the time, and will, it is said, necessitate his removal from Minneapolis."

Sam was still uncommunicative to reporters a month later, on his return from a brief trip to England " . . . to accompany Mrs. Hill home after her tour of the continent." He did say that " . . . he owned a house in Seattle and would probably spend some of the winter months on the coast."

The news of his resignation from the Great Northern was thus released in piecemeal and reluctant fashion, but the die had already been cast several weeks earlier. A letter from Sam to his father-in-law, written on July 30, 1901, on his return from an adventuresome and seemingly carefree jaunt to Russia (Chapter 19), strongly suggests that his resignation had been requested:

> Dear Mr. Hill:
>
> I herewith hand you checks of the St. P.M. and M. Ry. Co. [St. Paul, Minneapolis and Manitoba] and G.F.W.P. and T. Co. [Great Falls Waterpower and Townsite Co.] to which I do not think myself entitled.
>
> In returning the checks I wish to thank you for the great generosity shown me while connected with your service and to assure you that no one regrets more than I my inability to meet your expectations.
>
> While it is no defense to my shortcomings, I believe no one has ever been more loyal to you and few have ever had for you a more affectionate regard than I. That I have often been an embarrassment to you I am sorry for, but no one has ever lost any money through me, even those enterprises which at one time looked doubtful, being, I trust, now established. Your great ability (for I believe you to be the man most gifted in all ways whom I have ever met) places you beyond the need of asking the aid of anyone, but it does not preclude my offer to serve you should occasion ever arise.
>
> Together with my grateful recognition of your generosity I cherish the fact that I believe I have the friendship of all who are in any way connected with the Great Northern Railway.
>
> Yours,
>
> Samuel Hill

We don't know what "shortcomings" of Sam's or "embarrassments" to J. J. Hill Sam refers to. One would think that any serious defects in Sam's judgment or performance in his fourteen year association with J. J.'s enterprises would have led to an earlier parting of the ways. J. J. was too shrewd a businessman to give Sam large responsibilities simply because he was a son-in-law. Whatever grievous errors Sam may have made, they are not to be found in the available correspondence. Sam's tone implies the finality of his resignation, rather than a plea to be taken back into the fold. It can be argued that Sam hoped to placate J. J. and avoid the damage to Sam's career that J. J. could effect if he chose, but there is no evidence that his father-in-law held any grudge for personal or business reasons in later years. Nor is there reason to think that Sam bore "the President," as he was usually called, any ill will; on the contrary he continued to revere the particular genius of his father-in-law. As he wrote a friend early in 1903, "The President is, perhaps, the greatest living example of a man who knows how to save and yet with the same hand spends lavishly. The history of the Great Northern road demonstrates this fact. He used to say to me so often, 'Never throw away the old dollar 'till you have the new one in your hand.'"

Again, Sam wrote to a man inquiring about the Great Northern's "Railroad School" for training management in St. Paul: "Railroading, as I understand it, is only about 15 years old and was invented by Mr. James J. Hill. Other men had played with it, but he first reduced it to an exact science. He was the first man, as far as I know, to lay down the proposition that a railroad is a manufacturing corporation. It makes one commodity and offers it for sale. That commodity is transportation, divided into freight and passenger. The problem is, what does it cost to run a train a mile? — what does it cost to move a ton of freight a mile? This exact information is put in the hands of the people who sell transportation, that is, the traffic men. The problem is not to make more transportation than you can sell. To learn modern railroading it is necessary to begin at the accounting end, to find out what it costs."

It was rare for Sam to refer to his father-in-law irreverently, but he did so in writing A. B. Hepburn, a banker friend, in 1902: "We are looking for President James J. Hill here in a few days in order to tell us about farming and I have no doubt he will be able to convince us that it is a good thing for the farmers to raise wheat at a cost of 25¢ a bushel, pay the railroads 25¢ a bushel for hauling it to market, and for the farmers to live off the experience gained in the work."

Sam definitely was not fond of Louis Hill, who succeeded J. J. as head of the Great Northern. In 1923 Sam wrote Joseph Blabon, then with the Texas Company in Cape Town, South Africa, "I resigned from the Minnesota Club in St. Paul because I found the club enthusiastically for L. W. Hill, and I know of no reason why I should have to listen to talk like that." Sam's hostility was probably related, at least in part, to the unseemly squabble over the estate of Mrs. J. J. Hill, beginning in 1921, in which Louis and Sam's wife were allies in a fight with her other children (Chapter 11).

Frank Branch Riley, a long time Portlander and raconteur who knew Sam well, wrote this about the relationship between Sam and Louis: "Sam Hill was a great guy. He was charming, filled with enthusiasm, the complete extrovert. He was blessed with a vanity that was captivating. I fancy that Jim Hill's harder-headed, and maybe harder-hearted, son Louis was often bemused, possibly often annoyed, by the performance of this handsome, virile, and volatile brother-in-law, with his tremendous flair for the dramatic and spectacular."

In a biography, unlabeled speculation is as unacceptable as peculation in finance. Unfortunately, we must turn to speculation about the decisions made in the fateful year, 1901. Perhaps J. J. had detected in Sam signs of instability which would make him unsuited to sharing the rule of empire, signs which would become floridly evident years later (Chapter 26). It may be that the estrangement of Sam and his wife influenced J. J. in his decision, or that the senior Hills gave Sam some kind of ultimatum about his family situation which Sam failed to follow. It seems likely to the author that Sam's later aversion to visiting Minnesota arose in part from the reaction of some of the Hill clan to the disintegration of the relationship between Sam and Mamie.

The author thinks that Sam and J. J. Hill came to some kind of amicable understanding leading to Sam's official resignation from the Great Northern in November 1900; amicable because Sam continued to correspond with his father-in-law in friendly fashion about business matters in which they had a mutual interest, such as the Minneapolis Trust Company and the Seattle Gas Company, as well as those in which J. J. had only an indirect financial interest, e.g., good roads matters and the establishment of a planned town at Maryhill, Washington.

Whatever the reasons that Sam left St. Paul for a new life in Seattle, he appears to have done so without regret. Here was an opportunity to achieve success on his own merits and not on the coattails of his father-in-law; a chance to change the predictable course his life would have taken had he remained in the Twin Cities as president of the Minneapolis Trust Company. Although he does not say so, Sam may even have thought that moving away from Mamie's family would improve her mental outlook and broaden her interests, and thus help to save their marriage.

There may well have been an element of bravado, too. If he was dismissed from railroad service, it must have been secretly shattering to his confidence and self-esteem, and one suspects that it made him more prone to gamble to restore them. One way to achieve this was to make a lot of money, as he proceeded to do in the stock market in the next decade. Another was to win admiration through his famous friends, public service, and success in business. One thing seems sure; Sam emerged from that year changed, if not chastened, with different goals in life and different designs for achieving them.

7

The Spur to Russia

In May and June 1901, Sam undertook a great adventure, crossing Siberia to Stretensk on the then unfinished Trans-Siberian Railway and by boat and train to Vladivostok. He returned to Minneapolis by way of Japan in mid-July. He later told Lockley that the purpose of the trip was to inspect the railroad and report to French investors before they took the construction bonds of the Russian government. On his return, the *Minneapolis Journal* said he had been investigating " . . . new commercial and transportation opportunities for the Morgan-Hill syndicate." At any rate, Sam was well qualified for such an assignment, but if he made a report in writing, no copy of it seems to have survived.

Occurring as it did so soon after his momentous midlife decision to sever many of his ties with the Twin Cities and begin a new career in remote Seattle, and shortly before he brought his wife and children there, it is likely that this trip represented more than a combined business and pleasure junket to Sam. One suspects that in part it was a defiant gesture to proclaim severance from J. J. Hill and connections to the past, and a declaration that the rest of his life would be played by different rules. One of these strained ties was to Mamie. He apparently bore their three month separation with equanimity; in his letters he does not express a desire to be back with his family and one gathers that he was enjoying himself too much for this to cross his mind.

Sam had visited Russia once before, in the summer of 1899, when he went as far as St. Petersburg, leaving his family in France. He was asked to write an account of these two trips for the short-lived periodical *Opportunity*, published by the Passenger Traffic Department of the Great Northern Railway. This appeared in 1902 in a five part series, illustrated with drawings and Sam's own photographs, titled, "The Problem in the Orient." The "problem," according to Sam, was whether the new railroad would put Russia ahead of the United States, Canada, and Britain in competing for trade with the Orient.

Sam dictated a long account of his second trip and made additional observations in letters to his wife, letters which were mostly impersonal, as one might write to a good friend interested in travel. Combined, they make a well-written and captivating narrative, unfortunately too long to include in this book.

On his second trip, he traveled with Robert Lebaudy, a well-to-do French businessman, with whom he inspected the luxurious coaches of the railroad at an exhibition in Paris in 1900. He told the *Minneapolis Journal* reporter that this was " . . . the most comprehensive panorama of the world's progress ever presented to mortal eyes," and that the cars in the exhibit of the Trans-Siberian railroad were " . . . equal in every respect to those operating between Minneapolis and Chicago."

Through the U.S. ambassador to Russia, Charlemagne Power, Sam met Prince Khilkov, Minister of Communication, and Rothstein, president of the Russo-Chinese Bank, both of whom furnished letters of introduction which opened many doors for Sam.

Sam commented at length on everything he saw; his (excuse the expression) fellow travelers; the countryside, which often reminded him of places in the American Northwest; the birds and flowers; the exotic cities and towns; the hotels and public baths; the military maneuvers of the Cossacks; the deep religious feelings of the Russians in the west and the superstitious regard for lamas in the east. He paid particular attention to the construction and operation of the railroad, which he found up-to-date in some ways and quaintly backward in others.

The Trans-Siberian was finished as far as Stretensk, from whence he and Lebaudy took a boat down the Amur River to Khabarovsk. Sam describes a poignant episode following the death of a small child of one of the immigrants on the boat:

> The captain ran the boat ashore at a small town and he had evidently sent a wire ahead from the last station, for when we got there at dusk, the church on the bank of the river was all aglare with lights. Four sailors without caps and with solemn faces bore the tiny coffin followed by the mother with a boy holding either hand. The father was dead, and the Captain, with a pair of black cotton gloves, followed the mother and everyone who chose to join the procession. It slowly wound up along the bank of the river toward the church through the beautiful meadow covered with flowers, and from time to time those in the procession would leave the ranks, gather flowers, run forward and throw them on the coffin. It was indeed a strange yet a simple sight to see these people of different races all joining in this tribute of respect to a little child. The coffin was then placed in the church in front of the altar and services were said; then it was taken out where a grave had been dug and was buried, and then everyone filed back to the boat.

From Khabarovsk, Sam proceeded by train to Vladivostok, where the governor of the province had arranged an elabrate excursion to the island of Askold. There a splendid buffet had been prepared, supplemented by vodka and four kinds of wine. Sam wrote:

> I ate and drank just what the gentleman next to me did. Imagine my horror at the conclusion of the repast to have the President arise and apologize for the fact that dinner was ten minutes late! I had supposed that we were eating the principal meal. Not so!

By this time Sam had learned enough Russian to respond to the frequent toasts during the meal which was then served. What was more remarkable, when he was invited to shoot at a champagne bottle, he broke the neck of the bottle on the first shot and modestly deprecated this feat by saying that a real American would have hit the cork only.

There were other gala dinners and parties in Vladivostok. At one of these, Sam graciously acknowledged Russian and French friendship with the United States and so delighted the governor's wife with his gallantry that " . . . she declared I must be a Russian and sent for her brother's picture to show my resemblance to him." One of the guests was the commandant of the French battleship *Guerin*. He invited Sam and Lebaudy to lunch aboard and during the meal received orders to sail immediately. The warship steamed to Japan in thirty hours and dropped off its two passengers. Sam was entertained at dinner by the Harvard Club of Tokyo on the Fourth of July.

He was back in Minneapolis some three weeks later, bringing kimonos for his in-laws and "an exquisite silver vase" for Mrs. J. J. Hill. He was soon off to France to escort his wife and children back to the Twin Cities in early October. Later that month they were off to make their new home in Seattle.

After his trip, Sam wrote letters of introduction for several friends about to visit Russia. In Vladivistok, he had met one Valeria Amosova, who did translations. She wrote asking Sam about writing a book on Russian history for American youth. He responded by inviting her to teach Russian at the University of Washington, where he proposed to endow a chair of Russian studies. She regretfully declined because she was about to be married, but she hoped to go abroad and meet Sam again " . . . and we will once more cosely [*sic*] talk as we did a year ago. . . . Goodbye, Mr. Hill. Do you not think that in the battle of life one needs sometimes more bravour than in battle of war? I try to be brave." We hear no more of the brave Valeria Amosova.

What does Sam's story of his Russian travels tell us about the man? In the first place, how many established businessmen of that day would have undertaken such an aventuresome and possibly dangerous journey? He was a keen and appreciative observer of people as well as railroads, his specialty. His sense of humor and savoir faire are evident throughout, even if one allows for the opportunity to improve one's image in a retrospective account. He comes off as a knowledgeable traveler and citizen of the world. Who knows whether the history of the Trans-Siberian Railroad might have been different had he been a high born Russian engineer when it was being planned and built? Certainly Russia had a greater impact on Sam than vice versa, but this was not due to lack of effort on Sam's part. The story of his unsuccessful attempt to change Russian history by his third trip there in 1916 is told in Chapter 20.

PART II

A FAMILY "UNHAPPY IN ITS OWN WAY"

8

Seattle and Estrangement

Thus far, Sam's story has been told chronologically, in the main. For the thirty years of his life from 1901 on, however, the author fears that a year by year account would serve only to confuse the reader completely, because in these decades, Sam hurried after all manner of pursuits concurrently. By 1910, for example, he had engaged in the gas business in Seattle and fought a bitter battle with a competitor; made millions in the stock market; bought a great summer house in Massachusetts and a large ranch in Washington State; begun a formidable campaign for good roads in the Pacific Northwest; built a mansion in Seattle; begun construction of a planned town and a system of experimental roads on the north bank of the Columbia; and purchased a telephone company in Portland. Meanwhile, he had worked for Harvard as an overseer and for other philanthropic causes; sent custommade world globes to various friends and institutions; hobnobbed and corresponded with numbers of the rich and famous; and traveled extensively. This frenetic activity did not abate during the following twenty years, witness his will-o-the-wisp ventures in the 1920's (Chapter 26) when he suffered from a manic state. If the gods were out to destroy him, they engaged in their traditional groundwork!

But Sam was no Job, pushed to the edge of despair, buoyed up only by faith and hope. He was sustained by many rewards and gratifying achievements, but he needed more than admiration and praise; he needed love. Was he loved, or loved enough, save by his poor daughter Mary Mendenhall, and, we presume, by the three mistresses who bore him children? Not if you hold with Maxim Gorky: "When one loves somebody, everything is clear — where to go, what to do — it all takes care of itself. . . . "

Marriages break up in all sorts of ways: the irrevocable snap resulting from a bitter quarrel; the recurrent fractures that fail to heal completely; the splints of children, religion, and social pressures that finally give way. In some marriages, there is no firm union to start with, only its appearance, and the realization of this is accepted gradually with reluctance or relief. The marriage of Sam and Mamie seems to have been of the last type. But a definite diagnosis is not possible from the incomplete history and only tentatively from the signs exhibited.

One suspects that it was with regret, and perhaps some stormy arguments, that Mamie left her family, friends, and the comfortable surroundings of St. Paul in October 1901, for the new milieu and challenges of Seattle. They lived in a rented house on Summit Avenue. Mamie and the children did not stay long the first time; she returned to St. Paul in the spring of 1902, ostensibly to visit her family because of her health.

What led Sam to move to Seattle instead of some other place? He knew the city because of his position with the Great Northern, which had extended its line there in 1893, and had an idea, which later had to be modified, of Seattle's golden promise. He came as president of the Seattle Gas and Electric Company, bought several years earlier by Minneapolis and Seattle investors.

In the last part of the 19th century, Seattle was a sawmill town, important for shipping lumber and coal to San Francisco. The Northern Pacific had completed its transcontinental line to Tacoma in 1883, but Seattle did not yet have its own connection with the East. Wheat from the Inland Empire went mainly from Spokane and Pendleton to Portland. Some entrepreneurs thought that the iron ore in the Cascade Mountains and the coal deposits around Puget Sound would be the basis for founding another Pittsburgh. There was hope, too, that Seattle would be the leading port for trading with the Orient and Siberia. But Seattle's development did not take the anticipated path. The coal and iron resources proved to be overrated. J. J. Hill undertook a survey, and in 1902 told Judge Thomas Burke, his agent in Seattle, that Hill was no longer interested in iron and coal because lumber would be the backbone of Seattle's trade.

Shipping from Seattle was also a disappointment at the time, in part because ships were beginning to use oil instead of coal, thus giving California an advantage over the Puget Sound region. Hill's large cargo ships, the *Dakota* and *Minnesota,* were embarrassing failures. The completion of the Great Northern's lines to Seattle in 1893 and the Klondike gold rush (1897-98) did increase Seattle's trade. Seattleites had resented the Northern Pacific's tactic of making Tacoma its western terminus, but now their city surpassed Tacoma and Portland in growth.

Sam had met Judge Thomas Burke, Edmund Meany, and others before the family moved to Seattle. As the quintessential extrovert, Sam made new friends and acquaintances at a great rate there. It is doubtful if Mamie kept pace or tried to. Her "rheumatism" was worse in Seattle and the polite fiction was maintained that the climate did not agree with her. People writing to Sam often courteously inquired about his wife's health. As Judge Burke wrote early in 1902, "Everyone in Seattle was anxious to see a good winter for the sake of Mrs. Hill and the children . . . for it was thought that good weather might entice her to make her home there altogether." He added, " . . . a man who gets up at six in the morning, is at his office at seven and doesn't get home to dinner until seven or eight . . . can stand any kind of weather that comes along." And so it might have been if the captain and his mate had stayed with the ship in stormy weather, or in perhaps what was more ominous, a dead calm.

While Mamie was in St. Paul in the spring of 1902, Sam dutifully sent her the floor and wall dimensions for carpets and wallpaper for their rented house. He discussed problems at his gas company and ended, "Everybody asks for you and the children and they are all anxious to have you back again." "They," not "I", one asks? About the same time, Sam wrote her, "I have asked Vernon Wright to call on you in St. Paul and talk over the plans for a house . . . I would like to have you give him your ideas and then have him block out something."

A month later, Sam wired Mary that he would see her at the J. J. Hill summer place at North Oaks in mid-June. She responded, "After two weeks of silence I had a letter from you this morning." She wrote of friends and family and of her current reading, *Far From the Madding Crowd* by Hardy. *Godolphins* by Lytton was "delightful in its natural artificialities."* She hoped he would have a good trip to North Oaks, and signed the letter, "Yours, Mary."

They came back to Seattle in July 1902, and Sam took his family and brother Richard on a steamship tour of the Inside Passage to Alaska. This, at least, was successful. Well-traveled Sam, who was not easily impressed, wrote his friend McLennan, "I have never seen anything yet to equal this Alaskan scenery . . . Mrs. Hill and the children enjoyed the trip very much." On their return, Sam wired his brother-in-law, Louis, on board J. J. Hill's private car on the Great Northern, "Mary expects all the family to stop at the house." Later, Sam borrowed Louis' house plans and he and Mary " . . . spent the evening looking over [them] . . . I hope to get our own plans out before the first of the year."

Sam had bought property for a new Seattle residence in 1902. That fall, he corresponded with Wright about plans. But his wife's leaving six months later called a halt to the project until 1906, when he started to lay out the ground for the house.

James and his mother were ill during much of the fall of 1902. Sam wrote his brother in September, "Since Clara [his sister-in-law] went away, Mary has had a setback and cannot sleep and is very nervous. As soon as I select a location for a house, I think her interest in life will return and she will have something to do in planning the house."

Later that year, James' recurrent tonsillitis improved, and his doctor assured Sam that he would outgrow his childhood asthma within two years. Sam wrote Beard, his brother-in-law, in January 1903, "My wife is not sleeping at all well and I may take her down to Portland and over to Spokane or to Victoria for a few days. She is not willing to go to California and she is not willing to go east or south."

A crisis early in 1903 did not help matters. Sam wrote, "The French woman who was acting as nurse for the children went insane and we had to send her to an asylum, all of which upset Mrs. Hill and the children a good deal. We now have a trained nurse."

Mrs. J. J. Hill was concerned about her daughter, and chided her son-in-law about the state of things. She wrote, "I feel very anxious about Mamie. I hear on all sides that she does not look well and that she is very nervous. She never mentions herself when writing, so I would know little of her but that I occasionally learn something from others. I feel all the time

---

*Could she have been reading Oscar Wilde, as well?

that Seattle is not a good place for her and I hope she will not have to remain there too long. I know she does not want to settle there indefinitely. Life is too short for either of you to sacrifice large portions of it unnecessarily." Gertrude, another of Mamie's sisters, took over from Clara in staying with Mamie, and a Miss Tweedy, the trained nurse from St. Paul, replaced Madeline, the deranged governess.

Heavy rains early in 1903 had severed train connections between Seattle and the east, and Sam had to miss a meeting of the Harvard Overseers for the first time. Late in January Sam wrote, "Mrs. Hill has been very ill with an acute attack of rheumatism." He visited the J. J. Hills in St. Paul early in February 1903. His wife wired him there that "James [is] much better. I also, no rheumatism." Was her recovery fortuitous or linked to Sam's leaving?

However wistfully Mamie may have looked back on St. Paul, it was not this wife's lot to turn into a pillar of the community in Seattle. She left there in March 1903, and never returned to the Northwest. One gets the impression that she was not easy to know, and this remoteness pervades her scanty correspondence with Sam during the next fifteen years. Perhaps significantly, she preferred sending him telegrams to writing letters.

Sam and his wife may well have had friends in the Twin Cities who regarded their union more as a merger than a partnership, but there is no basis for considering Sam a mere fortune hunter who would exploit an advantageous marriage in order to live in style with a minimum of effort. Sam had too much pride and self-confidence to limit his ambitions to such a shabby goal.

There is no indication that Sam ever offered to return to St. Paul to live with his family, or to compromise by moving to a warm climate for the sake of his ailing and unhappy wife. One suspects he was too much of a realist to feel these gestures would accomplish anything. The gradual disintegration of what had become a loveless marriage very likely had begun well before Sam set his face to the west and she to the east. As Francis Thompson's lines would have told them, " . . . 'Tis your estranged faces/that miss the many-splendored thing."

Mamie left Seattle by private rail car for St. Paul in March 1903, this time for good. The next month Sam went to New York to see his family off to Europe. In June he requested a Great Northern traffic manager in Seattle to " . . . have the Burlington transportation left at the ticket office at Union Depot, St. Paul; not made out in my name for it is not for me, but in an envelope directed to me. I cannot give you the name of the party for whom it is intended." This cryptic message, one suspects, was about "the other woman" and was related to the estrangement with his wife. One can only guess at the roles, or even the existence, of earlier infidelity or frigidity. The author thinks that Ben Franklin's epigram applies: "Where there is marriage without love, there will be love without marriage" — and if not love, at least the tireless pursuit of it by a tireless romantic like Sam.

It was an age when, in a failing marriage, it seemed more important than it does now to keep up the appearance of harmony; to plead the excuses of illness or pressures of business rather than admit that a marriage was on the rocks and beyond salvage. The conventional mores and social position of the J. J. Hills no doubt made preservation of the facade more desirable than might otherwise have been the case. It seems likely, too, that Sam and Mamie wanted to maintain a display of a unified family "for the sake of the children" as well as for others. Their purchase of the estate in Massachusetts is a case in point; another is Sam's acquisition of a ranch in northern Washington for James's sake. Before turning to these ineffectual gestures and the final collapse of all pretense between Sam and Mamie, let us turn to the stories of their children, hostages in a conflict which would scar them more deeply than the principals.

9

Mary Mendenhall Hill

Sam's daughter, Mary Mendenhall Hill, probably caused him more heartache than the estrangement from his wife or problems with James, his son. In his correspondence, he neither blames nor tries to exonerate himself for the increasing coldness in his relationship with his wife. In his letters to James, he admits spoiling him. His daughter's problems, however, were the sort that affection and money could ameliorate but could not cure.

Mary Mendenhall was born in St. Paul on July 3, 1889, ten months after her parents were married. We know little about her early childhood and education. Her grandmother wrote Sam about Mary's first communion in St. Paul in June 1902. "She has looked so well and is very happy. If you could have been here all would be perfect. She received a precious little gift yesterday from Father Keane, a souvenir of the occasion."

Sam's financial records in the Maryhill Museum files show that while the family lived in Seattle, his daughter went to a private school and took lessons in fencing and piano. Music lessons were continued in New York and she attended Miss Spence's School for Girls on West 53rd Street as a boarder in 1906-07. Bills for school fees, doctors, and clothes were forwarded to Sam.

There is evidence that Mary M. was somewhat mentally retarded as well as emotionally disturbed. In the numerous letters Sam wrote to her between 1905 and 1913, he nearly always refers to her in the third person and describes his travels and business and social activities in the simple but uncondescending fashion one might use with a young child. Occasionally, he uses the Quaker "thee." There are no scoldings or admonitions, as with James. In letters to Sam from his family, in-laws, and friends, there are many good wishes for Mary and inquiries about her health, but rarely a mention of any mental handicap.

Her early letters to her father are in an adult's handwriting, not her mother's — probably that of a governess or nurse. In correspondence, Sam never expresses doubt or fear that Mary would not develop into a normal adult. Honest as he was in most matters, Sam seems to have rejected, at least openly, a realistic appraisal of her prognosis and capabilities. Put more bluntly, to his friends, the fact of her bleak future was unspoken: for Sam, it was unspeakable.

In the earliest letter to her in his files (March 1905) he wrote that he would be coming to New York to take her back to Washington, D.C., where her mother and the children had moved upon leaving Seattle in 1903. He sent her a picture and description of Che-wil-o-kap, the ranch in the Methow Valley in north central Washington. In subsequent letters, he wrote about James's summer visits, their relatives and friends, his good roads activities, his travels, and plans for the Seattle house. "Everything here is very beautiful and green," he wrote in November 1906. "Mary has the place next to the ravine and overlooking the whole Sound and the beautiful Olympic Mountains beyond."

In 1906, at age seventeen, she began a letter, "Have you beaten anybody playing dominoes? I have not played since you left yesterday morning." She went on about skating with her friends, and added, "Mrs. Wheeler invited me to go to the White House with her and some girls. I could not go, but they did not see Mrs. Roosevelt, but Mrs. Longworth and the President."

Sam replied, "By the time this reaches Mary, the horses and yellow wheels will be in Washington. . . . I have Mary's picture on my desk and I like to look at it. . . . I am living at the Rainier Club [Seattle]." James was with Sam in July 1907, when Sam wrote about their vacation and planned trip to the Methow Valley. He and James would meet Mary and her mother in Ventnor, New Jersey, in early September.

In October 1907, he wrote Mary M. in detail about his discovery of the "Promised Land." For the next several years, he frequently sent her and her mother boxes of fruits from Maryhill. In the spring of 1908, he wrote, "The farmers there are all through with their plowing and most of the grain has been put in the ground. The nurserymen are trimming their trees and grapevines. The meadowlarks are singing and on the hillsides are great masses of yellow buttercups. The sun shone brightly, although when we left Portland it was raining."

Sam had been in Seattle earlier and expected that, " . . . the furniture that Mary and I bought in Chicago will be here today. . . . After I get in and settled, I will have a photograph taken and send it to Mary, especially [one] of her room."

He told her about the dinner he had given for the governor of Washington and the faculty and board of regents of the University of Washington. At the dinner, someone had told a story about an examination question given in the Seattle public schools, "Who was the Colossus of Rhodes?" Four or five of the children answered, "Mr. Samuel Hill."

For Christmas, 1907, Mary copied this poem in block letters for her parents:

> Mother and Dad
>
> In all the years I have known you both
> You've planned and strived for me
> Throu [sic] sacrifice of everything
> That could a pleasure be.
> This cluster of roses
> I am giving to you
> Just as a thought from me.

Early in 1909, Sam's mother-in-law wrote him that she had talked to Dr. Harry L. Taylor, a friend of Sam's who operated a "sanitorium for consumptives." He had had a "pleasant litle chat" with Mary in her room. Soon afterward, Dr. Taylor wrote Sam to say he " . . . wanted to talk about your Mary Mendenhall and find out how she really is, and what Mrs. J. J. Hill had accomplished in getting her away from Washington."

Sam replied that he had " . . . nothing to add about either of the Marys [that is, his wife and daughter]. You know the condition better than I. Mr. and Mrs. Hill were there and Clara. The program is as soon as Mary Mendenhall is well enough, for her grandmother to take her down to Jekyl Island [Brunswick, Georgia]. You will be glad to know that at least all of the Hill family — I do not mean the boys — are a unit with me." He meant that they approved the proposal of getting Mary away from Washington and her difficult mother. But Mary was back in Washington soon after this and wrote, "Mama had 22 people at dinner. . . . Mama doesn't seem to enjoy society, because she said, 'Isn't the view pretty out of the window!'"

Sam had a letter about Mary from Dr. Herman M. Biggs,* General Medical Officer for the New York City Department of Health, in May 1909. This was in response to a telegram from Sam about a consultation. Biggs was obliged to be out of town, but offered to have two other physicians see Mary, if Sam wished. The outcome is not recorded, but his brother wrote Sam a few days later, "I feel sure away from her mother and with proper surroundings she would be all right."

In the summer of 1909, her grandmother wrote, "Mary was looking better each week. . . . She is more energetic and interested. . . . I do not

---

*An old friend of J. J. Hill's, who, with the Mayo brothers, was called in consultation in J. J.'s last illness in 1916.

intend to send Dr. Peterson any word, for his visit disturbed her for days —
and what can he do?"

Mary wrote her father from the Jekyl Island Club in January 1910 to ask
if she could come out to Maryhill the following month. She was enjoying the
golf, tennis, and walks in the woods. She added, confusedly, "This is ideal,
but the same trouble has come here. My grandfather knows it was all right
when I was last here, but I remember something of the same that it is now.
Don't you think it would be well for him to know? I asked you first. I am
writing as well as I can. . . . I am going to stay with Grandma, as Dr. Biggs
thinks I will not be well in Washington."

The Jekyl Island visit ended badly. Mrs. J. J. Hill wrote Sam from there
in February 1910, concerned about Mary's mental status. "Although she
was looking unusually well, the weather has been cold and rainy and does
not agree well with Mary. . . . At times she seems disturbed as to what she
should do in the future and has talked to me about living out in the State of
Washington. I tell her that that would be impossible without her mother,
and it would. She could not be the responsible person nor would it be well
for her to be alone much. She is too inclined to turning things over to
herself."

A few weeks later she wrote:

> My stay . . . was shortened by Mary M's condition . . . she had a few
> days indisposition before I reached Jekyl — it was thought to have been a
> bilious turn. . . . Poor Mary had quite an ordeal as we were leaving the island
> — an acute case of hysteria. By the time we got here [New York City] she was
> much better and has been, since Dr. Biggs says it is entirely physical. Poor
> Mary's mind apparently is never at rest — too much of the time she is inclined
> to be listless. You will have to be very careful not to hold out promises to her
> that cannot be fulfilled for her. Her memory is excellent. All the time that I was
> at Jekyl, she was turning over something in her mind. It eventually came out.
> She said you had told her she could go to Seattle in February. I told her I was
> sorry if you had, for that would be impossible for so young a girl to do under
> the circumstances. . . . I hope I have made the situation plain; Mary is very
> nervous. She is about as she was when you left here. She lost some weight at
> Jekyl the last week there. She is getting that back fast now, as her illness was
> entirely physical. . . . I have decided that Mary will need a companion for her
> best chances. She should be out much, and driving does not seem good for her
> so walking is next best. . . . It is difficult for her to concentrate her mind for
> any length of time. She reads a little and is read to some.

The phrase, "entirely physical" was no doubt intended to reassure
both Sam and Mrs. Hill. But as Albro Martin puts it, she " . . . fared poorly
in the strained domestic atmosphere . . . By 1910, Mary Mendenhall had
begun to suffer the severe and recurring depressions from which she would
be released only by death."

Two of Mary's aunts, Clara and Rachel Hill, wired Sam in Portland, in
April 1910, "Father and Mother would release Mary [to her mother]. We
strongly protest in regard to proposed change ill-advised. Physicians agree
with us. Action must be immediate. Come at once — answer." J. J. Hill also
wired Sam (in code) asking him to come to New York as soon as possible.

Sam took the train east the next day. A few days after he arrived, J. J. telegraphed him that Mary Mendenhall had " . . . always improved very fast in St. Paul when she has opportunity to visit her relatives and a few friends with whom she feels quite at home. Her few setbacks have been her fear of returning to Washington [to her mother]. . . . "

But Sam decided to get his daughter and bring her west with him in May. His brother thought this was a mistake. "I wish thee might have seen fit to come on this far and have it out with the family. . . . I am sure thee can't go to New York again, as Mary was under the order of the court and by taking her away was in contempt of court. Mrs. J. J. is very hostile. . . . I think on her account, thee made a mistake to leave her with this matter hanging over her. . . . Neither of you can go back to New York till the matter is settled and Cohen [Sam's attorney in a later court suit] will work it to the limit."

The air had cleared a few days later when Dr. Taylor called on Mrs. J. J. Hill. He found her worrying " . . . because she fears you are letting Mary do too much. I assured her that the resident physician would not allow Mary to become exhausted. J. J. expressed himself as well satisfied with the present arrangement. He thought Mary looked on Washington, D.C., with horror and said he could not blame her for attitude toward the place." He added, "Mrs. Hill [Sam's wife] must have felt deeply grieved at first, but has evidently been talked around." These were his impressions, he said, but he was " . . . not anxious to probe deep. . . . Dick [Sam's brother] telephoned me that I would get well tanned when I was there, but the atmosphere seems to have cleared."

Sam was happy about his decision to bring Mary M. to Seattle and Maryhill. He wrote his brother that Mary had enjoyed her trip west and was " . . . perfectly delighted with the place. Dr. Burris and Miss Marte are here with her. Whatever may come in the future, I feel I have certainly done the right thing in bringing her to Seattle."

He expressed the same feeling to his friend and Harvard classmate, Francis McLennan. "I have had a great deal of trouble and sorrow but have decided at last to act hereafter on my own responsibility. I have brought my daughter west. . . . Both the doctor [Burris] and nurse [Miss Martel] complain that they have nothing to do since coming west except to enjoy themselves. Mary seems very delighted with Seattle and with the place here at Maryhill. She has been riding over the hills on horseback. . . . I do not know whether I shall feel like going abroad this summer, although I ought to attend the Congress at Brussels. You will hear all manner of things to my discredit, but they will not be half as bad as the things I could tell about myself."

The controversy over Mary M's custody was not made public until the *New York Times* carried a story in August 1910, headlined, "Hills in a Fight for Granddaughter":

> Though closely guarded, news got out yesterday that for many weeks
> until a few days ago a referee appointed by the Supreme Court of this county

has been quietly taking testimony in an action by Mrs. James J. Hill to get the custody of her granddaughter. Not even the name of the referee would be disclosed by any of the lawyers connected with the case, nor could the court's order of reference be found at the County Courthouse. [The author's search of New York Supreme Court records for 1910 failed to turn up any reference to the custody suit.]

Mrs. James J. Hill has been represented first by Anson McCook Beard — and later by Mr. Beard and ex-Supreme Court Justice Henry A. Gildersleeve . . . whom Mr. Beard brought into the case. [Beard was Mrs. J. J. Hill's son-in-law. He and Sam had had a run-in in 1904 over legal fees in the sale of Sam's gas company. Perhaps Beard regarded this suit as a way of getting back at Sam.] Samuel Hill . . . is represented by ex-Supreme Court Justice William M. Cohen.

Mr. Cohen declined yesterday to say anything about the suit involving the Hills other than that it could not possibly interest the public. . . . "

Beard told the reporter, " . . . when resort was had to the courts, the granddaughter was not of age, but that she had gained a majority while the referee was taking the testimony, and therefore could do as she pleased." He would not say why a referee had been used or why Mrs. Hill wished to have her granddaughter brought up under her direction, rather than under the guidance of the girl's father. " . . . The referee had not made his report and might never do so in view of the girl's becoming of age." Attorneys for both sides denied that Mrs. Samuel Hill was seeking a separation. The reason for the grandmother's action " . . . was her desire to have her granddaughter educated in the Catholic schools and brought up in the Catholic faith to which both she and her husband belong."

In a statement about ten days later, Sam declared that the latter part of the report was not relevant, because he was "friendly with representatives of that faith."

One's first impression from the news story is that the J. J. Hills brought the action because they considered Sam to be a bad influence on their granddaughter. Considering Mary M's "horror" of returning to Washington and her mother's peculiar personality, it seems quite likely that the senior Hills were trying to get Mary away from her mother, preferring that she live with them or with Sam.

After returning from a visit to Maryhill in the fall of 1910, following the court hearing, Dr. Taylor wrote Sam, "The more I think over my warning to you about letting your daughter return to Washington, the more convinced I am that it was good advice. With her [Mamie's] staff of paid doctors, she could have herself appointed as Mary's guardian — don't take the risk."

Sam assured his brother that Mary was happy at Maryhill, "making jelly, riding, having a good time." He was . . . "inclined to think that she would like to take a trip to see her mother. If she does, there is no reason why she should not go. The only question would be, who should go with her."

But soon afterward, Sam expressed reluctance to have either of his children in Washington, D.C. He wrote his brother in November 1910, "Since James's experience, I hesitate to try Washington for Mary." What

Mary Mendenhall Hill and companion (probably Dr. Burris) at Maryhill, about 1910. Friends Meeting House in background. (Maryhill Museum files.)

"James's experience" was, we don't know, but presumably it was related to his mother's behavior. At any rate, Mary stayed with Sam at Seattle and Maryhill from May 1910 until early in 1912. She went to Washington, D.C. the following year and returned in 1913. Why these decisions were made, we don't know.

Muriel (Mrs. Zola) Brooks recalls visiting Sam and his daughter in his Seattle house on an occasion when Mary was to accompany a noted violinist on the piano. However, Mary was having one of her attacks of "melancholia," and would not appear for the guests.

Sam's letters to his daughter take on a more adult tone from about 1912 on, and Mary's letters to him also are more sophisticated. About that time, Mary began writing letters in her own hand. In March 1913, she wrote, "This writing looks third class but I thought you would like to see it. Affectionately, thy daughter, Mary."

She wrote about a cartoon of Sam in the *Minneapolis Tribune* which one of her aunts had sent to her. She was practicing music and was " . . . learning more about music all the time. . . . I was playing Bach, 1700, and it's all right to know about his works but more modern music is much more worthwhile and beautiful. I wish I could have my piano in Seattle at

Maryhill if I should happen to be there for the summer." She was reading *The Marble Faun*, had heard the Boston Symphony play in Washington, D.C., and expected to go to *H.M.S. Pinafore*. That summer, she wrote from Easthampton about a dance at the club where, "You never saw such funny dancing in your life. . . . the Bunny Hug and Gaby Glide." She and her companion, Miss Donavan, were enjoying auto excursions. "I will never enjoy anything more than that California trip in 1911."

Once while playing golf alone, she wrote, "A man about 50 came up. I got out of the way and asked him to go ahead. He said, 'Would you mind playing nine holes with me?' Of course I didn't, as he was a perfect stranger and astonished me very much." It must have been a rare and thrilling experience for Mary.

In response to a suggestion from her father that they go to Europe in July 1912, she wrote, "If I were old and ugly, I might enjoy Europe much more than just now." They did go the following summer and motored through England, while James and his mother went to Aix-les-Bains. Later, Sam wrote of her cottage at Maryhill, which he was having fixed up, " . . . so that when you come again, you will be a very surprised little girl. The roads are simply wonderful. Rex, your saddle horse, is in fine shape, and I have been riding him. . . . I have only been in the Seattle house to stay one night in a year."

Mary went to the YWCA in Portland for swimming and gymnasium classes in the summer of 1915. In January 1916, Sam wrote to his friend Mrs. C. A. Dolph, later one of the first trustees of Maryhill Museum, "Mary is very well." Mrs. Dolph replied that she " . . . was glad to hear that Mary was better. She was so sweet to us when we saw her just an evening or two before we left [Portland] for the East. She wanted us to promise that if we went to Washington [D.C.], we would call upon her mother and ask her to show us her room. . . . She laughingly said, 'And if mother is not at home, just tell the butler that I say you are to see my room.'"

But a crisis developed in the summer of 1916 when Mary was put in St. Vincent's Hospital, Portland, for about three months under the care of Portland's leading surgeon, Dr. Kenneth A. Mackenzie. At Sam's request, Mackenzie wrote Dr. Richard Hill, Sam's brother, about Mary's condition: "She has been under my treatment for several months and the treatment has been directed to the improvement of her general condition and has been largely hygienic and dietetic. A marked improvement is taking place but we seem to have reached a stage where there is no longer any response. . . . I find there is stagnation in the intestines which is not relieved by treatment of any kind. Feces are held up for a long period in the large intestine, especially in the cecum. This may be due to bands or adhesions . . . [or] to some intrinsic disorder of the intestine. . . . I'm very seriously thinking, and have suggested so to Mr. Hill, that it might be a very good plan to explore the abdomen."

In that era, the concept of "autointoxication" was in full bloom. Many an appendix, tooth, gall bladder, or pair of tonsils were removed and many a paranasal sinus drained for the treatment of arthritis, anemia, or ill-defined fatigue. Dr. Mackenzie apparently was not immune to the toxin of this theory.

Dr. Hill replied, urging a nonsurgial approach. His friend Dr. Willson of the Mayo Clinic had reported that " . . . their operations in such cases have not been satisfactory. . . . The whole Hill family . . . has been under the Mayos and they're all convinced that their opinion on a case is the best to be had in the world, and I am sure that they would all insist that she go there, if they knew about the matter."

In his answer, Mackenzie sniffed, "The Rochester Clinic . . . has never given very much consideration to this type of case. . . . Their attitude in such cases as Mary's might therefore be highly critical rather than simply pragmatic. . . . They would assume the highly conservative attitude which is so typical of them and deny Mary the one hope that is offered to her for the relief of what previously has been regarded by everybody as a hopeless malady. My attitude would also be conservative, but I would take a position of a pioneer in the case who has called attention to the physical tort and the mental obsession, and offering by way of its solution an exploration which might lead to unexpected developments. Of course I would welcome a consultation with Dr. Mayo but . . . anyone participating in it should be familiar with the more recent literature of dementia praecox which calls attention to the association of the malady with the faults that exist in Mary's case." He was, however, " . . . disposed to continue the treatment indefinitely until there are signs manifest to enable us to say it has found its limit."

His letter contains the first mention of schizophrenia (dementia praecox, as it was then usually called) in connection with Mary's behavior. In a letter to Sam's wife, Mackenzie went into more detail. "At the beginning she was silent and sullen, had a wild uncanny stare and refused to speak to anybody . . . but the contrast of her present to the past condition . . . is very marked; she is full of animation and keeps up a continuous conversation and is quite lucid in her expressions and quite logical. Now and then there might be an eccentric expression used which might be regarded as being out of place, but generally speaking, her conversation is normal." He again brought up the possibility of abdominal surgery and of trying " . . . at the proper time suggestion under hypnotism."

Dr. Mackenzie also wrote Sam, noting Mary's improvement in recent months. But the prognosis was clouded: "Your daughter cannot take care of herself; she will have to be guarded for a long time to come . . . it would not do for her to embark on any life in which there was excitement and too much activity . . . institutional treatment I deem entirely contraindicated in her case . . . the home life in Seattle would not be adapted to her nor would the isolation of Maryhill. I am inclined to think that she would thrive in some quiet resort in Southern California," preferably under the care of some family member and her own nurse.

That is almost the last we know of poor Mary's life. The author heard a report that she lived out her days in a Catholic institution for the mentally ill. She was considered incompetent when Sam's will was contested by her mother and brother in 1931. She died in 1941 and was buried in the J. J. Hill family plot in St. Paul.

Sam never expressed any ambitions he may have had for his daughter. He never mentioned the possibility of her marrying and having children; presumably he was resigned to the fact that she would have to lead a sheltered and limited existence. Their correspondence did not reveal any resentment for the poor hand which fate had dealt Mary: not on her part, because she was probably unaware of it; not on Sam's because it was too sad and hopeless to acknowledge.

10

James Nathan Hill

Most of our knowledge of Sam's relationship with his son, James, comes from their correspondence between 1905 and 1913. Sam wanted very much to be proud of James; to send him to a good prep school, to Harvard, and then into the world with every advantage money and influence could provide. He did not say that he expected James to follow in his footsteps as a celebrated entrepreneur, philanthropist, and friend of the great and near-great, but his ambitions for his son certainly extended beyond the limited horizons of a secure and innocuous existence dependent on inherited wealth. One can only assume that James was a cruel disappointment to a man whose whole approach to life was to attack it with zest and confidence.

James Nathan Branson Hill was born in St. Paul on August 23, 1893. Nathan and Branson were the given names of his paternal grandfather. Presumably, he was named James to honor his maternal grandfather, James J. Hill. We know little of his early childhood, except that he was sickly, subject to frequent sore throats until a tonsillectomy was performed when he was fourteen, and to mild asthma in childhood. One of the first references to James in Sam's correspondence is a letter from Sam explaining that he would have to miss a meeting of the Harvard Overseers because of James's illness.

Sam always dictated his letters to James or sent telegrams. In his early letters, he refers to him in the third person, as he did in writing to Mary Mendenhall.

Sam's interest in things Japanese and a desire to strengthen James both physically and mentally led him to seek instruction in judo for ten-year-old James and three of his friends. Sam sponsored a trip to the United States for Professor Yamashita, head of the Department of Physical Culture at the University of Tokyo. Mr. Shibata of New Haven, a friend and admirer of the professor, acted as intermediary in the negotiations. Sam wrote in February 1903, about a month before Mamie took the children from Seattle to St. Paul, "I want him [James] to come to know and like Japan as I like it. I wish him to be thoroughly imbued with the ideals of the Samurai class, for that class of men is a noble, high-minded class. They look beyond the modern commercial spirit."

After some brief negotiating, terms were agreed upon and the professor and his wife left Japan for Seattle in September 1901. He gave exhibitions for Sam and his guests, including Mrs. J. J. Hill, who was in Seattle on a visit, and Senator Alger, Secretary of War during the recent Spanish-American War. Sam accompanied Yamashita east in November. Since James was then living with his mother in Washington, D.C., Sam encouraged the professor to give judo lessons in Cambridge to Harvard students. This venture had an unsatisfactory ending, the professor defecting to teach Annapolis cadets (Chapter 18).

In May 1905, soon after he and Mamie bought the Stockbridge estate, Sam also bought a ranch in Okanogan County in north central Washington. He intended it to be a retreat where he could bring his friends to fish and hunt, but more important, a place his son would enjoy with him and cherish after Sam's death. His plans for both Stockbridge and the ranch, Che-wil-o-kap, went awry, the first because of the estrangement from his wife, the other because of alienation from his son.

Sam became interested in the Okanogan area in a roundabout way. With the intention of helping to rehabilitate Leavitt Rand, the alcoholic younger brother of two of Sam's friends in the Minneapolis Gas Light Co., Sam had invited him out to Seattle early in 1903. He then arranged for George Abbott, a Harvard man in Sam's employ, to take "Leav" on a scouting trip to evaluate possibilities for investments in mining, gas companies, farming, and lumbering. Guy Waring, who in 1894 had founded the town of Winthrop in the heart of this region, had sent Sam a promising sample of iron ore, and Sam had sent it on for analysis to Louis Hill, his brother-in-law and assistant to J. J. Hill. The sample, incidentally, showed 5.22% titanic acid, a finding which would be of greater interest today than in 1905.

Apparently, it was on the basis of information gathered on this trip that Sam decided to buy land around Pearrygin Lake, five miles north of Winthrop in the upper Methow Valley. The lake, formed in the glacial age, was some 200 acres in area and 50 feet deep, with no outlet. The valley, named after an Indian tribe, had been discovered by fur trappers and traders and later became a mining region, but the mining boom came to an end in the early 1900's. The Great Northern extended its line to Wenatchee in 1892 and there was boat service on the Okanogan River, making the area relatively accessible.

James Nathan Hill and trophy, probably near Che-will-o-kap. (Maryhill Museum files.)

The place which Sam bought for his son James was called Che-wil-o-kap. Sam does not explain the name, but there is a Che-wil-iken Creek, a tributary of the Okanogan River, named after a Nez Percé chief. Sam had the Pearrygin mortgage purchased in May 1905, and sent James documents to sign in November. Waring was to operate the farm on the property.

Sam described his acquisition in a letter to his daughter in the spring of 1905 and sent her a picture of the lake. "There are fruit ranches near it and a big forest of trees on the mountainside. The lake is about one and one-half miles long by one-half mile wide and full of trout. . . . I have some wild rice and will have that sown on the shore of the lake. There are many birds and waterfowl coming there. There are two trout streams running to the lake. . . . Snowcapped mountains in the distance are very beautiful. Just beyond the upper end of the lake is the Methow River. The place runs almost to the river bank. Plans are being drawn now for the house which I hope to build there this year."

Sam traveled to the area several times between 1905 and 1908, usually to hunt and fish with friends, taking Sam Finch along to cook. Sam described his most adventuresome trip in a long letter to James. Heavy rains had caused a landslide which blocked the rail line just west of the summit of the Cascade range. Sam and several companions manned a handcar to go west, carrying it around other slides and washouts, and proceeded by engine, on foot, and with a team and wagon to the flooded town of Snohomish. Finally, they obtained a rowboat to get as far as Everett on the swollen Snohomish River, and then took a streetcar and ferry to Seattle.

James came west to spend the summer of 1906 in Seattle and paid his only visit to Che-wil-o-kap ranch. Sam wrote a friend, "I cannot tell you how much I enjoyed the trip which we had together, and what a great thing it was for James . . . Nothing has happened in many years which has given me so much pleasure as to see him come to love the West as I love it."

At thirteen James entered Middlesex School at Concord, Massachusetts in the fall of 1906. There were some difficulties from the outset. Apparently James complained that he had written to his father "a half a dozen times" about getting clothes for athletics and nothing had been done. Sam replied that he had certainly not received half a dozen letters from James altogether, and that he wished "to caution him to be extremely careful not to make overstatements." Sam wrote to the school, "I am very stern with him but have never caught him in a deliberate untruth. He will evade things, as many boys do."

Sam wrote James about his talks for good roads; progress on the new house in Seattle; people James had met there; his discovery of "The Promised Land"; and news of a boulevard being built on the high ridge between Tacoma and Everett, reminiscent of " . . . the Corniche which James remembers so well, or La Tourbi which James liked in Italy." He did not miss an opportunity to urge him to work hard in school, to be polite to the headmaster, and to write to his mother. He also took pains to tell James some of his business affairs, "so James will understand that I have begun the work which he is to carry on."

James was with his father in Seattle again when Sam wrote to his daughter in July 1907 about sailing on Mr. Stimson's yacht and visiting the flagship of the United States Pacific Fleet. Some anti-Semitism shows in Sam's remark that, " . . . James does not think the picture of himself and Mary very good. James puts his hands up and says the picture looks like 'Ikie.'"

In the fall of 1907, James was in trouble with his grades at Middlesex School. Sam heard about this indirectly and was hurt and upset. He wrote:

> You found time to do that [i.e., write to the Hanford boy]; you did not find time to write to me. To make it easy for you, I told you you need not write to me often. That was not because I did not want the letters for I want them very much indeed, and now you are in disgrace and unless an immediate change is made will be expelled from school. . . . Unless you go on through this school, your career is at an end. All my plans and hopes, all the work I am undertaking for you will be nothing. Can you not realize what you are doing? Can you not see it? Why this indifference and affected superiority to everybody and everything? Why did you insult my friend Dr. Hobart by failing even to acknowledge her invitation to dinner, and secondly, sending her a postal card which reached her at the dinner hour? You know better than that. . . . I cannot tell you how deeply humiliated I am. . . . How proud I wanted to be of you. You must know how much I love you. All my work is in vain; you could help me; will you? Will my Christmas present from you be your disgrace and dismissal from school? You have the ability, the strong will, which rightly directed means so much to your friends, so much to the world, so much to me, so much to yourself. I have not spoken of your mother; what are you doing to

help her? . . . If you do not change and change at once your whole mental attitude toward the school, you will have disgraced yourself, your mother and me and will have proved untrue to the traditions which have been handed down in my family from father to son. . . . I wish I could be with you and put my arms around you and talk to you.

There was a mixed message here: you have disgraced me — I love you. But Sam made up his mind to be more cheerful when he next wrote. He had seen Dr. Mary Hobart who had said " . . . many nice things about James and is very fond of him." Charlie Chamberlain had told Sam that James was " . . . not a bad boy but that he was put in too narrow a stall; he ought to have a box stall. I said to him that I could not afford a box stall now and James would have to stay in a narrow stall."

James did not share his father's concern about his grades. He wrote, "My marks for the last two weeks have averaged about 65 so I don't think there is any danger of my being expelled. . . . . I will try to average about 72 at the end of next week."

Despite his reassurances, James was expelled from Middelsex in December 1907. Sam wrote his brother, "One of two explanations is possible; either owing to the fact that James is growing so rapidly he cannot concentrate his mind on his work, or that by reason of his strong self-will and his great dislike of his teachers he has refused to study." Sam favored the second possibility: "I shall want you to meet with James and me somewhere and have a talk. . . . He has hardly had a fair show, and I am probably more responsible for this than anybody else."

Sam went to the school at the start of Christmas vacation to take James to Washington, D.C. to see his mother, and then to Goldendale, Washington, where James stayed at the home of attorney N. B. Brooks. While in Goldendale a Mr. Kramer, a young Harvard student, was retained to tutor James. At this point, Sam was living in the Perry Apartments in Seattle and coming to Goldendale frequently to see James and to tend to matters at Maryhill.

Sam bought additional land at Che-wil-o-kap for James in the spring of 1908, in fact, all of the land surrounding the lake except a parcel of 158 acres, for which Sam's offer of $6,000 was rejected. He wrote James that he would make the payments on the land for him but he wanted James to learn about contracts and such things as easements. He added, "With this land you will always have a nice place to go to and it will get better every year, and when you are a man you can take your friends up there and have some fine shooting when the shooting elsewhere is all gone." Sam had a postcard made showing a wheatfield on the "James N. B. Hill ranch." But James showed no enthusiasm for returning to the ranch. After Sam's efforts and investment, this must have been a great disappointment, and was probably the reason that Sam himself did not visit the place in later years.

Dr. Mary Hobart wrote in May 1908, that she had "absolute confidence in James's ultimate development." Sam replied that "James is very tall and stoops a little and has a slight bronchial irritation. [Sam did not mention his severe facial acne.] The great trouble with him is his lack of exercise, and he does not feel equal to taking any and yet he must. I have grown very fond of him all over again and am just back from Goldendale where I spent a week with him. I have bought him a beautiful horse."

Sam did not fail to advise James about taking regular exercise, going horseback riding, and avoiding smoking. Sam's letters to James, in fact, are full of admonitions, expectations, and encouragement: apart from gifts and other material blessings received, it is problematic how well James understood his father's fondness for him.

It was arranged that James would go east in June 1908 to go fishing with J. J. Hill and later stay with his mother. Sam visited James in St. Paul on his way to New York and Europe.

Kramer, James's tutor, wrote Sam in August that Middlesex would not readmit James, but that he would tutor James intensively in the hope that he could get into another good prep school. James was admitted to Philips Exeter Academy in the fall of 1908. It was not long, however, before reports of unsatisfactory school work were coming to Sam. Sam wrote to urge the instructors " . . . to remember that the boy's training heretofore has been such that he has never been used to systematic work. I believe he is in earnest and I believe he will work out all right." Sam was cheered, at least, by his improved marks in faithfulness and effort.

Meanwhile, James's letters were mainly about visits with family and friends; frequently there were requests for money. He went to Washington, D.C., to see his mother for Easter vacation in 1909. "I hate to go back to New England. Everybody looks happy and prosperous here [in Washington] and up here they all look unhealthy," he wrote.

James now became excited about automobiles. He sent his mother catalogs for Packards and Locomobiles and advised Sam to turn in his old car and get a 30 horsepower Locomobile for $3,500. Sam was quick to respond to the hint. He promised to buy James a car in New York and have it shipped to Seattle, without so much as exacting a promise of better school work. Alas, James was on probation again after Easter 1909, for violation of the rule that he be in his own room without visitors after 8:00 p.m.

Sam may have had an ulterior motive in inviting Mr. H. P. Amen, principal of Philips Exeter, to visit him in Seattle in the summer of 1909. Sam had sent the school a world globe and mentioned talking to Edward Everett Hale " . . . regarding the assistance which the right kind of man could render the boys at Exeter." He expressed gratitude for "the great improvement in James" since he had come to the academy.

Amen rose to the bait, acknowledging that, "It seems very hard to have a famous old school like this crippled in its work from a cruel lack of funds, while the colleges in the country are so well cared for." He enclosed a pamphlet giving " . . . exact information on the state of our funds" and citing the increased costs of operating the school. There was no mention of quid pro quo for the academy's determined efforts to get James ready for Harvard.

That summer, Headmaster Amen visited Seattle and thanked Sam for "the most delightful vacation of my life." Later he wrote, "I could say confidentially that if I had not been here at the close of the term, James would have been excluded from a return." A Mr. Cleveland would continue tutoring James in Latin. "I hope and believe that you will be willing to spend considerable money if necessary, to discover whether or not James's failure is due to lack of ability or merely to lack of effort . . . For the sake of discovering the exact condition of James's case, I would cheerfully use a part of your very generous contribution . . . and I shall be most grateful to you for the gift of bonds which you mentioned. May I add your name with this amount [$5,000] in my 'little red book?' . . . I am most grateful to you for speaking to Mr. James J. Hill." Sam had also contacted Edward Tuck, a wealthy friend of J. J.'s, about a donation to the academy.

James spent his 1909 Christmas holidays in St. Paul, stopping at the Auto Show in New York on his return to Philips Exeter. He did not thrive under the heavy program of study in 1909-10. He wrote, "I have not been so well lately and have been over to the infirmary twice a week. . . . I think it is the study hour that is the trouble. It keeps you in the house all day and in the study hall two hours every night but Sunday." Amen reported with satisfaction that James's report card was free from unsatisfactories, though he had three D's and three C's. For this crumb of comfort, Sam sent James a congratulatory telegram and added, "Don't rest on your oars." He did not need to tell him not to pull too hard.

James was back on probation again in May 1910, with extra study hours, because he had been out for a walk one evening when he should have been studying. This, according to James, " . . . was not square, but I won't give them a chance to work it again."

Mary Mendenhall was now with Sam in Seattle. Sam proposed that James come west again for the summer of 1910 with his Uncle Richard and Cousin Louise. James declined: "I am going to stay East this summer with Mama as she is very ill and nervous and wants me to be with her. . . . It has been about three days since she has been able to eat anything except raw things and such. . . . However, Miss Donovan is taking good care of her." James and his mother intended to supervise closing their house at Stockbridge, Massachusetts, before going to Huntington, Long Island, for the summer. James did not often express concern for his mother, or for his sister, either. There is no information about his mother's feelings for him. It must have been difficult for a boy living in no man's land between two such dissimilar parents, alike only in being strong minded.

James passed his classes, except for mathematics, and the Philips Exeter faculty voted to permit his return to the academy in September 1910. He managed to pass two of his exams for Harvard and in September went to Cambridge to be tutored for three other Harvard exams.

A month later, James was advised to leave Exeter by the academy physician. The doctor earlier had advised that he quit gymnasium classes because of a functional heart murmur, but the main problem was that he was " . . . still nervous and strung up. . . . Permit me to say that I think if he felt his family were all right that would straighten things out for him. The reason I suggested his keeping away from Washington is that his boy friends there seem to be of such a character that they would not help him much. . . . He has apparently lost his dread somewhat of losing his mind." James had suffered a minor abdominal muscle injury in September, and " . . . when he has a twinge there he immediately thinks of appendicitis." But James reported that a Boston specialist had told him that "it was nothing but an extreme case of nerves." After the doctors discussed the matter, it was decided that he should stay at the academy after all.

James spent his spring holiday in 1911 at Maryhill. Sam wired his brother that James " . . . has been doing remarkably well. Returns for two Harvard examinations and another year at Exeter."

There is a gap in the correspondence until Christmas 1911, by which time James, eighteen, had entered Harvard. He wrote Sam, "I think when you come back you ought to spend some time with Mama and Mary. I think it would do you a lot of good and it would give you an opportunty to see how she is." In his letters, James never discussed his parents' separation. Undoubtedly, he felt a greater sense of duty to his mother than to Sam. James never even mentioned the possibility of living in the West or becoming associated with Sam in business.

One of James's instructors sent Sam an encouraging report early in 1912. "I think he is going to be a case of a lad maturing very late but in a way that will make him a thoroughly creditable member of society." But bad news from Harvard came soon afterward. James had three unsatisfactory grades for mid-year exams, and the administrative board voted to sever his connection with Harvard. James was disappointed because he " . . . thought I had the work and everyone else did, and no one had the least suspicion that I would be dropped except Mr. Nolen" [his tutor]. James planned to go to Washington for a rest, then return to Cambridge to work with Nolen again before spending the summer on Long Island with his mother.

Sam asked James if he could bring his sister west in the fall of 1912. James replied, "It is utterly impossible to bring Mary west without sacrificing a whole college year. I also am wholly unwilling to take the responsibility." He seemed to be implying that it was unfair of Sam to suggest that a brother had a duty in this situation. Sam had telegraphed his wife that Eben Wells, a phone company associate, could go east to bring Mary and Miss Donovan, her nurse-companion, west with him. But he told James this offer was rebuffed; "She replied that Mary was well and Miss Donovan was not available. She did not offer to get anybody else." James did not comment on this evasion.

By now, James had 23 out of 26 points needed to be readmitted to Harvard as a sophomore in the fall of 1912. He got by his mid-year exams in the spring of 1913 and spent his vacation in Washington, D.C. and New York. He expressed (in correspondence at least) his first interest in girls, noting, "There is a very pleasant girl about 22 years of age who is Mary's companion. She is doing very well, but I am afraid Mary is very rude to her as she was to Dr. Burris." He " . . . found it impossible to make out on my present allowance, because of room rent, tuition, and $9 a week board. Being broke, there is not much to do except study and exercise." Unfortunately, he was not fond of either.

Sam paid his outstanding bills but was not happy about it. He wanted James to manage his finances better. After all, James received $1,500 every six months as income from bonds of the Home Telephone Company which Sam had turned over to him. "You will have to regulate your affairs so as to live within that amount; I do not intend to pay any bills on the side . . . . [You now have] a bank account which most fathers would regard as excessive." He added gloomily, "Next birthday I shall be 56 years of age; my father died before he was 57, and I have not a great deal of time in which to work. There is much to do, but I feel sure you are going to do your share."

James and his mother went to Europe in the summer of 1913. Sam accompanied Mary Mendenhall separately. While in England, James and his mother visited Lord Strathcona. Much more interesting to James was news about the coveted auto. He wrote, "I was so overcome when you told me I could have the motor car that I could not thank you. . . . I cannot begin to tell you how much pleasure I will take in having it."

In April 1915, Mr. Briggs of the Faculty of Arts and Sciences at Harvard wrote Sam that J. J. Hill had seen James in New York and advised him strongly to finish his course at Harvard. Briggs estimated it would take a year and a half to do this and advised that he take only four courses at a time. He commented that James was " . . . one of the most courteous people with whom I have had to deal, and I believe that he is fundamentally earnest. . . . He has a good deal to overcome in a poor start, and as he says, he has not known how to study."

For some reason, Sam was still paying the property tax on James's 840 acres in 1915. Perhaps James had let them become delinquent as a manifestation of indifference. Che-wil-o-kap is not referred to in the correspondence after that.

The ranch eventually was sold in the settlement of Sam's estate. Washington State acquired about 580 acres of land and lake surface for Pearrygin State Park in 1957. The rest of the land around the lake is held by the State Game Department and two private owners.

Che-wil-o-kap was one of Sam's dreams, a Shangri-la he had discovered, remote and unspoiled, to leave to his son. But when James evinced no interest in it, a retreat "exempt from public haunt" was not what Sam's own restless spirit wanted. Sam knew the way back to the earthly Shangri-la well enough, but the one he had built in his imagination could not be recaptured.

James was called "Jimmy" or "Jaso" at Harvard, where he was a non-graduating member of the class of 1915. His activities after leaving Harvard are summarized in his notes to the class secretary for the twenty-fifth anniversary report in 1940:

> Prior to the World War, my home was in Washington, D.C. After being put upon the inactive list of the U. S. Naval Reserve, with the rank of ensign, and fourteen months overseas service, I moved to New York City in 1919, and was employed for a time in the export department of the Texas Corporation [James N. Hill, his uncle, was a director], then went into the banking business, which with a side venture into manufacturing, I followed until January 1st, 1930. During the period 1930-38, I took part in political work as a Republican election captain in the 15th Assembly District of the 17th Congressional District. . . .
>
> In the summer of 1930 I went abroad, combining business with pleasure. . . . The following year, I became interested, through inheritance, in a tract of timber with quicksilver under it, out on the Pacific Coast, and after looking it over, decided that the world of geology and mining, like the life at sea, is a thing apart. I, therefore, moved up to Boston January 1st, 1932, where I had always wanted to live, and entered as a special student in the Graduate Schools of Harvard and the Massachusetts Institute of Technology, in order to study economic geology and geophysical prospection.
>
> In the summers of 1932 and 1933 I went prospecting for gold in Western Quebec and Eastern Ontario. This was very interesting and on a small scale resembled the days of '49. In 1934, I returned to financial work again. In the summer and autumn of 1937 I made another trip abroad. . . .
>
> During the autumn of 1938, I dipped into politics again, and worked for Leverett Saltonstall of the Class of 1914 in the gubernatorial campaign . . . playing a small part in organizing the Polish voters, who number around 125,000 in Massachusetts. In June of last year [1939] I made a business trip to the Pacific Coast in connection with the quicksilver industry.
>
> The only activity connected with Harvard University that I can claim to be engaged in is that of being a member of the Visiting Committee of the Peabody Museum in Anthropology for several years. I am also a member of the Visiting Committee on Alumni Relations at Middlesex School. I was also treasurer of the Federation of the Alliance Francaise of the U. S. and Canada while a resident of New York City. For ten years, since 1924, I have held a commission in the Organized Reserve of the Army of the United States, and during that period made many good friends and had a most interesting time. While a resident of New York City, I joined Navy Post No. 16 of the American Legion, resigning, as did most of one's friends, when the bonus forays began. Shortly after the declaration of the Second World War, I joined the American Legion in Boston, in order to be in touch with World War veterans once again.
>
> My chief interests outside of plying my trade are golf, lawn tennnis, court tennis, sailing, ice-skating, bird shooting, fishing, and going down to North Carolina as frequently as possible. During the predepression years I used to indulge in small boat sailing and was keen on horse racing. . . .

He then commented on "the virtual dictatorship" of F.D.R. and " . . . every degree of radicalism from New Dealers down to the Communists . . . " and advocated building a large U.S. Army and Navy while keeping out of the war in Europe.

He listed memberships in several clubs in New York and Massachusetts. For the fiftieth anniversary Harvard class report, he simply wrote that he had nothing to relate.

In 1958, he sent the Minnesota Historical Society five large envelopes of letters and records, among which were " . . . records of the Minneapolis

Athenaeum Library of which [my] father had been vice president," and letters from Archbishop John Ireland and Ignatius Donnelly to Sam. James chose to ignore Maryhill Museum, which he was said to have regarded as a "big fake."

Francis Hines was 87 when he responded to the author's request for information about James. He had not known him at Harvard but met him in 1940 when Hines handled a legal matter for James. At his mother's death in 1947, James inherited $5,788,000, and Hines helped with his legal affairs. He described James as " . . . something of an enigma to me. . . . He lived in a world of fancy." He was a Francophile, and " . . . would spend a whole lunch hour talking about his friend, de Gaulle." His mother's death was a blow to James, but he did not mention his father or sister, except once when he showed Mary's picture to Hines. He was very hard of hearing and became a recluse in his later years. Hines added, "Though I liked Jimmy and I am sure he had a warm spot for me, he was not a man who trusted anyone."

James was at his father's side in the hospital when Sam died in 1931. Whether they saw each other or even corresponded from the time James left Harvard to join the Navy in 1917 is unknown, as is the reason for their estrangement. It may well be that James and his mother learned of Sam's affairs with other women and his illegitimate children, and that this knowledge was the reason that James joined with his mother in the prolonged contest of Sam's will (Chapter 28).

Many years later, Robert Campbell, then the director of Maryhill Museum, wrote to Mr. Lawrence Coolidge of Boston, who was handling James's financial affairs, enclosing photographs for identification. Mr. Coolidge replied that this reminder of the past was somewhat upsetting to James, who had been bedridden for a number of years at the Ritz-Carlton Hotel in Boston. James died on September 17, 1975. He was buried at the J. J. Hill family plot at Resurrection Cemetery, St. Paul. Hines was one of the two executors of James's will. James left to the Pasteur Museum, Paris, the gold headed cane of Dr. Louis Pasteur. The oil painting and crayon study of Sam done by Gabrielle de Clements in 1889 went to Mrs. John M. Cabot, a cousin. Portraits of his mother were left to Mr. Louis W. Hill, including the equestrienne portrait by Jan V. Chelminski. He left other pictures, mostly of the Barbizon School, to the Louvre, including the Corot painting, "Greek Girl with a Rose." The Widener Library at Harvard received his books. Various personal belongings, including jewelry, engravings, furniture, wine cellar, and two Guyot shotguns were left to Dorothy McWiliams, another cousin. The remainder of his property, including that held in trust for him under his mother's will, was added to a trust he had set up in 1966.

Except in James's prep. school days, Sam's letters did not express his disappointment with him. Sam was accustomed to imposing his will on people and events in business; it must have been frustrating for him not to be able to influence James's attitude and behavior. For James, the ultimate weapon against his father's ambitions for him was not rebellion but indifference. Unfortunately, James did not seem to have the intelligence, talent, and initiative to carve out a satisfying career of his own. Instead, he drifted into various pursuits: sports, conservative politics, veterans' affairs, art collecting.

James did not marry, nor does he seem to have formed any close personal relationships. Perhaps he felt unloved by his fond but domineering father and remote neurotic mother, and was all too aware of the lack of love between them. His sister, who might have helped him had she been normal, was doomed.

Highways and concrete monuments alone could not fully satisfy Sam's desire for immortality. His wife would not dissolve their marriage; his children would not procreate. Would there be no one to carry on his name? Surely by design and not through accident, he sired three children by other women as a defiant answer to a fate bent on thwarting his dreams.

11

The Long Goodbye

After Mamie and the children left Seattle in March 1903 Sam rejoined his family at Millbrook, New York, in June. By this time, he may have been sure that Mamie would not return to Seattle: at least, he gave up their rented house there in July. In October, he sent a freight car to St. Paul with furniture, which Mary soon had shipped to the house she had bought in Washington, D.C., at 1712 Rhode Island Avenue.

Sam visited his family at St. Paul again at Christmas 1903. He wired New Year's greetings to Wells, his associate at the Seattle Gas Company, adding, "Wife's indisposition keeps us in St. Paul." At least Mary was not disposed to return to the West. As Albro Martin writes, her parents " . . . watched sadly as the marriage of Mamie, their first born, and Samuel Hill died in all but name. Sam was in love with the Pacific Northwest and spent more and more of his time there, but Mamie had formed an attachment for the kaleidoscopic social life of Washington, D.C., and determined to live there permanently."

Sam wrote wistfully to his sister-in-law, Gertrude, early in 1905, "I shall be very much dazzled by Mary's new house when I get back to Washington, I suppose. . . . If I could see the prospect of having her and the children here in the state of Washington I think life would assume a very pleasant aspect. Everybody here speaks of her with kindly remembrance and admiration whenever they speak of her." Late that year, after the gas war was settled, he wrote to his friend Farrell, "I have not done anything in the business way at all. . . . I sometimes feel if I had my family here and was in a comfortable house and hard at work, I would be a contented man." The comfortable house and hard work were soon obtained but contentment eluded him.

Sam implies that he had no choice but to remain in Seattle and that it would have been fruitless to move east to live with his family. Although their marriage was coming apart, Sam and Mamie did make an attempt to keep up appearances. Since Sam would not leave Seattle and his wife would not live there, they could compromise on visits from Sam from time to time and purchase of a summer place appropriate to their station. Perhaps they intended it as a sort of neutral ground.

In 1905, they decided upon a large estate at Stockbridge, near Lenox, Massachusetts. The 30 room main house, "Manor of Beckwithshaw," had been designed as a summer residence and built in 1892 by Leonard Forbes Beckwith, a Boston architect. Ralph Forbes, an attorney who owned the adjoining estate, handled the sale.

In September 1904, Forbes declined Hill's first offer of $40,000. Sam wrote in the style of a typical wary buyer, "I looked over the property. . . and find that the place is, as you are doubtless aware, considerably run down, both the land and the house. On the other hand, I think, by expending a considerable sum of money, that the place could be put into a habitable condition. My experiences with such places is that they are very hard to dispose of. I have a house in Minneapolis, Minnesota, which cost $60,000 and which we have not been able to sell for $15,000. I do not know that Mrs. Hill would care for the place . . . I would be glad if you would wire me your lowest cash price, then I would submit the matter to Mrs. Hill, and give you an answer . . . as I would not wish to dicker in the matter."

Forbes then quoted a price of $90,000 for three parcels: one of 214 acres with the large furnished house, farmhouse, and farm buildings, including a long frontage on Lake Averic and a three acre island; another of 180 acres between Interlaken and Lenox with pasture, woods, and farm land; and a third of 420 acres of mountainside and pasture. Forbes and Sam would share the use of the reservoir and water pipeline and the wages of a caretaker. Forbes admitted that the house was lightly built and rambling, " . . . almost impossible to live in perhaps between December 1st and April 1st." There was water in the basement which would have to be drained before freezing weather set in.

Forbes sent the house plans to Mary Hill in Washington, D.C. A price of $60,000 was agreed upon, with the deed running to Mamie. Sam does not say why she held title to the property; perhaps it was paid for by money of her own. He renamed the place "Shaughlin" but does not explain why.

Almost at once, Sam had regrets about his purchase and had little good to say about it thereafter. In the spring of 1905 he wrote, "I regard real estate as a liability and not an asset . . . I have, however, recently bought a place at Lenox, being actuated with the desire to help out the tax gatherer in that part of the country." After the Hills had spent their first summer at Stockbridge he wrote to a friend, "Unfortunately, I cannot congratulate anyone who moves into the state of Massachusetts. It has been my misfortune to spend three months there this summer. But I am glad to know that the state is being improved by immigration."

Before going to Montana to buy some thoroughbred Morgan horses for the estate, Sam expanded on his disenchantment with the residents of New England generally in a letter to his friend, Charles Chamberlain, gratuitously including those of Washington, D.C.:

> I am going away tomorrow, stopping a day in Montana to get some horses and I am very sad in consequence. Being here, seeing all that might, makes me feel like Moses who was permitted to see the Promised Land but never entered. So I have to go back to all the littlenesses and smallnesses and trivialities of New England life, the striking feature of which life is dishonesty, just as the characteristics which stand out most prominently in the life at the capitol of our nation are the characteristics of insincerity, dishonesty and graft. The city is composed of 300,000 souls, 100,000 Negroes who have all the bad characteristics of the race and 200,000 whites who are trying to see each day how they can defraud this Government out of an hour's work, or in some other petty way. I have lived almost everywhere and under almost all known conditions, have been the guest of kings, lived with Buriats, Ostiaks and Goldis in Siberia, but give me the waterfront of Seattle, or the main street in Butte, Montana, in preference to New England or Washington, D.C., for the reason that the people on the waterfront and in Butte are only sporadically or occasionally bad, but as Hetty Green said to me the other day in New York, 'Down there they are consistently bad all the way through' and Hetty ought to know. [Hetty Green (1835-1916), the greatest woman financier of her day, was born in New Bedford, Massachusetts. She managed her large fortune in stocks, bonds and real estate.]

Headaches accompanied whatever heady pride of ownership of Shaughlin he may have had. Late in 1905, one of his employees wired Sam with admirable brevity, "Lynch on drunk. Don't know what to do. Will I draw gravel and sand?" Sam had to correspond frequently about taxes, water rights, insurance, installation of telephone poles, road improvements, and general maintenance. The stables had to be remodeled. His chauffeur, Dickson, while driving Sam's cook and two butlers in Sam's new Locomobile, struck a carriage, overturning it. The chauffeur was charged with intoxication and reckless driving. When Dickson applied to Mrs. Hill for a loan to pay the $100 fine, he was stonily refused. Sam wrote to the Massachusetts Highway Commission on his behalf, but gave up when it was pointed out that the chauffeur had no operator's license. Nor did the place fare better under a new manager in 1907. Sam wrote, "The neighbors stole a good many of the things, including a wagon . . . Then some of our men took to drinking and the accounts were mixed."

Sam and Forbes had agreed to share the operating costs and profit, if any, of their farms and annually consoled each other on the outcome. Sam's friend, William Porter, president of the Chemical National Bank, feigned concern at Sam's losses. He wrote, "I note with sincere regret your distressing report on the hay crop at Stockbridge. In case it should develop into a matter of financial embarrassment for you, we will try to help you out."

Sam went to Stockbridge briefly in June and December of 1907 but was away most of the summer on two trips to Europe while his wife and daughter went to the seashore. The following year, Sam began efforts to bail out of Shaughlin. Forbes was able to rent the house for him in the summer of 1908 while Sam was in Europe. Sam wrote him, resignedly, "I hope you will make the sale of the land at Stockbridge. Do anything that you wish regarding the matter."

In these years, communications between Sam and his wife mostly concerned the children, about which they did not always see eye to eye. Mamie usually sent telegrams, which she had taken to signing "Mary Hill Hill." Sam wrote his brother in June 1908, "Mary desires to go abroad and wishes both children to go with her, sailing July 2nd. Her mother would much prefer that Mary Mendenhall should remain in St. Paul. Neither of the children care to go abroad. I shall do all that I can to meet her [Mamie's] views as I wish her to have a good time."

From 1903 to 1908, Sam visited his family at St. Paul, Stockbridge, or Washington, D.C., two or three times a year, usually at Christmas and during James's vacations. James visited Sam in Seattle in the summers of 1906 and 1907 and was at Goldendale during the school year of 1909-10. Mary Mendenhall was at Seattle and Maryhill much of the time between 1910 and 1916. By 1909, however, Sam's visits to his wife had become infrequent, and soon they ceased. Sam wrote Cass that Mrs. Hill would not be going to Stockbridge that year and that two of the employees could be discharged and their fare home paid.

In 1909, Sam and his wife declined an offer to trade their country place for a residence off Fifth Avenue and Central Park in New York. The realtor added, "As this is not an idle inquiry, we would appreciate an early reply." Sam must have wished more than idly that the millstone of the Stockbridge place was his own to trade.

Perhaps from unconscious rejection rather than oversight, Sam did not pay the manager's wages from November 1910 through January 1911, and other bills were also delinquent. Mamie sent Cass a check for his wages and Sam an indignant note. Sam's secretary paid Cass and asked him to reimburse Mrs. Hill. The truce between Sam and his wife was obviously strained.

In 1912, Mamie frostily reminded Sam that she again had had to pay Cass overdue wages. Furthermore, she had paid taxes on the place although she did not know they were in arrears until she wrote the assessor. She added, "If, however, as the property is in my name and has become nothing but an investment, you feel that I should meet the burdens attached to the ownership of the place, I will do so."

Early in 1913, Eben Wells, Sam's associate in the Home Telephone Company of Portland, complained to Sam's son, James, at Harvard, of

Aerial view of the "Dan Hanna Estate," owned by the Sam Hills from 1905 to 1916. Their house, "Shaughlin", is in the foreground; the barn built by Hanna in 1917 and destroyed by fire in 1955 is in the background. (Photo courtesy of *The Berkshire Eagle*, Pittsfield, Massachusetts.)

constantly receiving bills from Lenox, and asked if James and his mother could dispose of the horses, since Wells had not been able to get instructions from Sam. Later that year, however, Sam finally sent a man to board up the house and accompany a shipment by rail of three horses, farm wagons, and household furniture from Stockbridge to Maryhill, Washington.

The place then stood vacant until it was sold to Dan R. Hanna in 1916 for $500,000. Mrs. Hill, who had legal title, thus realized a handsome profit. The estate, renamed "Bonny Brier," was given by Hanna to Molly, his fourth bride, as a wedding gift. The following year, Hanna built the largest barn in New England. After passing through many hands and alterations, the main house is now the De Sisto School.

"Shaughlin" brought Mary Hill some unneeded profit but little joy for her and Sam. They may have anticipated entertaining some of their prominent friends there, but if so, they soon gave up the idea. Sam does not refer to Stockbridge in his correspondence in later life, no doubt wanting to forget the whole affair. His heart was never in it; otherwise the house might have become an enduring monument, as are his great houses in Seattle and at Maryhill. Sam was to return many times to New York and Washington, but for him the Northwest was always home.

We don't know when Sam and his wife last saw each other. In November 1912, after Ernest Lister had been elected Governor of Washington, Sam wired her, "Governor's first reception will be at our Seattle house Nov. 23rd." Surely he must have known she would not come; perhaps it was a wistful gesture toward reconciliation.

Their last communication found in the files at Maryhill Museum was a telegram from Sam to his wife reading simply, "August 13, 1887-1915." The significance of the date is not clear; the message may have been a sentimental reminder of the date they became engaged.

So far as we know, Sam never referred to the option of divorce from his Roman Catholic wife, nor is it likely that she would have consented to a divorce had he wanted to marry again. It seems nearly certain that she knew of Sam's mistresses and illegitimate children. We can imagine the depth of the bitterness and the affront to herself and her family, and that it was this which led to the contest of Sam's will in 1931, joined by their son James (Chapter 28).

One of the few hints in Sam's correspondence about the mental problems of his wife and daughter is in a letter Sam received from his friend, Charles Ames, in August 1907: "When I last saw you eight months ago, you were going eastward full of sorrow and anxiety about your daughter. I hope that with her recovery, your domestic skies would be clear again, but [Dr.] Harry Taylor told me yesterday, briefly but circumstantially, of the unhappy condition of your wife. . . . We feel very badly about it all." His long-time friend, Charles Babcock, touched obliquely on Sam's family problems three years later. "My thoughts have frequently turned in your direction during the last two weeks and especially since the long talk I had with Dr. Hill [Sam's brother] on Friday, May 20th [1910]. For the first time in all these years we discussed your trouble. . . . After all, however, there are some things which we have to bear alone and your trouble is of that nature. . . . There are things too sacred to be discussed by anyone other than the two directly concerned."

After the legal dispute over the custody of Mary Mendenhall was settled (Chapter 9), Sam's brother, Dr. Richard Hill, wrote Sam that he had talked to J. J. Hill, who " . . . had recently seen Mary [Mamie] and she seemed more reasonable that he had seen her and thought if thee would go with Mary and make a visit . . . being careful to do nothing to start an argument, the chances were good for reconciliation." Sam did not go east on such a mission; perhaps he had a dimmer view of its chances than did his in-laws. In a unique reference to the J. J. Hills, Sam once told Clarence Barron, "There is a singular streak in the Hill family. Hill would not speak to his wife sometimes for a whole week. My wife would not speak to her mother for a year."

From their marriage until his death, Sam provided Mary Hill with a monthly allowance of $1,000. At times he sent her six months' payment in a single check. Mary would briefly acknowledge with thanks receipt of these payments.

Mamie Hill. Portrait by Jan Chelminski at North Oaks, the J. J. Hill summer home, about 1890. (Photo courtesy of Louis W. Hill, Jr.)

We know very little about the last 35 years of Mamie's life. She acquired an estate in North Tarrytown, New York, and a brief report in the *Minneapolis Journal* in 1921 noted that she was being sued by W. and J. Sloan for $292,029, the "balance on the construction and furnishing of her country place in North Tarrytown."

Though she did not emerge in person, Mamie's name came out of obscurity after Mrs. J. J. Hill died in St. Paul in November 1921, leaving an estate of about $15,000,000, including real estate valued at $350,000. There was an immediate nasty squabble amongst the heirs,* leading to a legal battle between Mamie and Louis on one side and their seven brothers and sisters on the other. The St. Paul *Pioneer Press* noted that Mary Hill Hill was " . . . virtually an invalid and has not given testimony. . . . One of her letters, however, had played an important part in Louis's case." She confirmed that Mrs. J. J. Hill had told her that she intended to leave North Oaks farm to Louis. The lawsuit brought by his siblings against him was finally dropped in 1928 after four years of litigation.

In the end, one must say that much of Mamie's relationship with Sam is unknown. For that matter, except for the superficial glimpses afforded by correspondence, so is the whole personality of this unhappy disturbed mother of disturbed unhappy children.

Mamie's six-line death notice in the St. Paul newspapers of April 18, 1947, read, "Hill, Mary Hill, daughter of the late Mr. and Mrs. James J. Hill. Private graveside services at Resurrection Cemetery . . . please omit flowers. . . . " Any mention of Sam was also omitted.

---

*Who seemed disposed, if not actually eager, to whack the necks of kin.

PART III

THE PACIFIC NORTHWEST

12

Seattle and Gas Warfare

For a man with Quaker upbringing, Sam had an unbefitting fondness for a fight. He was no doubt pleased to come to Seattle in December 1900 as president and principal owner of the Seattle Gas and Electric Company, his first business venture distant, if not quite removed, from the power and patronage of his father-in-law. But it was the struggle with a wily and worthy adversary which lent exhilaration to the affair, absorbing his attention and energies for several years. Although at one time he averred he would fight for 50 years, the struggle was not so prolonged that he became bored with it. Probably more important than financial gain was the sense of power in directing a battle of wits through legal stratagems, publicity, political influence, and the gamble of potentially ruinous price cutting.

What led Sam to move from Minneapolis to Seattle instead of somewhere else? He knew the city because of his position with the Great Northern, which had extended its line there in 1893, and had an idea, which later had to be modified, of Seattle's golden promise.

In the latter part of the 19th century, Seattle was a sawmill town, important for shipping lumber and coal to San Francisco. The Northern Pacific had completed its transcontinental line to Tacoma in 1883, but Seattle did not yet have its own connection with the East. Some thought that the iron ore in the Cascade Mountains and the coal deposits around Puget Sound would be the basis for founding another Pittsburgh. There was hope, too, that Seattle would be the leading port for trading with the Orient and Siberia. But Seattle's development did not take the anticipated path. The coal and iron resources proved to be overrated. J. J. Hill undertook a survey, and in 1902 told Judge Thomas Burke,* his agent in Seattle, that Hill was no longer interested in iron and coal, because lumber would be the backbone of Seattle's trade.

Shipping from Seattle was also a disappointment at the time, in part because ships were beginning to use oil instead of coal, thus giving California an advantage over the Puget Sound region. Hill's large cargo ships for the Pacific trade, the *Dakota* and *Minnesota*, were embarrassing failures. The completion of the Great Northern's lines to Seattle in 1893 and the Klondike gold rush (1897-98) did help, and the city soon surpassed

---

*Sam's venture in Seattle utilities is well told, albeit with a somewhat jaundiced view, in Robert Nesbit's biography of Judge Thomas Burke (1849-1925), a long-time friend of Sam. Burke arrived in Seattle as a young attorney in 1875, when the population was about 2500. He became a probate judge the next year and soon was elected to the state legislature. He spent most of his working years as a representative of capitalists, both local and absentee, accumulating on the way a fortune in real estate investments. From 1890 to 1902, he was J. J. Hill's agent in Seattle.

Tacoma and Portland in growth.

How did Sam get into the utilities business? The Minneapolis Trust Company, in which J. J. Hill and William Dunwoody, a Minnesota grain elevator owner, had substantial interests, looked for opportunities to develop and underwrite securities for utilities and other businesses, and found one in Seattle.

The first gas company was organized in Seattle in 1873 and given an exclusive 25 year franchise, later changed to permit the sale of electric current purchased from the powerhouses of the Street Railways Company.

In 1892, on behalf of the Minneapolis Trust Company, Sam wired Burke to send him a confidential evaluation of the existing gas plants. Burke gave this at between $700,000 and $750,000. In 1895, Burke acted for Sam and his associates in consolidating the Union Illuminating Company and the Union Electric Company into the Seattle Gas and Electric Light Company. "Light" was later dropped from the name.

In December 1895, it was announced that a syndicate led by Sam Hill had obtained control of the new company. His associates were W. J. Murphy, a Minneapolis newspaper publisher; Judge Thomas Burke and H. C. Henry of Seattle; and two directors of the Minneapolis Trust Company, H. W. Cannon, president of the Chase National Bank, and William Dunwoody.

The original franchise of the gas company expired in 1898, but it continued doing business without renewing its franchise No one made much of this until 1900, when the Seattle *Star* campaigned against the going rate of $2.00 per thousand cubic feet, pointing out that in other cities near a source of coal the rates were in the range of $.75 to $1.30 a cubic foot. Utilities, especially if unduly greedy, were attractive targets for a crusading newspaper, and the attacks helped to sell papers. The *Star* challenged the City Council on the legal right of the gas company to expand without a renewed franchise. Burke, as attorney for the utility, responded that the franchise was perpetual, and only its exclusive character had changed in 1898.

Sam had brought guests, including Sir Stafford Northcote, later Governor of Bombay and of Australia, to Seattle in a private car in April 1896, and no doubt did some reconnoitering. He returned in December 1900 with Dunwoody and other associates from Minneapolis. On that visit Sam told the newspapers, on behalf of the bondholders, that he wanted to continue to expand the company and give the best possible service to its customers. The matter of the franchise should be left to the courts. Sam thought it " . . . curious that certain parties should wish to prevent the company from extending its business so that by increasing its volume, it might serve the public at a reduced rate, and at the same time were calling on the company to reduce the rate." He added that he felt "a little piqued" about being termed a nonresident by some. "Where a man's treasure is there will his heart be also," he said. "I have never taken away a dollar from this city, and I believe that I may state, without exaggeration, that I have been instrumental in bringing many millions of dollars here," referring to his past work for the Great Northern Railroad.

In an attempt to mollify the *Star*, he called on the editor and offered to show him the books of the gas company in order to justify its rates. When the editor pointed out that the company was overcapitalized and claimed that it was hiding its profits by paying interest on a mortgage of $2,500,000 to the Minneapolis Trust Company, Sam blamed it all on the previous utility owners, and furthermore warned against the danger of antagonizing the powerful men who were holding the mortgage bonds.

The *Star* hoped that a new company would come in to reduce rates, and through its editorials, persuaded the state's attorney general to test the legality of Seattle Gas and Electric's franchise. Late in 1900, the Seattle City Council passed an ordinance repealing the franchise. Burke's junior partner, Shepard, promptly went to a friend of the company, Judge C. H. Hanford in Spokane, and obtained an injunction against repeal of the franchise. Embarrassingly, it was soon revealed that the ordinance for repeal had actually been drawn up in Burke's office. Burke cooperated in this way because he was sure he could block the repeal of the franchise through a decision in Judge Hanford's court. Sure enough, in the spring of 1901, Hanford handed down the decision that the company's charter was perpetual, and that the Council's attempt to repeal the franchise was void.

Sam was at Aix-les-Bains when he heard of Judge Hanford's decision. "I shall endeavour to see that the citizens of Seattle are in all things fairly treated," he wrote E. F. Wells, the company's secretary. "Wednesday night I am dining with Mr. Andrew Carnegie and I may be able to put in a good word for the (Seattle) library." He had previously wired Blethen, editor of the Seattle *Times*, that he would subscribe $500 toward a new library.

Nesbit's book relates a story told by Joe Smith, the *Star* reporter who covered the gas war, including the fight over extending the franchise. The *Times* had editorialized that $500 in the right places in the City Council could have settled the problem in Sam's favor at any time. Later, when asked what confirmation of the perpetual franchise had actually cost him, Sam answered, "thirteen cigars." But, he said, they were not just ordinary cigars: they were tinfoil wrapped. Whereupon Sam laughed and offered the reporter a noncorrupting brand.

During his first year as president, Sam corresponded from Minneapolis and abroad with Wells on the most minute details of operation of the gas company. In January 1901, he authorized an increase for advertising in the *Star* from $4.00 to $8.00 per week, a move scarcely suspect as an attempt to influence editorial policy. While in Europe in the spring of 1901 before going to Russia, he wrote of visiting gas works in Rome, Florence, and Milan, which may well have been of more interest to him than the twentieth church on the tour. He also sought the advice of the presidents of other gas companies, especially the Minneapolis Gas and Light Company owned by his friends the Rands.

Sam's company actively and successfully promoted the sale of gas for cooking and heating, and extended its mains throughout the growing city. It sold gas lamps, cooking stoves, water heaters, and gas grates at attractive prices in order to get new customers. Its principal product was "coal gas" distilled from soft coal, consisting of hydrogen, methane, and carbon monoxide. The coal, 60 tons or more per day, was obtained mostly from the Roslyn mine, in which Sam later had an interest, located on a four mile spur of the Northern Pacific near the Snoqualmie Pass in the Cascades. The company also owned a small plant using steam and incandescent coke, operated only when necessary, to make "water gas," composed principally of carbon monoxide and hydrogen. The processing of the coal yielded coke, ammonia liquor, and tar by-products. Some of the coke was used for the company's boilers, and the rest sold, mainly to the Pacific Coast Company to which Sam had a track and trestle constructed. An ammonia plant was added in 1901.

Late in 1901, Sam heard that Lyman C. Smith, the typewriter magnate of Syracuse, New York, was arranging a short term mortgage for $450,000 on his Seattle office buildings to finance a rival company in Seattle, the Citizens' Light and Power Company. Sam reflected darkly that the mortgage would mature in February 1904, adding, "I am satisfied we can keep his kind occupied until that mortgage comes due."

In 1902, the Seattle City Council granted a franchise to sell gas to the new Citizens' Light and Power Company. To add insult to injury, Smith's associates in this venture had previously been associated with Sam's company, Collins as manager and Clise as a trustee.

The prospect of a price war was looming. Sam told Wells to reduce the price of gas to $1.50 per cubic foot " . . . if it should become necessary as a last resort in the final settlement of the gas controversy." He wrote to a friend, "You remember that the unjust steward said on a certain occasion, 'Take thy bills, sit down quickly and write fifty,' and you also recall that when the time of trouble came the unjust steward had friends."

The coal stokers struck briefly on New Year's Day, 1902. In the circumstances, the company thought it best to accede to their demand for a steep twenty five cents per hour wage. It was a time of bitter feelings between management and unions. Aldrich, secretary of the Spokane Falls Gaslight Company, which had been struck by the stokers that year, wrote Sam that it was "suicidal" for gas companies to recognize a union, and complained, "It will not be long before they will be demanding an eight hour day." Sam replied sympathetically, "If you give in, you might as well turn over your plant to them. You must run your business and the sooner they find it out the better for all parties concerned." Aldrich sent Sam the names of seven of the strikers so that Sam would "know how to treat them" if they came to Seattle; the laborer, it seems, was worthy of his ire.

Charles Babcock, head of the land department of the Great Northern Railroad, wrote long earnest letters to Sam in the hope of modifying his reactionary ideas about unions. Sam protested, "You know me well en-

ough, Charles, to know that I try to sympathize with all classes of people*
and with all sides, and out of the result to have a true judgment. All that we
must do, though, is to try to do our part well."

In April 1902, Sam wrote his wife in St. Paul, "The Western Central
Labor Organization Walking Delegates and I have had many sessions. Thus
far they have resulted in my favor. I was down at the works at two o'clock
this morning and am keeping after the thing pretty sharply."

He told her of a customer who " . . . had his meter taken out about
eight years ago and bypassed the gas. We discovered it . . . We had him in
and I made Mr. Coleman, one of the best known citizens here, arbitrate in
the matter . . . Coleman finally decided that he ought to go [to the
penitentiary] but recommended that he should not be sent on account of his
family . . . Of course, if we had prosecuted him it would have a very
salutary effect here in Seattle, but what are you to do?"

Expansion and competition were proving expensive, so expensive
that in May 1902, Sam had to send $31,000 of his personal funds to the Chase
National Bank to allow payment of the company's bond coupons. New
second mortgage bonds for $1,300,000 were issued that year.

Furthermore, Sam's rivals in the Citizens' Light and Power Co. were a
trial in many ways. They hired away some of his men. They laid pipelines
parallel to those of Sam's company, sometimes within a few inches, and
took over some of his customers. His plant manager, too, was having a hard
time with various problems. Sam wrote, "Our gasworks looks like a
barnyard full of chickens, all running in different directions."

He invited William Thomas, who had been manager of the Vancouver,
B.C., gasworks since its inception, to visit Seattle late in 1902 and then to
tour the Minneapolis gas plant. Thomas complied, and after his visit to
Minneapolis, wrote a letter to the superintendent with some frank criticisms and suggestions which were not received kindly. The superintendent
wrote Sam ironically, "As for your sending this man to Minneapolis, I
should not like to have him with me . . . He knows a great deal more about
the business than I myself." Thomas had more diplomatically offered con-
structive criticisms about Sam's plant, which impressed Sam enough to
engage him as the new manager.

Meanwhile, the electric power side of the business was not prosper-
ing, partly, at least, because Sam did not give it his full attention. He sold
the assets late in 1902, and agreed not to reenter the electrical business.

By December 1902, the Citizens' Light & Power Company had laid
some twenty miles of pipe, some of it in the heart of the city, and began
delivering gas. Sam reduced the price of gas to 80¢ a cubic foot in competitive territory. He got so worked up over the tactics of the opposition that he
redrafted his will to provide that, in the event of his death, " . . . while the
other parties are in the field, gas will be sold at cost during the life of their

---

*One of Babcock's friends, incidentally, had incurred a loss of $2,200 in the Seattle
Piping Company, a supplier of Sam's, which Sam generously agreed to pay.

franchise, if in opposition to our own." E. C. Cooke, vice-president of the Minneapolis Trust Company, and J. J. Hill were named as executors.

Through newspaper publicity, Sam seized upon the greater danger of asphyxiation from water gas compared with coal gas because of its higher content of carbon monoxide (about 26% versus 7%). He did not stress the point that his company also produced water gas, amounting at times to about one-fifth of the total output. In a couple of instances at least, when customers had changed over to the opposition, Sam wrote them letters warning them of the dangers of " . . . the introduction of dangerous or poisonous illuminants" and holding the customer " . . . responsible for such damages as may ensue by reason thereof."

To counter Sam's warnings about the higher carbon monoxide percentage in water gas, a letter was printed in the Seattle *Sunday Times*, signed by three physicians from the Seattle Board of Health, no doubt motivated by nothing but the public weal. They claimed that water gas was no more explosive than coal gas, and furthermore, that in the event of accidental leakage in a home, " . . . water gas, as sold by the Citizens' Gas Company, has a noticeable pungent odor as well as an irritating effect upon the air passages when inhaled," and that therefore the customer would be warned of danger.

Sam was aware of the hazards of alarming the populace too greatly about the hazards of water gas. "People will finally say they [had] better use electricity and drop out the gas entirely if there is going to be any question about it," he reasoned. Business improved, for all that; the company's sales in 1902 were 155 million cubic feet as compared with 109 million in 1901, and its net profit was over $62,000.

As a stratagem for cutting the price of gas in competitive territory, Sam decided he would contract to buy gas from his own company and sell it to the customer "at the burner" for whatever price he chose. Meanwhile, to show he was in Seattle to stay, he let it be known that he had purchased land and planned to build a house.

The opposition found ways of fighting back. Sam protested to Blethen, editor of the Seattle *Daily Times*, that " . . . an anonymous, scurrilous, and libelous circular . . . " was being distributed in Seattle about the gas situation in which personal reflections on Sam were made.

One of the questions Sam seized upon in 1903 was the legality of Citizens' Light and Power Company doing business in Seattle, since it had been incorporated in New Jersey. He filed suit in the U.S. District Court in January 1903. Sam engaged in lengthy correspondence about this with Anson M. Beard, his brother-in-law and a New York lawyer.

Beard pricked up his ears when he learned that Sam might finally be willing to sell his interest in the Seattle Gas Company to Lyman Smith, who for years had been a client of Beard's firm, Gifford, Stearns and Hobbs. Beard wrote that Gifford and he " . . . rather hoped that we might be able to get you and Mr. Smith together if the time ever came when you did not feel in such a fighting mood." Beard enclosed " . . . a little bill for services park at the international border. Tourists want three things; a good road to drive on, something worthwhile to see and something worthwhile to eat. I recently put up two restaurants 300 feet long and 32 feet wide at the international border. I bought a strip of land a mile long and a half a mile wide. I have installed cook houses, a golf course, an auto camp, and a hotel system where the tourist could get the best of food and the best of service at a reasonable price." Sam was proud of his " . . . traveling food wagons which are really steam chests on wheels. We can feed one thousand people at a time. No, I did not go into this with the idea of making money. If I break even, I will be more than satisfied. It is my contribution toward establishing and maintaining the good will of the people who travel back and forth between our country and Canada." Sam did not mention a star attraction, alcoholic beverages, but his establishment was probably one of the first restaurants accommodating large numbers of auto tourists; actually, a fast food emporium on a grand scale.

In 1927, Sam contemplated building a replica of Anne Hathaway's cottage on the grounds as a tourist attraction, and wrote to Prof. Edmond Meany about it. Meany had a student do a drawing for the project, but Sam soon abandoned the idea.

Hanna notes that in 1928-29, the restaurant was the only liquor outlet in the district, so that Merrill had to use the liquor permits of his staff members to get an adequate supply. He tells of one thirsty member, who lived near the fifth tee, often being seen at night holding onto the tail of his black Labrador dog to be guided home, a literal use of "the hair of the dog."

The gross income from the golf course during 1935 was only $4,000 and it was evident that a lot of money would need to be spent for machinery and labor to get the course into proper shape. Accordingly, the board of trustees of Maryhill Museum voted to turn the property over to Edgar Hill so that he could, if he wished, recoup "in part some of the funds due him," namely the $25,000 interest in the development Sam had conveyed to him after Edgar's nominal marriage to Sam's mistress, Mona Bell (Chapter 28). Edgar retired because of illness in the summer of 1944 and returned to Indiana, where he died.

The old buildings housing the restaurant were being torn down when the author visited the club in 1979, but there was a new clubhouse and the place was thriving.

Solomon's Temples

Most of Sam's visions had a way of being realized, sometimes incompletely or belatedly, but one flamboyant dream was so beyond fulfillment that it deserves mention. Late in 1925 the *Minneapolis News* carried the startling headline, "Samuel Hill Visions World Chain of Solomon's Temples";* Huge reproductions of ancient structure conceived as peace symbol

---

*One is tempted to ask, "Franchise, anyone?"

257

by former Minneapolitan." Construction of three great counterparts of the temple in this country and five more in world capitals was contemplated. The first replica, shown in a newspaper drawing, was to be on thirty acres at the Philadelphia Sesquicentennial Exhibition of 1926, and was to be the site of a world peace conference. Sam was to tour the world in 1926 at his own expense, visiting all nations and inviting leaders of people to attend. He was acting on behalf of " . . . the syndicate of New York financiers [which] has underwritten the first few millions for the colossal undertaking." The building committee was headed by Harry Walker, former lieutenant governor of New York.

Solomon had built his splendid temple, Sam said, " . . . as a means of unifying all the discordant elements of his people around the one faith and the one God." The story continued, "Mr. Hill and his associates find the people of the world in exactly the same condition in which Solomon found the tribes of Israel . . . Mammon, the god of greed, is all powerful." The advocates of his plan " . . . believe to have found a permanent and tangible symbol of the abstract conception of universal peace, for which the world will lay down its arms." A $10,000 prize would be awarded for an international peace anthem.

In Seattle, Sam referred reporters' inquiries to Col. John B. Rose, who hastened to explain that King Solomon's original lavish decorations, including 100,000 talents each of gold and silver, would not be duplicated. The architect, Harvey W. Corbett, said he would ignore existing models of the temple and rely on more recent archeologic findings to recreate the exquisite citadel, great banquet hall, and Porch of Judgment at a cost of three million dollars. The original temple had not heard the sound of a hammer, " . . . which would be a bit difficult rule to enforce upon modern labor," Sam added. Still, it would have extended the work and labor might not have knocked it.

We don't know when this project was abandoned: probably immediately. The exposition itself went five million dollars in the hole. Perhaps with the gold of Ophir, the Queen of Sheba, appropriately costumed, could have pulled it off, so to speak, as Sally Rand did for Chicago's World Fair.

Speaking of the Century of Progress Exhibition, held in 1933 in Chicago, Sam mentions in a letter of July 1930 that he had been " . . . very busy trying to launch the Century of Progress Excursion," apparently a promotional venture to increase attendance at the Fair. Sam died before he could fulfill this plan.

The Alabama Coal Mine

In 1923 Sam wrote his former secretary, "I am looking into things in Alabama, which promise well and in a few years should give a good income." Three years later he wrote, "You will be glad to know I am president of the Deepwater Coal and Iron Company, Jasper, Alabama. I get no salary.

I am to have an interest in the stock which will be of value if I live. Col. Bowlby [introduced in Chapter 16 as Major Bowlby, later the first Oregon Highway Department engineer] is also with the company. I live in a tent at Nahvoo, a little town eighteen miles north of Jasper." After the queen's visit, he would go back to work at Jasper. "My young man secretary says I work nineteen hours per day. I mean to get on my feet again. . . . It looked as if I was down and out. You remember our old fight in that gas company? Well, I'll win again."

In a 1927 letter to Loie Fuller, he told of his tribulations: "I have worked as never before . . . Three times I have had it financed and three times it has been knocked over by parties seeking to control the company. But I am fighting on. . . . "

Sam had invested in coal mines in the early 1900's, but we don't know how he got into the business in Alabama. Included in his estate was " . . . an interest in 4,733 acres of coal lands" there.

Movies

In 1921, Sam made a movie, "The Sacred Faith of a Scrap of Paper," featuring the dedication of the Peace Portal in Blaine, Washington, and celebrating more than a hundred years of peace between the United States and Canada (Chapter 21). English Quakers had given him a piece of a timber from the "Mayflower Barn" at Jordans in Devonshire.* When Sam arrived in New York, he announced that the film was being made and that his old friend Frank Terrace would carry the wooden relic to Blaine to be placed in the cornerstone of the Portal.

The movie showed excerpts from the Mayflower Compact; William Penn's treaty with the Indians; and the Treaty of Ghent in 1814. Scenes included presentation of the wood relic to Sam by Friends in England; the Treaty House in Ghent with portraits of the signers; the burgomeister of Brussels; Cardinal Mercier giving his blessing; Joffre in Paris in civilian garb to symbolize his stand for peace; the party on the *Olympic* crossing to New York; the arrival at Blaine of the chest containing the relic; and the ceremony of the dedication in September 1921.

In Paris, Sam had addressed an emotional request to Joffre to " . . . take in your hands this piece of wood. . . . We see in this gesture a token of your constant devotion, and the evidence that a great soldier, such as yourself, may be equally fervent in his striving for peace. . . . When one displays your portrait, at the very depths of America, there is but one cry: 'Father Joffre!'"**

It was announced that the movie titles would be translated into French and prints of the film given to Marquise de Chambrun of Paris and Mme. de

---

*It's too bad no movie was made of the movie-making. One can picture Sam and Loie Fuller invading the quiet Friends' service as Sam " . . . took over the role of motion picture director."

**To invoke the *New Yorker* again, may one submit this to the Department of Doubt That But One Cry, etc.?

259

Wairt, wife of the Prime Minister of Belgium, for use in connection with their charities. A note in the *New York Times* a year later (September 1922) announced the release of the film.

Sam had asked a friend to show the movie to Will Hays, president of the Motion Picture Producers Association in July 1922. Sam wrote Hays to ask if it were true that Hays might " . . . be disposed to take my cinema and spend whatever money is necessary to put it in the shape that you thought best and produce same?" Sam also had " . . . some of the film which has not yet been put together . . . taken on the tour of Marshall Joffre around the world. . . . Expenses incurred in these two enterprises [the trip and production of 'The Sacred Faith of a Scrap of Paper'] up to date possibly will run as high as $200,000. If you would care to undertake this, I would be willing to turn the same over to you, you to bear the expense of putting it into shape and producing same, and I should wish one third of the net profits. . . . My personal expense in connection with the creation of the Peace Portal amounted to a little over $100,000." Mr. Hays' reply has not been preserved, but it was probably brief.

In the same letter, Sam had proposed that Hays might wish to buy the American rights to Queen Marie's movie based on her short story, "The Lily of Life." Whether Sam had helped to finance the production is unknown. He wrote, "I have seen the representation in Paris and I have never seen a movie which interested me so much. . . . Miss Loie Fuller's School of Dance appears. It is so graceful and beautiful that by decree in Greece, she alone is allowed to use the great stadium in Athens." In case Hays agreed, and providing all expenses were paid, Queen Marie and party would come to America and be present at performances in some of the principal American cities. Hays did not hasten to exploit this opportunity, either.

Sam was not destined to be another Cecil B. DeMille. "The Sacred Faith of a Scrap of Paper," transferred from nitrate to modern film at Maryhill Museum several years ago, will no doubt remain a historical curiosity. Apparently no print of Queen Marie's movie has survived.

Writing Projects

Early in 1923 a Minneapolis reporter was told, "Mr. Hill is now writing three books, all of which, he says, will be published within the next year. One is on the 'Life of James J. Hill'; another on 'People I Have Known'; and a third on the war policies and administration of President Wilson." It is likely that the J. J. Hill biography would have been a eulogy; the Wilson book a diatribe; and "People I Have Known" a best seller — at least if Sam told the whole truth. He flirted seriously only with the first of these projects and none actually got between the covers.

Sam made a start on the biography of his father-in-law in February 1923, discussing the project with J. J.'s brother, Alexander Samuel Hill of Fergus, Ontario. Addressing him as "Dear Uncle Alexander," Sam wrote, "You once paid me the great compliment of saying that I knew your brother better than anyone else, in that I had caught his point of view in many things . . . I never met his equal in the universality of his knowledge. The thing that troubles me now more than anything else is my inability to portray his character as I saw it, to describe his work, and to indicate the widespread influence which he had upon the affairs of our time. . . . If people enjoy reading this book as much as I enjoy writing it, they will have great pleasure."

In a flurry of letters in February 1923, Sam sent some advance sheets of the biography to a former Minnesota legislator and an inquiry to the governor of Minnesota to have certain points checked. He wrote to the iron works which had built J. J. Hill's cargo ships for the Great Lakes to obtain the name of an engineer. He sent to Putnam and Sons for a copy of the James J. Hill biography it had published and promised, "I will hurry and get my book finished." (The author could find only one page of Sam's typewritten text in the Maryhill Museum files, headed, "Threatened Receiverships, page 7, 12/24, 1922." It describes Sam's early acquaintance with Lt. Gov. Ignatius Donnelly of Minnesota.)

The Maryhill Museum files yielded ten pages which look like page proofs for a biographical sketch of J. J. Hill, as might have been prepared for a dictionary of biography. The proofs bear the imprint of the Knickerbocker Press and indicate tha material was submitted in 1906 and re-edited in September 1910. Blanks had been left in the printed text for data filled in in Sam's handwriting. The article is full of praise for J. J.'s ingenious planning, organizing, and supervising every detail of his enterprises, and for his service to the country in bringing settlers to the West and creating for them " . . . two billions worth of wealth in real property, which great achievement is without parallel in the history of American railroads." Sam might have been able to describe incidents not found in the "Empire Builder's" official biographies. On the other hand, J. J. was a hero of Sam's, and we could not have expected an unbiased view from Sam's pen.

In February 1923, Sam wrote Gen. Clarence Edwards and Marshal Joffre that he intended to publish a " . . . little book entitled 'Woodrow Wilson and the World War'" to supplement Robert Lansing's book (which he had sent for) and the letters of Ambassador Walter Page and Franklin Lane. He told his friend Edward Tuck, a financier living in Paris, that he had arranged for its publication while in New York. It would be "dedicated to the women, wives, and widows of the United States." He asked Charles Babcock " . . . to ascertain the date that Wilson made the decree that nobody should speak his name except in praise . . . and get, as far as possible, the wording of that statement. Senator Poindexter [of Washington] will get it for you if he is there. If not, George Chamberlain [an Oregon senator] will get it." One doubts that Sam quoted Wilson correctly, but there is no doubt about Sam's resentment. He wrote Joffre dramatically, "After its publication I may have to leave the U.S., so please keep a place open for me there in France." Just what Wilson had done to incur Sam's displeasure is unknown; no text of the Wilson work has turned up, and it is unlikely that Sam ever finished it. Another item of unfinished business turns up in the stack of letters Sam wrote in February 1923. He addressed A. R. Francis, governor of Missouri: "I am planning to print a little account of my trip around the world in 1916 and enclose a few lines which refer to yourself. Do you see any objection to my printing what I send?" The only account we know of about this trip is the one Sam sent to the Secretary of the Harvard Class of 1879 (Chapter 20).

In March 1923, Sam talked to a local reporter in Goldenale about his writing plans, not mentioning the J. J. Hill work, but adding another project in which he would relate his world-wide travels. Miss Genevieve Sunderland of Goldenale was his stenographer and judging by Sam's prodigious output of letters in several weeks early in 1923, she was kept very busy.

It is regrettable that Sam did not record reminiscences of the famous people he had known. He did relate some of them to Clarence Barron, references to whose recollections are scattered through this book. Perhaps Barron omitted some scurrilous or juicy items from their conversations on shipboard and in Paris which would have made the best reading of all!

The Trip Around the World with Joffre

Entertaining in the grand style has become a habit of royalty through the ages, their subjects picking up the tab and sometimes even being granted the privilege of looking on. The robber barons in the pre-income tax era could and did rival, or even outdo, royalty in this kind of display. Sam's hospitality was enthusiastic and lavish, but of more modest proportions. Most of the cost of Queen Marie's tour was borne by the railroads and steamship companies and the cities visited. When Sam accompanied Joffre, his wife, daughter, and aides around the world in 1922, however, Sam picked up the check. Just why Sam admired Joffre enough to do this for the "Hero of the Marne" is not clear.

Most of the correspondence about arranging Sam's junket with Joffre has been lost. He wired Senator Miles Poindexter of Washington in December 1921, that he would soon leave for Japan to meet Joffre. "He visits the Phillipines, China, and Manchuria as my guest. . . . I plan on our return in March [to] visit Washington to pay our respects to President and Mrs. Harding." Poindexter's office notified Charles E. Hughes, Secretary of State and Hughes assured the Senator he would assist in any way he could. Sam was reported to have " . . . journeyed to Paris especially to invite the hero of the Marne to undertake the tour." The details of their itinerary are not known.

A news story from the *North China Star*, Harbin, Manchuria, dated Febraury 27, 1922, reviewed Sam's career, including the 1916 trip through Siberia and his good roads efforts. He was to " . . . leave tonight for Peking and thence for Shanghai . . . In Peking, he will, if he can, get a hearing [to] urge upon the government the importance of good roads in the development of China." The story noted that he was accompanied by R. R. Earle of the Pathé Company who would film the trip with Joffre. "When General Joffre steps on board the Admiral Line ship at Shanghai, he will automatically pass into the care of Sam Hill who will see him to America, across the country, and [be] the last man to shake his hand when he leaves New York. . . . "

A dispatch from Tienstin, when the group was enroute to Peking, gave a more complete report of Sam's career and the Peace Portal; "Mr. Hill has come out to China for three reasons. In his brief visit he hopes to further the cause of international peace and stimulate the good roads movement. But his main object is to meet Marshal Joffre who accompanies him to America. . . . "

A reporter from *Le Journal du Pekin* interviewed Sam in Peking. The reporter called him the "King of the Road" because he had " . . . made a fortune in constructing roads in America [sic]." He had somehow gotten the idea that Sam Hill was still a power in railroad circles and that he had " . . . numerous residencies [sic] in all the cities in America." Even counting Sam's clubs, it was a pardonable exaggeration. He regarded France as his second fatherland, Sam said.

The reporter noted the resemblance between Sam and Joffre. Sam admitted graciously, "That's somewhat true from a physical standpoint . . . and I find it flattering, but I couldn't be compared to one who has 'saved the world from barbarism. . . . '" Then they all drank toasts to France and America with vintage Bordeaux.

The China press reporter in Peking sympathized with Joffre in the grueling round of banquets and speeches: "Anyone who succeeds in completing such a tour deserves all the orders of the striped tiger . . . and a medal from the Physical Cultural Society besides. . . . Also, the Order of the Rising Sun, that being the time that one is usually allowed to go home. . . . When the Marshal first entered the hotel at Peking to the dislocated strains of the 'Marseillaise' as tormented by a Chinese brass band, he seemed a worn old man almost too weary to salute. . . . 'I am very tired' were his only words to the correspondent. . . . " The reporter observed, "He combines the vigorous mind of a Roosevelt with the enlightened pacifism of a William Penn," which Sam probably considered half insult and half compliment.

They returned by way of the West Coast, visiting the Peace Portal, which Joffre rededicated, then Victoria and Sam's home in Seattle. There was a story in the *Seattle Daily Times*, revived at the time of Queen Marie's visit, that the Marshal " . . . refused to permit his host's huge baggage labels to be placed on his luggage." Another concerned " . . . a silk hat kicked with the skill of a varsity punter across the lobby of the Hotel Empress in Victoria by the favorite of kings and queens, in a time of stress over final arrangements for the Marshal's entertainment." This was illustrated by a drawing of Queen Marie with Sam alongside, kicking his topper over the Peace Arch. Still another tale was told of " . . . a misty morning in Blaine, following the dedication of the Peace Arch . . . when adamant and unsentimental railway officials refused to start a train until certain fares to Seattle had been paid, which they were with a gallant wave of the fountain pen of Mr. Hill."

After the Marshal's death, a reporter recalled his visit to Portland on April 4, 1922. Joffre, his wife, and daughter Germaine arrived in the morning in Sam Hill's private car. Joffre spoke little English and an aide supplied by the War Department acted as interpreter.

Oregon's Governor Olcott and Mayor Baker of Portland accompanied Joffre and Sam to the Interstate Bridge between Portland and Vancouver to dedicate the Pacific Highway. Five Indian chieftains dressed in tribal costume, who somehow always managed to get in on this sort of ceremony, were present at the exercises. There was a tour of the Coumbia River Highway, with John Yeon telling Joffre the history of the highway and pointing out its highlights.

In May 1922, the party was in San Francisco. Sam, Alma Spreckels, Marshal Joffre, and President Milharaud of France gathered before the portrait of Washington to be hung in San Francisco's unfinished Palace of the Legion of Honor. Milharaud thanked Mrs. Spreckels for constructing the building, and Sam for his courtesies to Joffre. The " . . . visitors left donations to a fund for the safeguarding of French art." Joffre probably heaved a sigh heard 'round the world on the completion of his second most arduous assignment. Sam saw the Joffres for the last time when he visited Paris in May 1929.

Helen Stone, daughter of former Governor Os West, recalls being invited for tea at the Spreckels mansion while the party was in San Francisco. She was attending nearby Mills College at the time and was driven to the house in Sam's car. Since she spoke French and had met Sam previously, she was asked to come because Joffre's daughter, who was about the same age, was there with the daughter of Mayor Rolf. Mrs. Stone recalled Joffre's daughter as a shy, subdued, convent-trained girl. Sam was charming, Alma Spreckels formidable. One memory that lingered was of a spun sugar basket with petit fours.

Miscellany

One of Sam's more obscure enterprises was to get a house in Victoria, B.C., apparently a bolt-hole to avoid the relentless pursuit of the Soviets. In the February 1923, letter to Gen. Edwards he wrote, "Just before the government closed up my coal mines and reduced the dividends on my railroad stock, I went over to Victoria, B.C., and got a place called 'Gibraltar.' In this I placed 'much goods laid up for many years,' and have a Chinaman who is a dead rifle shot in charge." This house was probably at View Royal, several miles from downtown Victoria, but we don't know how and when Sam disposed of it.

A three-man group with the impressive title, "Central European Trust," headquartered in London, had been referred to Sam by Loie Fuller rendered" which he would not have sent, " . . . except for the fact that it is a part of the firm's agreement to charge everyone for work done, whether friends or family connections." Sam cheerfully paid the bill, remarking only that it was too small. His attitude was to change later on.

Sam was enjoying the contest in spite of the turmoil. He wrote, "The fact of it is, Anson, I have become fascinated with the business and with the place . . . I have no feeling against Mr. Lyman C. Smith, but I am a little bit like yourself, when I get set, I stay set. I do not care so much about making money as I do about having my own way. . . . I have put the price of gas down and mean to keep it down so that Smith cannot make any money during the lifetime of his franchise. If I can knock him off quicker, so much the better. Knock him out I must and will."

He wrote Farrell late in 1902, "If I have to, I can take up the entire share capital and bonded debt of the Gas Company." He promised that, "If the time ever came when I wanted to sell out my interest," he would take it up with Beard, but he did not anticipate that this would happen.

Sam resented Collins and Clise defecting to Smith and forming a rival company with the intention of " . . . purely and simply injuring the old company." He told Beard indignantly, "I was shown certificates of stocks signed by him [Smith] issued to members of the [city] Council direct, without the formality of having them signed in the name of a stool pigeon." Sam felt it was up to him to teach his opponents a lesson they would not forget. "It is true it may cost us several times their investment to destroy them, but when they are destroyed others will be very slow to seek a similar investment in that line."

Sam had also appraised M. D. Grover, general counsel for the Great Northern Railway, of the law suit challenging his rivals' right to sell gas. Grover wrote to ask Sam what he expected to gain by it. If Sam prevailed, the Citizens' Light and Power could simply organize under the laws of Washington instead of New Jersey and get a valid franchise to sell gas. Sam, as owner of two shares of C.L. and P. stock, replied in that event he would go to court to prevent transfer of the property from the old to the new company.

Beard asked Sam about the value of Smith's plant. Sam put this at $150,000 but admitted that his rivals claimed to have invested $400,000. He added, " . . . but I would not believe any man connected with the company under oath." Gifford, Beard's partner, learned at a conference in Syracuse with Clise and Smith that they had already spent $200,000 and were under contract to spend $400,000 more. Beard pointed out that they would then have a new plant, while Sam's was obsolescent.

One of the options Beard dangled before Sam was that he could become president and director of a combined gas company in Seattle. The board would include Smith's representatives and, " . . . one director to represent our firm which would hold the balance of power and see that justice was done to both sides in case of any dispute." Beard had obtained J. J. Hill's approval of the scheme. Furthermore, wrote Beard, it was " . . . the best possible solution for Mary. I mention her because I have understood that she did not like to live in Seattle." If Sam and Smith could not agree on the respective values of their properties, Smith suggested that they could submit to an evaluation by some expert selected by J. J. Hill.

The gas price war was taking its toll. Sam confided to a friend in the gas business that, "There is not at this time in the treasury of the company a sum sufficient to pay the interest of the bonds July 1st."

After consultation with J. J. about the terms, on May 1, 1903, Sam finally did the unthinkable: he quoted a price to Lyman Smith for the Seattle Gas and Electric Company, namely, $1,750,000. Soon, Sam met with Smith for the first time in New York City and concluded a gentleman's agreement to the effect that both properties should be examined with a view to bringing about a settlement.

A Mr. Witherby was the expert summoned to Seattle for the evaluation. He wanted to see the company books through May 1, but Sam balked at giving out the figures for the first four months in 1903. For one thing, there was a second mortgage against the company's property, and there were $20,000 in bills payable which Sam held personally. Witherby found Smith's plant up-to-date and well located. It could be duplicated for between $400,000 and $450,000; Sam's plant could be replaced for $1,450,000. Beard was upset because Sam would not permit an examination of current accounts, but neither would Smith's company, probably because both sides were now losing money. There would be difficulty in getting underwriters for the bonds of a combined company unless there were good prospects for profit.

Witherby's report did not make a hit with Sam. He complained that Witherby had not made a sufficiently thorough investigation of his property, and that Witherby had agreed to leave examination of the books to an auditor. Sam stoutly defended his projections for a profit in 1903. He suspected that the request to obtain recent financial data was " . . . made more for the purpose of ascertaining our condition than for the purpose of placing bonds."

Smith wrote Sam that, in view of Witherby's report, he regretted that his bankers could not provide financing. He added politely, "I do not want to dismiss the effort at this juncture, and if you can make any recommendations or suggestions, I should be most pleased to have you do so."

Sam, miffed because Smith would not meet his price, wired Beard that he was coming to New York to " . . . inaugurate a war of extermination." Beard was about to leave for a fishing trip with his father-in-law, J. J. Hill, but encouraged Sam to continue negotiations and make some concessions. Beard hoped that Sam would not come to New York while he was gone, probably sensing the possibility that a deal might be struck without the benefit of his good offices.

Sam, still intransigent, wrote to Smith firmly but politely to justify his asking price. He had " . . . used every effort which I have at my command to meet your views. . . . It is probable that July 1st I shall make another reduction in the price of gas. This will undoubtedly be met by a reduction in the price of electric current and will entail a loss on all concerned. I regret this, but feel that I am not to blame in the matter." Sam went on to express pessimism about business conditions in Seattle.

Smith was sorry that Sam had nothing to suggest to resolve the impasse but added, "Something may occur to you later on. . . . I am a little fearful, friend Hill, that you are depressed at times. Pardon the suggestion." He might have asked why Sam seemed to be losing his head while all about him were keeping theirs!

Understandably, this reply failed to mollify Sam. He initiated a policy of selling gas ranges at less than cost and giving free gas when customers signed a contract to use the ranges. The rate in noncompetitive areas was reduced from $1.60 to $1.35 per thousand cubic feet.

The attorneys for the two sides, however, stipulated to an armistice on rates until September 1903. Sam was much displeased at the performance of his own attorneys, complaining to Beard that, "I've got a roomful of lawyers, and confidentially I sometimes think they know less law than I do — and you know how little that is."

Nevertheless, he planned to act as his own attorney. A year earlier, he had arranged for admission to the bar in Washington by reciprocity with Minnesota. He wrote Beard, "I have fooled away enough time with the lawyers when the whole thing ought to have been settled in sixty days . . . Up to the present time I have paid out $1,500 and will probably have to pay out as much more." A week later he paid attorneys fees of $5,000 and told Beard acidly, "Your guess of $300 was a little off as to what it would cost to get a determination of the case."

Beard righteously deplored the high fee, particularly because " . . . this was entirely thought out by me, and I do not see why the Seattle lawyers should charge you for advice that you had received from me . . . Anyone here would have obtained the injunction for you at an outside fee of $500." He advised Sam not to have so many counsel and not to conduct the case himself, as he had not practiced for so many years. He added, "I suppose it is your last name which has gotten you into so much trouble."

Sam now wavered and grudgingly held out hope for consolidation. He offered to meet Beard and Smith at the Great Northern offices in New York. " . . . with the understanding that Mr. Smith has selected you to act for his interest. . . . I am not willing to hold a town meeting. . . . This will probably be the last time that I shall be willing to take the matter up. I am so much annoyed by daily receiving letters and telegrams from different parts of the country asking me to put a price on the gas company, that I have decided, after this interview, unless disposition of the company is made, to take the plant entirely out of the market except on the lines of consolidation."

Peace was not advanced after Smith wired Sam that he would meet him at the appointed place and time in September 1903, but did not appear. Sam, in bad humor, caught a train for the West. His representative Farrell, president of the Great Northern Steamship Company, and Smith's Mr. Clise did meet soon afterward, however, and arranged an accord which finally led to amalgamation of the two companies.

Nisbett writes that " . . . the Dawes brothers, Chicago bankers, bought control of both companies and consolidated them. It was claimed that James J. Hill and J. D. Farrell made the decision to sell out without consulting Sam Hill." This is hard to believe, since Sam was the principal bondholder, unless he had resignedly given power of attorney to Farrell to complete the negotiations. If he did so, there is no mention of it in the correspondence.

It is difficult to say how Sam came out financially on the sale. Nowhere does he record how much of his own money went into the business and how he shared in the final settlement. The author's guess is that Sam's profit was not less than two or three hundred thousand dollars, an amount useful to Sam in now increasing his ventures into the stock market.

Articles of incorporation for the new consolidated Seattle Lighting Company were drawn up and the final financial arrangements completed in the spring of 1904. Sam could write on April 1, "I am out of the gas business." The Manhattan Trust Company loaned Smith and associates $400,000, of which Sam advanced one half in exchange for notes of the company due in six months. Farrell agreed to manage the properties until Sam's loan was paid, which was done on schedule. The bonds of the old company, of which Sam was the principal owner, then amounted to $729,000. Not long afterward, the new company sold the property on which Sam's gas works and holder had stood to the Harriman interests for one million dollars.

After the settlement had been agreed upon, the correspondence between Sam and his erstwhile enemies became polite and cordial to the same degree that it soured with Beard. Sam did not say so, but he probably admired Smith's coolness and acumen, though he was certainly not a match for Smith in the former. Sam was confident that the business of the new company would grow rapidly. He even offered Clise some advice about effecting economies and more efficient operations. It was none too soon; electric power was making large inroads upon the gas lighting business.

What of Beard, ignored in the final settlement? At the news that the agreement had been consummated without him, he became alarmed and indignant. He wrote Sam in October 1903, "I hope now that the deal has gone through, that you won't forget me in the final settlement . . . I have worked long and earnestly on the matter in your behalf and . . . spent a great deal of time on it for the last year and a half . . . . Unfortunately, Farrell and Clise did not inform me that any negotiations were pending the last couple of days in which the deal was closed . . . . I think under the circumstances . . . it is very modest on my part to suggest that if and when the money is paid to you, that you pay our firm $5,000 and a like amount to me personally for my outside personal attention to the matter. . . . . I do not see any reason why I should present Gifford with this additional sum and get practically nothing myself. He has already made sufficient money out of me. I am also going to request Smith to pay a fee of $5,000 and probably $10,000 . . . I know any other firm in New York would not hesitate to put in a bill for $50,000 in a case where so much money was being paid over as a result of their efforts." His estimate of attorney fees prevailing in New York City had apparently changed.

He wrote again in injured tones, "I do not feel that you and Mr. Smith treated me in the transaction with that courtesy which your situation called for . . . I think that you and Smith should be pleased to pay a reasonable fee for what was done for you." He sent another bill for $5,000 for his firm, but reduced the fee for his personal services to $1,000. He asked that Sam send the reply to his home, " . . . as I do not like Mr. G's attitude, and want to keep him out of the transaction entirely." Beard's alarm turned to anger when Smith did not pay his bill for $5,000. "Smith seems to think we were acting for you and not him in the gas deal . . . We intend to start actions forthwith against both of you, if our bills are not paid . . . We feel that we are being sawdusted and will not stand for it."

Beard had second thoughts about suing Sam for his fee. Farrell informed Sam that Smith had paid Beard a fee of $2,000. Beard was surely not anxious to have it come to light that he had proposed a private fee for himself in addition to billing Sam for his firm. Sam suggested that Farrell make Beard a personal gift of $1,000 after Beard had dropped his lawsuit. Sam would, of course, repay Farrell, but Beard was never to know the source of the money.

In spite of Beard's unethical billing, one can't help feeling that he was, in fact, "sawdusted" by Sam. Sam was nearly always fair in financial dealings, but perhaps this opportunity to one-up his attorney brother-in-law proved irresistible. Their friendship and correspondence ended with the "gas war." In 1910, Beard probably relished a reprisal when he represented Mrs. J. J. Hill in her legal action to obtain custody of Sam's daughter, Mary Mendenhall.

The utility fight had only a transitory effect on Seattle's economy. What of its effect on Sam? His absorption with the business perhaps contributed to the estrangement from his wife, but this consideration does not seem to have daunted him. His turbulent involvement in this first semi-independent venture into business gives us insights, not always attractive, into his character. Under the pressure of rugged competition and personal criticism, he had shown excitability, instability, even vengefulness, but not the all-around strength of character he no doubt wished to portray to J. J. Hill, his model and father figure. The compulsion to prove himself on his own merits would continue.

13

A House for a Prince?

The *Seattle Daily Times* headed an August 1909 story, "Built Palace Here for Royal Guest; Samuel Hill Spends $250,000 to Entertain Belgian Heir Apparent; Now Prince Can't Come — European politics keep him at home — but Mr. Hill will finish the house." Sam told the reporter grandly, "I wanted to help the town entertain the Crown Prince of Belgium on his visit here to the Exposition, that's all — just to help out."

While touring Europe in the summer of 1908, he and Albert had " . . . completed arrangements in Brussels for the Prince to visit the Exposition and get set to take a trip to Alaska. . . . Because of complications in the Congo, the Crown Prince cannot come," Sam said, "but I shall finish it as soon as I can, for I shall need it for my other guests."

In dozens of news stories and magazine articles after that, writers have taken Sam at his word. But it is certainly probable that the connection between Prince Albert's proposed visit to the Alaska-Yukon-Pacific Exposition in 1909 and Sam's decision to build a residence was an afterthought. He may well have hurried the work after Albert told him he planned to come, but in his announcement, it would seem that he wanted to give the public a reason for building the grand house he had envisioned for several years. Sam was prepared, however, to believe his own press interview. Early in 1910, he thanked General Jungbluth, Albert's aide, for the King's photograph: "I have prepared a place for [it] on the walls of the house that should have been his, and which I shall always think of as being built for him."

In December 1900, when Sam came to Seattle to be president of the Seattle Gas Company, he let it be known that he intended to be a permanent resident, not a fly-by-night capitalist. He and six of his friends soon bought five acres overlooking a ravine near East Highland Drive and Volunteer Park. As he wrote a friend in Minneapolis early in 1902, "I have just purchased a place for a home here and am much delighted over it. I look to the north and see Mt. Baker; to the south and see Mt. Rainier; look down at the foot of the hill and see Lake Union; look out to the right and see the big ocean; down to the left and see the shipping in the harbor, and look straight ahead and see the great Olympic Mountains, covered with snow all the year around. The weather yesterday was so warm that we went around entirely without overcoats and I counted twenty robins in the dooryard across the way. Come west, young man!"

Sam expected his friends to build on adjoining lots; J. D. Farrell, Walter Oakes, Judge C. H. Hanford, and Thomas Burke among them. He wrote his brother, "It is the only place in Seattle where I can drive from the office to the house without taking the horses out of a trot . . . Street car service is fairly good, cars every ten minutes . . . Two blocks from the place is a big city reservoir and Volunteer Park. From this point, the driveway will be built by the Park Board, running around Lake Washington."

In 1902, he asked an architect friend, Vernon Wright of Fergus Falls, Minnesota, to call on Mary Hill in St. Paul to discuss house plans. After Sam's wife and children left Seattle in the spring of 1903, he lost interest in building a house for several years.

He had been living first in an apartment, then at the Rainier Club in Seattle and probably wanted a showplace complete with servants, suited to his station, in which he could entertain his guests properly. He may have been thinking, too, of a proper home and refuge for Mary Mendenhall after she came of age.

In November 1906, Sam wrote to his daughter, then seventeen, "Sam [Finch] is living out in the little shack on the estate. Four of the Italians are here and pretty soon I shall begin to build Mary's house. We are surveying the ground now." As he told Lockley, he remembered that there were about 200 Italians doing concrete work near his house at Stockbridge, Massachusetts, who were " . . . being paid $2 a day and boarding themselves. I learned the name of one of the most expert of these men and told him to select 20 of his friends — that I would pay them $2 a day and board them and would pay their railroad fare from Lenox to Seattle and return. I built a boarding hall near where I was going to build the house. I installed a cook [Sam Finch] and boarded the men. They were working by the day and their instructions were to take their time and do good work." Later, some of these same men were employed on the Columbia River Highway to build stone retaining walls.

Sam engaged the architectural firm of Hornblower and Marshall of Washington, D.C. The firm had designed the Army and Navy Club, the Natural History building of the Smithsonian group, the Custom House at Baltimore, and a number of large homes in Washington.

Sam paid their bill ($750) for drawings and specifications late in 1908. How much of the residence was planned by the architects and how much by Sam is not clear, but Sam was prepared to take credit. He told the *Daily Times* reporter, "I planned the house entirely . . . I studied all the styles of architecture and found the Grecian Doric best for this climate and the site. The house stands on the edge of a deep ravine and I had to build a wall 65 feet high, 10 feet wide at the base, reinforced with 90 pound steel rails. I had to build my lot before I started to build the house." He expanded on this to Fred Lockley years later: "I went out to an old coal mine and they sold me for almost nothing a huge cable. I put 90 pound steel rails upright, wrapped this cable around the rails from bottom to top, and then poured the concrete, so that if a burglar wants to come in he would have to chisel through the thick concrete wall, cut the cable and then cut the 90 pound rails. It would probably take him a week or ten days and by that time he would probably get discouraged. I wanted to buy six inch steel girders, but the man from whom I wanted to buy them had some 24 inch plate steel girders that he wanted to get rid of, and which he gave me at the price of six inch girders."

Construction of the house did not actually begin until September 1908. Sam continued to Lockley, "My home is 52 feet square. In the whole house you will not find a crack, a knot, or a blemish in any of the beam ceilings or the woodwork. I had been working for weeks selecting the material to go into the house. When James J. Hill was here visiting me, he went over the house, figured very carefully, and when I had told him I had built it very cheaply, he bet me that I could not have it built for less than $150,000. He lost his bet." Sam told his father-in-law about getting the material and labor for building the foundations at a bargain and J. J. said, "Building your house was a donation party — not a legitimate business enterprise."

The Seattle *Daily Times'* estimate that building the house had cost $250,000, whatever its source, was even wider of the mark. Actually, the total, as given in a memo in Sam's handwriting, was modest indeed: $37,828. Of this about $16,000 went for payrolls and $10,000 for steel and concrete. The furniture, mostly from Marshall Field and Company, Seattle, came to about $2,600. The construction materials were from the Northwest, " . . . except the cement, which was Belgian," according to another newspaper story. Oddly, though Sam kept every bill for materials, the plans for the Seattle house have not been preserved.

With elaborate understatement, Sam told the Seattle reporter in 1909, "There is nothing unusual about my house. I wanted to make it a plain substantial affair . . . two stories high with servants' quarters and a garage in the basement and a subbasement — and a roof garden," he added as an afterthought. He explained that giant girders supported the roof, on top of which was an eight inch layer of cement composition and then " . . . five applications of pitch and tar paper alternating, each one-half inch in thickness. That is covered with a two inch layer of cement composition and surmounted with an application of boiled linseed oil. Above this are . . . a one inch layer of mastic red lead; three inches of agricultural drain tile; four inches of clay, filled and tamped; eight inches of soil; four inches of loam; and on top of that the sod for the roof garden."

It is no wonder, with such stupefying specifications for architectural overkill, that he told Lockley that he wanted the building " . . . to be here a thousand years after you and I are gone." He added, with some satisfaction, "I have built a good many houses in my life and this is the seventieth, I believe." The house had its own gas plant for heat. Sam once told his valet that if the house toppled over into the gulch and landed right side up, he would only have to connect up the water and go right on living in it.

The front door led to a large reception room and dining room communicating with a library, living room, and small bedroom. Georgia Patterson, who visited the house with her family in July 1914, recalled that the dining room had " . . . inside shutters faced with mirrors to give a feeling of greater space." Another reporter noted that " . . . on the molding in the dining room and hall, set in flush with the walls, are transparent colored photographs of Northwest land and seascapes, which can be illumined by lights behind. These, . . . as large as [street] car cards, cast a soft, comp-limentary light upon his women guests and pleased them immeasurably."

The second floor contained six bedrooms and baths. An elevator gave access to the roof garden, in which he could entertain as many as 100 people. There were no call bells in the rooms; rather, an intercommunica-ting telephone system was used.The exterior windows were fitted with bars of chrome steel and the wire netting outside these was electrically charged. Sam got another bargain on his chrome steel, the owner of the mill selling the bars to Sam at cost to keep his work force busy at a slack time. There was a steel-lined vault for valuables, including the large silver service.

Sam gave a lot of time and thought to the outside of the house, as well. He had a florist in Portland send men to plant a floral design of the American flag. Sam sent the exact latitutude, longitude, and elevation of the property to Mr. R. M. Hazard, at whose home in Rhode Island he had seen a sundial designed to be accurate within a minute. Sam had this verse inscribed on the instrument he ordered:

"I mark no hours but bright.
Steadfast through gloom I stand
Waiting 'till God command
Shine on me this light."

Reed and Barton, silversmiths, made the dial to Hazard's specifications.

Paul Douglas tells of encountering Sam, "a most unforgettable charac-ter," while out for a walk one evening in 1920: "I saw moving toward me a huge gray-clad man with a cloak and Quaker hat crowning a shock of white hair." After they had introduced themselves, Sam took Douglas to his house for a talk — actually a monologue — lasting until four in the morning, about Sam's travels: " . . . where the best snails in Paris were served and the best seafood in Naples . . . how he had picked out the site upon which Bryn Mawr College was built, and how one morning at 10:15 A.M., in a three minute conference with railway and shipping executives, he had cleared up the confusion on the Jersey City waterfront." Sam put the rhetorical question, "Who had the corners of Seattle sidewalks made to slope gradually down to street level?", and many another about his innova-tions and exploits.

Douglas thought it must have taken fifty years for ivy to have covered the walls of the great house. Sam explained that he had expected Albert of Belgium and his wife to come the summer of 1909, and in order to make them feel at home, " . . . after scouring the Cascade and Olympic Moun-tains, he had finally found an abandoned log cabin over which ivy had been growing for over half a century. He had the ivy dug up and fastened to wire netting and its roots planted in deep boxes. Then he had a trench dug around the house and had strong hooks coming out from the bricks. Drop-ping the ivy into the trench, he fastened the netting to the hooks and instantly had an ivy-clad mansion fit for royalty."

In going through the house, Douglas was surprised to see several trucks loaded with furniture in the basement garage. Sam told him he sometimes had the trucks follow him when he went to other states to talk good roads, so he could be sure of comfortable quarters. Sam took him past lighted photographs of the Columbia River Highway, Queen Elizabeth of Greece, King Albert, and Queen Marie, " . . . across whose largely bare bosom was written in glowing words, 'To my darling Sam, Marie of Rumania.'"

To add to Douglas's bemusement, "As his car started to take me home, a huge spout of water gushed through the pavement of his driveway, rising at least thirty feet in the air. I said to myself that it was another of Sam Hill's stunts. He had probably arranged this for his royal visitors and was trying it out on me." Only the next day did he read that a bolt of lightning had struck the sidewalk, hitting a water main: "Even nature had collaborated to heighten the drama at his house."

Sam lived in the house intermittently until his death. It was closed for long periods when he lived in Portland as president of Home Telephone Company. Much of the time his valet, Sam Finch, lived there with Sula, his wife. Finch was formerly head waiter at the Hotel Lafayette at Lake Minnetonka, Minnesota. Clara and Lucy Wetherby, Sam's two housekeepers in the Seattle house, went to Maryhill to operate the Meadowlark Inn after Sam's death.

Finch told a reporter that he often received telegrams from Sam in Portland, Vancouver, B.C., Spokane, or the East, telling him that the house was to be prepared for guests the following night and that a car was to meet them at the railroad station. Finch said he never knew how long Sam would remain at home; "Usually it was not more than five days."

Lockley tells the story of Sam's happening to meet a young man and his wife at the Seattle railroad station. "The young man said, 'Mister, my wife and I are on our wedding trip. Can you tell us where we can find a good place at reasonable rates to spend a week or ten days?' Sam Hill pointed to his car and said, 'Step right in. I can take you to a place I think you will like. Rates are a dollar and a half a day, but I'll make it $2.50 for both of you.'

"He assigned them to one of the view rooms in his home and his housekeeper served them all the luxuries of the season. When the young man and his bride left, he said to Mr. Hill, 'This is sure a swell joint and mighty reasonable. I'm going to recommend it to all my friends.' Mr. Hill thanked him, shook his head and said, 'I'm glad you both enjoyed your stay here, but we're going to quit taking guests. I'm planning to move to my farm at Maryhill on the Columbia River.'" Sam was not given to practical jokes, and the few recorded are of the kindest variety.

Finch described Sam's system for ordering meals. A number one dinner for four guests was the best, with four or five kinds of wine. A number two dinner meant that there would be 12 guests for a simpler meal. The number three consisted of plain American cooking for up to 40 people. "He never ordered dishes himself," Sam said; "He left that to me after he had given me a rough idea of the sort of dinner he wanted." Hill's favorites were roast suckling pig; saddle of lamb; corned beef and cabbage; and beans and brown bread, Southern style.

A reporter noted that Hill " . . . carried his enthusiasm for Northwest

Seattle house. Sam with members of the Belgian military mission, 1918. (From glass slide, Maryhill Museum files.)

products to the point of refusing to let oranges come to his table. Oranges, he argued, came from California. Seattleites ought to eat apples.''

In the 1920's, Sam developed a paranoia about burglars and Soviet spies. When he stayed at the house, he slept in a little room between the dining room and the lobby. There was a button at his bedside which would turn on every light inside and outside the house. Sam Finch told of sitting in his master's bedroom when Sam was having "anarchist trouble." Occasionally Hill would forbid entry to the house even to the milkman and iceman, so that Sam Finch would go outside to bring in their deliveries when the men were out of sight.

Sam did not often entertain in the Seattle house after the first years following its completion, and was seldom seen in Seattle society. However, one glittering, if not warm, occasion was the dinner Sam gave during Queen Marie's visit in 1926, described in Chapter 25. He was host also for members of a Belgian military mission when the group visited Seattle during World War I, probably in 1918. A reporter recalled the " . . . carpets that Belgian hares once hopped around.'' Whether they were pets or an emergency food supply, the reporter did not say.

In 1922, Sam entertained in grand style Marshall Joffre, his wife, daughter, and staff of aides. There was a report of a contretemps when the officers were assigned two to a bedroom. "It appeared a major would not consent to share a room with a captain, the captain would not possibly occupy a room with a lieutenant. So Sam Hill sent the whole staff down to the new Washington Hotel where he gave each man a room and an un- limited expense account. According to the story, the boys took a little advantage of him, having their shoes resoled, their uniforms repaired, and their clothes laundered — charging all to their hotel bill."

In 1920, Sam was much upset by the city council's decision to build a reservoir in Volunteer Park. He wrote tendering his resignation as honorary city policeman No. 505. He had appeared before them " . . . for the first and only time in 20 years and urged the city council not to place [the] reservoir . . . as I believed it would endanger all the property underlying it to the shores of Lake Union. . . . Knowing as I do the dangers incident for the residents below this reservoir, it would be improper for me to dispose of this house to one not conversant with the situation; I shall therefore comply with the law and take down the house." Sam did not estimate how much dynamite would have to be used if he were pressed to this extremity. He based his concern on his " . . . qualifiations as an engineer, having on one occasion received an engineering fee in a sum larger than, I believe, any engineer in Seattle has received, when I changed the channel of the Mississippi."*

Sam went on to review with some bitterness the things he had done to help Seattle: promoting paving of streets and boulevards before the 1909 Alaska-Yukon-Pacific Exposition, with the aid of Thomson and Lancaster; protesting the use of Lake Union as a source of city water; favoring school inspections by doctors and nurses; erecting the Good Roads Building and endowing a chair in road engineering and another for the study of the Russian language at the University of Washington; promoting Seattle as a Pacific port for trade with Russia and the Orient; and constructing the Peace Arch at Blaine, in which, " . . . outside of a few personal friends, no one in the city of Seattle has shown any interest. . . . " He concluded, "For myself I never claim infallability, but yield to none in my loyalty and devotion, whatever cause I may espouse."

From then on, pique at his accomplishments being appreciated less in Seattle than in Portland no doubt contributed to his hanging his hat more often at the Arlington Club in Portland than at his Seattle mansion.

In July 1921, Sam wired Charles E. Hughes, Secretary of State, "Please consider Seattle's facilities and accessibility for holding disarmament conference. My residence at government's disposal, therefore." The reply, from the Third Assistant Secretary, indicated the government did not contemplate holding the proposed conference on the Pacific Coast.

After Sam's death, his cousin, Daniel B. Hill, occupied the house until a purchaser could be found. Under the newspaper heading, "Mysterious Old Mansion For Sale — Home Built for Prince Renewed," the reported cost of the building had shrunk to $50,000: after all, it was 1932. The iron bars were removed from the windows, and for some reason, the ivy adorning the house was clipped to the roots. As an ironic sidelight on Sam's fear of burglars, three determined young man had broken into the house when it was untenanted and stayed there for several days undetected. They pulled books from the library shelves, emptied the drawers, and prowled through

---

*This is not explained in Sam's correspondence, but probably refers to his railroad days and the construction of the railroad bridge between St. Paul and Minneapolis.

the contents looking for money.

It was not until 1937 that movers came to load up the household furnishings and take them to Maryhill Museum. The heavy oaken leather chairs, massive tables, and carpets were put into four large vans. In the garage was a jinricksha, a carriage, and an old Studebaker. James, Sam's son, took two grandfather clocks and the Curtis pictures and books on North American Indians. The silver, linen, plate, and china were to be sold and the proceeds divided between James and the Maryhill Museum.

Once the contest over Sam's will was resolved, the house was sold to Mr. and Mrs. Theodore Pletscheef, who converted it into a duplex. They found the floor plan unsuitable and had the elevator removed, the entrance and interior extensively remodeled, and the house beautifuly furnished with French furniture.* The house is a historic monument and a monument, too, to Sam's Pharaonic compulsion to be remembered by a structure which will stand for centuries. It was more refuge than residence in the last twenty years of Sam's life.

As a girl, Helen Stone, daughter of Oregon's Governor Oswald West, heard Sam refer to his mansion in Seattle as his house. She asked him why he did not call it "home." "Ah," he replied, "When you are older you will know the difference."

14

Spinning the Wheel of Fortune

The stories of the founding of great fortunes are often interesting, if only to support one's convictions about the rapacity of the rich and the inability of wealth to bring happiness. The index of interest is, perhaps, roughly proportional to the size of the fortune: if $100 million or over, high; if around $10 million, slight to medium; if several million, minimal, unless one is the millionaire himself telling the story to a rapt circle of listeners. Sam Hill's fortune belongs in the third category. He was not considerate enough to leave annual summaries of his net worth. Most of his fortune was made in the halcyon days before income taxes, so there are no copies of tax returns to snoop into.

In 1888, the wedding present from his wife's parents of $200,000 in railroad stocks and bonds was a respectable start on the road to wealth. Sam did well financially in law practice and as president or director of various

---

*The author visited the house in 1978 and was shown about by the gracious chatelaine, Mrs. Plestcheef.

railways and president of the Minneapolis Trust Company.* In spite of his displeasure with some of the officers of the trust company, he did business with them until his own U.S. Trust Company was set up in Seattle in 1907. He concluded a final financial agreement with Minneapolis Trust that year and sold two-thirds of his stock for $33,325 in 1906 and the rest in 1909.

His principal income, however, was from other securities, especially those of railway companies, and profits from stock trading. He made money from the sale of the Seattle Gas Company but lost a good deal on the Maryhill venture and the Portland Home Telephone Company. Various other business ventures rewarded him, but it is difficult to determine to what extent.

Being a profligate spender, Sam needed a fortune to make his means fit his ends. There were the great houses in Seattle and Maryhill and the estate at Stockbridge. He must have spent a staggering amount on travel; the cost of taking Joffre and party around the world in 1922 alone must have been considerable. Although he was popularly supposed to have picked up the tab for much of Queen Marie's tour in 1926, most of the burden actually was borne by the railroads and her hosts in various cities; still, his share was substantial, nearly $20,000, and had to be paid at a low point in his fortunes.

Sam was generous in the support of his children, legitimate and illegitimate. He settled on James a $3,000 annual income from bonds and paid for his attendance at expensive preparatory schools and at Harvard. Beginning with their marriage, he gave his wife an allowance of $1,000 a month. Sam belonged to fashionable clubs in the East and Northwest. He spared no expense when he was host to friends in the United States and abroad.

His efforts for good roads were quite expensive. One spectacular gesture was taking members of the Oregon Legislature and the press on a special train to Maryhill in 1913. The experimental roads at Maryhill alone cost about $100,000 to build and his tireless journeys on behalf of highways nearly as much. The attempt to establish a town at Maryhill was his most disastrous financial venture, the loss being in the neighborhood of $600,000. The costs of his philanthropies and other gifts, such as globes, surely totalled more than $100,000. Add to these the expenses for constructing the Peace Portal and Stonehenge Memorial, and one arrives at a total of not less than two or three million dollars. Perhaps this biography should have been subtitled, "Profile of a Profligate"!

His estate was reported to amount only to about $500,000 at the time of his death in 1931. It is likely that Sam expected to leave a much larger amount, but the Great Depression had wrought havoc with the value and proceeds of his stock and bond portfolio and with his real estate. Inheritance taxes and a prolonged legal battle over his will further eroded the respectable fortune he had accumulated.

The first years of the twentieth century were happy times for financial manipulators, or rather, for some of them. The famous Northern Pacific

---

*In 1913, the company became affiliated with the First National Bank of Minneapolis and other mergers occurred in the next twenty years, eventuating in the First National Bank and Trust Company of Minneapolis.

"corner" of 1901, which caused a Wall Street panic, confirmed the public image of the ruthless depredations of the "robber barons." E. H. Harriman of the Union Pacific coveted the strategic and profitable Chicago, Burlington and Quincy Railroad, owned by the Northern Pacific in which J. J. Hill and J. P. Morgan held a substantial interest. They bought more stock when they learned that Harriman and J. D. Rockefeller were attempting a takeover of the Northern Pacific, thus driving up the price. Short sellers, not privy to the struggle, were badly hurt in the resultant credit crunch, and the stock and bond market fell sharply. An armistice was arranged, with Hill and Morgan the acknowledged victors, now able to buy the C. B. & Q. system.

In a long conversation with Paul Douglas in Seattle in 1920, Sam asked the rhetorical question, "Who outwitted E. H. Harriman in the Northern Pacific fight?," implying that J. J. and J. P. were not the sole strategists. Sam, however, had resigned from the J. J. Hill railroads six months before the event, and the author could find no evidence that Sam played a role in the epic struggle.

The Northern Securities Co., a holding company for the common stocks of the Great Northern and Northern Pacific Railroads, was incorporated in 1901. The company was judged in restraint of trade and was dissolved three years later. Just before that, Sam held 15,015 shares of Northern Securities. He traded actively in the stocks of the two railroads through 1909, often using the stocks as collateral to buy more. At times when he had a large cash position, he would make short term loans to brokers.

In May 1907, Sam filed articles of incorporation for the U.S. Trust Co. in Seattle, to serve as a personal holding company to receive dividends from his stocks and bonds and to dispense funds for Sam's various ventures. The *Wall Street Journal* reported that he intended to set up a "U.S. National Bank of Seattle" as well. Together, they would have a " . . . paid up capital and surplus of $1,100,000, and are believed to be the largest financial institutions in the Northwest. Samuel Hill is president of the trust company and Hervey Lindley president of the bank.* Business will be begun late in the fall."

But it did not. Sam went so far as to rent quarters for a bank and to offer shares of its stock to Frederick Weyerhaeuser and other friends, but soon decided not to go into the banking business. The approach of the panic of 1907 no doubt discouraged him. He wrote, "My own idea is that we are now going into a 'hungry' period and it is best to go a little slow."

Most of Sam's voluminous correspondence with New York banks about his Wall Street ventures is found in the years 1903 through 1909. There are some humorous asides in these letters. He had lived with the Krech family in Minneapolis before his marriage. During the 1907 financial panic, he wrote Alvin Krech of the Equitable Trust Co. to ask him to " . . . file for me a homestead south of Canal Street, or take up a claim under

---

*Neither the bank nor the trust company is listed in the Seattle directories of the time. Sam used his Seattle office and later his residence as the mailing address of the trust company. It was not until 1928 that he moved his trust company matters to the First National Bank of Seattle.

the Desert Land Act." He had promised A. B. Hepburn, vice-president of the Chase National Bank, a shot at a grizzly bear if Hepburn would come west. Confronting bears in the canyons of Wall Street did not prepare Hepburn for this and he feigned disappointment when a tentative hunting date had to be canceled. In another letter, Sam told a story predating the Robert Benchley version:

> A man who was prone to the bowl was discussing with friends the transmigration of souls. He imbibed very freely one night and his friends took him and put him to bed, took some molasses, took the feathers out of the pillow and stuck them over him. Next morning when the man woke up he was rather dazed. He . . . looked himself over and said, "In hell, and a bird!"

Sam also kept copies of correspondence from friends and acquaintances asking for loans; jobs in railroading, banking, and utility companies; and for financial advice. People asking for advice not only often credited him with financial sagacity but also assumed he continued to be an insider in matters concerning the Great Northern Railroad. Paul Douglas heard the story that Sam " . . . had made three successive killings in real estate by letting Everett, Tacoma, and Seattle each in turn believe that they were to be the western terminus of the Great Northern. He had an unfailing ability to buy land cheap and sell it dear." The correspondence does not substantiate the railroad story, and one doubts that Sam would claim "unfailing" acumen in real estate matters; the Maryhill venture was a disaster.

Stocks and bonds were Sam's solid financial base. But he was an inveterate entrepreneur, and not only frequently sought business ventures, but was besought to invest in many others.

After his return from Russia and Japan in 1901, Sam received offers to invest in projects in the Orient. One concerned the "China America Co." and C. A. Jameson, who " . . . has associated with him in some degree another important engineer, Mr. Hoover*, who has been very successful in the matter of the Taiping coal mines combination recently." Sam did not pursue these offers, at least in part because of his deep involvement in the Seattle Gas Co.

Among his investments were three coal mines in Washington and British Columbia. One of these was at Rosalyn, located on the west side of the Snoqualmie Pass in the Cascades, on a short spur line of the Northern Pacific, which furnished the coal used in the Seattle gas business. A by-product of the latter was liquor from which ammonia was made, leading to the purchase of an ammonia plant in San Francisco. His friend Forbes, who had arranged the purchase of the Stockbridge place, persuaded Sam to buy a share in a nitric acid business, also. Another minor involvement was partnership with his cousin, D. B. Hill, in a hotel supply business in Seattle, which allowed him a discount on furnishings for his Seattle house and for the buildings at Maryhill.

Sam wrote a number of letters inquiring about buying farm and timber lands and purchasing stock in various utility and coal mining companies. He wrote to ask if the Portland Gas Company was for sale and considered buying into the Spokane Telephone Company. The reasons he did not

---

*Herbert Hoover spent three years in China (1889-92) overseeing coal mining near Tientsin, before going into gold and silver mining in Australia and Burma.

follow through on these various projects often are not clear from the correspondence. He did own some timberlands in Lewis County, south of Mt. Rainier, and stock in a British Columbia coal mine at the time of his death.

Sam toyed with the idea of going into newspaper publishing in 1905. He wrote his friend Farrell about Blethen, the editor of the *Seattle Daily Times*, with whom he had had some heated exchanges during the recently concluded "gas war": "Friendly relations exist between Col. Blethen and myself, at least so far as his taking lunch with me at my expense is concerned . . . My idea is that we should take the *Reveille* [a paper not doing well under the ownership of Sam's friend, Charles Chamberlain] and the *Herald*, put the two together on the basis of fifty thousand each, and take in the Blethen papers on the basis of twenty five thousand, all to be paid for in stock — then run one morning and one evening paper." It is not likely that Sam brought this proposal to the choleric Blethen, who might have resorted to the traditional horsewhip.

In 1906, he looked into starting a cement plant. He wrote that he had " . . . been visiting different parts of the state and inspecting quarries of lime so as to fix on the final location for a cement plant. . . . I have now in prospect one on the banks of the Columbia River." James Norman Hill, J. J.'s oldest son, had offered to help Sam in this regard after Sam sold out the Seattle gas business. But Sam did not pursue this opportunity. James wrote, "All I wanted was to get you in an independent and good-paying business where you would stand by yourself, and not have too much father-in-law."

On one occasion, Sam loyally acted as an unpaid intermediate in a complex deal involving Hervey Lindley, a high school classmate of Sam's in Minneapolis, who owned timber lands southwest of Klamath Falls, Oregon, and who was president of the 24 mile logging railroad serving these holdings. Sam arranged to buy a locomotive and car for the little railroad, and in 1906, engineered the sale of the timber lands to the Weyerhaeusers of St. Paul.

U.S. District Court Judge C. H. Hanford wrote Sam in 1905 about a land irrigation project on the Columbia near Kennewick in southeastern Washington. He and associates eventually bought 12,000 acres of land from the Northern Pacific, expecting the construction of J. J. Hill's railroad on the north bank of the Columbia to raise prices considerably. He wanted Sam to recommend the investment to his friends and offered to have him " . ... take charge of it personally," but Sam declined.

A year later, unworried about a possible conflict of interest, Hanford wrote Sam about condemnation hearings he was about to conduct on the right-of-way for the Spokane, Portland and Seattle Railway. The Hanford Irrigation and Power Company was making progress, he said. "We will build a city which will be next to Spokane, the finest and richest city in eastern Washington and it is to be named 'Hanford'*. . . . " Sam did not

---

*There is indeed a town named Hanford near the larger Tri-Cities of Pasco, Kennewick and Richland, but the name is more likely to be connected with the nearby Hanford Project, where materials were made during World War II for the production of atomic bombs, than with commercial development.

purchase stock in the company, which he considered undercapitalized, but offered to furnish without cost the many reports of his investigations of the company.

Sam had loaned Judge Hanford $27,500, part of which had been used for improvements and assessments on the Judge's house when he was strapped for money. Could there have been a delayed connection between the loan and Judge Hanford's convenient injunction in 1901 in the Seattle gas war (Chapter 12)?

Sam did not leave railroad management without a backward look. In 1905, he considered undertaking construction of a "Tacoma Northern Railway" to connect with the Columbia and Puget Sound Railways at Renton, Washington, to link Tacoma and Seattle. He hoped " . . . ultimately to have the Puget Sound Terminal Railway so as to do business between Blaine and Portland." Sam continued to Farrell, "The Tacoma Northern ought to be built and the Northern Pacific ought not to oppose it . . . as a matter of fact, if the directors of the Pacific Coast Company will exchange trackage rights, I am strong enough to build this road, I think, even with the opposition of the Northern Pacific." Perhaps fortunately for Sam, he thought better of this and did not try to reenter railroading.

Otherwise, Sam's subsequent interest in railroads was primarily that of a stockholder. That is not to say that he did not have convictions based on principle, as well. He frowned on the Seattle Y M C.A. when it passed a resolution in favor of a railroad commission in Washington in 1903. "Nothing is so vitally important to the city of Seattle, in my opinion, as to be on friendly terms with the transportation interests."

He had more than a passing interest in the construction of the Spokane, Portland and Seattle Railway on the north bank of the Columbia, owned jointly by the Great Northern and Northern Pacific, because the route would pass between his proposed town of Maryhill and the river. In 1903, the Columbia River and Northern Railway Company completed a 43 mile line from Lyle, on the river, to Goldendale, which line the S.P. & S. acquired in 1908. By that time, construction of the S. P. & S. was completed beyond Maryhill, and trains ran from Spokane to Portland in 1909.

Late in 1909, Sam took the initiative in a very large project. He wrote a long memo to Lazard Frères Co., Paris, about forming a syndicate to buy its immense land grant in Central Oregon.

A note of explanation is in order about the acquisition of vast tracts of land in the West by railroads and wagon road construction companies. In the latter half of the nineteenth century, Congress was profligate in disposing of these territories, nearly empty except for Indians, who, of course, were not considered. Between 1860 and 1890, at least 80 million acres were given away, mostly to transcontinental railroads which received grants of alternate sections on either side of their tracks as a way of financing construction. The largest of thirteen grants made to wagon road companies was that of 800,000 acres to the Willamette Valley and Cascade Mountain Wagon Road Company, which had been organized in May 1894. Its goals were to

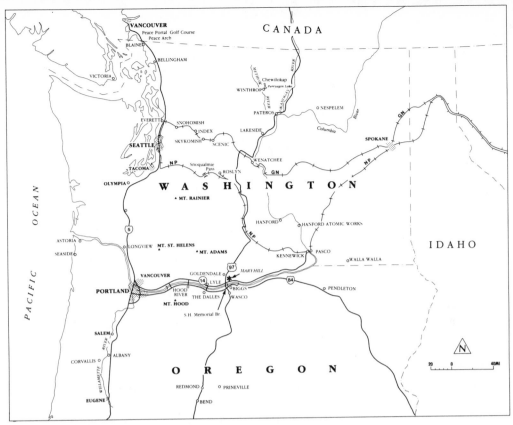

Map of present-day Oregon and Washington.

provide a toll road across the Cascade Mountains, over which ranchers in the Willamette Valley could drive their stock to graze in Central Oregon, and to sell land to settlers. By 1903, the company had passed into the control of Lazard Frères. Col. C. E. S. Wood was the company's agent in Oregon.

The syndicate Sam wished to organize would include several of Sam's personal and business friends, including R. H. Thomson, Seattle City Engineer, with whom Sam and the senior partner of Lazard Frères had met in 1908, and John S. Stevens, the engineer then in charge of constructing a railroad for J. J. Hill through the canyon of the Deschutes River in north central Oregon. Completion of this railroad was expected to enhance the value of the land grant.

Sam proposed that his U.S. Trust Co. act as attorney for the proposed sale. The syndicate would develop and irrigate the lands, probably over a period of 15 to 20 years, sell them, and split the net proceeds with Lazard Frères. Sam cited lands sold by the Northern Pacific 20 years earlier which were later provided with irrigation and then sold at $500 an acre. But he reminded them that "a very moderate price should be placed on the grant" because the syndicate would bear the sole risk in developing land to which it did not hold title.

Thomson wrote Sam, "I think you and I ought to get busy. Mr. [C. E.

115

S.] Wood now wants $300,000 to be paid down and a total of six million . . . If you can get someone to advance the money to handle this proposition, I would be willing to quit the City of Seattle and give my time exclusively to the management of the proposition . . . I am fully satisfied that I could net seven and a half million dollars from the land within a period of five years."

We don't know why the French bankers found Sam's proposal unsatisfactory, but they no doubt scented bigger game. Thomson noted this sarcastically: "As I understand it, Mr. Wood's insinuation is that the party about to close with him for the land is a Mr. J. J. Hill of St. Paul, who has for some time been in the railroad business."

Sam still had hopes early in 1910. He wrote Thomson that he had seen Wood " . . . and the matter has impressed him very favorably indeed and he will recommend it." But the J. J. Hill interests had already moved in. In 1909, J. J. sent Stevens, who used the alias John F. Johnson, into the Deschutes Canyon country to buy up ranches and the charter of the Oregon Trunk Railway, a paper entity. Harriman surmised that Hill intended to push south into Harriman's fiefdom, California, and so started construction of a railroad on the opposite bank of the narrow canyon, to connect with the Union Pacific line on the south bank of the Columbia Gorge at Biggs, Oregon. There were fights between the rival construction gangs in the canyon, worthy of any Western movie. Through a compromise, joint occupation of a line south of Bend, Oregon was negotiated.

A syndicate of Minnesota capitalists acquired an option to buy the land grant from Lazard Frères, the largest area of land sold in the United States up to that time, and proceeded to sell parcels to settlers and some of the timberlands to the Hill interests.

If Sam had been able to conclude the deal with Lazard Frères, his subsequent financial history would certainly have been different. He did not forget opportunities in Central Oregon, but had no better result in 1921 when he contemplated engaging in a large reclamation project there (Chapter 26).

There were other proposals, some of which sound interesting today, which Sam presumably rejected out of hand. One was an offer to sell 2,500 acres of oil land in Alaska. Another man offered to " . . . secure a monopoly of the lighterage of all freight in Manila," and needed the first " . . . $500,000 within 20 days in order not to miss an unusual opportunity. I enclose a copy of my letter to your father [he meant J. J. Hill]. Will you not send him a telegram telling that Hardy is worth the hearing? . . . Perhaps you will consent to be one of the most important springs of the machine if not its head." His friend Farrington, a vice-president of the Great Northern, was more than half serious when he wrote Sam about investing in a new method for harnessing energy from ocean waves.

From his correspondence about the various business enterprises mentioned in this chapter, one might get the impression that Sam was overambitious, indecisive, and obsessed with making money. It was not as simple as that. He probably wanted to show his friends in Eastern banking and corporate circles, as well as the J. J. Hill clan, that he could on his own become a power to be reckoned with in the Northwest. The intense and thwarting experience with the Seattle Gas Company probably heightened his compulsion to succeed in other ventures which would be both challenging and satisfying.

There is another explanation of Sam's frenetic business activities in this period, namely, that they foreshadowed more egregious activities in the 1920's, manifestations of a manic state. That later era, described in Chapter 26, makes the enterprises outlined in the preceding pages seem downright conservative.

In summary, one can compare Sam's financial career to a roller coaster: there was a gradual and satisfying rise in his law and railroad days; a steep and exhilarating climb early in the 20th century; and a slow and bumpy descent until his late years, when, close to ground level, he reached the end of the ride.

Sam could have secured his financial future by earning more or spending less; either way would have been out of character. Money, after all, was not his master but his busy servant, an overworked factotum for all his enterprises.

15

Ma Bell, Dame sans Merci

Several years after Seattle's gas war had ended in a truce in 1904, Sam entered the lists against another utility, this time a phone company in Portland. He seized the fallen lance from a distressed combatant to fight an opponent who did not appear as formidable then as later. Most of the onlookers cheered for Sam, the white knight, against the tyrant of monopoly. The tourney had its counterparts all over the land, but monopoly nearly always won; the fates seemed unable to distinguish the good knights from the bad.

Portland got its first telephone exchange, the Amerian Telephone and District Telegraph Company, in 1878. The connections then worked only in pairs, and a pharmacist was the first customer. Early in the century, operators responding with "Number please?" manned the switchboards of the Pacific Telephone Company in Portland, but a challenge to this system was now at hand. Charles E. Sumner acquired the right to use a newly patented automatic dial telephone, and in 1902 organized the Northwestern Long Distance Telephone Company as well as several local telephone companies in the Northwest. In 1904, he sought stockholders to invest in the "Home Telephone and Telegraph Company of Portland, Oregon."

The terms of the franchise, granted in June 1905, imposed some heavy burdens. The City of Portland offices were to get a free ride. The phone company had to be prepared to serve 10,000 customers within three years, and service was to be free to subscribers until the first 3,000 phones were connected. Until then, its rates were not to exceed $2.75 for a home phone and $6.25 for a business phone. If these conditions were not fulfilled, the franchise could be forfeited, in which case the city would own the part of the system serving the police force. Sumner and his backers had to post a $25,000 performance bond. Ralph Nader could have done no more.

The new company worked frantically in the next two years to install equipment, set up poles and wires throughout the city, and recruit and train employees. There was also the matter of getting the first 3,000 subscribers, and proving to them that dial telephones were superior to those requiring operators. Some phones were installed and used without cost to make the quota. Two employees of Home Telephone in the early days recalled that "The company was so underfinanced that most of the stockholders apparently did not have enough faith in the company to have a telephone in their own homes." By the time the construction company turned over the plant for operation on April 1, 1908, Home Telehone Company was in financial trouble. One could not easily ascertain this from the treasurer's report of November 1908, in which the net surplus was reported to be $33,710 and the number of telephones in operation 7,830. Moreover, some two millions in bonds were secured only by the company's equipment and three exchange buildings.

It is not clear how and why Sam became interested in getting into the phone business. In 1908 and 1909, he was already deeply involved in the Maryhill development. He wrote to three potential Spokane investors in September 1908, about " . . . taking over and completing the Spokane [telephone] plant. I have signified my willingness to take one-tenth interest [$50,000] and have signed the subscription list."

In March 1909, Sam wrote to his friend Ed Cooke at the Minneapolis Trust Company, "I have arranged to take an interest in the Portland automatic telephone company called 'The Home Telephone.'" On a Sunday visit, he had been impressed that the central office and exchanges each had only one boy in charge. He continued, "Also, we will take over long distance lines in Oregon, a long distance line to Tacoma, Washington and the plant in Bellingham, Washington. . . . There is some stock left in the holding company, although not of great amount, somewhere between $10,000 and $15,000. If you want some of it, send me a wire and I will put down your name. All these plants, except the Spokane plant, are growing concerns. The Portland plant last year earned its fixed charges and is now paying about $40,000 a year over and above the fixed charges. The plants in

Tacoma and Bellingham lacked $500 of paying their way. Long distance lines show a profit of $1,500. . . . "

This account does not jibe well with Sam's assessment in 1913 of the critical condition of the company affairs before he took over. The stock and bonds were then practically worthless and the company was in . . . "imminent danger of being thrown into the hands of a receiver at any moment. . . . At that time [1909] there were not 9,600 telephones in operation. Due to lax and inefficient methods of conducting the business, there were more than 400 telephones not producing revenue to the company . . . The indebtedness was then $255,000 and the liquid assets less than $5,000."

Sam took over as president and principal owner of the Home Telephone Company in March 1909. Charles Babcock and Abbott Mills were vice-presidents; J. B. Middleton secretary and manager; and Eben F. Wells treasurer. The directors were prominent Portlanders, including in addition to Mills, William Ladd; Henry and Elliott Corbett; Theodore Wilcox; and Edward Cookingham.

We don't know how much Sam had to invest to get control of the company. He had an uphill battle in selling stock and getting new subscribers. Home had 10,280 phones in its system at the end of 1909, and the number went up about 1,000 phones a year until leveling off in 1912. By that time, Bell's Pacific Telephone Company had some 34,000 subscribers.

The Bell System was on the march in the Northwest. When Theodore Vail, president of the AT&T, which then included the Western Union Company, came to Portland in December 1911, he said the public would be best served by a single system, and that his company would pay any reasonable price to consolidate the plants in cities in the Northwest. He announced plans to build a 12-story building at Southwest Park and Oak streets in Portland for $2,000,000. Within three months, acquisition of the Independent Phone Company of Seattle was announced by Pacific Telephone and Telegraph. Soon, Home Telephone of San Francisco was sold to AT&T.

The announcement of the Seattle merger touched off apprehension in Portland. Abbott Mills of the Home Company said there was "absolutely no possibility of combination with the competition." Sam sent a telegram to the U.S. Department of Justice filing a complaint against the merger. He feared that AT&T would refuse to accept long distance messages from his company, except at ruinous rates. Home took out ads in Portland papers reminding readers that it was an independent company, owned and controlled by Portland people. The same editions carried a report that Sam had been in Seattle consulting with officers of several independent phone companies. He announced that Portland would be the storm center of a fight which would be nationwide in its importance:

> It is a fight for independence. If there be any man in Portland who doubts the wisdom of competitive telephone service, he should take the train and go to Seattle at once and study the situation there . . . I believe that the

national government will take a hand in the matter and protect the rights of the people against this billion dollar trust . . . They have attempted to buy the Seattle Independent Telephone plant and are now engaged in making the service just as bad as it is possible to make it. I spent nine minutes trying to get my own telephone in Seattle, and was told by the information department that there was no such telephone, and had to give the matter up. It is no infrequent thing for an independent subscriber in Seattle to be told that he has no telephone. . . . Portland is the last place where a fight can be made against this great monopoly.

But the atmosphere was cheerful at the second annual employees' dinner of the Home Telephone Company in February 1912. A spokesman announced that Sam " . . . would from now on devote almost his undivided time to the building of the company." A reporter observed, "The spirit of the evening at times reached exuberance, although the bill of fare included nothing that should produce artificial hilarity." Each employee received a five dollar gold piece, which may have lifted spirits.

A month later, the Portland *Daily News* had a story headed, "Sam Hill, Quaker, Is Fighting Billion Dollar Phone Trust with a Steriopticon, and He Is Winning." Sam was quoted: "You see, we Quakers don't think one man should try to keep his neighbor from getting enough to eat, just to satisfy his greed, and that is why we don't like trusts. Thee understands that, does thee?" Sam had figured out a plan by which two clerks could do all the bookkeeping and still not work over eight hours a day. The article concluded, "He is a big jolly man and he can talk a chronic dyspeptic into good humor in two minutes."

The same paper carried a story about a baker who had a Bell System coin phone and was outraged by a demand for immediate payment when he had already sent a check for $4.05. The baker stopped payment on the check and ordered a Home Telephone automatic. "Thus does Sam prosper," the writer ended.

Sam did not neglect the public relations aspects of the business. He announced cash prizes for a public school essay contest on "The Telephone Situation in Portland: Would Public Ownership be Better Than Competitive Service?"— that is, public ownership versus service by two companies with separate exchanges which did not interconnect. One can imagine the inconvenience for business and professional people of having to subscribe to both services, each requiring a different directory.

New phone services were introduced. One innovation was a play-by-play description of Portland's baseball games carried on Home Telephone lines. Another story reported that Sam had awakened at 4:28 one morning and had called the officers of the company about his idea for free information telephones in booths on downtown streets during Portland's annual Rose Festival in June.

The Home Telephone Company's ads now pictured an automatic telephone with the legend, "Our telephone girl . . . She never sleeps nor talks back; her nerves are steel; she speaks all languages, 24 hours a day every day in the year; never gets tired or saucy; she never strikes, and can

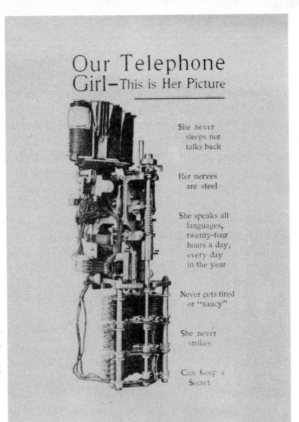

Our Telephone
Girl—This is Her Picture

She never
sleeps nor
talks back

Her nerves
are steel

She speaks all
languages,
twenty-four
hours a day,
every day
in the year

Never gets tired
or "saucy"

She never
strikes

Can Keep a
Secret

Newspaper advertisement for the Home Telephone Company's automatic phone, about 1912. (From glass slide, Maryhill Museum files.)

keep a secret." The ads stressed the value of competition and that the Home Company " . . . stands between you and the unendurable conditions of monopoly." Taking its cue from the Elks, Home began to use "B.P.O.E." (Best Phone on Earth) in its ads. The sale of six percent bonds of the company to the public was announced. Ads for these were also placed in Minneapolis newspapers.

In the summer of 1912, the battle focused on the hotel trade. Home Telephone signed up four Portland hotels but had to pay Pacific T&T a fee because of Pacific's contracts with them. Pacific won an injunction to restrain the Multnomah Hotel from removing its switchboard, citing its rule that it would not connect its lines with those of other companies. The mayor appointed a committee to investigate what he thought was an injustice to the Home Company. The hotels had to compromise by having the switchboards of both companies in their lobbies. Home and Bell each had its supporters in business, banking, and newspaper circles.

The telephone war extended to Oswego, a suburb south of Portland, when PT&T claimed that the owner of the exchange had not kept his contract and therefore withdrew its services. The Oswego manager complained that the charge for his four trunk lines had been raised from $8 to $15 per month, payable immediately. The Home Company, exploiting this opportunity, " . . . broke all previous records by laying four lines into Oswego from Portland in one day, and charged $6 per trunk."

Sam's report in January 1913 to the Home Company's directors outlined the sound financial position of the company as compared with its tenuous status in 1909 when the new directors took over. "Its only obligations are the bonds outstanding, amounting to $2,644,600." It owned plants at Albany, Corvallis, Oregon City, and Independence, Oregon, serving a total of 16,600 phones. In conjunction with the Postal Telegraph-Cable Company, long distance lines had been established to cities in western Oregon. The company was proud that there was an average of only eleven cases per day when a subscriber had had an interruption of service, due usually to "boys shooting holes in cables." The report admitted that the company's net earnings had been spent on improvements rather than dividends, but things looked promising for a dividend soon.

Later that month, Sam went to New York and San Francisco for conferences with MacKay and other officials of the Postal Telegraph Company. Sam, needing allies, hoped for a merger of Postal with independent companies, which would put the independents "on a pretty equal footing with the rival company."

Sam now filed evidence with the U.S. Attorney General to support an investigation of AT&T for trust violations. Bell's maneuver to buy the stock and bonds of the Northwestern Long Distance Telephone Company was cited as a possible violation of the Sherman Act. Vail of AT&T admitted that subscribers in Corvallis, Oregon, had been offered free service in order to build up Bell's business there. The Home Company took an ad complaining it had paid over $13,000 in franchise tax to the City of Portland from 1909 through 1912, as compared with Bell's $4,000.

Meanwhile, Sam was doing what he could to make things rough for Pacific T&T in Seattle. He attended a secret meeting at the mayor's office there about instituting municipal systems for Seattle, Spokane, and Tacoma to connect with Home's lines. Phone rates had gone up in Seattle when Bell took over the independent company. A federal grand jury in Seattle was investigating the "telephone trust" and the Department of Justice was about to file a suit for dissolution of AT&T.

A grand jury heard evidence that when Bell absorbed independent companies in Seattle, Tacoma, and Bellingham, it deprived Northwestern of long distance receipts, making takeover of Northwestern easier. Bell gave Seattle hotels a 15 percent discount on long distance calls over Bell lines and made it difficult to use Northwestern's service. Sam testified that he had instructed employees at his Seattle home to use Northwestern services but Bell telephone operators would instead switch calls to Pacific's lines.

There was trouble in Oswego, Oregon, in May 1913 when striking members of the Electrical Workers' Union taunted several non-union workers near the Home Company's exchange. The strikers threw rocks; one was wounded by a gunshot and a Home employee was kicked in the jaw. Thirteen pickets and three phone company employees were arrested. It developed that Ainsberry, one of the Home Company men, had broken parole from San Quentin prison. He said he had refused to join the union in

California and had left the state 30 days before his parole expired. The Home Company put up his $1,000 bail and he was released. The Home Company manager said he thought Ainsberry had been reformed by his recent marriage, and Home would continue to fight for him. Unfortunately, it was soon revealed that he had broken out of a Wyoming prison the previous year. A newspaper reported, "In an effort either to kill himself from poison or to relax the vigilance of arresting officers, Ainsberry chewed and swallowed two large plugs of tobacco on a streetcar. This made him very sick and he made several half-hearted efforts to throw himself out of the window but was restrained."

Sam's friend, Governor Os West, said Oregon had a primary claim on Ainsberry, and so did not extradite him to California. The Portland *Daily News* accused the Multnomah County Sheriff of favoritism when he took Ainsberry to Salem for an interview with the Governor to prevent extradition. Editorially, the paper said it was not afraid of the Home Phone Company, to whom it had always given a square deal in the past, after listening " . . . patiently to the somewhat diverse and self-congratulatory sermons of Sammy Hill." A grand jury declared Ainsberry not guilty of a felony at Oswego, but there were still the little matters of the prison escape and San Quentin parole violation. To confound the issue, another San Quentin graduate worked for the strikers in opposition to Home, and was arrested for cutting their wires to the Postal Telegraph system. Still, one must take one's employees as one finds them.

In 1913 Mead, former vice-president and treasurer of Northwestern Long Distance Telephone, for whom Sam had written letters of introduction in 1909, was accused of neglecting the company and misappropriating its funds. The U.S. Attorney General brought a successful antitrust suit against AT&T in July 1913, to dissolve its connection with Northwestern and other independent companies. In March 1914, the U.S. District Court ruled that Northwestern was to remain an independent, competitive long distance company, but authorized it to connect with the lines of the Bell Company in the Northwest.

Vail of AT&T, aware of the need for some public sympathy, wrote a letter to the *Oregon Journal* stating that over 85 percent of its shareholders owned less than a hundred shares, and that a majority of the shareholders were women. There was no mention of widows and orphans.

Antitrust hearings were also proceeding at Chicago. Late in 1913, in what was called a great antitrust victory, AT&T agreed to connect all other telephone companies in the U.S. to its toll lines and to give up its interest in Western Union.

The Home Company itself was not free from slings and arrows. There were charges that Sam had tried to put Northwestern and the Sunset Company of Tacoma out of business so he could consolidate them with the Postal Telegraph Company. In October 1913, a complaint was filed with the State Railroad Commission, which then regulated utilities, alleging Home was using iron wire; was not putting its wires in conduits underground; and not giving service to all parts of the city. The competing phone companies in Portland were not beautifying the skyline, either; a reporter counted fourteen poles at one street intersection.

During 1914 and early 1915, the Home Company put on drives for new subscribers. One ad read, "How to be a princess on $2 per month," citing the army of people ready for instant phone service. A flyer was put out offering children a dollar for each new Home subscriber they obtained. The 25 children enrolling the most subscribers would be sent to San Franciso's Panama-Pacific Exposition. Another flier offered $20 of stock in the Home Company for each new subscriber secured by a current customer. In 1916, Sam's memo to telephone users was almost conciliatory: "The Bell Telephone service is good, the automatic is better and secret as well. . . . The automatic sells its service at a lower price than Bell and reached every station the Bell does."

In October 1916, Sam finally admitted that his company was in financial distress and not able to meet its bond interest due to the business depression and Bell's competition. About $3,000,000 in stock and about $2,600,000 in bonds were outstanding. Sam held over half the stock and a large share of the bonds. He said, "I am unwilling to proceed further in the matter unless I find the people of Portland more responsive and more appreciative of the service given . . . Continued lack of support to the company can have no result but a return to the deplorable telephone conditions which prevailed when this company was chartered." He reminded subscribers that he had received no salary or expense money as the president of the Home Company. He continued, "This is the last stand of independent telephony on the West Coast and it is for the people of Portland to decide whether they wish it to continue or not."

Early in 1917, Sam used his last ammunition. He offered six months of automatic service free on the condition that Home was the only telephone used. He announced that the Portland School Board had voted to use automatic phones in the schools and that automatic phones were being installed in Portland at the rate of forty per day. He reserved 150 automatic telephones for " . . . the best colored families in Portland to use at his expense until July 1st." He was sure that they " . . . would be more than willing to pay the regular rental of $2 a month after that date."

All his efforts were to no avail. The Home Company passed into the hands of a receiver, ex-Governor West, in June 1917, on the petition of Sam, who held the company's overdue note for $50,000. Soon after that, West sent a memo to Home Telephone customers stating that " . . . receivership will in no manner affect the splendid service which the Home has rendered its patrons in the past." Receivership was a "preliminary step in a reorganization . . . for the protection of its many stock and bondholders . . .[which would] ensure to the public an improved and extended service at the lowest possible rates."

In August 1917, the *Oregon Journal* editorialized that the company's capitalization was at least double the value of the stock, and this had contributed to the failure of the Oregon Trust and Savings Bank. The paper claimed that blocks of stock had been given free to promoters, and decried "the wreckage along the way." In short, it felt that Sam was more to be censured than pitied.

Sam was not quite ready to surrender. The following month, he announced he was retaining his holdings in the company; earnings were exceeding expenses, and "a few thousand more phones in Portland" would help the situation.

But Home's loss in 1917 was $163,800. The mortgage was foreclosed and a public sale of the company was held on the steps of the Multnomah County Courthouse in February 1919. The only bid was $500,000, made by a trust company by arrangement with the bondholders. Judgments against the company totaled $3,289,000. The war was over. The Home Company's properties in Portland, Albany, and Corvallis were transferred to PT&T for "a consideration of slightly more than $2,000,000." This netted the bondholders about 70 cents on the dollar, most of which they were to receive in the five per cent bonds of the Home Telephone Company of Spokane, principal and interest being guaranteed by PT&T. The stockholders received nothing.

Home Company subscribers were allowed to retain their automatic phones. In 1921, PT&T began the long task of bringing dial service to all of Portland's telephone users. The city did not lose, receiving a $5,000 franchise fee and an arrangement to have free phone service: you can't beat city hall.

No correspondence survives to tell how Sam felt about this defeat by his giant rival, or for that matter, about the losses sustained by his stockholders. His own losses after years of effort were considerable, but the partial payoff in Spokane Telephone Company bonds was of some comfort.

Why did he lose the battle when some other independent telephone companies in this country came through? There was still hope in 1913 and 1914 that the surviving small independent companies could merge with the Postal Telegraph Company and produce a formidable rival for the Bell System. But it was manifestly impossible for two separate systems to operate efficiently in the same city without interconnections. If Sam had had the financial muscle to organize the independent companies of the Northwest before they were picked off one by one by PT&T, things might have been different. Like King Canute on the seashore, he found he could not halt the waves (on rival wires).

He could probably have cut his losses by selling out to his adversary, as he had done in Seattle, before it was too late. The combination of stubbornness and ego led to another casualty, wounded pride, unpublished but none the less telling.

PART IV
GOOD ROADS

THE PACIFIC HIGHWAY
IN 1915

16

The Long Crusade

Like so many other features of the contemporary scene, the great network of roads and freeways in the United States is likely to be taken for granted by the young. Oldsters can remember when touring was for the adventuresome. Motor trouble and flat tires were accepted risks. Rural roads were often miserable, narrow, winding, dirt tracks, upgraded little from the wagon trails of the early settlers. Cars would get stuck in small streams or in mud holes, and the motorist would be obliged to call a farmer and his team from the plow to pull him out. The streets of towns and cities were not much better. In many a town, dirt roads were encountered only a few miles outside the city limits. At the turn of the century, the roads of Western Europe were superior to ours, although some dated from the famous Roman roads, others from the military routes of Napoleon.

The invention of the automobile spurred the efforts of a few enthusiasts for good roads. Population growth, increasing industrialization, and movement of farm people to the cities made the need for good roads greater. Nowhere in the United States was the need so obvious as in the West. The transcontinental railroads with their many branch lines could not, after all, go everywhere. Vast regions of the booming Pacific Northwest, particularly, were without any connecting roads, making transportation of the products of farm, forest, and mine almost entirely dependent on the proximity of the nearest railhead or ship dock. Only train travelers could enjoy briefly the beauty of the mountains, lakes, and rivers of the West, so that tourism, too, was an undeveloped resource, the privilege of the few.

Two things boosted road development in the United States tremendously. One was the discovery of petroleum in abundance as a cheap engine fuel. The other was mass production of the automobile, bringing its cost within the reach of people of modest means. As Samuel Hill remarked to Lockley, "Did you ever stop to think how large a debt of gratitude Henry Ford and John D. Rockefeller owe me? I have had a great deal to do with making them two of the richest men in the United States. Unless we had good roads, Henry Ford wouldn't have been able to sell millions of his cars. Without Henry Ford's cars, John D. Rockefeller wouldn't sell quite so much gasoline."

As an apostle of good roads, Sam said truly, "Good roads are more than my hobby; they are my religion." He was indeed a zealous evangelist, preaching the gospel to a country slow at first to receive it.

He liked to recall his father's interest in roads, when, through his influence, 44 miles of plank road were built in North Carolina. Sam himself was interested in road building before he came to Seattle. He wrote a friend,

"There are 85 miles of road out of Minneapolis which I planned some years ago. They were never finished nor surfaced, but they do run through some beautiful parts where you will get plenty of dust."

His father-in-law, J. J. Hill, had a continuing and practical interest in developing roads as feeders for his Great Northern Railroad. Sam differed with him on the order of importance of the methods of transportation. J. J. put this as "waterways, railways, and highways." Sam replied that highways should not be put last. "You told me once, Mr. Hill, that a railroad without terminals was like a human body without arms and legs. . . . You forget that you need more than arms and legs for your railroad systems; you must have toes and fingers, to reach the men on the farm."

Near the end of his life, he told Fred Lockley of his first vow to work for a Pacific Highway. About 1894, James J. Hill and he " . . . drove by team from Brownsville, at that time a five house town opposite New Westminster, B.C., to Blaine, Washington. There was no bridge across the Frazer River. We crossed it on the ferryboat. The distance from Brownsville to Blaine was 34 miles and much of the road was corduroy. It was a hard all-day drive over this waffle-board road, and I was sore inside and outside when we reached Blaine. I protested so vigorously that Mr. Hill said, 'Sammy, what do you propose to do about it?' I said, 'If I live long enough, I am going to see a highway built through British Columbia down our own coastline, clear to Mexico and it's going to be a hard surfaced road.' He smiled and said, 'Well, if you say you are going to do it, you will, all right.'" In 1929, Sam added, "302,000 autos crossed the borderline at Blaine and they carried over a million passengers."

The Good Roads movement in the United States was started by bicyclists, the League of American Wheelmen, which was organized in 1880. In the 1890's, the movement was taken over by automobile enthusiasts and a revolution in American travel began. In 1892, New Jersey passed the first state-aid road act, providing one-third of the cost of construction, about the time the first autos were appearing. The United States Department of Agriculture established an Office of Road Inquiry in 1893, and published a map of improved roads in this country two years later.

In September 1899, Sam and a few friends formed the Washington State Good Roads Association. He became its president through 1910, and later its honorary president for life. At the first meeting, " . . . not a soul was present but those on the platform." Among these was his longtime friend Frank Terrace, a farmer from Orilla, Washington, and former English sailor and Newcastle miner. He would fight along with Sam in a crusade which would continue for another quarter of a century. The association had its first annual convention in 1901. It gradually evolved a policy favoring a highway system built and developed by the state, rather than by the uncoordinated efforts of counties.

Sam had no axe to grind in his efforts to promote good roads. A possible exception was his campaign to have a road constructed on the north bank of the Columbia which would serve his planned town of

Maryhill. No doubt he wanted people to see it and his chateau, which he intended to be his monuments, but he began his roads campaign years before these developments, and certainly invested more time and money in the experimental roads around Maryhill (1909-1912) than he could ever have hoped to realize in return. He relished showing the roads to visitors, along with lantern slides taken before and after their construction. He must have enjoyed the response of his audiences. News stories frequently reported his listeners entranced by his pictures and promises of things to come in highway travel. Whatever the accompanying frustrations, he thrived on the political maneuverings necessary to see his dream of a good road system fulfilled.

His first effort for good roads on a national scale was an appearance before a U.S. Senate Committee in 1900, the year of the first National Auto Show. He lobbied for an appropriation of $35,000 to provide the Secretary of Agriculture with funds to conduct experiments in road building. In his pitch to the committee, Sam contrasted the large appropriations made for federal buildings and for river and harbor improvements with the lack of financial support for roads for the farmers. He invited the Senators to come out to central Washington and ride with him in a wagon and "suck in the alkali dust . . . It will be a great pleasure to you doubtless . . . to reflect that Congress in its wisdom has seen fit to erect public buildings in cities which the farmers may never see, and to leave unaided and uncared for the roads which they must daily travel." Senatorial wit being no less keen then than now, Senator Foster of Washington interrupted; "There would probably be something in the wagon to neutralize the dust" [Laughter].

Sam countered by recalling a meeting where an old man had questioned him about where he lived. Sam replied, "I live in Washington, sir." the old man then asked, "Which Washington, tax eating Washington or tax paying Washington?"

Sam said he had ridden horseback across the northern part of Washington State and that he had not met ten automobiles on the journey. He cited the high hauling costs of $1.00 per ton per mile for the farmers in northern Washington, a burden which could be removed by the construction of adequate roads. "If you go back to the people you represent," he continued, "you will find that they are behind us . . . We have confidence that you will see the right and do it . . . If you do not gentlemen, I stand here today and tell you that others will come after you who will."

Well, they did not see it nor do it until years later, but Sam did not give up. In 1902, he corresponded with Martin Dodge, Director of the Office of Public Road Inquiries of the U.S. Department of Agriculture. Dodge proposed a plan whereby the federal and state governments would contribute to a fund, " . . . say ten millions of dollars to start with," to be distributed among the states for highway improvement along lines approved by the federal government. This proposal, like Sam's, was farseeing, but its time had not yet come. The first Federal Aid Highway Act was not passed until 1916. One of its aims was to provide funds for the states to improve county roads for rural free delivery. Sam would surely have been amazed and, one supposes, pleased, could he have foreseen that the government would spend many billions on freeway construction in the second half of this century.

He continued to lobby for good roads in Washington State and nationally. In 1903 he wrote, "I have sent out letters to all the country press and many of the school teachers in the state and believe the combination, together with the transportation companies, can effect a radical change in highway building." At the request of the Great Northern Railroad, he represented it at the Good Roads national convention at St. Louis that year. Sam later told Dodge that his plan was " . . . to take a house in Washington, D.C. this winter and do a little log rolling for the good roads bill." Although he was engrossed in the business of his gas company in Seattle from 1900 to1904, he found time to attend a great many state and national road meetings. In 1903 he was invited to address the Washington legislature, which soon passed a law authorizing employment of convicts on road construction, an idea which Sam had espoused.

In 1904, good roads enthusiasts from King County, who later came to be known as the "old guard," met in Seattle. Sam Hill, of course, was among them, along with Judge Hanford, Alfred Battle, and Frank Terrace. These four men formed a committee to study the road laws of other states as a basis for developing a state highway organization. The following year, the legislature created a state highway board appointed by the governor.

Early in 1907, Sam was invited to address the highway committee hearings for the Washington legislature and brought Samuel Lancaster, a road engineer, with him. In March 1907, Sam Hill could write, "Our legislature has passed all the measures we asked for, ten laws in all, which give the state of Washington the best road laws of any state in the Union."

Lancaster (1864-1941) played an important role in achieving better roads for the nation. He had worked as a railroad construction engineer until 1886, when he contracted typhoid fever and severe poliomyelitis. His lower extremities were paralyzed for eighteen months, but he learned to walk again, using a wooden frame on wheels to support him. He was still on crutches when he returned to work. He was city engineer for Jackson, Tennessee, from 1889 to 1906, where he developed a system of hard surfaced roads which brought him to the attention of the U.S. Secretary of Agriculture. In 1904, he was appointed consulting engineer for the Bureau of Public Roads. A speaking tour and article in the *Yearbook of Agriculture, 1904* about his macadam highways in Tennessee made him nationally known to good roads advocates. He came to Los Angeles County in 1906 as a federal consultant and met Sam Hill later that year.

As Lancaster told Fred Lockley years later, the Secretary of Agriculture, James Wilson, had wired him to meet Sam Hill at a roads meeting in Yakima, Washington in 1906. Soon afterward, "Mr. Hill sent word for me to meet him in his beautiful home in Washington, D.C. [actually, the house belonged to Sam's wife] to talk over the road situation in the state of Washington." Sam wanted Lancaster to spend six months helping him to get started on a road program. Lancaster said he did not want to leave his family for that long a time. Sam immediately said, 'Bring your family with you.' Going to his desk he wrote a check for $500 and handed it to me."

Lancaster did not think Wilson would allow him to stay so long in one state, but Hill called on Wilson to overcome any objections. Sam said. "Make a proper start in some one state as an example for the rest of the country . . . Let the government pay his salary. I will pay all other expenses." Wilson was won over and Lancaster was detailed to spend six months in Washington State. But six months scarcely saw the work started, so Lancaster resigned his federal job and was employed to design a $7,000,000 system of boulevards and parks in Seattle, in preparation for the Alaska-Yukon-Pacific Exposition of 1909.

In 1907, Hill was instrumental in persuading the Board of Regents of the University of Washington to establish a chair of highway engineering, the first in the country, with Samuel Lancaster as professor in 1908-09. About 200 young men enrolled in the course. C. H. Hanford, the judge's brother, wrote Sam to congratulate him on this innovation; "We are certain to profit by the knowledge which has cost other states millions to acquire and which has come to us free, thanks to your wisdom and generosity." Not everyone was so impressed. A. J. Blethen, the sour-tempered editor of the *Seattle Times*, wrote Sam, citing opposition to " . . . this boulevard scheme [in Seattle and] . . . the expenditure which we are now making on good roads."

In 1908, when Lancaster went to the Mayo Clinic because of an abdominal problem, Sam volunteered to conduct the course, because, as he said ironically, "Time hangs heavy on my hands." He relished his role as Professor Hill. "You know how tonsorial artists and others grasp at that title," he wrote. "You have not any idea of how much fun it is . . . I look away ahead to the time when these young men will go out, back to the farms and all over the state, and when the grafter in the person of the road supervisor comes along, there will be a young man at his elbow who will say, 'That is not right; it did not cost that amount of money.' In other words, I am scattering wildfire in the form of good practical education."

Sam, as president of the Washington Good Roads Association, was commissioned to represent the state of Washington at the first International Road Congress in Paris in October 1908. He took with him, at his own expense, R. H. Thomson, City Engineer of Seattle, and Lancaster. All three were named U.S. delegates to the "International Congress on the Adaptation of Roads to the New Means of Locomotion," a title surely composed by some French bureaucrat.

"We traveled all over Europe by automobile," Lancaster told Lockley. "This was Mr. Hill's 32nd round trip. To my surprise, he knew the porters and bellboys and the proprietors of most of the hotels at which we stopped." He was also surprised that Sam spoke German, French, and Italian fluently, making their journey easier. They took a boat trip down the Rhine, and Lancaster asked who had built the rock retaining walls as terraces for the vineyards. Hill replied that Charlemagne had done so, realizing that if rich river soil were carried up to make the terraces, it would be an ideal spot for vineyards. Prophetically Sam added, "I want you to notice those walls closely, for some day we are going to have similar walls along the banks of the Columbia River. We will build a great highway so that the world can come out and see the beauties of the land out of doors . . . [and] we will realize the magnificence and grandeur of the Columbia River Gorge."

The first American Congress of Road Builders was held in Seattle in July 1909, in connection with the Alaska-Yukon-Pacific Exposition. Experts on road building came to the Congress from Europe and the United States. Sam treated the delegates to the ferryboat ride from Seattle to Victoria and to dinner at the Empress Hotel. A "Good Roads Building", the first of its kind, was erected to display exhibits of road construction methods. After the exposition, the building became the home of the Dept. of Highway Engineering of the University of Washington.

Sam thrived on all of this activity, and found time to chide a friend for not joining in. "I am in the middle of a Good Roads Congress and do not have time to sleep. I do get time to eat. I feel very badly to think you would take advantage of this time of year to have appendicitis, in the busy season. It would not make any difference along in the fall if you felt you had to indulge in this luxury. . . . I will not write you at greater length now, partly because, as you know, I am always bothered for something to say."

In London, late in 1909 just before sailing hom on the *Lusitania,* Sam gave an interview to the *New York Times* correspondent. Sam had come from Brussels, where he had been concluding arrangements for the second International Road Building Convention to be held in July 1910. He had talked with Prince Albert, a trained engineer, for an hour and a half. The Prince had agreed to send out personal invitations to the convention delegates representing every state in the Union. At the first conference in Paris in 1908, only 20 of some 2,150 delegates had come from the United States.

In the *Times* interview, Sam deplored the condition of the roads in the United States, saying we ranked with Turkey as " . . . one of the worst roaded countries in the civilized world." Roads, he said, were more important that the Panama Canal, then under construction. He urged state legislatures to follow the example of Washington, which had voted one-third of its 1909 revenues for roads. He predicted that Washington would have the best roads in the nation within five years. He put in a word for the establishment of chairs of road building at state universities, as had been done at the University of Washington.

As much as Sam liked to give interviews and talk at meetings, he also knew how to listen. As he wrote Thomson regarding the program for a 1909 Washington Good Roads Association meeting, "My idea is to have the Governor and . . . farmers do all the talking. Let us go once and listen and give the people a chance."

In Sam's view, there was a moral as well as an economic reason for

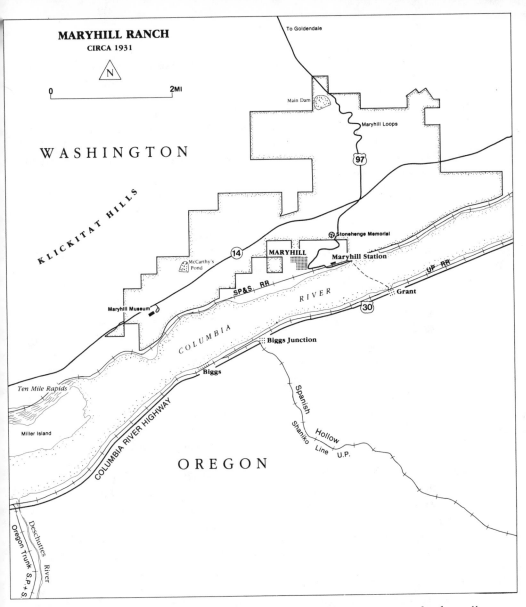

MARYHILL RANCH
CIRCA 1931

N

0   2MI

To Goldendale

Main Dam

Maryhill Loops

97

WASHINGTON

KLICKITAT HILLS

Stonehenge Memorial

McCarthy's Pond

14

MARYHILL

Maryhill Station

UP RR

SP&S RR

RIVER

Grant

Maryhill Museum

30

COLUMBIA

Biggs Junction

Ten Mile Rapids

Biggs

Spanish

Miller Island

Shaniko Line U.P.

Hollow

COLUMBIA RIVER HIGHWAY

OREGON

Deschutes River

Oregon Trunk S.P.+S.

helping the farmer, namely, keeping the young folks "down on the farm." His puritanical side showed through in a 1922 interview with Lockley: "I believe in man on the land. We cannot afford to have our producers leave the land and come to the city and become parasites. We want our girls to stay on the farm and become the mothers of a virile race of men and not just go to the city and become manicurists, stenographers and variety actresses. We want our boys to stay on the farm and not succumb to the lure of the Great White Way or become chauffeurs and clerks*. . . . . We cannot keep the ambitious boy or girl on the farm unless we make life attractive and comfortable."

*Here he sounds more than a little like his namesake, Professor Hill of *The Music Man*.

135

Sam began his own road work at the planned town of Maryhill in 1909. He had a rock crusher set up, a bargain at $100. He brought in wagons, rollers, and screens for crushed rock, obtained from the vicinity. Heavy oil, 80 percent liquid asphalt, was shipped by rail from California to the Maryhill siding. The asphalt was heated and pumped into tank cars to be sprayed on the crushed and steam-rolled rock and gravel.* Typically, the roadway was first covered with macadam six inches in depth and rolled to four inches, then covered with oiled rock and rolled again.

In 1911, Sam invited Lancaster to Maryhill " . . . to build him a road up from the river to his home and to build roads about the place." Seven types of experimental roads, totalling ten miles in length, were built, costing Sam over $100,000. These extended from the townsite of Maryhill north up through a canyon to join the old road to Goldendale (see map). Sam liked to compare the cost with the $28,000 a mile for which the roads around Seattle had been built.

Sam's roads were the first in the state to be paved. One stretch, the "Maryhill loops," ascended 850 feet in some 3.6 miles up the canyon in a series of tortuous curves, in the fashion of alpine mountain roads, keeping the gradient of ascent low. (This route was used until 1948 when a shorter road was built on the opposite side of the canyon. For some years thereafter, the "loops" were used for sports car hill climb races.)

The purpose of the roads, constructed with proper drainage and gradual grades, was to demonstrate the best types of binding material and rock to withstand wear and great variations in temperature. The roads intentionally varied in composition and construction and were not equally successful. Several years later, when Sam invited the mayor of Kennewick, Washington, to inspect the roads he wrote, "All the ways of showing how not to do it are exhibited there, as well as how to do it. . . . I have never yet seen one mile of road or one block of street built by government engineers worth going to look at the second time, not do I believe there is a man in the government employ who knows a road from a hole in the ground. This road business is a business all by itself, like painting pictures is one all by itself."

Lancaster designed a horse-drawn wagon,with tires six feet in diameter having a six inch tread,which could haul four cubic yards of crushed stone treated with asphalt, and Sam had two such wagons built.

Sam wrote an article for *Collier's* in 1909 on his favorite theme of the deficiencies of American roads, felt most severely by farmers, who then constituted 35 percent of an estimated 30 million working population. (Sam evidently was not counting housewives as workers, a mistake not uniquely his own.) It was unfair to put most of the burden of building rural roads on the farmer, whose products feed the people of towns and cities, he said. The Washington Good Roads Association had given out forms to farmers haul-

---

*A. L. McAdam,. 1756-1836, a Scottish inventor, originated the use of broken stones for road building. Early in the 20th Century, bituminous macadam roads, made of hot asphalt mixed with various types of aggregate, became popular. The British term "tarmac" derives from this process.

The "Maryhill Loops" looking south down Maryhill Canyon. Undated photograph, probably early 1920's. (Maryhill Museum files.)

ing produce to railroad stations throughout the state. The farmer was to fill in the distance of the haul, weight of the load, the number of horses required, and to compute the average cost per ton or bushel per mile versus the railroad freight to tidewater. The average cost of hauling a ton per mile by railroad was three-fourths of a cent, but on the country roads at that time it was thirty cents. Good roads would reduce this cost by twenty cents, Sam said. "Freight rates really begin at the farmhouse door," he told Lockley.

Progress in road building was being made in Washington. In an interview in the fall of 1910, Sam noted the work planned on three important roads in the state: north to south, from Blaine to Vancouver, to become part of the Pacific Highway; from Vancouver east along the Columbia and then northeast to Spokane; and from Spokane through the Snoqualmie Pass to Tacoma and Seattle. For 30 years, farmers had had to contend with the 15 percent grade in Hangman's Gulch, south of Spokane. The Washington agency planned and built the road there with a three and a half percent grade. A state highway policy was established whereby no state road would have a grade exceeding five percent.

The use of convict labor to build roads in Washington State received national attention. In May 1910, Sam and Henry Bowlby, the Washington State Highway Commissioner, took a party of Portland and Seattle citizens to inspect the work being done near Lyle, Washington. About a hundred convicts were sheltered in wooden buildings surrounded by a portable stockade constructed of heavy timbers. The reporter noted with wonder, and possibly apprehension, that a prisoner who had been in jail for dynamiting was in charge of the explosives. Armed guards were on hand but no one had tried to escape. Bowlby stated that three convicts would do as much work as any four men he could hire because of the convicts' fear that if they were not industrious they would be returned to the penitentiary.

One of the visitors from Oregon said the men looked happy and contented to him, unlike their attitude in prison where many had worked in jute mills. The state lost money in selling the jute bags at five cents each, but made about $2.00 per day on convicts doing road labor. Penologists of today would shudder at the thought of returning to the system, but on the other hand, they do not often point with pride to their own successes.

In 1913, Sam expanded on the idea of convict labor in a full-page article in the *New York Times* about the Pacific Highway from Canada to Mexico, then under construction. He said that Armour, the meat packer, had told him that no great manufacturing corporation could prosper unless it used its by-products. Sam added, "One of society's by-products is the convict. Our utilization of him in the construction of our roads is strictly along efficiency lines . . . The convicts are treated like men in these well-ordered, beautiful camps and many of them are rehabilitated."

He reported a conversation with a pessimistic contractor who complained that the state was taking work away from honest men and giving it to convicted crooks at starvation wages. Sam replied that the families of the convicts got their pay, or it was saved for them until they had served their terms. The visitor was concerned about the dangers in convicts handling tools and explosives, but Sam reassured him that there had been no trouble. Once a trusty, put in charge of some concrete construction, was missing at dinnertime. Sam was worried and, with a guard, went out to search for him. They found the man so interested in his work that he had forgotten to knock off for dinner.

After his return from the Good Roads Congress in Brussels in the summer of 1910, Sam was vexed because the Klickitat County commissioners refused to appropriate money to keep Washington convicts at work on the roads near Lyle. Sam campaigned throughout the county for five days and at an election, persuaded 90 percent of the farming community to approve continuation of the work. A modest one-mill levy raised $10,000 for the purpose. Sam expected that completion of the road would permit the farmers to haul millions of bushels of grain to the steamboat landing at Lyle, and to save two cents per bushel. However, only about a mile of the road was completed, cut into the rocky cliffs east of Lyle. Today, remnants of the road have been nearly obliterated by rock slides and washouts.

In 1911, the legislature increased the highway board from three to five members, with the governor and his appointees in full control. At the meeting of the Washington State Good Roads Association in Wenatchee in October of that year, Governor Hay gave " . . . valiant assurance that he favored using convicts to build state roads." He soon changed his mind, however, and withdrew the convicts from the roadbuilding camp at Lyle and put them in the Walla Walla penitentiary. He was soon to rue this.

Sam relished his part in foiling Hay's attempt to be reelected in 1912 in a campaign hinging on expenditures for good roads. He told a *New York Times* reporter, "Our good roads candidate for governor was Ernest Lister. It was an astonishing campaign. Every newspaper but one, every railroad but the Northern Pacific, and every professional politician in the state opposed him without regard to party — but he was elected. The old governor, Hay, had 3,000 appointees, organized as ingeniously as ever Tammany was organized for a political battle in New York. But the good roads slogan led their enemies to victory."

Sam endorsed federal aid for research in road building. He envisioned three transcontinental highways which would " . . . tie its east and west together with good roads," as Lord Strathcona had done with the Canadian Pacific Railway. "The big broad plan is a necessity," Sam contended, but it would require direct taxation, bond issues, and convict labor.

But even Lister would not go along with Sam's pet project of building a highway on the north bank of the Columbia. Because of the terrain, construction was " . . . costing $30,000 a mile, [so] both Governor Lister and the legislature developed cold feet [and] cut out more of the appropriations. . . . " This blow and the withdrawal of convicts from road work led Sam to vow he would never return to live in Seattle until a Washington governor put state convicts back on the road. Sam did not make good on this promise, but he soon turned his time and energies to improving Oregon's road system.

Early in 1912, Sam returned from a month's stay in Europe, where he inspected roads in England, Belgium, and France, photographing them to record changes from previous visits. On his way west, he told an audience in Minneapolis, "Switzerland is a joke when compared with our great country. Nowhere in the world is there such magnificent scenery as can be found along the Columbia River. I have . . . yet to find anything more impressive than what lies at my front door." What was more, he wanted tourists everywhere to share this natural wealth.

As president of the Home Telephone and Telegraph Company of Portland, Sam had become a great booster of Portland, which was not only the terminus of transcontinental railroads but was near the Columbia River and Pacific Ocean. He advised Oregonians to stand behind Governor Oswald West in developing roads in Oregon. California was spending $30,000,000 for highways, he said, and Oregon roads connecting with these would bring a great many tourists to the Northwest.

During 1912 and 1913, Sam was tireless in traveling about Oregon and Washington to give talks on good roads, using his now famous slides* of

---

*One portrayed a poem of Robert Burns (1786):
I'm now arrived — thanks to the gods! —
Through pathway rough and muddy,
A certain sign that makin' roads
Is no' this people's study:
Altho' I'm not wi'
 Scripture cram'd,
I'm sure the Bible says
That heedless sinners shall be damn'd
Unless they mend their ways.

roads and Northwest scenery. At Corvallis, Oregon, it was reported that his slides "brought out frequent cheers." When he appeared in Albany, Oregon, he was pleased to find that a street had been named for him. He had employed an artist for two years to hand-color his slides of the mountains, waterfalls, and rivers of the Northwest, and some of the pictures had cost as much as $500 each. In 1915, a reporter marveled that Sam had " . . . delivered his famous illustrated good roads lecture . . . before 20,000 Portland school children, taking them in classes of twenty at a time." That representated 1,000 sessions; one has reason to marvel at Sam's zeal, not to mention his stamina.

On other occasions, he talked to civic and church groups on "Americanism," "Young Men and the Republic," and even on "Essential Elements in Homebuilding." He seldom missed an opportunity to berate Washington's Governor Hay for his decision against convict labor on roads. He also chided the federal government for doing so little about highway development, saying in 1913, "For 12 years, I have spent more each year in the construction of good roads than has the national government."

Early in 1913, Sam brought off one of his best public relations stunts. He invited Oregon's Governor West and the entire legislature to be his guests on a visit to Maryhill to inspect the experimental roads and view his slides. The group of 88 met at the Portland office af the Home Telegraph Company and was taken by a special train, well provided with food and drink. The legislature passed a concurrent resolution of thanks for the excursion and " . . . the unselfish work that is being done by Mr. Hill in the cause of good roads."

Soon afterward, Sam was guest of honor at a banquet in Portland attended by its most prominent citizens (all male, of course). The affair was organized by Julius Meier, a well-to-do department store owner in Portland, who later figured in promoting construction of the Columbia River Highway. A massive loving cup filled with champagne was passed around. The numerous guests offered toasts and gave Sam the title "Oregon's friend," because of his work for good roads. C. S. Jackson, owner of the *Oregon Journal*, was toastmaster and said Sam " . . . is more generous with his money than any man I ever knew who had earned it." Sam responded that he was proud to be of service to Oregon, "a state I love."

Sam and the governor made a great team in getting the Portland establishment interested in good roads. As West told it years later, after Sam's campaign for a highway on the north bank of the Columbia was rejected by Governor Hay, Sam came to call. "Before he had a chance to say much, I said, 'Listen, brother; you don't have to waste your breath on me. I am a hundred percent for your good roads program . . . You know little about the people of this state, but I know a lot. They are fine, but damned peculiar. One often is obliged to resort to strategy in order to induce them to do the things that are really in their interest.'" The well-to-do members of the Arlington Club, Portland's equivalent to the Union League Club in New

York, were purportedly shy of publicity, but actually would relish it. "Throw a few dinners for them, and make some good roads excursions where pictures can be taken for newspaper use. They will follow you because you smell of money and have not only dined with the King of Belgium, but held the Queen of Rumania's hand. . . . ' So through his use of the Arlington Club and my use of convicts, we had the public pretty much good roads minded by the time the 1913 session of the legislature rolled around." As one step, West appointed a "Harmony Committee," its members each pledging $500 toward promoting bills for state road bonds, the appointment of a highway commissioner, and convict labor measures.

Sam's gift of $10,000 for the preparation of a comprehensive outline for Oregon state highways also helped. He was reported to have worked quietly on this for months, studying routes, topography, and the population to be served.

When Sam defected to Oregon, he brought his own troops with him: Major Bowlby, who became the first Oregon state highway engineer; Sam Lancaster, who was put in charge of construction of the Columbia River Highway; and Charles Purcell, bridge engineer. In the fall of 1912, in campaigning for a state-wide highway system, Governor West had run into the opposition of the state Grange to issuing state bonds, but he persuaded the 1913 legislature to impose a tax levy of one-fourth mill to fund a state highway commission and employ Sam's experts for the highway program. Initially, the annual levy brought in a modest $248,000.

Bowlby was directed to prepare a map proposing several main state highways. The Pacific Highway was the most important of the several north-south highways approved and the Columbia River Highway the major east-west road. The plan was along the lines that Sam had proposed to Rufus Holman, then a Multnomah County commissioner, in May 1913, when he convinced Holman of the necessity and practicability of a road through the Columbia Gorge. Sam recommended a pitchfork-shaped plan, the tines being a coastal highway; the Pacific Highway; and a route through central Oregon to California, all united to the north by the Columbia River Highway. Within a decade, these highways were completed.

The idea of a paved highway traversing Washington, Oregon and California seems so logical and inevitable that it may be surprising to some that the oldest motorists now around can recall that even in 1925, a hundred mile stretch of such a highway in northern California was still unpaved. Ten years earlier, it was only the most adventuresome who set out to drive from the Canadian to the Mexican border between the months of November and April, when some stretches were often impassable because of mud and snow. America's love affair with the automobile made it necessary to provide roads on which to consummate it. Sam Hill was one of the few who anticipated the rapidly expanding need for good interstate and international highways.

A. E. Todd of Victoria, B.C., has been called the father of the Pacific

Highway Association for his pioneer efforts. In the summer of 1910, Todd and his wife drove 2,000 miles from Tijuana to Vancouver, B.C. in 17 days. Two months later, in September, the Pacific Highway Association was formed in Seattle and Sam was named president. Convention delegates from British Columbia and the coastal states had been instructed by chambers of commerce and automobile clubs to make plans for a Pacific Highway, hurry its construction, and publicize it in the press and through community meetings. Existing county roads often were not suitably placed for a north-south highway, so the association directed its efforts at state government support.

In the summer of 1912, Sam, accompanied by Charles Chamberlain and Charles Babcock, drove from Portland to San Francisco, where he gave an address before the Pacific Highway Association. The association had already erected direction signs " . . . at every turn and crossing between Vancouver, B.C. and Redding, California."

California was the most farsighted of the Pacific states in planning for a good highway system; a Bureau of Highways was set up in 1895. The California State Highway Act was passed in 1910, provding for $18,000,000 in bonds and construction of 3,050 miles of road.

In 1913, the *New York Times* carried an interview with Sam headlined, "Great Highway from Canada to Mexico Underway". By that time, contracts for roadbuilding had been let for segments in Washington and Oregon.

Until then Oregon had lagged behind its neighbors. Todd, who drove through the state in 1912, observed there were " . . . only a few miles of good macadam or gravel roads" and "not 35 percent of the total distance" was properly graded. "All the rest is mud and boulders, impassable in winter and difficult in summer." The only tollgate on the Pacific Highway in place was in Oregon, " . . . and that is on a very bad section of road, too!" He concluded that the notably independent, if not always progressive, Oregon voters had to be persuaded of the need for change.

The change came suddenly in 1913 when Sam and Governor Os West convinced the legislature of the need to plan and construct key highways. Sam's grand gesture of taking the whole crowd to Maryhill was the turning point, and the speed and success of building the beautiful Columbia River Highway helped further the more gradual completion of the Pacific Highway through the state. In 1917, the legislature passed a $6,000,000 bonding act, the first of a series which permitted Oregon, like the proverbial tortoise, to make up for its slow start. By the end of 1922, 345 miles of the Pacific Highway had been constructed through Oregon, nearly all of it paved.

In 1913, Sam took his friend Charles P. Chamberlain, editor of the Bellingham *Reveille* and a supporter of good roads, on a whirlwind trip to Europe, in part to attend the International Road Congress in London. The *New York Times* interviewed the bewildered Chamberlain on his return. Touring in Europe with its different currencies and the difficulties with the language had not been easy. Sam's schedule had kept Chamberlain's average night's rest to five hours, " . . . and I took my feed out of a nosebag like a horse, you might say." Sam took him on a quick tour of buildings, parks, churches, galleries and museums, doing all of the necessary parlaying in French. Sam had given a dinner in London for the delegates to the congress from the United States and Canada, with Lord Strathcona, formerly Donald Smith of the Hudson's Bay Company and Canadian railroads, presiding.

Sam told Lockley these anecdotes about the faithful Chamberlain:

> On numerous occasions he has saved the day for me. One day we were going to hold a meeting advocating good roads in the Public Library in Portland. We got word that a lot of objectors were coming to try to break up the meeting. Chamberlain told me not to worry about it — that the meeting would be held, and there would be no trouble, and there would be an enthusiastic audience. When I and the other speakers arrived the hall was packed, and there wasn't room for another person in it. There were scores of husky looking men outside the library. We had a very successful meeting and the resolutions for good roads were pased unanimously and the papers played up the enthusiasm of the public for the good roads program. I asked Charley how he had done it. He said, 'I sent a big bunch of railroad men to go there an hour early and occupy all the seats, so when the objectors came they couldn't even find standing room.'
>
> At an election in Seattle, we wanted to put in some officers who were favorable to good roads and to the issuing of bonds. We counted noses pretty carefully, and to my despair I found our opponents had colonized four rooming houses. They were going to vote all these men, which meant we would lose out by a small margin. The city officials and police force were against us but the sheriff was with us. Charley told me not to worry — that it would come out all right. The day before the election, Charley slipped a man with a varioloid* into one of those rooming houses, notified the sheriff that there was smallpox there and next day, all four of these rooming houses were guarded by deputy sheriffs, who wouldn't allow any of the men to break the quarantine for smallpox. We won the election, got in the officials we wanted, passed the bonds, and got our good roads.

In the early days of motoring, especially from about 1910 to 1925, newspapers frequently had special sections and articles on automobiles and touring. There was a scramble to record the first and the fastest trip from here to there and to discover the most scenic — and least bumpy — route. Tourists often would stop at newspaper offices in the cities through which they passed to bring and ask for information, and perhaps to brag to the automobile editor of the fast time they had made. A 1915 scrapbook prepared by Chester Moores, automobile editor for *The Oregonian*, gives interesting sidelights on the pleasure and perils of the venturesome motorist; some selections follow.

There was considerable interest in driving from the Northwest to San Francisco for the Panama-Pacific Exposition of 1915. Sam, as an inveterate road explorer, wrote an article advising tourists on the best routes. He did not recommend taking the Pacific Highway south through the Willamette Valley because that road was not yet properly graded and drained. Instead,

---

*A mild form of smallpox resembling the real thing. Charley's rash behavior did not endanger lives but no doubt tested tempers.

the new Columbia River Highway route would be mostly finished for summer travel. Sam noted that, "I shared with the County of Klickitat the expense of building a road from Goldendale to Maryhill on a 5 percent grade, which will be finished in 20 days. I am now building at my own expense a ferry to run from Maryhill to Spanish Hollow . . . Some years ago I had a survey made at the expense of $3,000 for a road up Spanish Hollow to Wasco [Oregon]. That road will be opened to traffic by April." The automobilist could then continue south through Central Oregon, detour to see beautiful Crater Lake, and proceed to Medford and to northern California. Sam also described alternate routes and pointed out the need for restaurants and other tourist stops along the routes. Tent cities would be established along the route from Seattle to San Francisco, a trip expected to take about six days.

The same issue of *The Oregonian* noted that a gasoline war in Portland had forced the price down to ten cents a gallon. There has also been a recent 25% cut in tire prices which " . . . has materially lessened the cost of upkeep on the cars."

On one of Sam's speaking tours, accompanied by Fred Lockley, they stopped at a small town in southern Oregon. The proprietor told them it was after closing time, and did not budge when Sam offered to pay him well for getting some ham and eggs and coffee. Sam said, "I guess you don't know who I am. My name is Sam Hill, and we are cruising through your country to try to promote better roads." "I don't care who you are," answered the hotel man, "the dining room is closed." Lockley then introduced himself and the hotel man recalled that Lockley had written up "one of my kinsmen a year or so ago, and it was a humdinger of a good story." He thereupon offered to cook the pair a couple of good steaks and the best meal in the house.

Sam had the laugh on Lockley on another trip when they were lost on a road in eastern Oregon. They stopped at a farm where the housewife knew all about Sam Hill and offered them lodging. When he introduced Lockley, she said, "I like your writing so much and I thought you would be tall and slender and have curly black hair, instead of being a big fat man like you are."

Sam was a picturesque figure on his tireless tours. As Lockley wrote, "If you saw him in his broad-brimmed gray hat with a red bandanna around his neck, wearing his well-worn corduroys, stopping his auto to shovel a sharp-cornered rock out of the road, you would think he was a road supervisor. He works on the roads as if he were on salary and afraid he would lose his job if he didn't put in full-time at hard work. I have ridden a good many thousand miles with him over the highways, over mountain trails and through the sagebrush and desert and he is always the same — start at from 4:00 to 5:00 a.m., stop somewhere for breakfast at about 7:00 o'clock, eat some doughnuts and raisins for lunch, stop for supper, and travel a couple of hours after supper. If he doesn't work or travel sixteen hours a day, he feels he has wasted the day."

Sam's first car, a Locomobile, " . . . bought at the dawn of the automobile industry, carried him 265,000 miles as he pioneered the roads of the entire Northwest." He bought two more Locomobiles after that, and in 1915, a Hupmobile which he considered "the finest article built for touring." A reporter credited him with being the first to drive over the Snoqualmie Pass road between Seattle and Spokane, and the first to drive the full length of the Columbia River Highway before its completion.

In 1916 Sam plumped for construction of another north-south highway from British Columbia to Mexico, paralleling the Pacific Highway, but, " . . . as near as can be on the shores of the ocean . . . hard-surfaced all the way, which will permit the carriage of heavy materials of all kinds in time of war . . . and which can be used as a wonder drive for pleasure, particularly in time of peace."

In 1912 and again in 1915, Sam had offered to build at his expense a connecting link from the Maryhill roads to the top of the Klickitat Hills, if the county commissioners would construct a proper road from Goldendale to meet it. The commissioners did not act or even seek his advice. Sam wrote to chide them for wasting money on poorly done repairs. He was still scolding them in 1926 for simply putting gravel on the county roads west and east of Maryhill, and invited comparison with his own sturdy roads on the ranch. Sam pointed out that increased tourist travel would result from construction of the Stonehenge Memorial and completion of his museum, but he did not propose to finish the museum until the North Bank Highway was completed. The legislators from the Seattle area, however, were against putting a large part of the state's highway fund into an area where heavy traffic was not expected.

In the early 1920's, Sam extended his campaign for good roads to Japan (Chapter 19). His part in the construction of the Columbia River Highway is told in the next chapter.

He continued to be active in state and national highway organizations. In 1922, the Advisory Board in Highway Research of the National Research Council thanked Sam for his part in getting a $1,000 contribution from the American Road Builder's Association, of which Sam was president. Not all of Sam's dreams for great highways came true, at least not at the time. At the 1926 convention of the association, for example, he plumped for a "Great South Way" which would connect Detroit and the Midwest with Key West, Florida. A tribute to Sam written after his death mentions his invitation to representatives of highway associations of the U.S. and Canada to investigate the feasibility of extending the Pacific Highway into Alaska. Had he lived, he might have succeeded in getting this plan underway long before construction of a military highway through northwestern Canada and Alaska began hurriedly in 1942.

Sam could indeed take pride in his part in promoting completion of the Pacific Highway. In 1923, it was " . . . the longest continuous stretch of paving in the world." Its length from Vancouver, B.C. to Tijuana was 1,687 miles at that time. The *Washington Motorist* called it "the most colossal roadbuilding feat in the history of the world," and rhapsodized, "Its wonders will be the writers' theme, and poets will sing of its glories. A 1,600 mile avenue!" Perhaps only Robert Service could have done it justice, and he did not choose to do so. Sam called it "the best single highway in the world." He commented sourly on certain New Jersey delegates who travel " . . . up and down the land and tell each state that they have the best highways in existence." This was an usurpation of Sam's prerogative not to be tolerated!

Late in 1927, there was a news story on Sam's announcement of the formation of a "Memory Gardens Association," the president of which was to be Mrs. R. P. Butchart of Victoria, B.C., the developer of the famous Butchart Gardens there. The ambitious object of this association was beautification of the Pacific Highway from Vancouver, B.C., to Mexico. Soon afterward, Sam confirmed this at a luncheon he gave in Paris for forty persons, including the Butcharts, Joffres, Paul Verdiers, Albert Tierman (French Counselor of State), M. Guiffrey (Curator of the Louvre), and Gaby Bloch, the companion of Loie Fuller. Queen Marie, Sam said, had chosen the name and accepted the honorary presidency. Clubs would be formed for various sectors of the highway, and $1,000 in prizes given to the organization having the most beautiful segment. "The thought is," he said, "that this proposal will result in practically making one garden of the whole Pacific Highway." Sam wrote a few letters about the organization of the association, but it appears there was no follow-up on this very large undertaking. The time for landscaping and beautification of highways on the West Coast was years away.

Today, Interstate 5 carries most of the traffic which once used the Pacific Highway. The motorist can get to his destination faster and have less fun than in 1925. Sam probably would gulp and approve if he could see the fruition of his dreams of a great international highway, now the Pan-American highway, extending from Alaska to the Panama Canal and into South America. He would frown on the great speeding trailer trucks, but smile in wonder at the efficiency of it all; the engineering marvels, the gradual grades and curves, the signing system and safety measures. The landscaping along the freeways and the parks and rest areas would certainly get his approval. And perhaps, having seen it, he would sympathize with those who would not mind exchanging it all for a less hurried time when gasoline was cheap and plentiful and motoring was an adventure.

In the last years of his life, Sam began to be concerned about the damaging effects to highways of heavy truck traffic. In one of his last letters, Sam said he had " . . . pointed out to the President [Hoover] the location of the forts on the line of the Great Northern Railway and told him that $5,000,000 would connect up the highways leading to them. . . . Of course the main object of the call was to discuss the truck and bus damage. The President is with us, and I think realizes the danger to the country. . . . The President said, 'Good work, keep it up!' "

True to the indomitable call of duty, Sam tried to ignore abdominal symptoms in order to address a joint session of the Oregon legislature on the truck regulation problem on February 9, 1931. He was on his way to this appointment when acute symptoms led to his final hospitalization.

Sam's yearning to be remembered after his death was manifested in a number of ways. For the best, one can echo the inscription to Sir Christopher Wren in St. Paul's Cathedral; "If you would see the man's monument, look about."

17

The Columbia River Highway

If Sam Hill's campaign for good roads was a long crusade, the beautiful Columbia River Highway was to Sam the Holy Grail. His earlier efforts had been devoted particularly to improving road transportation between farm and railroad station, but he had long been aware of the potential of tourism for bringing dollars as well was an influx of new people to the Northwest. For all its immense territory, the Northwest then had few roads, and those beyond the limits of cities were poor. Few envisioned a highway through the Columbia Gorge to Astoria at the mouth of the river, providing a virtually all-weather route to the eastern part of the state, and connecting eventually with proposed transcontinental highways.

A serious objection to construction of roads through passes across the Cascade Mountains was that they were subject to closure by snow blockade. Early settlers used the Barlow Trail, opened in 1846, to bring their wagons from eastern Oregon across the Cascade Mountains south of Mt. Hood. The Columbia River was the logical water route through the mountains, but there were dangerous rapids at The Dalles (The name "Dalles" derives from the French word for flagstone, "dalle." The flat basaltic rock in the riverbed apparently reminded French trappers of that used to line gutters.) A wagon road, and later a four mile portage railroad, were built parallel to the Lower Cascades in the 1850's, supplanted by the line of the Oregon Railway and Navigation Co. in 1883. This rail line used the right of way of the wagon road around the rapids on the Oregon side for the next thirty years, so that immigrants had either to use the railroad or take boats below the Cascades to get to the fertile Willamette Valley. River travel was made easier by a canal around the Upper Cascades, completed in 1910, and locks adjacent to the Lower Cascades. Both of these were engulfed by the pools formed above

The Dalles and Bonneville dams, respectively, in later years.

The Oregon legislature appropriated $50,000 in 1872, and a like amount four years later, to build a narrow dirt road from the mouth of the Sandy River east through the Gorge to The Dalles. This road had steep grades, and double teams were necessary in places. It was often impassable in winters because of mud. The terrain was difficult for road building on both the north and south banks of the Columbia because in many places there was scarcely room at the base of the basaltic cliffs for both railroad tracks and a road. Sam Hill later recalled that James Allen, Washington's capable highway commissioner from 1915 to 1925, once had warned him, "You can't survey a road along the Columbia River, let alone build one."

Nevertheless, in 1909, Lewis Russell, a Portland auto enthusiast, at his own expense had a preliminary survey made for a road through the Gorge on the Oregon side. The estimated cost for a road sixteen feet wide with grades as steep as 17% was only $42,000. He was joined by E. H. Wemme, owner of the first automobile in Portland, in petitioning the Multnomah County commissioners to undertake the project. The idea was approved, and in May 1910, Philo Holbrook, the county surveyor, mapped out a wider road with grades not over 9%, to cost some $150,000. Beginning in the spring of 1911, county workers constructed 1.8 miles of road east from Bridal Veil Falls (see map), but it had to be rebuilt two years later to conform to the standards of the newly formed Oregon State Highway commission for trunk roads. The segment completed was not only steep and winding but also encountered right-of-way problems with the railroad, whose officials did not relish the prospect of rock slides onto their tracks.

In the spring of 1912, Sam Hill,Bowlby (now executive officer for the Pacific Highway Association), two Multnomah County Commissioners, the county surveyor, and the road superintendent took a two-day trip, most of it on foot, over a proposed route between Portland and Cascade Locks. The elderly Mr. Pittock, publisher of *The Oregonian*, gamely went with the group. Ropes were often needed to get up and down precipitous rocky slopes on the route.

A breakthrough came in March 1912, when a millionaire Portland lumberman, Simon Benson, became interested in the project and gave Governor Oswald West $10,000 to build a difficult segment of road in Hood River County between the base of Shell Rock Mountain and the Columbia. The governor released Oregon State prisoners for the work, following Sam Hill's example with Washington convicts across the river at Lyle, Washington. The Shell Rock Mountain road later had to be rebuilt, also, but its construction was a demonstration of what could be accomplished in the difficult terrain.

The next step was the planning and construction of the two-lane Columbia River Highway, accomplished in a relatively short space of time (1913-15). (Nowadays, two years would scarcely see completion of the environmental impact studies.) This feat is a tribute to the talents and generosity of an unusual group of devoted men.

148

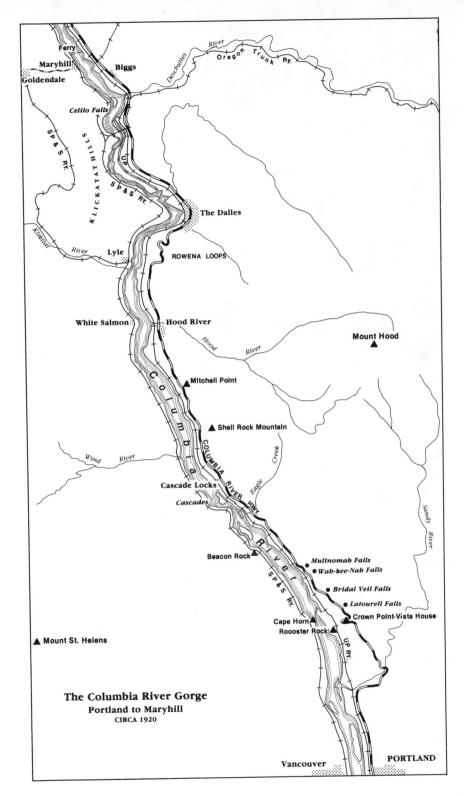

Ferry
Maryhill
Goldendale
Biggs
Oregon Trunk Ry.
River
Deschutes
Celilo Falls
SP & S. RY.
KLICKATAT HILLS
S P & S. RY.
Up
Klikitat
River
Lyle
The Dalles
ROWENA LOOPS
White Salmon
Hood River
Hood
River
Mount Hood
Mitchell Point
Shell Rock Mountain
Columbia
COLUMBIA RIVER HWY.
Eagle
Creek
Wind
River
Cascade Locks
Cascades
Sandy
River
River
Beacon Rock
Multnomah Falls
Wah-kee-Nah Falls
SP & S. RY.
Bridal Veil Falls
Latourell Falls
Crown Point-Vista House
Cape Horn
Roooster Rock
Mount St. Helens
UP. RY.

The Columbia River Gorge
Portland to Maryhill
CIRCA 1920

Vancouver
PORTLAND

Plaque at Vista House on the Scenic Columbia River Highway. (Author's photo.)

The first is Sam Lancaster, introduced in the preceding chapter, for whom the highway was to be the crowning achievement of his engineering career. He possessed a rare blend of roadbuilding know-how, an almost religious aesthetic sense, and conservationist convictions. On a preliminary survey, while standing waist deep in ferns, Sam Lancaster recalled his mother's admonition to him in childhood; "Oh, Samuel, do be careful of my Boston fern!" It was then he pledged himself " . . . that none of this wild beauty should be marred where it could be prevented. The highway was so built that not one tree was felled, not one fern was crushed, unnecessarily." He felt it his duty to bring the natural beauties of the Gorge within the view of the average motorist. When he and Sam Hill saw the terraced vineyards on the steep banks of the Rhine in 1908, he scarcely believed Hill when he said they would see something like that on the Columbia some day, but within five years, Lancaster had begun to direct just such a project.

Secondly, there were a number of well-to-do Portland businessmen, in addition to Simon Benson, without whose support the project would have found heavy going. Julius Meier, a wealthy department store owner in Portland and later governor of Oregon, contributed money and influence to get the project done. One of the most devoted backers was John B. Yeon, a millionaire businessman who had come from Canada by way of the lumber camps of Ohio to Portland in 1885. The remarkable thing about Yeon's contribution was his two year service as unpaid roadmaster. Amos Benson was his unofficial assistant and right-of-way agent, who persuaded many of the property owners in the Gorge to donate land needed for the highway and parks along the way. Among these was Charles Coopey who had bought a three and a half mile stretch of land between Bridal Veil and Wah-Kee-Nah Falls (see map), intending to use water power for a woolen mill.

Civic pride was an important factor in the support of Portland's prominent citizens for the highway. By 1910, Seattle had surpassed Portland in population and economic importance. Some Portlanders realized that the new road from Tacoma to Mt. Rainier National Park would bring more tourists to their northern neighbor than Oregon could expect for the near future. Then, as now, there were some who looked with distaste on the prospect of an influx into Oregon of people who would come as tourists but decide to stay, but their objections were swept away by the enthusiasm of the boosters.

Thirdly, there were the politicians who obtained the necessary backing of the Multnomah County commissioners and the Oregon legislature. Governor Os West's alliance with Sam Hill is described in the preceding chapter. Rufus Holman, later a U.S. Senator, was then a Multnomah County commissioner who introduced a resolution in July 1913, setting up a County Advisory Board on Roads and Highways. Amos Benson was on this board, along with C. S. Jackson, publisher of *The Oregon Journal*. Multnomah County includes not only Portland, but a 40 mile stretch extending eastward up the Columbia.

Then there was Sam Hill, the catalyst for all of these. He had brought Lancaster and Bowlby into the picture; his Arlington Club connections had given him an in with the Portland establishment; and his grand gesture of bringing the Oregon legislature to Maryhill in February 1913 had paved the way for state support. Holman called him " . . . the playwright and director, the great mind of the enterprise." Holman later recalled that in May 1913, "Just as the sun was setting behind the Cascades and the long shadows of the mountains were falling across the gorge of the Columbia to the west of Maryhill," Sam had led him to the edge of a cliff overlooking the river and said, "Envision for me a wonderful road through that wild canyon . . . a road such as no one had yet seen. . . . " Holman's own grandfather had " . . . lost by starvation in that very gorge every head of livestock which he had brought across the plains. . . . I realized that there was infinitely greater use for a road through the gorge of the Columbia in 1913 than there was in 1852 . . . and I assured him that I would do whatever my opportunities permitted me to do to bring to a realization what was then only a vision in one man's brain."

Governor Hay of Washington deserves mention in a different connection. Had it not been for his objection to the use of Washington convicts on road projects and his thwarting of Sam's efforts to promote a north bank highway, Sam probably would not have turned his considerable energy and talents for persuasion to the Oregon side of the river.

In August 1913, about a month after the Advisory Board on Roads and Highways had been set up, its members met with the county commissioners and several local backers at Chanticleer Inn, located on a bluff overlooking the western end of the Gorge. Sam Lancaster came as Hill's guest. At that meeting, Commissioner Lightner objected to the expense of hiring Lancaster, proposing that Holbrook, the county surveyor, supervise the construction. Holbrook considered Lancaster's plan too costly, based on his own 1911 survey for quite another type of road.

Lancaster calmly recommended that there be a 24 foot roadway with no grade over 5% and no curve with a radius less than 100 feet. The board accepted his recommendations, but because of friction introduced by Holbrook and Lightner, the county commissioners soon voted to turn over a fund of $75,000 to the newly created Oregon Highway Commission to undertake surveys and other preliminary work for the highway. The objections of the economy-minded were understandable in those days before federal aid for highways. There were then only 11,800 motor vehicles in Oregon, and to many people the automobile was still a rich man's toy, a concept which Henry Ford was in the process of abolishing forever.*

Sam Lancaster was appointed consulting engineer late in August 1913, and with Herbert Nunn as engineer, began surveys for the new highway. Construction began in October 1913, and the labor force was enlarged from 100 to 500 or more by June 1914. The work was done in part by convicts using pick, shovel, and wheelbarrow. Sam had movies made, now at Maryhill Museum, of the various stages of construction. April 25, 1914 was proclaimed "Good Roads Day." Five hundred Portland businessmen came up the Gorge on a special train, paying $0.75 each for the privilege of working for five hours, thus saving the county $1,000.

Multnomah County road funds ran short in the fall of 1914, so Lancaster and Yeon appealed to the sponsoring group to loan $50,000 to the county without interest until the tax levy of 1915 was available. This loan permitted completion of grading of the highway on schedule.

The highway construction was completely up-to-date for its time. Reinforced concrete was used in the seventeen arched bridges and viaducts, many of which were of novel design, intended to place the structures into a natural setting on the steep slopes and cliffs of the gorge. The retaining walls were of dry masonry, modeled after the walls Lancaster had seen with Sam in Italy. The Italian masons had worked on Sam's house in Seattle earlier, and at Stockbridge before that. At one point just east of Multnomah Falls, there was so little room between the railroad and the cliffs that Lancaster designed a concrete viaduct 860 feet long so as " . . . not to disturb the mountain and ruin the trees and flowering shrubs which are so beautiful."

C. H. Moores, motoring editor for *The Oregonian*, fervently promoted an upcoming bond issue for paving Multnomah County's part of the highway through the Gorge. He and a party made the trip by auto to Multnomah Falls and found John Yeon, the only man working that Sunday. Yeon told

---

*Or at least until OPEC took a hand.

Columbia River Highway under construction, April 1914. Note retaining wall. (Photo courtesy of Oregon Historical Society.)

them, "The $600,000 spent on the Columbia River Highway isn't worth a snap of the fingers until it is paved." They were convinced of this on their return trip when they were caught in a deluge of rain. The road became a quagmire, with tire chains needed to get out of the mud, a foot deep in places. They ran out of gas and had three tire punctures to round out a perfect day. As a happy ending, the $1,250,000 paving bond issue was approved in April 1915, and contracts were let two months later. The "Warrenite" pavement, a tarmacadam made of broken stone mixed with asphalt and rolled, cost about $15,000 per mile.

The high point of the road is Crown Point, about 23 miles from Portland, located about 725 feet above the river, commanding a marvelous view of the Gorge. The highway passes alongside some ten beautiful waterfalls located close to the river. Simon Benson gave a 400 acre park to include the most spectacular one, Multnomah Falls, over 900 feet high. The park also includes Wah-Kee-Nah Falls ("most beautiful" in the Indian language), named after the daughter of a Yakima Indian chief. A rock tunnel about 125 feet long was required two miles east of Multnomah Falls.

Criticisms of the project by Lightner and Holbrook continued, and early in 1915 they actually refused to honor Lancaster's salary vouchers. Lancaster therefore quit in April 1915, but by then, fortunately, the engineering work was practically completed.

The Columbia Gorge portion of the highway, 48 miles long, was completed in the summer of 1915. In August, the Columbia Highway through the Coast Range to the sea was ready for travel. Julius Meier, president of the Columbia Highway Association, led a caravan of autos from the Hotel Benson in Portland on August 12. The party set out at 7:00 a.m. and made it to Gearhart on the coast for dinner, at which Sam Hill presented a silver loving cup to John Yeon.

A month later, the highway was opened to Hood River and soon it was possible to drive 363 miles from Seaside to Pendleton in eastern Oregon. Sam was in the party made up of state officials, Lancaster, Benson, Yeon, Meier, and others, who drove from Portland to Hood River. They had to detour around Mitchell Point west of Hood River. A tunnel there, 390 feet long, with five great rock windows cut in the north wall, was completed in late November 1915. H. W. Mitchell, in his Mitchell Six, was the first to drive through the tunnel when it was partially finished. The generous Benson had guaranteed Hood River County that he would pay any deficit over the $75,000 provided by the sale of bonds to complete his work. He was stuck for $13,000 as a result.

The Columbia River Highway was officially dedicated on June 7, 1916, at a ceremony at Multnomah Falls, to coincide with Portland's Rose Festival. Later that afternoon there was a ground-breaking ceremony for Vista House, to be built on Crown Point. President Wilson at the White House pressed a button which unfurled a flag to signal the event. The Rose Festival Queen poured rose petals and loganberry juice* at the site. A bronze plaque at the entrance to Vista House now commemorates Lancaster's role in building the highway.

Although no longer employed by Multnomah County, Lancaster continued to do all he could to protect and publicize his beautiful creation. He campaigned against billboard advertising along the Columbia River Highway. To promote travel on it, he raised money for an exhibit of paintings and enlarged photographs at the Panama-Pacific International Exposition in 1915. The same year, he wrote a history of the Columbia Gorge and its highway which ran to three editions. Portland newspapers urged their readers to send copies of the book to friends and relatives in other parts of the country. He dedicated the book to "Samuel Hill, roadbuilder, who loves this country and brought me to it. Who showed me the German Rhine and

---

* A temperance beverage of the time, which does not seem to have caught on.

The Columbia River Gorge, looking east. Sawmill and Rooster Rock at the lower left, below Crown Point on the right. About 1913. (Maryhill Museum files.)

Continental Europe. Whose kindness made it possible for me to have a part in planning and constructing this great highway."

Lancaster went on to other projects, including designing a scenic highway along the north rim of the Grand Canyon and the park near the site of the Bonneville Dam. Ironically, a large house which belonged to one of Sam's mistresses, reported to have cost $50,000, had to be condemned for the park (Chapter 28).

In 1928, Sam recalled to Lockley, "When the Columbia River Highway was being built and I prophesied that the time would come when, instead of having five- or seven-passenger cars, there would be regular stages and buses, carrying as many as 12 people at a time, to Seattle and to The Dalles and to other points in the state, I was jeered at and called a dreamer and visionary."

In the 1940's the need was evident for a wider highway at river level through the Gorge. Such a route was not feasible in Sam's day, before the introduction of massive road building equipment and massive expenditures of federal money. The first ten mile western segment, the freeway now called 84N, was completed in August 1949. The new route through the Gorge was about six miles shorter than the winding scenic highway and permitted a large volume of high speed traffic.

Segments of the scenic highway between Multnomah Falls and The Dalles, including the dramatic "Rowena Loops," are open today, but the Mitchell Tunnel is closed. Apart from residents who live on it, the "old highway" is traveled mostly by out-of-state tourists, who choose to take

Sam Hill, roadbuilder. (Photo courtesy of Oregon Historical Society.)

time to travel the unique, winding shunpike road with its magnificent views of the Gorge. Some stop for a few minutes at the memorial to Sam Hill, located on a high viewpoint about two miles west of Crown Point. The memorial was dedicated on Sam's birthday, May 13, in 1932, the year following his death. Probably few are aware of the effort, determination, and devotion of Sam Hill and others who made their journey an inspiring one.

PART V

AT HOME AND ABROAD

Chapter 18

Harvard and the Three P's

To relieve at once the curiosity of the reader, the three p's of the title refer to Sam's philosophy, philanthropy, and politics. All three were influenced to some degree by his single year at Harvard: many of his political convictions were no doubt shared by his classmates; his long time efforts on behalf of the college exemplify his philosophy of working full blast for something he believed in; and Harvard was one of the most important of his philanthropies.

In fact, one would be hard put to name anyone who had attended Harvard for only one year but who did as much for the school financially and took such a continuing interest in its affairs as did Sam Hill. A cynic might contend that Sam's efforts on Harvard's behalf reflected his wish to be identified with some of the wealthiest and most influential individuals in the country, and that he was simply an extrovert who loved to talk and mingle with congenial people and be admired by them for his generosity. Perhaps these factors did explain in part his long advocacy of the university, but he felt a genuine bond with all Harvard men, especially with his classmates. He wrote many letters of introduction to his business associates on behalf of Harvard graduates and hired others on his own.

After his graduation in 1879, Sam wasted no time in going to work for Harvard. In that same year, he helped organize the Minnesota Harvard Club and became its first president. He wrote Charles Eliot, president of the university, after attending dinners of the New York and New England Harvard Clubs, of his concern that Yale was making relatively more headway than Harvard in the West and Northwest. "However," he added in a later note, "It may be that Yale men make so much noise that we fear them just as we did the Populists before the election."

In 1897, Eliot asked Sam who could best fill the requirements of a lecturer on railways at Harvard. Sam responded in an eight page handwritten letter whch was practically a lecture itself, proposing William T. Clough, vice-president of the Great Northern Railway, and praising J. J. Hill's methods. Sam's fervent advocacy of instruction in scientific railroading makes one wonder if he would have accepted the post himself had it been offered.

Sam promised to talk to his father-in-law about the proposed lectures. But it was not until 1907 that Professor Taussig of the Department of Economics at Harvard wrote Sam, "We are adding this year a new course on railway practice." He wondered if Sam would approach J. J. Hill for a donation to provide a library on railway subjects, as he had done for the University of Wisconsin. Sam suggested that Harvard give J. J. an honorary degree, but this was not done — an oversight of a wealthy potential contributor which does not often occur today.

Sam had been president of the Minnesota Harvard Club for three years (1896-99) when he was nominated for overseer by the Associated Harvard Clubs, which consisted of several midwestern Harvard groups. He was elected to the Board of Overseers in June 1900, as one of five elected for five-year terms. Only once previously had a Westerner been made an overseer. Sam received more votes than any other candidate. He had to promise to be present at the regular meetings, held four times a year. This was not easy for someone living in distant Seattle who was deeply involved in a business enterprise, the Seattle Gas Company.

In March 1902, Sam was host to thirty Harvard alumni at a dinner and smoker at the Seattle University Club, in its " . . . .handsome rooms . . . appropriately decorated with college colors." Harvard's president, Charles Eliot, had accepted Sam's invitation to be the guest of honor, but later had to decline.

Sam tried again unsuccessfully to persuade Eliot to come west in 1902. He offered to arrange travel in a private railway car, with the help of officers of several railroads. In his letter of invitation, he mentioned President Hadley of Yale, graciously admiring his " . . . frank statement of what Yale wishes to do . . . if it could, take second place to Harvard." Eliot declined the invitation but spoke kindly of Hadley as a " . . . frank and progressive colleague . . . although he sometimes comes to conclusions too quickly."

Sam definitely blundered when he remarked at a meeting of the Associated Harvard Clubs in the fall of 1903 that he had been more faithful in attendance at the Board of Overseers than had President Eliot, who was not about to let this claim go unrefuted. Eliot's secretary countered that the president " . . . was puzzled by your statement." Of fourteen regular meetings held from 1900 through 1903, Sam had attended only nine. Sam had to eat a portion of crow, but explained that one absence was due to an illness of James and others to trips abroad.

As related in Chapter 10, Sam brought a Professor Yamashita from Tokyo to teach judo to his son, James, and his friends, and later encouraged the expert to give lessons at Cambridge. The professor, however, was lured away to instruct midshipmen at Annapolis. Sam did not take kindly to this breach of contract by his protégé; he growled to his friend Bacon, "Your classmate [Theodore Roosevelt] has taken away from Harvard my judo man without my permission or even asking."

In 1904, Sam was asked to address the Harvard Political Club. He received an appreciative letter from Henry James II saying, "We have never had a better meeting at all." In June of that year, Sam presided at the dinner marking the 25th anniversary of the Class of 1879.

Sam gave a number of bequests to Harvard, including $50,000 in bonds, "which J. J. Hill thinks are good bonds," for the Teacher's Endowment Fund early in 1905. He wrote his friend, Robert Bacon again, "I have not any money due to the fact that your classmate [Theodore Roosevelt] has prevented my getting any income for more than a year. . . . However, the fact that we have failed in one instance does not prove that the University is not doing good work. . . . " Other donations were made to the Harvard Riverside Associates, set up to purchase land between the Harvard Yard and the Charles River; the Guaranty Fund; the Harvard exhibit at the St. Louis Fair; $5,000 toward a new stadium; and to various departments, the heads of which had approached him for money. He set up an essay prize contest on the advantages of attending Harvard, to be directed at boys aged 12 to 16. A Cambridge photographer made Sam a set of lantern slides of all the Harvard buildings, along with cartoons depicting student life, which Sam displayed from time to time, and which are now at Maryhill Museum.

In 1905, he wrote his sister-in-law, Gertrude, "I am much swelled up owing to the fact that the Harvard Club of Seattle is giving a banquet in my honor . . . They decided to do this while I was out of town so I can not be accused of instigating it . . . We now have the largest Harvard Club on the Pacific Coast and the Harvard men are coming by stage, on foot, and on horseback." There were probably times when Sam thought each was bound for his door, hat in hand for a job reference or other favor. Even Yale men were sent to him.

Sam's interest in Harvard did not flag in the years after he completed his stint as overseer. He was made the first president of the London Harvard Club in 1913 and addressed the Harvard Club of Tokyo on several visits. He was an active member of several Harvard clubs from New York to Seattle, as well. He was put on the committee to visit the Harvard Library, the chairman of which was Herbert Putnam, his friend from Minneapolis Athenaeum days and now Librarian of Congress.

He entertained Wells, Dean of Harvard, at Seattle and Portland in 1913, and went with him to San Francisco, " . . . as I want James's [his son James Nathan] boss to understand that his poor old father has some standing on the Pacific Coast." James had made it to Harvard after heroic exertions on Sam's part, and it was no doubt a disappointment to his father that he failed to graduate with his class in 1915 because of grades.

If a year at Harvard could inspire this kind of devotion, what would four years have done? Will Rogers said, "Every Harvard class should have one Democrat to rescue it from oblivion." Many an alumni treasurer would settle for one man like Sam per class, whatever his politics!

Philosophy

Sam Hill's philosophy is more truly expressed in his conduct than in his words. If he had a system of principles, he didn't put it in writing, and whatever faith he had he did not express in a creed. One cannot say that he always followed the Golden Rule, nor was he one to turn the other cheek. He was usually tolerant of the conduct and principles of others, but in a selective way. His tolerance did not extend to trade unionists, government bureaucrats, or social radicals of any stripe. He gave voice to anti-Semitic sentiments at times and these feelings, like those of many a clubman of his day, affected his choice of friends, if not his conduct of business. He looked down on Negroes except for his servants, Sam and Sula Finch, whom he regarded highly; it is true they "knew their place." His admiration for Indians was probably limited to the old time chiefs, who exemplified courage, integrity, and the ability to lead, characteristics to which Sam himself aspired.

He was born a Quaker, but the influence of this background seems superficial and certainly not abiding. George Fox bade his followers "tremble at the word of the Lord," and so they came to be called Quakers. Sam was not known to tremble at the word of anyone. He used the Quaker form of address in writing to his relatives and to other Quakers, but by middle age he had gradually dropped this mode. A lecture given by a Quaker minister at Guilford, N.C., inspired him to establish a Quaker settlement at Maryhill, Washington — an idea he soon had to abandon because of the discouraging response. Apparently he was not a regular church goer except in his youth. Part of his heritage, however, was knowledge of the Bible, especially the Old Testament, from which he liked to quote in his letters, usually to make some humorous point. He does not speak of an afterlife except in this vein. His real convictions about the Almighty are, in fact, not discernible and the author has chosen not to list Him amongst Sam's famous friends.

UnQuaker-like, he resorted to belligerency in business, exemplified in the "gas warfare" in Seattle and in the losing battle with the Bell Telephone Company in Portland. He was not a pacifist, as manifested by his anti-German sentiments in World War I. Sympathetic as he was to the Russian people, late in life he considered the Soviet government an implacable, and even personally dangerous, foe.

Neither friends nor relatives voiced misgivings about the mixed marriage when Sam and Mary Hill, a Catholic, were wed. However, the usual promises to bring up any children of the union as Catholics and not to interfere with his family's religious observances were no doubt obtained. In 1910, when Mrs. J. J. Hill brought suit for custody of Sam's daughter, the ostensible reason was that she wanted to have her educated in Catholic schools. Sam denied any implication that he may have interfered with this intent, and in fact, both in St. Paul and in Seattle, he had been both friendly and generous with a number of the Catholic heirarchy. His wife probably had something to do with these friendships; at least his contacts with the white collar workers of the Catholic church mostly ceased when he entered business in Portland in 1909.

He was friendly with Bishop James McGolnich, mentioned in Chapter 4. McGolnich recalled the " . . . pleasant remembrance that we met in Rome and stormed the Vatican so outrageously." He had sent Sam's wife a little lamp from Pompeii and a " . . . little work of art in ivory from Rome . . . " when he asked Sam to beg a pass for him on the Great Northern from J. J. Hill.

Sam was also friendly with Archbishop Ireland of St. Paul, whom he helped bail out of difficulties in an archdiocesan land purchase. Sam told Barron that the Italian cardinals were " . . . rather against Archbishop Ireland," and Sam did what he could to get his friend a red hat. Bellamy Storer, ambassador in turn to Belgium, Spain, and Austria-Hungary, had received a letter from Theodore Roosevelt who hoped that Ireland, who had helped T. R. politically, would be elevated by the Pope. Storer asked Sam to arrange a dinner with Cardinal Mercier of Belgium and Albert, then Crown Prince. Storer went to Rome with Mercier full of hope, which, anticlimactically, proved unfounded.

Sam was under no obligation to follow the dictates of the Vatican, but as an American, resented the domination of the church in America by Italian cardinals. "I've waited patiently ten years for some recognition on behalf of the church with the great men who lead it in the United States," he wrote in 1905, after three cardinals had been picked from other countries, but none from America. "Frankly and bluntly, it occurs to me that the church in Rome is being run as a political machine, to perpetuate the power of a certain clique in Rome . . . The revenues of the church derived from the United States are second on the list. I do not find that Italy can or does make any great contribution to the revenues of the church [and] one might ask for a voice in the spending of that revenue." This kind of businessman's approach to the selection of cardinals is still heard today.

After Sam moved to Seattle, his prosperity and Catholic wife made him a natural target for a contribution to building a cathedral there. In 1907, he asked Archbishop Ireland to come from St. Paul to dedicate it. He invited his friend Monsignor O'Connell, later a bishop at Richmond, Virginia, to come from San Francisco to give the invocation at the first American Congress of Roadbuilders on July 4, 1909. He had met a Monsignor Antonini in Rome, and from time to time sent friends to him with letters of introduction. It was probably Antonini who showed him places Sam later talked to Barron about: " . . . things underground that nobody outside the church knows the existence of — churches in Rome a hundred feet underground. Indeed, one of the original watchtowers on the walls of Romulus and Remus is perfectly preserved underground. Even the key to the entrance of these places is not kept in Rome. If the Italian Government knew the existence of these things they would seize them for antiquarian and research purposes."

What were Sam's real convictions? He told Lockley, "Good roads are more than my hobby; they are my religion." Through promoting them he unselfishly aided his fellow man; in this regard, he could not be accused of "doing well by doing good."* It is true that a highway on the north bank of the Columbia, for which he campaigned, would have brought visitors to Maryhill had the road been completed in Sam's lifetime. But his efforts for good roads and promotion of tourism began long before 1917 when he decided to found a museum, and continued until Sam was an old man.

---

* As did "the old dope peddler" in Tom Lehrer's song.

If a single phrase can sum up Sam's reason for being, "hard work and dreams" does as well as any. There is abundant evidence for both dreams and a workaholic personality in his career. He usually slept six hours and got up at 5 a.m. He wrote a young lawyer, "I do not believe in vacations. I do believe in change of occupation. . . . There's nothing to me harder in the world than to try to 'vacate.' It produces a condition of mind very closely allied to insanity whenever I try it." Apparently Sam was not considering his trips around the world and many visits to Europe to be vacations, and indeed, he nearly always had good roads or some other project in view on his expeditions.

Sam tended to be sententious on such favorite subjects as making good use of one's time and resources, and the importance of sturdy, happy farmers in the economy. His weakness for punditry and preaching when a reporter was within earshot does not seem to have been discouraged by the press of his day. For him, money was a fool's goal. At age 58 he told Lockley, "I have come to the conclusion, valuable as money is, the most precious commodity we have is time. The longer you live the more you appreciate how exceedingly brief one's span of life is and how much there is to do. I haven't much sympathy with a man whose highest conception of life is . . . to make money. I long ago came to the conclusion that money was only a means to an end. The real value of time is in the ability it gives you to be of service to humanity. . . . Strong nations have their roots in the soil. The only way for our country to grow and thrive is to get the people back on the land. We must keep more of them from becoming parasites in the city. We must make more of them producers in the country . . . [by making] the country desirable." This could be done, Sam said, by giving them good roads, good mail and telephone service, and education in farming. In a similar vein, he told a reporter that once a young man had been assured how best he could make a living, the next question was how to make best use of his life. One wonders how Sam, at the end of his life, would have graded his own answer to the question.

Sam himself was not one to put down roots in the soil. One did not often catch him down on the farm except when he had to tend to business at Maryhill. And while he frequently espoused the Protestant work ethic, the same can scarcely be said for thrift and other simple virtues of the poor.

Surely Sam intended to be a good husband and father. The reasons for his shortcomings in either respect can only be guessed at, because he guarded his private life strictly. In middle age, he had affairs with at least three women by whom he had illegitimate children. Whether things would have been different if his wife had divorced him so he could have remarried, one can only conjecture.

Sam believed in the virtue of competition in business, or at least in making a virtue of the necessity of competition. "The secret of efficiency, to my mind," he told Lockley, "is system organization and competition." Mind you, that did not preclude striving to overcome the opposition, sometimes by questionable methods, as he did with his gas and telephone companies. Surrender to the Bell monopoly must have been an especially bitter pill for him to choke down. It is hard to commend competition unless your competitor believes in it, too.

In the same interview, he named J. J. Hill and several other tycoons, "graduates of the 'University of Hard Knocks'" who had not had a college education. "I have employed and fired a lot of college graduates," he said, "and I have employed and promoted a lot of men who had a minimum of education but a maximum of energy, horse sense, and loyalty." He did not imply that it was downright deleterious to graduate from Harvard and marry the boss's daughter.

Philanthropy

Many of Sam's good works are mentioned in other chapters: the gift of at least $5,000 for Belgian war relief; endowment of chairs in road-building in 1908 and in the Russian language at the University of Washington in 1916; gifts for Professor Edmond Meany's projects; substantial donations to Harvard and later to Phillips Exeter Academy, where his son James was enrolled; and the major monuments of the Peace Arch, the Stonehenge replica, and Maryhill Museum. By acquiring all of the stock of the Minneapolis Athenaeum Company, he was able to transfer its land and a large collection of books to the Minneapolis Foundation (Chapter 4).

He did his bit for the Quakers, also, making a contribution of $5,000 to the Guilford College endowment fund in 1901 and "several thousand dollars" to the construction of New Garden Hall at Guilford. He gave $5,000 to his first alma mater, Haverford College, in 1903. With Hervey Lindley and R. H. Stuart of the Carnation Company, he contributed money to build the Puget Sound Quarterly Meeting House of Friends in Seattle. In their long conversation in 1920, Paul Douglas says that Sam told him he wanted to establish a Quaker college in Seattle with Douglas as its president; Douglas declined.

Though large, these donations do not compare in magnitude with those Sam made to the good roads movement. Apart from the $100,000 or so he laid out on construction of experimental roads at Maryhill, he must have spent a staggering amount on travel to meetings in the United States and abroad, and on the preparation of slides to show at hundreds of meetings.

Nor did he stint on aiding people in unfortunate circumstances. Often, Sam made loans which he knew would not be repaid. One such "loan" was in response to a pathetic letter from a minister who had never earned more than $600 a year, who asked Sam for a loan of $60.

The invitations to contribute which Sam turned down would easily fill a page, but one of the wilder ones will suffice. A man wrote that Blessed Theresa had appeared to him, with Mrs. J. J. Hill and Dr. Richard Hill, to direct him to form an order of priests whose prime mission was to " . . . fight perverted immorality amongst the younger generation." He needed a loan of $500,000 immediately and later planned to raise $11,000,000 for this purpose. Sam's reply is not preserved; it may be that he considered the sum totally inadequate.

Politics

Sam was a political animal, a gregarious, persuasive extrovert with an ability to conceive and organize great projects. The wonder is that he did not try for state or national offices. His friend Hepburn, vice-president of the Chase National Bank, probably was only half kidding when he wrote in 1902, "If you expect to become president of the United States, as of course you do — we all know you do — [you must] lay the foundation for your presidential boom . . . Kindly try to remember that your humble servant was one of the first to contribute in paving your way to greatness. Try to save for him, as a souvenir, some second class post office."

His activities as a young lawyer pointed the way early to a political career. He was president of the Young Men's Garfield and Arthur Club of Minneapolis in the campaign of 1879. (Garfield was assassinated in July 1880 and Chester Arthur served out the term.) His friendships with prominent Harvard men of the time and his national reputation as a good roads advocate would have been helpful in politics. Instead, the only political campaign in which he was a candidate was a humble one, that for the Klickitat County representative for the Washington State Republican Convention in May 1912. He was proud to say that he received every vote cast.

Why did Sam not try to become a U.S. senator or representative? He admitted, "My long association with the railroads has probably barred me from [public affairs.]" He expressed a distinct distaste for Washington, D.C., also, notably in a 1912 letter to James: "I do not think you quite understand my extreme distaste and dislike for the city of Washington . . . . The moment I land there they have scouts out at the depot, not only for me, but everybody else that comes to the town; they then promptly rush to the house to borrow money. I regard Washington as a town containing but three classes of people; Negroes, clerks, and grafters. Of course there are a few nice people there, but I did not vote for Taft. I did vote for Wilson. I helped the electorate to elect the Democrat, Mr. Lister, as Governor of Washington to succeed Mr. Hay. . . . I do not care to go to Washington and be told to make way for Paymaster Merriam, wretched little Jack Merriam." The fact that his estranged wife lived there then was an unadmitted, but possibly important, factor in this outburst.

One wonders, too, if plain restlessness did not prevent Sam from pursuing a career filled with much boring routine, and whether even being a U.S. senator could have held his interest or absorbed all of his energies. This does not imply that he wold have been a shoo-in as a candidate; he did not by any means charm all the people in Washington and Oregon important to a politician's advancement.

His interest in state and national politics began early in his career. He told Fred Lockley, "When I was 21 years of age, I was at the head of the Republican Party in Minnesota." His feud with General Washburn, a Minnesota politician, carried over to Washburn's son during Queen Marie's visit many years later (Chapter 25). Sam professed, "Personally, I am a Republican and desire the election of Republicans; but others of the Great Northern Board are not of the same political faith, so that as far as I know, the G.N never takes sides with any party in politics." He did not add that nevertheless it knew how and when to reward its friends.

He had met Judge Thomas Burke before he moved to Seattle, and favored Burke's election to the Senate in 1896, despite Burke's Democratic affiliation. He recommended a lawyer of Norwegian descent who would make campaign speeches in either English or Norwegian on Burke's behalf. In writing to a friend about Burke's defeat, he reflected piously, "It seems strange that men will seek after office and honors, which after all is a form of selfishness, because it is not always from a desire to render a public service but rather a desire for personal glory." Otherwise, he seldom went to bat in political campaigns. In 1902 he asked Sen. Mark Hanna (Ohio) to use his considerable influence to get W. Cameron Forbes appointed to the Panama Canal Commission. Later, Forbes helped to sell Sam the estate at Stockbridge, not exactly an even exchange of favors.

Sam was personally friendly but politically opposed to Ignatius Donnelly, the Minnesota Populist, who advocated the nationalization of railroads, an end to the tariff on wheat, and an increase in the money supply. Donnelly once complained, in a remark borrowed by more than one stand-up comedian, that the Minnesota legislature " . . . was the best that money could buy." Sam was in agreement with him about the appointment of a certain imcompetent bank examiner. He wrote Donnelly that it would not help if he (Sam) remonstrated with the Governor; "Just now a cloud seems to have arisen and shut out from my view the illuminated countenance of the chief executive of the state."

In 1897-98, Sam was a member of the executive committee of the Indianapolis Monetary Convention, an organization in favor of bimetalism, or parity between gold and silver, as a backing for currency. In that day, the old fashioned idea prevailed that currency should have some sort of backing.

Sam backed McKinley in 1900, but never liked Teddy Roosevelt who succeeded him. Roosevelt's trustbusting activities, witness the dissolution of the Northern Securities Co., did not endear him to Sam. If T. R. took notice at all, the feeling was probably mutual because of Sam's previous connections with the Great Northern. Sam wrote, "When he gets through being president I am going to take a trip east to tell him what I think of him. . . . You do not know what command of the English language I have when I am thoroughly aroused."

In 1903 he growled to Herbert Putnam, chairman of Harvard's Library Committee, "I had expected to make a contribution of considerable size to the library this year, but the attitude of President Roosevelt toward invested capital put it out of my power for some years. . . . I sometimes wonder if he knows what he is doing." Near the end of his next term, he wrote to his friend Edgar, "How much longer must we endure 'tackhead Teddy?.

... This period in history will be known as the Roosevelt hunger period. . . . I know the common people are with him, the unthinking people, but when their stomachs have been empty for awhile, they will return to the fleshpots. . . . " He gloomily predicted, "There can be no permanent improvement in the attitudes for the railroads here for at least two years . . . there have been 'Rosenfeldts' sown like dragons' teeth all over the United States . . . but of course the fever must run its course and until Roosevelt is out of office the United States, in my opinion, will not be a safe place to make investments. . . . " In the spring of 1908, when there seemed to be a possibility Roosevelt would be renominated, he wrote, "If they nominate Roosevelt, me to Canada. I am near to the line here and have established friends on the other side and I'm carefully looking up the extradition treaties. I understand the remarks made in one sovereign territory against another are not extraditable, so I can get over there and call him everything I think of — and I think of a good many things during the day."

The nomination of Taft in 1908 was even worse in Sam's view. He wrote Gavin, his brother-in-law, "I believe the election of Taft more dangerous to the country than that of Roosevelt, and I prefer . . . Bryan to either, because with the Republican Senate, Bryan could not do the harm that Roosevelt and Taft will and can do." He concluded that "Rooseveltism has not yet been killed off. . . . If I were a czar and had control of the business of the country, I would absolutely quit and go on a farm until Rooseveltism and Bryanism were thoroughly dead." It seems safe to conclude that Sam took presidential politics very seriously.

Even after he left the railroads, Sam plumped for their political interests from time to time. He was, after all, a substantial stockholder and these efforts were not entirely disinterested. He was against giving real power to the Washington State Railroad Commission, for example. In writing in 1902 about a candidate with the same conviction, he could say humorously, "He was willing to sacrifice himself for the railroads. Not being a direct descendant of Isaac and having no knife ready, and not representing the railroads, I thought it best to spare his life."

Sam's ultraconservatism extended to trade unions. His sentiments against hiring union men are discussed in "Seattle and Gas Warfare." But he took some comfort that " . . . the curse of unionism has not touched the farmer or lumbering people." Paul Douglas notes that in 1920, Sam, knowing Douglas' labor sympathies, told him that he " . . . had been one of the Northwest leaders of the Knights of Labor" early in his career. The author could not find corroboration of this; if true, Sam had a change of heart after he became an employer.

Sam's most successful impact on political matters was in the field of good roads, notably in helping to frame model laws passed by the Washington legislature and in coordinating efforts to complete the Columbia River Highway in the remarkably short span of two years. He began a campaign for regulation of motor trucks on highways in the year before his death.

At first, Sam was a supporter of Woodrow Wilson, president from 1913 to 1921. He turned against him after World War I, but the reason is not clear from his letters. In 1923, he intended to write a book critical of Wilson but did not do so (Chapter 26). He told Joffre, drolly, "After its publication, I may have to leave the U.S., so please keep a place for me there in France."

Sam's political acumen did not increase in later life. He wrote President Harding in 1922 expressing support and noting Harding was " . . . facing difficulties which were second only to those which President Lincoln faced." Perhaps a comparison with those of U. S. Grant would have been more apropos.

Sam did not live to see the election of F. D. Roosevelt; if he had he might have been carried off by apoplexy instead of an abdominal infection. He was not so black a Republican as to support all the members of that faith, but he did not fail to be enraged when he discerned the faintest hue of red.

19

The Globetrotter and his Japanese Scrapbook

There must be many reasons for a person to aspire to becoming a world traveler. Some writers, scientists, diplomats, and businessmen are paid for it. Insatiable curiosity or crashing boredom may motivate others. Some who call travel a hobby are rewarded by one-upping their poorer or more timid acquaintances.

Sam Hill was a world traveler, all right, and for each of his many trips he could no doubt supply a plausible reason. Some of his fifty European ventures involved attendance at good roads congresses or observation of road building or visits to famous friends. In the case of Japan, he went primarily as an evangelist for good roads. On his three trips to Russia, he traveled successively as tourist, railroad observer, and transportation expert (Chapters 7 and 20). But from these constant peregrinations one gets the impression of a profound restlessness, amounting to compulsiveness, akin to his passion for building a wide range of structures, from a cottage for his daughter at Maryhill to his Peace Arch at Blaine. These kinds of obsessions raise again the question of the presence of a hypomanic state, which in the 1920's would escalate into a full-fledged problem.

Sam even had a sort of personal trademark for his penchant, to use a non-pejorative word for travel—that of preparing and presenting world globes to friends and institutions.

It is likely that Sam had seen and admired the globes, 80 cm. in diameter, in Germany after his trip across Siberia in 1901. He had more than two dozen of them made to order for him by Dietrich Reimer, Berlin, a publisher of geographies and nautical charts.

Sam's orders began in February 1902. Reimer agreed to add the connecting routes of the transcontinental American railroads and the soundings of West Coast harbors, the latter data to be furnished by the U.S. War Department.

During the next ten years, Sam ordered batches of these globes for friends in railroad, banking and shipping circles, notably James J. Hill; Baron Kondo, President of N.Y.K. Lines; and William H. Porter of the Chemical National Bank, New York. Others went to educational institutions, including Phillips Exeter and Harvard, and to several clubs to which Sam belonged, including the Arlington Club of Portlad, the University Club of Seattle, and the Cosmos Club of Washington, D.C. One went to Thomas Edison and another to Justice White of the U.S. Supreme Court. He cautioned one recipient, F. D. Underwood, president of the Erie Railroad, to be careful in assembling the globe, noting that, "It is all there, but it is like a watch and you may have something left over after you get it together."

Sam got a reduction in price for the first five globes, his bill amounting to 1,350 marks. Thereafter, he added so much data to the globes from year to year that their cost rose from about $250.00 to $400.00 by the time war began in 1914 and the globes became unobtainable.

The Chief Signal Officer of the U.S. War Department obliged Sam by sending him the harbor sounding data of major Pacific ports, a map of telegraph lines in the Philippines, and submarine cable connections of the world. Sam sent Reimer other additions and corrections for the globes from time to time. He complained that Seattle should be in larger letters because of its rank as the largest port on the Pacific Coast next to San Francisco. He wanted the steamship lines of the Pacific Coast and Alaska Steamship Companies shown, along with the location of several cities in Alaska and the railroad to Dawson. He hoped Reimer would label the globes with English words instead of German. He insisted on the inclusion of at least the high and low harbor soundings of various Asiatic and West Coast harbors. "It will not be difficult to put on these soundings . . . and put them on such part of the globe where there is no land . . . If you have all these soundings from the U.S. Government charts, you may proceed at once," he instructed Reimer. At the time, Sam was the only American member of the Geographic Society of Germany, which may have impressed the map maker.

Reimer did not object to putting the Seattle harbor data on a sidemap in the Pacific, adding, with Germanic thoroughness, 'If this place [Seattle] is represented in a larger scale and with the soundings, this is because you yourself are staying at this place. On the other hand, it will not be under-

Sam Hill with globe. (Photo courtesy of Oregon Historical Society.)

stood why the other harbors you mention should be placed on the globe while more important harbors do not appear."

At Sam's request, Kondo directed N.Y.K. ships to record the surface and subsurface water temperatures " . . . when any occasion arises for them to stop at sea . . . with a view to determining the direction of ocean currents." In the later globes, isothermal lines and population figures were added.

Sam liked to use the globe to bring home facts often overlooked. He told columnist Fred Lockley this story:

> J. J. Hill, Admiral George Dewey, John F. Stevens and myself had just finished dinner. I had one of my large globes in my library, and walking back to it, I told Jim Hill to put his hand on the equator, and I told John to revolve the globe very slowly. As it passed around, I had them notice the amount of earth area south of the equator. When they discovered that less than five percent of the population of the entire globe is south of the equator they were absolutely astonished. Taking Admiral Dewey's hand, I placed it over another small place

on the globe including the British Islands, part of Europe and Norway and Sweden and told them that nine-tenths of all the manufacturing in the world was taking place under his hand, which also was an astonishing fact to them.

Sam considered ordinary atlases deceptive as compared with globes. As he told Barron during their long talks aboard the S.S. Olympic in May 1921, "One of the troubles in this world is that people do not know that this world is round. They are improperly educated to it by flat maps on Mercator's projection. Most of the congressmen that voted to build the Panama canal did not know where it was. They did not know that it was in the longitude of Pittsburgh. Dewey was surprised when I asked him to tell me which ship would arrive at Seattle first — the *Oregon* from Panama Canal or a similar warship from Yokahama. He was astonished to find that Yokahama was a day nearer than the Panama Canal."

It is easy to understand Sam's fascination for globes and other maps. He was an indefatigable world traveler from the time of his first trip to Europe in 1881 until late in life. News stories noted that he had gone around the world seven times. He crisscrossed the United States innumerable times. One could almost conclude that he had time to read nothing but railroad and steamship schedules and financial reports!

When interviewed after Sam's death, Sam Finch, Hill's butler-valet-cook, told a reporter of a special sort of suitcase " . . . made by the dozens and completely outfitted with evening clothes, business suits, golfing costumes, shoes, neckties and shaving apparel. These he placed in leading clubs and hotels throughout the world. When he traveled, he carried only a little black bag. For a change of clothing and linen he depended on these suitcases, placed at strategic points along his route."

Sam's extravagant habit of presenting globes to people and institutions important to him deserves comment. Sometimes, as in the instance of his gift to Phillips Exeter Academy when his son was in attendance, there probably was a quid pro quo intention. Subconsciously, the gifts may have been a symbol of possession and control of the earth: call it megalomania if you will, but at least he was willing to share the feeling. His frequent modifications of the globes to show changes in means of travel and communications imply the hope of manageability of a planet then not too large for one man's knowledge to encompass. But above all, the globes were princely gifts, and gifts from princes have been known to reflect the esteem of the donor for himself rather than for the grateful recipient.

A Japanese Scrapbook

One of Sam's favorite spots on the globe was Japan. The account that follows of several of his trips there is not a systematic compilation because there is little or no information about some of his earlier visits.

A Japanese newspaper noted in 1922, "Altogether, Hill has made nine trips to Japan, the first being around the year 1897, the 30th year of Meiji reign." Sam's long love affair with Japan began with that visit. J. J. Hill had sent Captain James Griffith to Japan in 1896 to invite the Nippon Yusen Kaisha Line to establish service to Seattle and so to connect with his Great Northern. The first N.Y.K. ship was welcomed in Seattle that summer.

At the turn of the century, Sam shared with his father-in-law the conviction that there were prospects for lucrative trade and opportunities for investment in the Orient. J. J. Hill founded his own shipping firm for this purpose, the Great Northern Steamship Company, in August 1900. He had completed building two great cargo ships of 28,000 tons each at New London, Connecticut, the *Dakota* and the *Minnesota* in 1904. Sam had attended the launching of the *Minnesota* the previous year. The ships were completed in time to send supplies to Japan during the Russo-Japanese war. However, the large ships were hard to navigate; the *Dakota* sank in March 1907, after hitting a rock in Tokyo Bay. Both the Harriman and Hill interests decided to abandon the pursuit of markets in the Orient when they had to eliminate preferential freight rates in the U.S. (Chapter 5).

In 1922, Sam recalled his first trip, telling the *Tokyo Times* reporter, "25 years ago I brought to Japan a message of greeting and good will and an assurance that the city of Seattle, now the gateway to the Far East, and, we hope, the best loved American city in Japan, wished Japan's friendship and trade." In 1901, he had hitched a ride from Vladivostok to Yokahama on the French battleship *Guerin* and visited Tokyo, as related in Chapter 7.

Sam admired the Japanese, at least those in the upper stratum whom he met, and vice versa. One can imagine the charisma this tall, impressive, confident, gray-haired man had for the Japanese. They may well have pictured him as a model of the western capitalist and industrialist to emulate in fulfilling their destiny. In the twenty-five years between his first visit and his last, Sam saw Japan come of age in the eyes of the Western world. Its victory in the Russo-Japanese war of 1904-1905 was an effective attention-getting device. Japan's painless participation in World War I and remarkable economic development led to achievement of world power status by the time of the Versailles Peace Treaty in 1919. The Japanese were not dragged, they rushed into the 20th century. They wanted to learn from the West, and Sam Hill helped so far as promotion of better roads and city streets was concerned. On his several visits, he met some of Japan's most prominent politicians and businessmen. Mrs. Yoshinari, who helped the author to research Sam's visits to Japan, wrote, "The list reads like a 'Who's Who' of the men who formulated and implemented the ground work of Japan's westernization."

Sam conducted an active correspondence with Japanese businessmen and officials who had become his friends, and entertained them from time to time in Seattle. Probably the first of the visitors was Marquis Masayoshi Matsukata, former premier and minister of finance, who had floated Japan's first war bonds in the war with Russia. Sam entertained him and his party in 1902.

For years, Sam corresponded with Rampei Kondo (later a baron), president of the Nippon Yusen Kaisha Steamship Lines. In 1902, Kondo wrote to ask if Sam could put in a word with J. J. Hill to place two of his protégés in a position to learn American railroading. Sam addressed letters of introduction to Kondo and other Japanese for a number of Americans visiting Japan on business or as tourists. Kondo was one of the first recipients of one of Sam's famous globes and to return the favor, he had his ship captains record surface and subsurface water temperature on their crossings " . . . with a view to determining the direction of ocean currents." Sam wrote, "I know that the Nippon Yusen Kaisha have got a strong hold on the water and I wanted, by sending you this globe, to show you that there was quite a piece of the world which does not yet belong to you."

Kondo was probably taken aback by Sam's proposal in 1905 that with the N.Y.K. Company, he organize a " . . . large corporation to do an express, transportation, banking, forwarding and commission business between Asia, Australia, Alaska, and America." Kondo politely bowed out: "The details of such an enterprise are so complicated and its general program involves so much that is quite novel, that I am unable to make any intelligent forecast. . . . It is very possible that my want of immediate appreciation arises from the failure to follow clearly the lines on which you propose to work."*

Sam was so impressed with the art of judo that he wanted his son James to learn it from an expert, Professor Yamashita of the University of Tokyo. He arranged for the transportation of the Professor and his wife to America in 1903, as related in Chapter 10.

With the help of his friend Walter Oakes, Sam helped to organize the Asiatic Association in Seattle in 1902. At the invitation of the Japanese Consul there, he attended a number of receptions and dinners in honor of the birthday of the emperor. The invitation for the reception of November 3, 1905 read, "In commemoration of the peace recovery," a delicate reference to the recent unpleasantness with Russia.

Unfortunately, no information is at hand about Sam's 1912 visit. He apparently stopped in Japan only briefly enroute to Vladivostok in 1916 to pick up an emergency passport at the U.S. Embassy.

In December 1918, *The Far East,* a weekly publication in English, reported on " . . . the first good roads meeting ever held in Japan. . . when Mr. Samuel Hill of Seattle gave a good roads dinner to his Japanese friends, under the auspices of Baron Shibusawa and Baron Kondo at the Banker's Club. . . . Never before in the history of the interchange between America and Japan has there been a clearer or more important message — that of solid highways so that the people, the humble and weak as well as the rich and powerful, may be benefitted." Among Sam's sixteen guests were the mayor of Tokyo and the ministers of communications and of agriculture and commerce. The bill of fare featured oysters a la Seattle; Columbia River salmon; peaches a la Sam Hill, and Washington honey candy.

Sam proudly showed lantern slides of the Columbia River Highway

---

*Translation: "Hold on a minute, Sam!"

and other scenic views of the Pacific Northwest. He told his audience, "Twenty years ago I got the idea of beauty in Japan; it remained with me and I never forgot. . . . I have brought out the seed planted twenty years ago." He pointed out the need for highways if Japan were ever to attract tourists. He had not seen "one single high road in all Japan,' he said, but rather, rickshaw men and farmers pulling carts and bearing burdens on roads "unfit even to walk upon." Someone asked him if he would like to own an automobile in Japan. "No! Rather give me a boat!" he said.

But he did not want them to think the problems of financing and building highways were insuperable; after all, Seattle had put in over 200 miles of paved streets in less than twenty years. Considering that Japan imported only 1,650 automobiles in 1918, his listeners probably doubted that an auto tax would go far to help Tokyo catch up.

Sam recommended forming a good roads association and suggested Matsukata as president and Kondo and several others as officers. If they agreed, Sam said he would " . . . gladly take up the office of technical advisor gratuitously." Sam escaped without having to make good on this promise. His talk was very well received, and Sam left his slides in Tokyo to help further the cause of good roads. Soon afterward, he left for Manchuria, returning to Japan at Christmas time and leaving for Belgium early in 1919.

When Sam returned to Japan in April 1920, he found that a "Japan Road Improvement Association" had indeed been formed. As president of the Pacific Highway Association, he intended to publicize the dedication of the Peace Portal at Blaine, Washington, scheduled for September 1921. While in Tokyo, he wrote letters of invitation to the Premier of Australia and certain officials in the Far East. Oddly, one was addressed to General Chai, military governor of Quan Tung Province. We do not know the General's reply, much less his thoughts on receipt of this invitation.

Sam stayed at the Imperial Hotel in Tokyo for several weeks and visited Nikko, Osaka, and Kondo's country estate. A Miss Alice Barton and her maid came over with Sam and J. C. Potter, one of Sam's associates in the now defunct Home Telephone Company. She joined her cousin, Lt. Arnal, in Tokyo.

The F. A. Vanderlip* party was visiting Japan at the same time, but for some reason, Sam took pains not to be associated with them, referring to Vanderlip as " . . . the very disagreeable reformer."

Sam gave a dinner for the Harvard Club of Tokyo and was host for another dinner at the Idaten Club. But the most impressive social occasion of his 1920 visit was the large farewell banquet he gave at the Imperial Hotel, attended by many of Japan's best known businessmen and politicians. Sam preserved the guest list, and Mrs. Yoshinari kindly has provided the information for the thumbnail sketches of the most prominent guests given below.

---

*Frank A. Vanderlip (1864-1937), banker, editor, author of articles on the political and financial problems of Europe. Just what he wanted to reform in Japan and why Sam disliked him are not clear.

In the guest house of the Toyo Steamship Co., *Shiunkaku* (House of Purple Clouds), 1922. Asano and Keiko are seated between Sam and the Joffres; Baron Shibusawa and Mrs. Asano on the right; Baron Soichiro and Bunjiro standing. (From glass slide, Maryhill Museum files.)

The Japanese peerage system was in effect from 1884 until it was abolished by the U.S. Government of Occupation after World War II. The five ranks of nobles included some of the descendants of emperors and feudal lords, and subjects who had made important contributions to Japan's modern political and business life:

Asano Soichiro (Baron)

Developed Asano Cement Co. and other enterprises, including Toyo Steamship Co.

Hara Kei (Premier)

Former minister to China, of telecommunication, and of interior; assassinated during second premiership.

Kaneko Kentaro (Viscount, later Count)

Harvard law degree. Helped draft first Japanese constitution. Held several ministerial posts and was president of Japan-American Society.

Kato Takaaki (Baron)

Mitsubishi and N.Y.K. executive; former ambassador to England, foreign minister, and premier (died in office in 1924). Was president of the newspaper *Nichi Nichi*.

Kondo Rempei (Baron)	President of N.Y.K.
Matsukata Masayoshi (Marquis)	Former minister of finance. Floated Japan's first war bonds in the Russo-Japanese War.
Okura Kishichiro (Baron)	Established Okura Trading Co., which owned the Imperial Hotel and other businesses.
Saigo Yoshinosuke (Marquis)	Banker, industrialist, member of House of Peers.
Shibusawa Eiichi (Baron, later Viscount)	Traveled in Europe before the Meiji restoration; became finance minister, founder of Daiichi Industrial Bank and many other enterprises. Involved in the industrial development of Korea, trade with China, and education within Japan.
Tokonami Takejairo	Minister of the interior.
Uchida Yasuya (Viscount, later Count)	Foreign minister in several cabinets, member of the House of Peers; ex-president of South Manchurian Railroad.
Yamagata Aritomo (Prince)	General of the Army in Russo-Japan War; former minister of justice and of the interior; former premier.

Mayor T. Fukii of Tokyo thanked Sam for making " . . . propaganda for the reformation of roads of Japan. Really, all the Japanese have been awakened by your speech and it seems that the reformation will be brought into concrete form* very soon."

He also proposed to the major of Osaka a memorial for Sam, " . . . according to your speech, to build your statue made of Japanese clay of about one foot high and of some five dollars worth, on the corner of the new road which we actually built under your advice by your engineer." The *New Yorker* magazine would no doubt have assigned this tribute to their "Mysterious East Department."

Enroute to Japan, Sam had written a note congratulating the ship's chief steward on the good food and service, and added, "Possibly you do not know that I am something of a cook myself, but my name is on menu cards in the cities of New York and Paris for dishes I myself have invented."

---

*Was this a none too inscrutable pun?

On the voyage home on the *Suma Maru* in May 1920,* Sam thought it prudent to write a letter to Baron Kondo, president of the steamship line, to explain a late party in the smoking room, following an impromptu entertainment by the passengers.Some of the missionaries aboard had expressed shock and dismay the following morning. "Many of the ladies, except the missionaries, went with us, and many amusing songs were sung," Sam said. He made it clear that no one was intoxicated and that " . . . some of the men who sang did not drink at all." He added, "If I were the power in the Japanese government I would make all other people keep their missionaries at home."

After his return to the United States in 1920, Sam wrote an article on good roads for Japan at the request of the editor of *Trans-Pacific* magazine. He seized the opportunity to take a swipe at the Soviet government, decrying its attempt to "set aside brains." He admired the railway and water transportation systems of Japan, but deplored its lack of highways. He cautioned his readers about the need for employing bona fide experts in road building: "There is no reason now why Japan should not profit by the experience and by the mistakes of other nations."

Sam returned to Japan for the last time in January 1922, with the impressive credential as Honorary Commercial Commissioner of the Seattle Chamber of Commerce. His prime intention was to meet Marshall Joffre as part of their round-the-world trip and escort him through China and Korea and then to the U.S., where Joffre was to rededicate Sam's Peace Portal at Blaine, Washington. The reporter said of Sam " . . . [He] has come to the Orient so often he is probably better known here than any other American." Another newsman noted that Sam was limping because of an accident which occurred in October 1921, when he fell down an elevator shaft,** resulting in " . . . severe bruises and sprains and he still walks with difficulty. . . . With Mr. Hill is Mr. Ralph Earle of the Pathé Company . . . . During the visit of Marshall Joffre, he will take reels of pictures which will be added to an ambitious motion picture which is being prepared under Mr. Hill's direction illustrating highlights in American history which mark the cementing of friendship between the United States and other lands." (Sam's movie making ventures are described in Chapter 26. So far as is known, the footage taken in Japan does not survive.)

On this visit, Uchida, minister of foreign affairs, forwarded to him " . . . the insignia of Third Class Order of the Sacred Treasure," conferred by the Emperor " . . . in appreciation of the inestimable services you have rendered for many years past in the cause of friendship between Japan and America." In reply, Sam professed surprise and pleasure, without, of course, commenting that he was not used to the third class of anything.

---

*Miss Barton had sailed home earlier. In July 1923, Sam wrote Loie Fuller, "I am waiting to hear from you about Maryhill. Are you coming? If so, when? I have finished with Alice Barton and naturally she will not like it."

**The mishap probably occurred at his house at Maryhill, where the elevator shafts were empty.

He again gave interviews to the Tokyo newspapers. *Yomiuri* reported that Sam " . . . if called on, will assist in construction of Tokyo's roads without profit; the only remuneration desired is a memorial plaque bearing his name and deed to be placed under roads he constructs. . . . * He has enough compassion toward the city he loves bluntly to offer his assistance. He is willing to send three of his engineers and five technicians and all the necessary construction machinery to assist Japanese counterparts in this project." Sam renewed his advice about rebuilding as soon as possible the streets of Tokyo; evidently they had not improved much in the preceding two years. He declared to the Industrial Club that, "If every Japanese is willing to bear one yen** each, Japan will have excellent highways through the country."

One cannot claim that Sam single-handedly persuaded the Japanese that their city streets and national roads urgently needed modern planning and construction, but he very probably had more influence than any other Occidental in bringing this about. It would have happened eventually, of course, but it was the time and place for a fervent evangelist. Sam relished the role of John the Baptist, not as a voice in the wilderness, but preaching to eager listeners: "Prepare ye the way . . . Make straight . . . a highway. . . ."

A final note about things Japanese: in 1925, Sam wrote an irascible letter to Judge Thomas Burke about Albert Johnson, " . . . whose plans to become Senator on an anti-Japanese platform should be nipped*** in the worm. . . . I've decided, in spite of the fact there are so many people I dislike here in Seattle, to do the city a good turn. Sometimes I feel sad to think it is so healthy — enough of them don't die!" Sam's Quaker forebears would have approved his defense of the Japanese, but not been edified by his misanthropy toward his neighbors.

In all likelihood, some of the happiest days of Sam's life were spent in Japan. How gratifying it must have been to be admired and sought after by Japan's elite as a successful representative of American drive and know-how!

In 1923, after his last trip to Japan, Sam wrote Kondo's son from Maryhill: "As I look out the window, I see Mount Hood, and the picture which you sent me of Fujiyama reminds me of the beautiful Japan which I came to know so well through the Kondo family, and to which I am proud to belong."

---

*Perhaps this appealed to Sam more than that $5 clay statue.

**Taxpayers of our day can testify ruefully that just a yen for highways is not enough.

***No pun intended, Sam?

World War I

Throughout the First World War, Sam was engaged in a number of frustrating battles of his own. One was the futile attempt to save his Home Telephone Company in Portland. The outbreak of the war in 1914 found him engaged in building his chateau at Maryhill. He stopped work on it in 1917. Operation of Maryhill Ranch, maintenance of his Seattle house, management of his investments, and concern over his daughter's illness in 1916 absorbed much of his time and energy.

There were three events between 1914 and 1918, however, which must have given him a good deal of satisfaction. One was the completion of the scenic Columbia River Highway in 1915. Another was his contribution of money for Belgian refugees, which won for him a decoration from their government. The third was an adventure involving practically every element Sam could have wished: a summons by King Albert to give expert advice on transportation to Russia, a floundering ally; a conference with the king and certain allied military leaders to that end; hurried journeys on a dangerous mission; and admiring press coverage of the scope of the assignment, if not of its eventual outcome. The only missing element was a damsel in distress, and indeed, Sam did find time to bring home with him a Miss Simeon, a teacher of the Russian language, for a chair in Russian studies he established at the University of Washington.

Soon after he left Victoria, B.C. for Japan and Russia there were news stories describing his assigned task. The headline of a June 1916 front page article in the *Seattle Post Intelligencer* indicated he would "Direct Operation of Siberia Line; picked by Allies to solve problems of freight congestion at Vladivostok and facilitate shipments into the interior." The story reviewed his career, adding, "It has been said of Mr. Hill that he has crowded into the 59 years of his life more interesting experiences and experiments than a hundred ordinary men, and with less ostentation."*

His account of this 1916 adventure to the secretary of the Harvard Class of 1879 is of such telegraphic compression, followed by such an elaborately casual paragraph, that it is worth presenting here in its entirety. He did not even begin the story with a new paragraph, the sentences preceding this narrative referring to his attendance at Harvard Club dinners in London and Tokyo. The account was directed to his aging, stay-at-home classmates; if they did not feel one-upped, it was no fault of Sam's.

> In 1916, on May 1, I landed at Liverpool, England, on the steamship *Philadelphia;* was the only man to leave the ship. Took the 9:15 train from

---

*The last phrase may be open to question.

Liverpool to London, met Major McKay who was in command of London and the district for ten miles around. Took the night boat to Havre, then occupied as Belgian headquarters, met M. M. Carton di Wiart. Arrived in Paris the same night.

Took the morning train for what remained of Free Belgium, passed through Newkirk and Dunkirk, arrived La Panne. I was received by His Majesty, the King, dined with the King and Queen and the Commanding General of the Army. The next morning at 4:00 o'clock was on the firing line. I remained for four hours, which was three hours and fifty-nine minutes too long. One minute was all I needed. Was invited to participate in the advance next day against Germany, but unfortunately, or possibly fortunately for both myself and the Germans, the movement of advance was postponed. I returned to Boulogne, crossed the Channel on a most exciting trip, took the night train for Glasgow, Scotland, examined the fortifications on the Clyde, returned in time to witness a night demonstration — the bombing of Glasgow —, caught the night train for Liverpool, spent part of the day with my friend, John Brodie who was in command there, and after having covered part of the four countries mentioned in five days, came back on the *Philadephia,* the same boat I went over on.

I met the leading railroad presidents of America on my arrival at New York, at the University Club, met many of our leading financiers next day at luncheon, came to Chicago and met many of the leading railroad presidents and bankers, arrived in St. Paul the next morning, saw Mr. James J. Hill, and started to go around the world. Arrived in Victoria and was called to St. Paul on account of the death of Mr. James J. Hill. I returned at once to Victoria, went to Japan, went across Siberia, traveling under an assumed name with a Russian passport, arrived at Petrograd; got information I had come for, traveled as courier carrying important dispatches for our very able ambassador, David R. Francis; went to Viberg, Tornea, Haparanda, delivered my first papers at Stockholm, had a narrow escape among the Germans there assembled. Went to Christiania [now called Oslo], Norway, then to Bergen. In boarding the steamship *Jupiter* was recognized by the captain and had another narrow escape from my German friends. Next day encountered a storm, such as only the North Sea can get up. Witnessed two German submarines show their periscopes, but as the *Jupiter* was a neutral ship, we were not attacked.

Arrived at London, saw Sir Edward Grey, met the leading members of both parties, was requested to again change my name. Was escorted by Wallinger, England's great detective, on my trip to Paris. Was recognized on attempting to land by the Commanding Officer of the Port, Baron Anton Mandat de Grancy, but as we were old friends, was allowed to proceed without delay. Secured the information I desired in Paris, returned to London, met David Lloyd George at breakfast, then returned to Washington, D.C.

But to turn from unpleasant things to more pleasant ones, I have, from time to time, met many of my classmates, and with some of them have formed or renewed a friendship which began at college, and have come to admire their work.

As a thoughtful anticlimax, Sam went on to praise a classmate who had founded a number of sailors' homes.

Without disclosing his mission, Sam added more details about the European part of his adventures to a *New York Times* reporter on his arrival from Liverpool on May 14, 1916. After reaching London, Sam said,

I drove at once to the French Embassy, presented my credentials from Ambassador Jusserand and the State Department, and obtained a special permit to travel that night to Paris via Southhampton and Havre, which is prohibited generally to neutrals, who have to go by Folkestone and Dieppe.

On my arrival at Havre on Tuesday forenoon I drove to the capital of Belgium, which is called Nice Havraise, and saw the Minister of Justice who telephoned to Paris and arranged for my visit to King Albert. Before taking the train to Paris, I was taken for a twenty-five mile automobile drive outside Havre, where the crops are abundant. Not a square inch of ground has been left uncultivated. I saw more vegetation in that ride than I did afterward in the whole of my trip through England and Scotland.

I slept in Paris on Tuesday night and started early Wednesday morning in the direction of Dunkirk. There were no cabs in the French capital and the porter had to carry my bag to the hotel while I followed on foot.

When I left the train at a small station, of which I may not give the name, I was met by an aide-de-camp with an automobile marked "S.M." in white letters on the front and side. There was a soldier chauffeur in front and the officer and myself sat in the tonneau. I do not know the make of the car but it went at a speed I had never traveled before over hills, streams, and plains, never stopping for nearly five hours. Our average speed was 55 miles an hour and we were 75 to 80 miles an hour on the down grades. At every main road crossing soldiers covered us with their rifles but fell back as the officer made them a sign. This worried me frequently, as I felt that he might make a mistake in the sign and that the soldiers would fire on us without waiting for inquiries.

It was about 4:00 o'clock on Wednesday afternoon when we arrived at the small village near La Panne where King Albert and Queen Elizabeth were staying at that time. I had a conference with His Majesty which lasted three hours, and then had dinner with him. The Queen and a Belgian general were the only others present. The meal was a very simple one, consisting of soup and roast chicken with salad and dessert. There was no wine on the table. After dinner I talked with the King until 10:30 o'clock and then drove off in the automobile to a small roadside house, where I slept until 4:00 o'clock the next morning in a sparsely furnished room.

At that hour, I was awakened by a rocking sensation accompanied by a heavy booming, which I discovered to be the Germans saluting the dawn. The King had promised that I was to see something of the firing lines, and he kept his word. After breakfasting on eggs, bread, and coffee, I drove some distance in the automobile until apparently we came quite close to the German guns and saw the Belgian soldiers in the distance, scattered in twos and threes, lying on the ground. I remained there until 8:00, when King Albert and his staff arrived, with the Queen, in the rear of the firing lines.

After leaving the Belgian battle front I drove in the King's automobile at the same terrific speed for about two hundred miles to Boulogne, where I had special permission to cross over to Folkstone on one of the British transports.

The people Sam had talked to on his brief trip to Europe apparently made him unduly optimistic. A *Minneapolis Tribune* article of May 16, 1916 was captioned, "War is Nearing End, Says Samuel Hill. . . . Teutons nearly bankrupt, he asserts, after short trip to the front. . . . Germany cannot struggle against the overwhelming financial strain and the economic conditions since the war. There will not be another winter campaign and peace will come just as suddenly as the war broke out." Perhaps the London fog had clouded the crystal ball without obscuring the light at the end of the tunnel.

Sam left New York for Washington to arrange for visas the day after arriving in the U.S. The U.S. State Department made it clear that Sam was not undertaking an assignment as a representative of the government. He hurried to arm himself with letters from prominent people in the field of transportation to expedite his mission of straightening out the tangled port and railway facilities at Vladivostok. Earlier, King Albert had furnished him with an elaborate commission as honorary Belgian Consul-General for the states of Oregon, Washington, and Idaho. Officials of the Erie, Chicago and Northwestern, and Northern Pacific Railways appointed him "Foreign Traffic Manager" for the occasion. The White Star and Japanese N.Y.K. Lines gave him letters of recommendation. Others were secured from the premier of British Columbia and Scotland Yard.

In later years, the tale did not lose color in the retelling. In 1921, Sam recalled for Clarence Barron other experiences on his trans-Siberian trip worthy of James Bond, or some might say, of Baron Munchausen;

> I speak German better than English and know it better than most Germans. They thought I was German when the war broke out. Wilson refused me passports, but after I talked with Baker [Newton D. Baker, Secy. of War] of my plan, I went around the world without a passport, I was so well known by the Chinese and Japanese. Orders everywhere from Wilson were not to issue me a passport, but I went through. I traveled with a man on the Siberian road who had orders for a £40,000 reward to kill me, and I arranged a plan how we would kill this Sam Hill. We would divide the reward. Then, of course, I slipped away.

Mrs. Ewing wrote a somewhat different version of this latter adventure (Chapter 27), the reward being £2,000. One can only conclude that James Bond would have had a less eventful literary career if his enemies had been so easily deceived.

William Edgar, editor of the *Northwestern Miller*, had written the Tsar in September 1916, at about the time Sam was on the way home to Seattle. Edgar had been received by the Tsar in 1892 after having been " . . . instrumental in delivering a shipload of flour to the suffering peasants of Russia during the period of scarcity." Edgar described Sam's experience in helping to build the Great Northern and said that Sam and John Stevens, the engineer who had worked on the Panama Canal and Great Northern Railway, wished to " . . . communicate to Your Majesty a plan which may be of vast importance to the cause of Russia in the present war . . . which may undertake to carry through without reward or compensation." Sam's efforts for Russia would likely have earned him a decoration from the last of the Romanovs had Nicholas' mind not been on other matters, such as the loss of empire.

The author could find little information about what, if anything, Sam was able to accomplish on his mission, except to have a splendid time. In an obituary fifteen years later, a St. Paul paper said, "Hill, in a single summer, reopened the port for the receipt of supplies and re-established the schedule of trains to the battle front." Sam, not famous for reticence, did not leave us an account of his activities in Vladivostok.

Late in August 1916, Lloyd George sent him an appreciative letter from the War Office in Whitehall:

> I am so sorry that owing to a slight indisposition which has kept me out of the office for days, I shall not have the pleasure of seeing you before you leave for the States. Having been absent from the office nigh onto a week, I have not seen the members of the committee, which had been appointed of the various departments concerned, to examine your proposal.
>
> My first impression was a favorable one; nothing which has occurred since has altered my view as to the undoubted advantage which would inure to the Allied cause if it had been feasible to put through your great scheme. The only thing that has shaken me has been the fact that the gravest doubts have been expressed by those who know Russia best, not as to the desirability of your plan, but as to the possibility of inducing the Russian Government to give it speedy acceptance and trial.
>
> I thank you heartily for giving me an opportunity of looking into it; but you know the difficulties without my dwelling upon them.
>
> Wishing you a good voyage and thanking you and your coadjutor for the very practical sympathy which you have shown to the Allied cause, I remain,
>
> Yours sincerely, D. Lloyd George.

Sam had glass projection slides made to copy this letter and the various letters of authorization and support mentioned above, possibly to confound anyone who might later doubt that his mission had been taken seriously by the governments involved.

In April 1917, after the United States declared war, Sam went to Washington, D.C. to confer with administration officials on aid to Russia in its eleventh hour. So far as is known, nothing came of this. *The Oregonian* reported, "Within the last year, Mr. Hill also escorted Nicholas Malinkoff, Chief Engineer of the Imperial Russian Government on a tour of the United States, when that official was studying transportation problems and remedies as he found them in this country." However, Malinkoff already knew about Russia's problems, and it was too late for remedies.

After the Bolsheviks had taken power, Sam wrote to the *New York Times* in June 1918, suggesting the appointment of an Allied Commission to help restore Russian railways and contract with ". . . the great cooperative purchasing societies of Russia to forward shoes, agricultural implements and other supplies essential to the lives of the people." These could be shipped by way of Vladivostok, primarily from Seattle where the shipyards were rapidly turning out freighters. "In the railway yards of Seattle are more than 20 million dollars worth of railway supplies, including one hundred locomotives ready to go across the Pacific to help restoration of traffic," Sam wrote. British and American troops would also be sent, with assurances that " . . . there will be no interference with the form of government that the people wish to maintain. . . . We have American troops available at Camp Lewis, on the shores of Puget Sound, twelve days from Vladivostok. . . . American railroad men, under Colonel Emerson, are now in Manchuria, and available at once to spread over the Trans-Siberian railways." He still had hope that such efforts would " . . . restore a great people to national srength and a great force in the east that will relieve the pressure on our armies in the west." He concluded that the United States should be " . . . preparing for prompt action that will save Russia and the world."

Sam found the final victory of the Soviets a bitter pill to swallow. He wrote Loie Fuller in February 1921, "The Soviet Government now reigns supreme from Vladivostok to Petrograd."

Sam Hill's exertions for relief of Belgian and Rumanian war refugees have been reported in obituaries and other accounts of his life, but it is difficult to document them. Sam had a slide made of a 1918 letter from King Albert thanking him for a gift of $5,000. Early in the war, he was "Chairman of the Oregon Committee for the relief of suffering Belgians." Major H. L. Bowlby, Sam's roadbuilding associate, wired the U.S. State Department in November 1914, probably at Sam's behest, recommending Sam if President Wilson were appointing a commission to distribute American supplies for Belgian relief. He listed Sam's qualifications: "Fluent knowledge of French, German, Italian; personal friend of King Albert; intimate knowledge of Europe; willingness to give time; ability to bear personal financial burden involved." The Department replied, "There will be no central committee appointed by the commission. . . . Suggest you consult Herman Hapgood, Chairman of the Committee of Mercy, New York."

At the time of his 1916 mission to Russia, a Seattle paper said Sam had " . . . personally raised a large fund for the relief of the distressed people, which he sent to the King of the Belgians. One of the donations to this fund was a check for $1,000 given by an organization of young women in Seattle who had been the guests of Mr. Hill once a year at an elaborate banquet. He requested them to devote the money that would have been spent on the banquet to the relief fund, and he sent forward the amount in their names."

In September 1916, after attending a conference of the Commission for the Relief in Belgium in London, he had harsh words, given to *The New York Times*, for the inadequacy of the American response. "It costs ten million dollars a month to provide for the refugees in German Belgium and Free Belgium alone, without counting the two and a half million in Northern France. The United States ought to be ashamed of itself for the half-hearted manner in which it has aided the people of this stricken country. Americans claim credit for supporting millions of refugees, while the burden has been carried silently by France and England." He considered American aid up to that point like " . . . sending them a Christmas dinner and then forgetting all about the people and their misery." What was more, "No arrangements had been made for chartering steamers to carry provisions to Europe because of lack of funds."

He also had a sarcastic comment on American unpreparedness: "It's hard to tell which is the weaker nation, China or the United States. We wouldn't last five minutes with any other nation." If Sam's crystal ball had been more oracular, he would not have been embarrassed a year later by its performance.

Sam's name is listed as a member of the Commission for Relief in

Belgium, but the Herbert Hoover Presidential Library could find no other reference to Sam Hill in its papers, nor is he mentioned in reports of the American Relief Administration or the European Relief Council from 1921 through 1923. Sam probably met Hoover for the first time in 1919 in San Francisco when Sam was made a member of the Belgian Order of the Crown, in recognition of his services. As prominent Quakers, he and Hoover were given honorary LL.D. degrees by Penn College in 1925, Hoover for war relief and Sam for his campaign for good roads.

Sam contemplated going to Rumania in August 1917. He wired Loie Fuller " . . . Saw Joe Leiter [a wealthy American grain broker] while enroute Washington, D.C. Believe you could persuade him to undertake Rumanian matter." But Leiter answered, "I find it impossible to join you in Rumanian expedition. I wired Loie Fuller today that I would do anything on your return to help out the cause." Sam was in Portland. " . . . suffering again severely in his arms and is going to deny himself of everybody and try to get well." The pain was said to be due to neuritis. At any rate, so far as is known, Sam did not go to Rumania until 1919.

George Hutton, who had met Sam in Seattle, where they had a mutual friend in R. H. Thomson, the city engineer, recalls something of that episode. He says that Sam was in Belgium in May or June 1919, when he received a message from Queen Marie saying she was trying to break up Prince Carol's liaison with Magda Lupescu. Hutton thinks that Carol had shot himself in the hand to protest his mother's plan of sending him to America with Sam. (Ellerby, Queen Marie's biographer, says that Carol shot himself in the leg to prevent his accompanying his parents to London. At any rate, the peril was not to life, but limb.)

Sam phoned Herbert Hoover in Paris, who suggested that he take passage from Marseilles on a ship leaving in a few days, carrying relief supplies to Constanta, Rumania. When Sam arrived at Constanta, he learned from officers on the docks the names of the U.S. military team which was surveying the need for, and distribution of, supplies. Sam sent a telegram to Hutton, then a 1st Lieutenant in the Seventh Division and a member of a six man team on a Herbert Hoover Food Administration mission, to invite him to meet Sam in Constanta. Hutton had gone to Turkey and was unable to leave in time to meet him.

The relief supplies were brought to Charnovitz, where the queen turned out the troops, dressed in British uniforms. The word was passed that the British military boots were not to be put on until the day of the parade. Hutton recalls that Sam received praise from the queen in the Rumanian press for taking part in the delivery of supplies, though actually he did not participate.

Although he favored the Allied cause early in the war, Sam did not advocate American military intervention before 1917 nor did he join with those who felt an all-out attempt should be made to defeat the Soviet government after the war. For a few weeks in 1916, the war had unexpectedly brought Sam a feeling of power and drama. He would never have said, "O, what a lovely war!'', but in this short interval, he must have felt that at last he was filling a role in the world ideally suited to his training and temperament.

21

Memorials to Peace and War

Monuments to people and events in our city squares and parks seem almost as numerous as the pigeons that treat them with so little reverence. Tyrants from Cheops to Stalin have had a weakness for monuments to themselves, most of which endure or which we endure. Memorials designed to commemorate ideals and events are less common, and like the great cathedrals of the Middle Ages, in part have their origin in pride and the desire to be remembered to history, however anonymously.

What were Sam Hill's motives in building two of America's most unusual monuments, the Peace Portal at the western end of the boundary between the United States and Canada, and the Stonehenge Memorial at Maryhill? Neither bears his name, but Sam knew that they would be lasting, if unspoken, tributes to him.

The International Peace Arch

There are celebrated gates and arches in the world commemorating victories in war, but perhaps only one celebrating peace between two nations. On July 4, 1915, at a celebration on the border at Blaine, Washington, in honor of a century of peace between Canada and the U.S. Sam said, ''Two Pacific Highways meet here today — the one reaching from Alaska to Mexico,* the other an invisible one reaching from the Atlantic to the Pacific, the highway of peace.'' In a 1922 interview in Japan, Sam gave credit for the idea of erecting the monument to A. E. Todd, a former mayor of Victoria and later life president of the Pacific Highway Association. We don't know when Sam engaged an architect (whose name has been lost in the shuffle) to design the arch.

Early in 1920, Sam had publicized the Peace Arch on a visit to Japan. From Tokyo and from aboard ship on the way home, he sent invitations for the dedication to several world figures, including Edward, Prince of Wales;

---

*Sam was looking ahead, of course; such a highway did not yet exist.

the Crown Prince of Belgium; the premiers of Australia and Japan; Marshall Joffre; and Queen Marie of Rumania. None of them came at that time, but Sam, a determined rededicator, persuaded Joffre to do the honors on their 1922 trip around the world, and Marie to do so in 1926, a respectable score even for such a large wicket.

Construction of the monument began in July 1920.* Like almost everything else Sam Hill built, the white Doric arch is of very solid, earthquake-proof construction. The footwalls of reinforced concrete are built on wooden piles driven 25 feet into the ground. The International Peace Arch, commanding a view of the sea, is aligned so that one side is on Canadian soil and the other in the United States. Some 800 cubic yards of concrete and 50 tons of steel went into the 67 foot high structure, which is topped by two flagstaffs.

The cornerstone was laid on September 6, 1921, with Canadian Premier John Oliver and other officials in attendance. The date was " . . . chosen because it was the anniversary of the sailing of the *Mayflower* from Plymouth, of the birth of Lafayette, and of the first battle of the Marne." President Warren Harding wrote Sam a letter to be read at the dedication: "The fact that a boundary line over 3,000 miles long remains unfortified — these are the testimonies that the world grows wiser and better. . . . I wish to convey to you personally my high appreciation of your patriotic service in providing a symbolic shrine to international peace."

The great bronze gates were then opened inward against the walls of the interior of the portal. On one gate is the inscription "1814 — Open 100 Years — 1914," and above the other, "May These Gates Never Be Closed." The plinth above the portal on the American side reads "CHILDREN OF A COMMON MOTHER" and that on the Canadian side "BRETHREN DWELLING TOGETHER IN UNITY." There is a bronze relief plaque of the *Mayflower* in the wall on the American side, and encased in the wall beneath it, a piece of wood from the Pilgrim ship and a print of Sam's movie, "The Sacred Faith of a Scrap of Paper"**(Chapter 26).He had commissioned the film to explain the treaty of Ghent and to show the "Mayflower Barn" in England from which the wood relic was transported to the arch by his friend Frank Terrace. On the Canadian side, the corresponding bronze tablet shows the *Beaver,* the first sail and steam-powered vessel to navigate the Pacific (in 1836).

The 1814 date on the portal commemorates the signing of the Treaty of Ghent at the end of the War of 1812 between the United States and Great Britain. Ironically, the agreement was not all that amicable. Clay, one of the

---

* An obituary of Sam's cousin, Edgar Hill, stated he was a " . . . banker and part owner of a paper mill in Carthage, Indiana . . . [who] came west in 1924 [sic] to supervise construction . . on behalf of his brother [sic] Samuel Hill." This is not the only news story mentioning Sam in which "sic" seems nearly semper.

** The title derives from Bethman-Hollweg's complaint about England's guarantee of the neutrality of Belgium in August, 1914: " . . . Just for a scrap of paper — Great Britain is going to make war."

The Peace Portal. Undated photograph, probably at the dedication in 1921. (Maryhill Museum files.)

peace commissioners appointed by President Madison, called it a "damned bad treaty." Britain wanted Canada to have access to the Mississippi and to have enormous tracts of land set aside for the Indians. New England wanted to renew rights to fish off Newfoundland and Labrador. J. Truslow Adams says, "In the end a treaty was patched up which did not mention any of the objects for which we had ostensibly gone to war," such as the subject of impressment of seamen.

These matters and the location of the 3,000 mile boundary, most of it on the 49th parallel, were left to another commission and another president, Monroe, to approve in the Rush-Bagot agremeent, signed in 1817. Nor was the boundary between Washington and British Columbia accepted without demur. "54-40 or fight" was for a time a popular slogan, the like of which we probably will not hear shouted on college campuses today.

In 1921, the U.S. Senate passed a resolution of thanks for Sam's contribution.Canada's Premier King added his felicitations, which did not quite mollify Sam, who replied, "I am greatly disappointed that the British Columbia Department of Roads has decided not to build a Canadian highway down to the Peace Portal and have built it a mile to the east on the theory, I suppose, that it will reach greater population. That is true, but independent of sentimental reasons, the Peace Portal would bring travel which I estimate at least 500,000 people yearly to this point. [In recent years, more than that number have visited the Peace Arch Park annually.] As it is now, they will drive by and never see it. However, the time will come when the importance of these things is recognized, and both the portal and I can wait." But Sam bore Premier King no ill will. He sent him a commemorative medal, designed by Pierre Rouche.

Sam returned from a visit to King Albert in Brussels just in time to attend the Dominion Day ceremonies at the portal on July 1, 1923. Pictures and medals of the arch were being sold at a concession, part of the proceeds going to the Pacific Highway Association.

It was not until 1929 that Sam could announce that Canada and Washington State had agreed that the main international highway would pass close by the portal. In 1932, the route, now Interstate 5, was diverted to

189

pass on either side of the arch.

The setting for the Peace Arch was not inspiring at the outset. Some people sneered at the idea of placing such a monument a mile distant from the main highway. Beginning in 1931, the appearance of the surroundings was greatly enhanced by the acquisition of land for Peace Arch Park in international territory, maintained jointly by Washington State and the province of British Columbia. The park consists of twenty-six acres on the American side and twenty-three on the Canadian side, acquired in part through contributions from school children. Annual programs are held, featuring attendance by war veterans of both countries and exchanges of flags by children. In 1936, on behalf of the Washington Good Roads Association, Frank Terrace, then 84 years old, unveiled a bronze plaque on the arch. It reads: "In commemoration of the life and works of Samuel Hill (1857-1931), eminent roadbuilder — a true Quaker — foremost in peace — always promoting world-wide unity — who ever sought to build up but never tear down." Lyndon Johnson and Premier Lester Pearson met there in September 1964, to sign the Columbia River Treaty.

Near the portal is a marker erected in 1940 by the Washington Division of United Daughters of the Confederacy, naming the former U.S. Highway 99 as "Jefferson Davis Highway." A stranger might conclude that this, rather than Gettysburg, was the "high-water mark of the Confederacy." At any rate, it is the I-5 Freeway, neither gray nor blue, which now passes the arch.

The elusive goal of peace between nations has not been achieved by the League of Nations or the U.N., but one can reflect that in at least one corner of the world, someone was grateful enough for more than a century of peace between two nations, and confident enough that it would continue, to locate between them a lasting testimonial of hope.

America's Stonehenge Memorial

Sam's other memorial was planned during World War I and its altar stone dedicated before the war's end. Its inscription reads:"To the memory of the soldiers and sailors of Klickitat County who gave their lives in defense of their country . . . in the hope that others inspired by the example of their valor and their heroism may share in that love of liberty and burn with that fire of patriotism which death alone can quench."

At least three servicemen had died by the time of the dedication on July 4, 1918. For the other nine dead who are commemorated on bronze plaques, it was an anticipatory memorial. Years went by before Stonehenge was completed and rededicated on Memorial Day, 1930, a delay due in part to Sam's being short of the money needed to turn his dream into thousands of pounds of reinforced concrete.

In an article on Stonehenge, Leverett Richards tells of Sam's inspiration for the monument: "It is April in England and war clouds swirl like a shroud around the globe of the world. Out of the morning mist that en-

Stonehenge Memorial looking south. (Photo courtesy of Pete May.)

velops Salisbury Downs comes a little party of men, including Lord Earl Kitchener, commander of 'Kitchener's.Mob,' and his guest, Samuel Hill, American. Across the endless sea of sod that is Salisbury Plain they gradually descry fingers of stone thrusting bleakly into the sky. That is Stonehenge.

"'Here the ancients 4,000 year ago offered bloody sacrifices to their heathen gods of war,' Kitchener explained.

"Sam Hill fell silent. After a while he remarked with meditative solemnity, '4,000 years. We have come that far. And still we are sacrificing the blood of our youth to the gods of war.'" Years later he told Lockley he had built the Stonehenge Memorial "to remind my fellow man of [that] incredible folly. . . . "

Newspaper stories of that day claimed that ancient Druids sacrificed war captives on the altarstone of Stonehenge to placate the war gods and achieve peace. In a memo to Professor E. S. Meany proposing construction of the monument, Sam mentioned " . . . the last [human sacrifices] being about 800 years before Christ . . .it seems fitting that this sacrifice which we have been called on to make to the war god of the heathen should be fittingly remembered in some permanent way." Archeologists now tell us that the Druids came long after Stonehenge was built, about 1700 or 1800 years B.C., and they doubt that human sacrifices were performed there.* No matter, Sam's memorial was a noble idea.

Ancient Stonehenge was laid out so that at the summer solstice, the longest day of the year, the rising sun would strike the tall hele stone, standing outside the double circle of great stones, and cast its shadow on

---

*The reader interested in what is known and what has been imagined of the history of ancient Stonehenge is referred to *The Enigma of Stonehenge* by John Fowles and Barry Brukoff, Summit Books, 1980.

191

Sam addressing crowd at the dedication of the altar stone for the Stonehenge Memorial, July 4, 1918. (Maryhill Museum files.)

the central altar. The outer circle of 30 stones, topped by flat stones, represents the days of the month. The inner circle consists of 40 smaller upright stones, not native to England. There are five other structures each consisting of two upright stones with another bridging them, rising in height from east to west. Computer studies have shown that there are careful alignments of the stones with observations of the sun and moon.

Sam's monument is a representation of what Stonehenge is thought to have looked like after it was built so laboriously over the course of three centuries. Sam asked Professor W. W. Campbell of the Lick Observatory, who later became president of the University of California, to fix the position of the altarstone. Campbell was in Goldendale at the time to observe a total eclipse of the sun, which occurred on June 8, 1918. The position and relative size of the other pillars to be constructed were carefully calculated. (The Klickitat Hills north of the memorial prevent the rising sun from casting its shadow at the precise time on June 21, but only men of the Stone Age would set their watches by Stonehenge. This unusual structure received mention in stories of the second total solar eclipse visible in North America in this century. Goldendale has the distinction of being the only town with an observatory directly in the path of totality of the eclipses of

Left to right: W. G. Collins, Edgar N. Hill, Sam, Charles Babcock, and J. C. Potter, at the dedication of the Stonehenge Memorial altar stone. (Maryhill Museum files.)

June 1918 and February 26, 1979. The observatory, with its 24.5 inch handmade reflecting telescope, was completed in 1973.)

Sam sited the memorial at Maryhill on a bluff overlooking the Columbia, some three miles east of Maryhill Museum. The St. James Hotel, now to be called Meadlowlark Inn, was moved to provide the best location for the monument. Only a few of the other original buildings of the planned town then remained (see page 210).

The outer circle of sixteen foot pillars is 108 feet in diameter. The pillars in the inner circle are nine feet tall, and the great altarstone is six by eighteen feet in area and three feet high. The forms were lined with crumpled tin and a finish was applied so the concrete would resemble hand-hewn prehistoric stones. The original plans and specifications for the memorial have not turned up. Oddly, it is not mentioned in his will, although the land on which it stands is part of Maryhill Ranch.

The dedication exercises of July 4, 1918 were held on the lawn in front of the Meadowlark Inn. It was reported that R. H. Thomson, Seattle City Engineer, in plain Quaker style, invoked the aid of the Lord in bringing a speedy victory to the Allies and righting the wrongs done to Belgium. Professor Meany noted that this was the first reproduction of Stonehenge to

193

be constructed. Frank Terrace, an ex-British tar and Sam's longtime friend, spoke for the sailors and Col. D. M. Dunne, a Civil War veteran, for the soldiers (in passing, denouncing American men " . . . who, by their actions, are not proving themselves 100 percent Americans.") Hill's staff then served refreshments and the guests toured his ranch.

America's Stonehenge has a lonely and incongruous look today, as stark and desolate as the bluff it stands on. It is accessible either from Washington Highway 14 or from the road east through Maryhill State Park at the north end of the Sam Hill Memorial Bridge. Near the monument is a stone fountain, long dry, which once stood in front of Meadowlark Inn, destroyed by fire in 1958. Like an untended grave, America's Stonehenge seems a more fitting reminder of our indifference to our war dead than of their sacrifices.

A throw-away society has no use for a monument like Stonehenge. As with the great cathedrals of another age, there are those who deplore the waste of money which could have been spent on alleviating the lot of the poor who are always with us. But whether one thinks that Sam's motive in building it was generosity or pride, or that it was simply the grandiose folly of an eccentric, it appeals to something in the human spirit that longs for immortality.

Sam's Peace Portal, 1979. (Author's photo.)

PART VI

MARYHILL

Chapter 22

The Promised Land

In 1907, Sam Hill began, with the highest hopes, the establishment of a new town in Klickitat County, Washington, about 100 miles east of Vancouver, near the north bank of the Columbia River. This was a consuming interest, in that it commanded — or demanded — a great deal of his time, money and prodigious energy for the next several years. But in reading this account, one should remember that, apart from family problems, Sam had many other things on his mind: speaking frequently to promote good roads; managing his investments; traveling about the United States and Europe (he went to Europe twice in the summer of 1908 alone); supervising the construction and furnishing of his great house in Seattle in 1908-09; and from 1909 on, running the Home Telephone Company in Portland. Still, he proceeded enthusiastically, planning every detail of the new model town and transforming the surrounding farms and orchards.

The small town of Columbus, Washington, located on the narrow flat land beside the Columbia, had been in existence since the early 1860's. There were ranches on bench lands several hundred feet above the river, and north of these were the nearly barren Klickitat Hills, 1,500 to 2,000 feet high. The view was dramatic. A short distance downstream began the rapids of Celilo Falls and across the river were the hills and cliffs of Oregon with the tracks of the Oregon Railroad and Navigation Company at their bases. Far to the west, the snowy peak of Mt. Hood loomed on the horizon. From the hilltops north of Columbus one could see Mt. St. Helens (intact) and Mt. Adams to the north, and glimpse Mt. Rainier in the distance.

Explorers of the Oregon country, among them Lewis and Clark and John Fremont, had remarked on the region just above Celilo Falls. Sam quoted an incident in Fremont's memoirs when on November 16, 1843, he met a " . . . Canadian immigrant . . .[who] was much chagrined at the change of climate and informed me that only a few miles above, they had left a country of bright blue sky and shining sun." Fremont pushed up the river, and " . . . though we made but a few miles, the weather improved immediately; and though the rainy country and cloudy mountains were close behind, before us was the bright sky; so distinctly is climate here marked by a mountain boundary." Sam added, "The place he found is now Maryhill."

The story of the founding and early days of Columbus is well told by Lois Davis Plotts. Amos Stark had " . . . wandered over the western states for several years, searching for the right place to stake his land claim, the bonus he was to receive for service in the Mexican War." In 1852 he traveled up river on a small steamer, and when he saw the green strip of lowland at the present site of Maryhill, he asked to be put ashore for a few days. He filed his land claim, then went off to the California gold fields. He returned in 1859, bringing livestock and supplies, and built a log cabin about two miles east of the site of the present Maryhill Museum. Other homesteaders had already arrived and staked claims in Klickitat County. They could earn money by hauling cordwood from the country to the north and selling it to steamboats to fire their boilers. The townsite was platted, named Columbus, and eventually recorded in 1878. There were perhaps a hundred residents twenty-five years later.

In 1868, a ferry began to operate between Columbus and Grant. The Oregon Railway and Navigation Company completed its line on the south bank in 1883. Transcontinental train traffic was established to Portland by the connection of this route to the Union Pacific by the Oregon Short Line. The railroad provided an outlet to the market for the fruit and produce of the ranchers in the Columbus and Goldendale areas. A crude wagon road linked these towns in 1873. Previously, livestock, wheat, and other produce were transported by river boat, but the ferry and rail connections made it feasible to transport freight on the Oregon side. Another ferry, a barge pushed by the tug *Waterwitch*, began service in 1905. The Spokane, Portland and Seattle Railway on the north bank was not completed until 1909, by which time Sam's efforts to found a town near Columbus were well underway.

How did Sam Hill come to know this area? He no doubt knew the projected route of the railway from Spokane to Vancouver, Washington and Portland from his association with J. J. Hill. Charles Babcock, his former law clerk in Minneapolis, had become a land purchase agent for the Great Northern railway and had mapped out much of Klickitat County in 1903. Babcock owned a farm in Oregon's Willamette Valley and visited it in 1907. W. J. Hilligoss, another Great Northern employee, had cruised the timber, because the railroad owned alternate sections along the proposed route of the S.P. & S.

But Sam's attention was first directed to the possibility of establishing a water power plant at Lyle, where the Klickitat River empties into the Columbia. In November 1905, he had discussed with a Mr. Culloch building a straw board factory. Culloch wrote him that this site would be ideal, not only because of the water power, but also because of the supply of straw, then wasted, from the wheat ranches around Goldendale; as well as the rail connection between Lyle and Goldendale and the expected construction of the S.P. & S. railway; and the proximity to Columbia River boats.

Sam engaged a lawyer, N. B. Brooks, to secure property near the mouth of the river with the idea of building a dam and powerhouse. The Klickitat Power and Electric Company was organized with Sam as its vice president. Nothing came of this project, or the straw board factory, either, but it was the beginning of Sam's long association with the Brooks family who lived in Goldendale, about twelve miles north of Columbus.

There is a story, perhaps apocryphal because it is not mentioned in Sam's correspondence, about a plan for Sam's town which went awry. The

Jewetts had a farm at White Salmon, Washington, situated on a bluff overlooking the river. They took in vacation borders at $9.00 per week. Sam is said to have visited friends at the Jewetts at a beautiful time of year. Much impressed with the scenery in the Columbia Gorge, Sam coined the slogan, "Where the rain and sunshine meet." He decided on the spot to make an offer to A. H. and Jenny Jewett for their place. A price was agreed on, and "Hill was so elated with the verbal agreement, he arose from his seat, ran to his cottage, and snatched up a bottle of Scotch. In his excitement he had forgotten, or ignored, the signs posted in each room and cottage. The signs pronounced: 'Absolutely no intoxicating beverages of any kind on these premises.' When Hill came running back, 'Let's drink a toast,' he proposed. It was a moment before he was aware of the icy stillness. 'The transaction is off, Mr. Hill. You may pack and leave at once!' . . . His first surprised bluster turned to loud protestations, but even the first explosion was lost, for Aunty Jenny Jewett had taken her husband by the hand and left the room."

Through his attorney, Sam reopened the offer and a meeting was agreed on. Mrs. Jewett offered to sell only on the condition there would never be any intoxicating beverages on the property, and if this proviso were ignored, the property would revert back to the Jewetts. Sam vowed he'd be damned before he would sign such a paper. The townspeople knew that he planned a new town and paved roads, and tried unsuccessfully to dissuade the Jewetts. According to this account, Sam then searched for and found the location near Columbus, preserving the catch phrase, "Where the rain and sunshine meet."

But what about the idea of establishing a town in the first place? This occurred to Sam in January 1906, when he was visiting his cousin, Mary Davis, a few miles from his birthplace at Deep River, North Carolina. J. Edgar Williams, pastor of the Friends Meeting at Greensboro, was holding a two week series of meetings at Guilford College. His preaching one Sunday morning favorably impressed Sam and his friend Lindley. At a reception that afternoon, Lindley whispered to the Reverend Williams, "Come out to Washington and help us build another Whittier." Lindley had prepared the way in 1878 when he bought a 2,000 acre barley field near Los Angeles and established the Quaker community of Whittier, California, where Richard Nixon, another entrepreneur, was raised. As Williams wrote Alma Spreckels years later, "That whisper . . . was the beginning of Maryhill."

At Sam's invitation, Williams, his wife, and three small children came to Seattle in July 1907. Williams became pastor of a meeting house paid for by Sam, Lindley, and Eldridge Stuart, president of the Carnation Milk Company. Sam invited Williams to visit his Maryhill townsite the following year, and in 1909 Williams returned for the dedication of the small Quaker meeting house. However, the Williamses, depressed with their lack of success in establishing a meeting in Seattle, eventually gave up and went to Indiana.

There were reasons for Sam's choice of a site about a mile northeast of the existing town of Columbus and about 400 above it. The Hood River district on the Oregon side, about twenty-five miles west, had been a successful apple growing area for thirty years. The prosperous wheat farming and stock raising community around Goldendale was only twelve miles to the north. Apart from realizing the great advantages completion of the North Bank Railroad would bring to the area, Sam had firm ideas about its geographical advantages. He wrote his father-in-law:

> I have examined to some extent the country on the north bank of the Columbia River between Pasco and Portland. I was led to do this from a study of the geography of the country, which showed me to the north of San Francisco, the Cascade wall was broken only at three points; the Fraser River, the Columbia, and the Klamathon River [now called the Klamath River]. My familiarity with the Fraser River and with the Klamathon River led me to believe if the place could be found where the rain and sunshine met, at the right altitude on the Columbia River, ideal farming conditions would be found. No map of Klickitat County had been published. I personally made an examination of the country and was convinced that land more productive than any I had ever seen before was there. The water finding its way from the mountains on the north bank through to the Columbia River subirrigates the soil. The country has been settled for something over forty years and resembles the country around Northfield, Minnesota. The sand is confined to the edge of the Columbia River and does not touch the upper benches. On one farm, I found nineteen varieties of grapes as good as any I have ever seen; peaches, plums, prunes, pears, apples, watermelons, quinces, apricots, almonds, walnuts, Indian corn of excellent quality, alfalfa growing without irrigation, etc. [This was the Gillenwater Ranch. It was well supplied with water from springs and its productivity may have led Sam to assume that the same results could be achieved on neighboring farms.] Heretofore the country was inaccessible, there being no transportation except by the Columbia River. . . . Columbus is some six miles below the point where your engineers have located the division point at a place called Cliffs. . . . I saw a country, averaging perhaps fifteen miles wide and one hundred miles long, reached by your North Bank Road, which is the finest country I have ever seen.

Sam cited the success of the Hood River orchard country and farms around Goldendale, Washington. He had been told by some of the orchardists of Hood River that the Columbus area was about ten days ahead of them in the fruit growing season. He continued, "Twelve miles back from the river there is excellent yellow pine of such high character that some of it is now being shipped to New York for finishing purposes. These facts may all be known to you but they were new to me thirty days ago."

Sam waxed more eloquent when he wrote to his brother Richard: "We have found the Garden of Eden. . . . It is the garden spot of the world — the most beautiful country I have ever seen. I took Mary [Mary E. Mendenhall Davis, Sam's cousin] up on the top of the mountain and showed her the kingdoms of the earth." Sam said he sat in his office and thought about finding a hole in the Cascades between the dry country to the east and the rainy country on the west extending to the Pacific Coast. "Just then Hilligoss came into the office and I told him my idea and told him to go down over the ground and try to find this spot. He went down and came back bringing grapes bigger than those shown in the Sunday School books at the time the two spies searched out the land. . . . I am going to incorporate a company called 'The Promised Land.' The only trouble is . . . I would like to buy it all."

The Gillenwater place of 240 acres, on which Maryhill Museum now stands, was acquired first for $11,000 and named the Maryland Ranch. Mrs. Gillenwater told Sam that she had 500 different plants, shrubs, and trees in her garden. Sam wrote that she " . . . gave one loud, earnest howl when Mr. Lindley insisted that they should stay there and work two months longer without pay." Sam sent Weyerhaeuser a box of apples from the Gillenwater Ranch and was told that they were the best Weyerhaeuser had ever tasted.

W. T. Collins, president of the Pacific Fur Company of Seattle, a would-be investor in the Klickitat Power and Electric Company with Sam, also bought a farm at that time. Sam hoped Collins and others would be stockholders in his land development, but for one reason or another, Sam eventually became the sole proprietor.

In the spring of 1908, Sam temporarily got cold feet about going further with his Columbus Land Company. He was afraid of a repeat of the crash of 1907 if Taft were nominated but he was convinced, "There is a great deal of money to be made in this land transaction if we were sure that our government would not destroy the business of the country."

Sam's optimistic nature soon triumphed, and he began planning construction of two dams, one large, the other small, for irrigation. He wrote to the Department of Agriculture for information about construction of reservoirs on volcanic ash land. He planned to run pipes from these reservoirs to the many ten acre plots. Buyers of the parcels of land would get a share of stock in the water company free. There were also springs in some of the canyons, including the large one above the Gillenwater Ranch.

Construction of the dams was begun in 1909. For once Sam was definitely not building for the ages. The floor of the main reservoir consisted of rock and clay. It persistently leaked water, and earth washed down from the hillsides above silted in the reservoir within a year of its completion. No correspondence could be found about this expensive and embarrassing error, except that years later, in 1930, Sam complained to attorney Zola Brooks that he was still being assessed by Klickitat County for taxes on the principal dam on a valuation of $100,000. "Will you give $100,000 for it, Zola? Don't you think the County Commissioners should rebate this tax?"

In April 1908, Sam wrote asking his congressman to approve a post office for the town he first intended to name Maryland, " . . . so called after Mrs. James J. Hill, my wife, and my daughter. I have somewhere between 75 and 100 men working there and am building a Quaker church, hotel, and other buildings."

Sam lost no time in organizing the "Columbus Land Company" and proceeding to acquire some seventeen farms and ranches. In December 1907, he hired W. J. Hilligoss to come from Minnesota to survey the area and to start securing options. Hervey Lindley, Walter Oakes and H. C. Richardson helped in closing later deals. Sam did not want to negotiate with the owners personally for fear of driving up prices. He enlisted Richardson, a U.S. Department of Interior employee from Okanogan, to manage the farms as they were acquired.

Sam wrote Babcock in St. Paul, "My idea is to organize a company of $100,000 capital and buy the fruitland and vineyards. . . . The plan is to sell a man a piece of fruitland and a piece of timberland so he can have material for fuel and boxes for his fruit. . . . I have set apart $10,000 worth of stock for you and Hilligoss. [There were no timberlands adjacent to the development. Sam may have been referring to " . . . several tracts of timberland on the side of the mountain near the town of Goldendale. . . . " In 1908, he contemplated forming a million dollar syndicate to buy these properties, but the deal did not go through.] I do not think we will have to call in more than $5,000 or 50 percent at once. . . . I am rather hard up myself just now, much to my regret. Trains will be running from Pasco to Columbus, our station, about the first of December, and as soon as the line [is completed], undoubtedly prices will advance very materially."

Sam's ideas were not grandiose in the beginning. He wrote Babcock, "The amount of land we can get is limited in quantity; there will not be over three or four thousand acres. Perhaps 7½ per cent of this will be in vineyards and orchards." He ended up with about 7,000 acres, much of it on the barren Klickitat Hills. The owners would not sell all the fertile bench land adjacent to the river which he wanted to own.

As Lois Plotts, who grew up in the area, says, it is hard to picture nowadays, when one drives by the mostly barren land between the highway and down by the river, now used only for grazing, that this was the site of prosperous orchards, vineyards, gardens, homes and farms. The changes in the next two decades call to mind what Charles Babcock said to his sons: "Why didn't Sam Hill leave the farmers alone? After they were bought out, some bought new farms, others couldn't stand prosperity. He ruined a wonderful country — nearly everything Sam Hill touched turned to gold; what didn't, he ruined." This judgment may be harsh, in that the country, with its low rainfall, winds, and cold winters, itself helped to ruin Sam's golden dream.

When the Spokane, Portland & Seattle Railway was being constructed through the town of Columbus in 1909, about half the houses had to moved north. The town had some 100 residents then, with three stores, two churches, a school, a post office, a railway depot, a small railway hospital, and two saloons. There was also "the house where the bad woman lived." Mystified children were admonished not to go near it. Travelers were met at the railway station by a horse-drawn stage, and later by a Stanley Steamer automobile which would take them to Goldendale.

In the summer of 1908, Sam had six horses shipped to Columbus from his estate at Stockbridge, Massachusetts. The next year the buggy and horses from his Seattle house were shipped by train to Vancouver, by boat to Lyle, Washington, and then driven over the mountains to Columbus, since there was no road along the Columbia east of Lyle.

Richardson soon began receiving frequent orders to ship boxes of apples and prunes to Sam's wife, daughter, the J. J. Hills, and various friends. He struck the first ominous note about the weather in January 1909; "The cold snap I think killed the greater portion of the peach and grape crop. . . . " Undaunted, that spring Sam sent him seed grain for "two fine varieties of wonderfully sweet corn" with detailed instructions for planting.

The time had come to seek buyers of the land. Early in 1909, Sam planned a campaign to attract Quaker farmers. He wrote Richardson, "I am getting in touch with Quakers all over the country." At Sam's behest, John Dillingham of Philadelphia, whom Sam had known at Haverford College, sent out a letter to several Pennsylvania and New Jersey Friends. The letter did not mention Sam by name, but stated that a man of wealth had purchased a tract of fertile land, and was " . . . desirous to people it with members of the Society of Friends, especially with those who have grown up within the limits of Philadelphia Yearly Meeting. He is about building an ample Friends meeting house there at his own expense, and wishes a Friends meeting to begin there in the coming summer." The letter asked for addresses of people " . . . who would be interested in receiving descriptive literature concerning the avantages of the colony."

Dillingham and his wife accepted an invitation to come at Sam's expense to attend the opening of the meeting. As a Quaker, he could not promise to give a sermon. Sam assured him that he would not care whether or not any words were spoken or if only a few people attended.

Lois Plotts was present at the first meeting held on August 29, 1909. Sam's brother Richard was there, along with several cousins from North Carolina and the Williamses from Seattle. She recalls the bare walls and benches and the elders dressed in their traditional clothes. After a long interval of silence, a prayer was offered, two of the elders shook hands, and the ceremony was over. No one can remember another service being held.

No Quakers came to live in the area, and Sam quickly abandoned that idea in favor of attracting other buyers for the tracts and homesites in the town which he had had platted, now called Maryhill. Sam later wrote Prof. Meany, "I desired to call the place Maryland, but the government objected, advising me to that effect by telegram at my expense. I handed the telegram to Jusserand [the French Ambassador, who, with his wife, was visiting Sam], who said, 'Call it Maryhill. You have the name right to your hand, after your daughter, your wife, and [her] mother.'"

Sam had Lindley prepare an illustrated folder promoting Maryhill in August 1909, featuring his slogan, "Where the rain and sunshine meet." J. J. Hill was quoted: "The shores of the Columbia River will produce more fruit and grapes than the Rhine," and there were other glowing commendations. The brochure compared the rainfall east of Maryhill to that of Los Angeles, and west of it to Portland's. The favorable prospects for prosperous farms, orchards, and stock raising were depicted. It was announced

Publicity folder, Maryhill land Co., 1909. (Maryhill Museum files.)

that a hotel had been built, the St. James, but that " . . . no saloon will ever be permitted in the town. No plans for a jail have been made . . . No speculators are welcome." The S.P. & S. Railway announced round-trip "home seekers" fares of from $52.50 to $57.50 from Midwest points to Maryhill.

The *Los Angeles Record* published a story about that time, perhaps planted by Lindley, on "Maryhill, Model City, Tribute to Three Women," picturing " . . . the most model city in the State if present plans are carried out. It will be in the midst of a farming community with all modern urban coveniences, such as daily mail delivery, daily newspapers, telephones, water and sewer systems, on a scale never before attempted on the Pacific Coast."

In the spring of 1909, Hilligoss left his job as a timber cruiser with the Great Northern Railway in Minnesota and came to help Richardson full-time. There soon was friction. Hilligoss wrote to Sam in Seattle that Richardson " . . . don't know how to plow or how to set a plow to make it do good work." Worst of all, he did not know how to harness a horse. He was taking out fruit trees and grapevines to put in alfalfa, and was behind in his spring work. Some of the ranchers were burning fence posts for fuel. "What I have written here I thought you should know," Hilligoss added. Sam agreed that Richardson knew only about orchards and had a Portland nurseryman send him quantities of walnut, spruce and cherry trees as windbreaks.

J. J. Hill and party paid Sam a visit at Maryhill in June 1909. Sam had the S.P. & S. train met by a wagon to drive from the station at Columbus up the hill to the hotel. He was afraid to have a car driven down to the depot because of the sand.

Sam's friend Cooke, now president of the Minneapolis Trust Company, wrote Sam about J. J.'s impressions of the visit: "He is very enthusiastic over your fruit land project and says he thinks five million dollars can be made . . . without a very large investment in addition to what you have already made. . . . He thinks it would be better for you, when you conveniently can, to dispose of your telephone interests and devote yourself to the fruit lands. . . . I think, however, it would be wise for you to sit down and talk the whole matter over with him." Sam apparently attended only to the first part of this message.

In the summer of 1909, Sam began to put in service roads (Chapter 16). The first road ran from the land office past the hotel to the store and on up to the church. Edgar Babcock recalls that the last piece of road built was from the sandpit near the river to Sam's new chateau. The rock used there was a poor grade so that the road did not hold up. Other types made of crushed rock covered with macadam stood up very well.

Sam originally intended to build access roads to all the parcels of land and to pave the streets of the planned town of Maryhill. The north-south streets were named after fruit trees and plants, and the east-west streets after shade trees, except for one named in honor of Ambassador Jusserand. This and Peach Street were the only ones actually paved. In addition to the stone store and post office, operated by Sam's cousin, Daniel B. Hill, there were the Maryhill Land Company office and weather station; a stable and blacksmith shop; a garage; and housing for men working on road construction.

Sam now had a substantial bungalow built for his daughter and her nurse companion, Miss Jean Marte, called "Miss Mary's Cottage." This was ready in July 1910, and his daughter lived there from time to time until 1916, mostly in the summer months.

Sam, who usually thrived on feverish activity, for once had too much on his mind. All of this was costing a good deal of money. By August 1909, about $166,000 had been spent for land alone, the largest parcel of which, 1,300 acres, cost $25,000. Equipment and operating expenses came to another $44,000. He wrote, "I am well but can hardly ever be said to be happy." He thanked a friend for sending a check for $8.75. "I have used the check to cover my payroll of $12,000 for this month and it was gratefully received."

Babcock had warned him that the cost of the dams for irrigation would be "out of all proportion to the cost of the land." He reminded Sam that people from eastern and central states had been stung by promoters of land schemes: "In my opinion, the cream has already been taken." He urged Sam to " . . . get the land on the market and force sales, provided you want to realize the profits which the location and character of the land certainly warrant." There is every indication that Sam deceived himself about the prospects for profitable farming at Maryhill, rather than trying to deceive others.

A few families were persuaded to lease the farms and farm houses. In some cases, a year's free rent was offered. Sam's employees were allowed to move into vacant houses rent free. Only one family besides the Babcocks and Richardsons bought land and built a house. Sam admitted to one prospect, "The drawbacks of the country are the facts that at certain times of the year the wind blows, and also that the fuel has to be brought in. Otherwise, I believe the land to be the best location anywhere in the country."

Sam's hopes of success continued for a couple of years. He even considered putting in golf links. A few dances and grange meetings were held at the St. James Hotel. Road workers were kept busy on construction of ten miles of experimental roads, except when snow and below zero temperatures held them up, as occurred in January 1912. There was talk of opening sales offices at Wenatchee, Seattle, and Yakima, but this was forgotten as sales proved to be few and far between.

The Maryhill Land Company was incorporated in April 1910 and in June 1912, the Columbus Land Company turned over all its property to it, including seven teams of horses, a team of mules, and road making equipment.

Sam tried for over a year to persuade his former law partner, Charles Babcock, to leave his job with the land department of the Great Northern Railway and come out as his assistant for the Maryhill project. Babcock visited Maryhill in May 1910 and finally agreed to come out to stay that fall at a salary of $2,500 a year.

Charles Babcock's son Edgar recalls that when the family came they stayed at the St. James Hotel for about a month before the furniture for their rent-free house arrived. There were solid orchards to the base of the hills and the farms were in good shape. Fire hydrants and a sewer line, one of the first in the county, were installed about this time, but there was no fire protection when the main reservoir failed to fill up.

The Babcocks built a house, finished in August 1914 with the help of Sam's head carpenter. Sam would stay at the St. James Hotel on his visits from Portland, usually on weekends, or sometimes with the Babcocks or with the Brooks at Goldendale. He and Babcock, Sr. would smoke many cigars as they talked. Sam limited himself to one drink before dinner. He would come by train or by way of the ferry from the Oregon side and often would bring visitors to Maryhill to show them the experimental roads and the chateau under construction.

There were then four or five families still living on the farms, working for Sam. Large quantities of peaches were packed in baskets in the orchards and hauled by wagon to the Maryhill railway siding. Minister Jordan, who had refused to sell out to Sam, raised beautiful grapes and would ship 80 to 100 boxes on the train each day in the season to the Italians at Roslyn, Washington, where Sam had an interest in a coal mine. Sam would send a wagonload of wheat to a mill near Goldendale and have four or five barrels of flour brought back. For a time in 1912, the ranch was supplying fruits and vegetables for the dining cars of the S.P. & S. Railway. In the fall of 1912, however, Sam wrote his daughter, "Unfortunately, we lost nearly all our [apple] crop owing to the fact that we had no means of shipping it out."

Early in 1912, Babcock furnished an overdue assignment of responsibilties. Sam Lancaster superintended the road work and water development; Sam's cousin, Daniel B. Hill, was in charge of the store, hotel, annex and stables; and W. W. Parris supervised the ranches. E. B. Wells, vice-president of the Home Telephone and Telegraph Company of Portland, took over disbursements. There was not much income to keep track of.

A county road improvement district was formed, and a contract for $35,000 let to construct a road, completed in 1912, from the town of Maryhill about three miles west to Maryland Ranch. Several property owners became delinquent in payment of assessments for the road, and presumably it was in this way that Sam came, willy-nilly, to own more property than he had anticipated.

Initially, Sam had ideas for a railroad spur from Maryhill to Goldendale, to be called the "Maryhill and Goldendale Railroad Company." This and the Maryhill Water Company were dissolved in 1913 and the Maryhill Growers' Association and Business Men's Association soon afterward. The Growers' Association showed a net profit of only $445 in 1914. The Maryhill post office operated from June 1909 through September 1913, when it was closed for lack of patronage.

Sam had not quite given up. In May 1913, he had a testimonial printed for prospects. "Any man skilled in his work should make a good living for himself and his family in growing vegetables and fruits for the early market on ten acres of land. . . . The locality is also showing marked adaptation for the production of alfalfa and other legumes . . . [so that] farmers may successfully add the production of milk, pork, and poultry to that of these products." In December 1914, he wrote Bishop O'Connell, "The grasshoppers have eaten us up for three years at Maryhill." This item aparently did not deserve mention in the flier.

But attempts to lure buyers were all of no avail. It finally became evident to Sam that it was futile to try to sell or lease more ranches at Maryhill. If the development was to make any money, it would have to become a cattle ranch. In May 1913, he had 70 head of beef cattle and two Hereford bulls sent from Montana by arrangement with his friend Stuart of the Carnation Company in Seattle.

Sam wrote a letter of complaint to the general manager of the O.W.R. & N. Railway in 1912. He had invested more than $600,000 in the Maryhill development, he said, but it was impossible to ferry across the river to land near the railway station at Biggs because of the nearby rapids. One had to drive a wagon east on the Washington side, cross the river, and then go west to Biggs, involving " . . . on each side approximately a mile through the blowing sand." He said that in 1910 he had, at his own expense, arranged for a ferry to Grant and expected the railway to put in a station there. He tried unsuccessfully to enlist the support of businessmen in Hood River and The Dalles in this campaign.

` In 1914, not noticeably daunted by failure of his dream for a new town, Sam began work on his great house (Chapter 23). He wrote his architect in 1915, "Owing to the scarcity of money and other things going on, I am proceeding very slowly with the house. He closed down the work in 1917, ostensibly because of pending plans for conversion of the house to a museum, but very probably because of lack of money, as well as America's entrance that year into the World War.

Sam inaugurated a new ferry service on the gas engine propelled side-wheeler *Governor West* in February 1915. The route was poorly located because winds blowing up river would tilt the craft and reduce its efficiency. In low waters, she tended to scrape bottom on a gravel bar, and the craft was later beached and abandoned, becoming to the local residents another of "Hill's follies." Fred Smith, a centenarian and former ferry boat operator, told Pete May that Sam's crew didn't know the river and hung up the ferry on a rock. Smith pulled them off and " . . . they got ashore and tied up and there they stayed. That was the end of Sam's ferry business." (Ferry service was operated by others until the Sam Hill Memorial Bridge was opened for traffic in the fall of 1962.)

Smith told the author that Sam had started the ferry service in a huff over the following incident: Sam had sent word to Smith to be ready to take his guests to the Oregon side at 10:00 A.M., but about 9:45, three cars appeared from the north to cross the river. As a public carrier, Smith felt he had to take them, leaving Sam's party to wait for half an hour, and Sam to come to a full rolling boil.

Sam foresaw the need for a highway bridge at Maryhill. He wrote to Zola Brooks years later, "You know, Zola, I sort of feel as if there is no use trying to help the public any more. . . . I am holding that land across there [on the Oregon side] for a bridge site so, when the time comes, the county won't be robbed." Sam didn't object to paying the taxes, $2.37 a year, but one Dinty Moore occupying the land did not pay Sam any rent. What was more, "The tax bill on the Maryhill Museum of Fine Arts is now $1,426.02, which is beside what I pay every month for the care of the place."

Maryland Ranch and the Meadowlark Inn continued to operate. (The name of the St. James Hotel was changed when the hotel was moved to make room for the Stonehenge Memorial.) Richardson, in charge of Sam's

The town of Maryhill, looking north across Jordan's orchard. Buildings, *left to right*: St. James Hotel, later called Meadowlark Inn; Annex; Maryland Land Co. office; stone store and post office; Friend's meeting house and "Mary's cottage" on hill. (From glass slide, Maryhill Museum files.)

ranches, had the help of a trio of hired men, Harp, Tharp, and Fields. Little correspondence survives about the finances of the Maryland Ranch in the 1920's, but what exists paints a depressing picture.

There is not to be found a mea culpa for the failure of the Maryhill development. Sam wrote his brother in 1912 to say fervently, if not accurately, "I always regard real estate as a liability and not as an asset." He managed some qualified enthusiasm in a letter to General Clarence Edwards in 1923: "Speaking of farming, if you think you are poor with a few acres, how would you like to have 7,000 acres around your neck, of which about 5,000 acres are rock and 2,000 acres are the best land that ever lay out of doors for raising fruits and vegetables?" Sam was trying to raise mules and added, " . . . I am trying to devise the best way to break eight mules and to do it in such a way as to keep away from the business end of the mule while he is being broken."

In October 1921, the property of the Maryhill Land Company was conveyed to the United States Trust Company, Sam's holding company in Seattle. Sam asked for a tax credit for a casualty loss of $59,180 for damage to fruit trees in the very severe winter of 1920-1921. Richardson reported to Sam in December 1922, that there were still about 3,800 peach trees and 234 pear trees on the property.

Sam wrote in 1923, "Things here went to rack and ruin during the war, as all of our young men went into the service. I am giving very considerable attention to Maryhill, and hope, in another year, to get things on their feet." There had been another bad winter, Sam said. "Our season here is about 30

Aerial view of Stonehenge Memorial and the remaining buidings at Maryhill about 1930. (Maryhill Museum files.)

days behind our usual seasons. . . . This morning, the temperature is seven degrees above zero, which is the coldest February that I have ever known in this country.''

Charles Babcock and his three sons, however, did well on their well-irrigated 250 acres. Edgar Babcock recalls that they would harvest up to 400 sacks of potatoes per acre, plus corn and other vegetables. Sam was interested in ditch irrigation and intensive farming and liked to vist their fields. He offered to deed some land to the Babcock boys for one dollar, provided they did not let their father know. The elder Babcock heard of the offer and indignantly declined it for his sons, though he did offer to pay the going price. Charles Babcock died in 1927; one son stayed on the place and the others went their own ways.

The Meadowlark Inn was operated for some years after Sam's death by Clara Carter and Lucy Weatherby, two maiden English women who had been housekeepers in Sam's Seattle residence. The two-story inn had a large kitchen with a massive wood-burning stove and a reputation for turning out good meals. Kerosene lamps were used until electricity was installed in 1939.

Most of the farm houses on the Maryhill tract were lost one by one to fires. Some were started from sparks from the brakes of railroad cars, others from cigarette butts thrown from passing autos. The winds and dry grass made control of the fires very difficult. The Quaker meeting house and

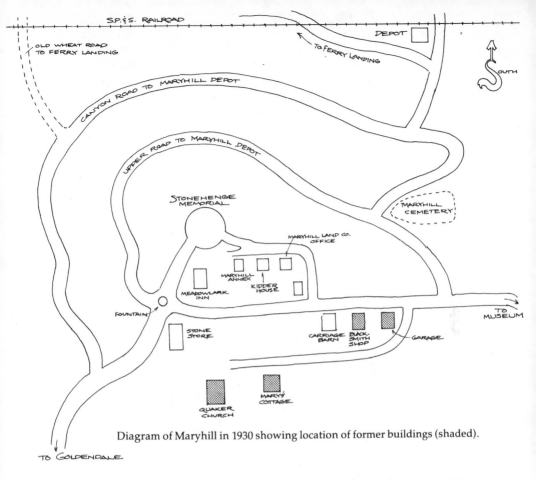

Diagram of Maryhill in 1930 showing location of former buildings (shaded).

Mary's cottage were torn down for lumber by employees of the Maryland Ranch during the Great Depression. A fire destroyed the remaining buildings in July 1958, so only the ruins of the concrete garage and stone store remain near Stonehenge Memorial.

Why did Maryhill fail as a farming community? One reason was the unfortunate selection of the site in the Columbia Gorge, unprotected from cold east winds in winter. The average annual rainfall at Maryhill is about 11 inches, whereas that at Hood River and White Salmon is about 30 inches. The low rainfall and the lack of an irrigation system were prime factors in the fiasco.

There are still orchards near the river bank at Maryhill, but they have subsoil moisture and are well irrigated. As Roger Pond, the Klickitat County extension agent, says charitably, "In today's economy, we wouldn't consider a dryland fruit orchard above Maryhill as a practical venture. However, in Sam Hill's time the impractical was commonplace and the impossible was accomplished daily."

But Sam's sometimes golden touch had failed him. When he discovered the Maryhill area, he exclaimed like Moses on the summit of Mt. Pisgah, "It is the Promised Land!" Moses and his people had wandered for forty years in the desert before they found the land of plenty. Within twenty years of Sam's discovery of the land of Eden, it had become a desert. One wonders how often he reflected on the time and money wasted. Had he not intervened, there would still be the town of Columbus with farms and ranches around it. To Sam's credit are the memorials he left in the area. One, the ten mile stretch of experimental roads, is of historic interest in that it gave momentum to establishing an excellent highway system for the Northwest. The other two, Stonehenge Memorial and Maryhill Museum, will endure.

23

Castle Nowhere

The residents of many an American town can point to some extravagantly built mansion or other and identify it, with a shake of the head, as "So and so's folly." The theme of the pride and ostentation of a newly rich millionaire, ending in ruin or disgrace, is found in a number of American and British novels of a bygone age — bygone because of taxes on property, income, and inheritance, and a future difficulty unforeseen in the grandiose planning, "the servant problem."

Sam Hill's lonely "castle," built on a ledge of the Klickitat Hills looking across the Columbia to the equally barren hills on the Oregon side, is unique. It was not completed in his lifetime and Sam never lived there. As was the case with his Seattle house, his wife never saw it. These two almost indestructible buildings were not envisioned as seats of a prestigious family, like the great houses of England, to be passed to descendants. They seem, instead, to have been intended as monuments to Sam himself, Pharaonic in intent if not in size, to be remembered after the memory of his deeds would fade.

The site he chose for his house at Maryhill, near the western end of his 7,000 acre ranch, did not make practical sense. It was miles from any good-sized town and inconvenient to reach. The highway on the north bank he had urged for so long was not completed until after his death. One either took the Spokane, Portland and Seattle train to Maryhill station and made the ascent up the winding road from the depot, or came by the Union Pacific on the Oregon side and took the ferry across to Maryhill. After the Columbia River Highway was completed in 1915, motorists from Oregon used the car-ferry.

The reason Sam gave for building his great house is difficult to accept. Fred Lockley visited the site while the house was being built in 1915. Waxing both practical and poetic, Sam told him, "I have planned it for a good, comfortable and substantial farmhouse. Here I can let the world wag as it will. My cold storage plant will keep my meats and farm products in good shape. It is large enough to have a few friends drop in and take potluck with me. I can keep them warm in winter and cool in summer. On the roof we will have our outdoor bedrooms throughout the summer months, and we can look up and watch the wheeling constellations swing across the night sky, or look down on the sea-seeking Columbia or at Mt. Hood in all its varying moods. . . . I expect this house to be here for a thousand years after I am gone."

The plans were absurdly grand for a ranch house for Sam and his daughter. Sam told Lockley that the dining room would seat 250 people comfortably. He expected it would cost between a quarter and half a million dollars. (In 1936, Zola Brooks, Secretary-Treasurer of the Board of the Maryhill Museum, estimated from the records that Sam had spent only $120,000. He reckoned that another $50,000 would have to be spent to complete the building.) There were to be long ramps at either end of the building leading up to the main floor. Guests could either drive into a garage under the west ramp and take an electric elevator to the main floor, or drive up the ramp and into the great reception hall to discharge passengers, and exit on the ramp at the other end. On the north side of the house, Sam planned for a large library, den, dining room, serving room, and his own bedroom. The great reception hall on the south side commanded a view of the river and the Oregon hills. The third floor was to be partitioned into eight suites with baths. In the small upstairs entrance hall, a warming oven was to be built into the wall so a man could leave a guest's breakfast to be picked up when he or she desired. Sam's probable intention was to entertain in style his prominent friends from the United States and abroad, but he nowhere says the house was built for Queen Marie or King Albert.

Sam again chose the architectural firm of Marshall and Hornblower of Wasington, D.C., which had planned his Seattle house, to design the large Flemish-style building. Work began in 1914. Sam wrote Marshall in April, "Our camp is in place and soon we will be at work, we hope by the 15th." Sam corresponded with him about details of planning, but Marshall did not visit the site until November 1915.

As in the Seattle house, the exterior walls were of very thick concrete reinforced with steel. The basement was to contain the laundry; furnace and boilers; pantry and other storage areas; refrigeration equipment; and five bedrooms for servants. Coal, wood, or oil could be burned in the furnace. In 1938, when work to complete the building was begun, it was reported that workmen filled the boiler with water and soon had it furnishing steam heat throughout the building. No wood was used in the structure. Through most of the building, steel studs covered with metal lath extended from concrete floor to concrete ceiling.

A mixture of gravel and sand, applied with a cement gun, was used for finishing the exterior walls. Massive double doors, ten feet tall, guarded the entrances from the ramps. These were made of heavy copper painted with green oxide to resemble green bronze. Even though the nearest source of electricity was the town of Maryhill over three miles away, the house was wired for it, including plenty of outlets in all the rooms. Current was not supplied until twenty years later. Every room was also piped for gas for heat and light. There were five miles of pipe for plumbing in the walls.

The house itself was 60 by 93 feet long, but the ramps, each with a circular turnaround for cars, extended the structure to about 400 feet. Twenty-four automobiles could be parked under each ramp. The structure was some 50 feet high, not counting the elevator towers at either end of the building. The doors and windows were covered with grillwork with a green bronze finish.

Had Sam proceeded with his usual speed and determination, the house would no doubt have been finished before America entered World War I. However, as Sam wrote Marshall in September 1915, "Owing to the scarcity of money and other things going on, I am proceeding very slowly with the house." He was referring to the financial difficulties of the Home Telephone Company in Portland and his preoccupation with the construction of the Columbia River Highway. Then too, he was away for several months in the summer of 1916 on the mission to Europe and Russia.

Sam did not get around to having plaster applied to the steel lath partitions of the rooms. He had mentioned going ahead with the plastering if it did not cost more than $3,000, but the workmen wanted to see the specifications before making a bid.

Sam returned from the East in June 1917, " . . . still suffering with neuritis." He told Marshall that only two carpenters were at work, " . . . and as I have not much money to spend, they might as well go ahead with the forms for the formal garden wall. . . . My idea is to keep the house going slowly until I can get some money to push it faster. Of course, if the Germans take it, they can finish it."

It was in July 1917 that Loie Fuller persuaded Sam to dedicate his unfinished chateau as a museum for French art. He did not mention the shortage of money when he wrote to her in November 1917: "I have closed down the work here until I hear from you, as I do not wish to put in any steel partitions which will have to be taken down. . . . I hope [by February 1918] to open up the work again and finish the house for occupancy in case it is not desired to use it for [a museum]."

Sam's financial status improved when his Home Telephone Company was sold to Bell. He had money to start construction of the Stonehenge Memorial in 1918, the Peace Arch in 1920, the restaurant and golf course at Semiahmoo, B.C., and the house near the Columbia River for his mistress, Mona Bell Hill. There were lavish outlays for the trip around the world with Joffre and party in 1922 and for other ventures in the 1920's. Why did he not instead proceed with plans to convert the half-completed chateau to a museum? The only reason appears to have been his pique over the failure of the Washington State authorities to construct a north bank highway which would give easy access to the museum for visitors.* Even the visit of Queen Marie in 1926, and the promises from her, from foreign governments, and from Loie Fuller for donations of art objects failed to persuade Sam to finish the house during his lifetime.

In a 1919 newspaper story, datelined Seattle, Sam was reported to have offered Maryhill ranch to the Belgian Cabinet " . . . with a suggestion that the farmland be utilized for colonization purposes and the big incomplete mansion that is part fortress and part residence be utilized as a museum, library, historical building and headquarters." Sam was said to be making this offering " . . . as a tribute to the defense Belgium made to the invasion of the German hordes in the summer of 1914." The article noted the popular fancy that the structure indicated Sam's " . . . vision of the point where America's first great defense would have to be waged against the invasion of an army landing on the Pacific Coast. . . . The roof was so strongly supported that great guns could be placed on it if necessary. The house itself would long resist attacks. Its water supply is brought by concealed methods from the mountains and the place could hold out indefinitely if it were required." Sam did not name the dreaded invader, or how this point so far inland on the Columbia could be of any strategic importance. He was not one to deceive a gullible reporter for the fun of it — it must have been another manifestation of his morbid fear of the Communists.

A newspaperman once asked Sam just what he would make of the unfinished chateau. Sam answered, "I may make it a museum, an international museum of fine arts. And a library. It will be a school of all the people. The farmer folk could come here to find solutions to their problems." The newsman mused to himself whether any "farmer folk" in Oregon or Washington could spare several days to get to and from Sam's remote "school." Stewart Holbrook concluded that Sam was " . . . thinking not of American farmers, but of peasants . . . It was just as obvious that this hulking fortress stemmed from his youthful memories of some castle on the Rhine."

The articles of incorporation of the "Maryhill Museum of Fine Arts" were signed by Sam, Edgar Hill, and Charles Babcock on July 4, 1923, and filed with the Klickitat County Clerk a month later. Its objects were "educational and scientific." There was to be a self-perpetuating five member board of trustees. The first board included Loie Fuller and Robert Tierman of Paris.

The "castle" received its first national publicity when Queen Marie came to dedicate it as a museum in November 1926. Sam surely had told her the building was only half finished, but except for the local residents who had become accustomed to its appearance, the people attending the dedication ceremony must have felt, in varying degrees, incredulous, amused, and embarrassed that this lonely hulk was to be taken seriously as a future museum.

---

* Any chess player would have told him he had castled on the wrong side!

But Sam did not lose sight of that goal. In 1929, he appeared before the Washington legislature and several civic organizations to campaign for completion of a paved north bank highway which would furnish easier access to Maryhill. He had received assurances that the road around Lyle Mountain to the west, where he had promoted convict work nearly 20 years before, would be finished within two years. On his return from Europe that summer, he told a reporter he had " . . . shipped his entire collection of paintings and relics gathered in the Old Countries to Maryhill."

The dream of a museum seemed far from fulfillment in Sam's last years. The chateau was the picture of dilapidation and must have been a depressing sight for him. Several buildings still stood near Stonehenge Memorial: the Meadowlark Inn; a guest cottage and one for Sam; and the caretaker's house. He was certainly aware of the label, "Sam Hill's Folly", applied both to the half finished pile and the near-ghost town of Maryhill.

"Mr. Hill doesn't like to have it called the castle," the manager of Maryhill ranch, Malcolm Flannagan, told a curious reporter in 1929. "No, there is nothing in the museum . . . The stuff brought by Queen Marie? It's been taken away . . . Why did Mr. Hill build the museum?" Flannagan waved at the Columbia Gorge. "Personally I have been around a great deal of the world and I never have seen anything like this." The manager had no authority to let the reporter enter the museum, and complained that, "I'm too busy to go. I have a letter a mile long from Mr. Hill telling me exactly what I am to do. He knows what is going on here, though he comes very seldom. I have been here since Stonehenge was started and he has made only four visits, that's in a year and a half."

The reporter saw the Celilo Falls of the Columbia a little downstream and could make out Indians moving about their shanties along the riverbank. Snow-capped Mt. Hood could be seen miles to the west. He entered the building through a window from which some intruder had broken the padlock. The wooden dais on which Queen Marie had sat was still in place in the main hall. He found a maze of rooms on the top floor and in the ground-floor basement, and was surprised that some of the rooms in the basement had no entrance or light except by a door opening into a hallway. (According to the blueprints, kindly furnished by Don Parks of Portland, these were intended for storage and refrigeration.) The stairs and floors were covered with rat dung and the wind moaned through the upper floor. Hundreds of mud swallows nested under the eves. The only other signs of life were cows grazing in a distant field.

Disturbed by this dismal report, the Portland *Spectator* took *The Oregonian* to task for committing " . . . a crime somewhat resembling burglary . . . [and] for holding up to ridicule one of our best known and useful men — Samuel Hill." But Sam was probably inured to it by that late date.

The title *The Prince of Castle Nowhere* has a fairy-tale quality. Those who are fond of fantasy may imagine that the castle slept while the prince lived (awakening only briefly for the visit of the queen), and for seven years after his death. Grim and uninhabitable, too sturdy to be a ruin, it was the home

Aerial view of Maryhill Museum, surrounded on three sides by vineyards and orchards. The remains of the old road to Maryhill Ranch can be seen above Highway 14. About 1940. (Maryhill Museum files.)

of rats and swallows, an object of wonder and ridicule by the people. It was seldom visited by the prince, who wandered restlessly on many a quest until his spirit departed for an undiscovered country. His ashes were buried near the castle in the domain he called the Promised Land, a country he possessed but could not bend to his will.

Loie Fuller, Professor Meany, and Other Famous Friends

Loie Fuller

The friends and acquaintances of Sam Hill made at home and abroad included some strange birds, of whom Loie Fuller was surely the most exotic. It was at her suggestion that Sam decided to convert his great house at Maryhill into a museum, and through her connections with Queen Marie of Rumania, Auguste Rodin, and Alma Spreckels that much of the museum's collection was acquired.

She was once the toast of Paris and celebrated by some of France's foremost artists and writers, but Loie's fame dimmed quickly after her death. As Peter Mooz, the director of the Virginia Museum, put it in the forward to the handsome catalog of its 1979 Loie Fuller exhibition, "The fifty-one years since her death in 1928 have left her an almost forgotten figure, shrouded in misinformation and obscurity. The primary tangible proof of her popularity and fame rests on the multitude of art objects produced during her lifetime and bearing her image." Margaret Harris has provided a well-researched account of her life for the catalog, on which much of the following summary is based.

Loie Fuller was born Mary Louise Fuller in Fullersburg, Illinois, near Chicago, probably in January 1862. She studied singing in Chicago and appeared in various theatrical productions in New York and on the road and later in London. She married a Col. William Hayes in 1889, a disastrous mistake ending within three years when Loie sued him for bigamy. In a play called "Quack, M.D." she wore a voluminous Indian silk costume, flitting about the stage like a butterfly in a dance she was later to call the "Serpentine."

The enthusiastic response of the audience encouraged her to invent other dances with the stage lit by projected lights of various colors and designs. She used aluminum or bamboo rods sewn into her silken costumes so she could swirl about with dozens of yards of cloth above and all about her, and introduced the use of lights below the stage shining through a glass floor. Another striking effect was achieved by having mirrors behind her and a wall of glass between the stage and the audience in the darkened theater. Some of her famous dances were called "Violet," "Butterfly," "Lily Dance," and "Fire Dance." She had many imitators during this part of her career, leading her to patent some of the stage effects and costumes she had designed and produced.

She read of the luminous properties of radium, newly discovered by

Pierre and Marie Curie, and wrote to them about the possibility of making "butterfly wings of radium." They explained that this was impossible, and Loie thanked them by dancing for them in their home.

She came to know other famous people of her day, including Auguste Rodin, Sarah Bernhardt, Alexandre Dumas, Camille Flammarion, Anatole France and many others. She became a favorite subject for a number of artists, among them Riviere, Larche, Roche, Whistler, and Toulouse-Lautrec.

She met Marie, then Princess Royal of Rumania, when she danced in Bucharest in 1902. Marie received her at the palace and they became life-long friends. She encouraged the queen to publish the poetry and fairy tales that the queen had written for her children. Years later, a movie featuring Loie's dance troupe was made, based on the queen's short story, "The Lily of Life" (Chapter 26).

Her real fame came in November 1892 when she made her debut at the Folies-Bergère. Her performances were not only a sensational success, but made the Folies a respectable place for parents to take their children for matinees.

She was briefly associated with Isadora Duncan on a European tour in 1902. Isadora said she left the company because she had been attacked during the night by a woman in the troupe. Loie's story was that Isadora had used the tour as a stepping stone to her own great success. In spite of this, they admired each other. (In the play, *Isadora Duncan Sleeps with the Russian Navy* by Jeff Wanshel, Dramatists Play Service, Inc., N.Y., 1977, there is a scene in which Loie invites Isadora to become a disciple of Sappho. Surprising, in this day and age, that anyone knew or cared.)

Loie paid the expenses of a Japanese dancer, Sada Yacco, and a troupe of thirty at the Paris Exposition Universelle of 1900, said to have marked the apogee of the Art Nouveau movement, and danced with this troupe in a theater especially designed for Loie. She later supported another Japanese troupe headed by a young woman dancer named Hanako, for whom Loie wrote several plays and pantomimes. She began a life-long liaison with Gabrielle Bloch after Loie's mother died about 1908.

One of Loie's important accomplishments was bringing the sculpture of Rodin, whom she had met several years earlier, to the attention of Americans. She put his works from her own collection in exhibitions in New York in 1903. Through Loie, Rodin was introduced to the Javanese and Cambodian ballets, as well as to the Japanese dancers Yacco and Hanako, inspiring him to do a number of sculptures and water colors.

In 1908, Loie started a dance school for young girls recruited from London, many of whom joined her traveling dance troupes. Janet Flanner wrote that in 1927, Loie had two ballet groups, members of which were paid 3,000 francs a month whether they worked or not. She added, "In case of Miss Fuller's sudden death, bonds in London assure each dancer of an inheritance. All her life she has displayed the same genius and generosity." (Generosity, yes: financial responsibility, no, according to Margaret Harris, who writes, "Not only were [her dancers] not paid when they didn't work, they were rarely paid when they did. . . . She took care of them . . . but nothing ever happened on a regular basis as far as money was concerned.") She had just opened at the Moulin Rouge at a contract of 25,000 francs a week. Her menage in Paris, located across the street from that of Prince Carol of Rumania, consisted of four secretaries, one French and one Japanese chef, and various underlings.

Alma Spreckels met Loie in Paris in 1914 and they became great friends. Loie introduced Mrs. Spreckels to Rodin at his country place in Meudon. The next year, the Pan-Pacific International Exposition opened in San Franciso. It was here that Alma Spreckles introduced Loie, who was there with her dance troupe, to Sam Hill. Sam had met the Spreckels through a mutual friend from Portland.

Rodin sculptures were exhibited in the French Pavillion, which was a replica of the Palace of the Legion of Honor in Paris. Loie encouraged Mr. Spreckels to buy six Rodins, including "The Thinker," "The Age of Bronze," and "The Prodigal Son." The Spreckels built the California Palace of the Legion of Honor, and at its opening in 1924, Mrs. Spreckels gave thirty-one works of Rodin to the museum.

In 1915, Loie persuaded Rodin to lend drawings for an album to be sold for the benefit of wounded French soldiers. Loie borrowed money, secured by her personal art collection, in the hope of publishing this album, but had to sell the drawings to pay off the bank loans. To help Loie out of her perennial financial mess, Sam Hill bought the Rodin drawings for $8,000 in 1921 and sent them to the Minneapolis Athenaeum. After his death, they were made part of Maryhill's permanent collection. It is believed that Sam bought all but three of the Rodin sculptures now at Maryhill Museum from Loie; however, the records have not been preserved.

Sam's correspondence with Loie Fuller consists mainly of a flutter of telegrams and letters in 1917, then only a few letters until 1927, when Loie repeatedly tried to get Sam involved in founding a "Loie Fuller Museum" in Paris.

In a series of telegrams sent from a transcontinental train enroute to San Francisco in mid-July 1917, Loie asked, "Shall I bring the young Rumanian officer who is accompanying me? . . . Have formed national committee with you as vice-president for the Rumanian and Belgian work together, Ambassador Herrick [as] president. . . . Received wonderful telegram from the queen."

Sam met her in Portland and they went on to Maryhill. He wrote, "After the eloquent pleading of today, I have decided to dedicate my new chateau at Maryhill, Washington to a museum for the public good and for the betterment of French art in the far Northwest of America. Your hopes and ideals shall be fulfilled, my dear little artist woman." He sent a confirmatory letter to the French Undersecretary of State, who promised a gift of tapestry and a Sèvres porcelain. Sam planned originally to have the first salon at the museum in the autumn of 1918, but the continuation of the war

Loie Fuller, about 1900. Drawing from *Tatler*. (Courtesy of Nicky Tom.)

prevented that. When he wrote Loie in November 1917 about closing down the work he did not mention that his Home Telephone Company was in serious financial straits and that lack of money was a problem.

Loie wrote Sam in December 1922, "I expect you about Xmas time." She was working on donations for Maryhill from France, Greece, and Rumania. "I leave for Rumania day after tomorrow. . . . I pray your brother is spared to you . . . also that you are keeping well for the great good you can do. With deepest regards, Loie."

Richard had died when Sam next wrote Loie after attending his funeral in Minneapolis. He added, "The Duchess of Vendôme sent me a picture for Christmas and I know it must have been at your suggestion. I had a nice letter from Marshall Joffre and one from the King of Belgium. . . . In writing to Rumania, be sure always to send my greetings."

Maryhill Museum was incorporated in 1923 with Sam as president and Loie as one of the trustees. Loie donated a collection of models of famous people's hands, cast by Rodin's molder. The inscription for the donation read, "Dear Mr. Hill: May these hands dedicated to your great work express what they have done for others as a symbol of your own." The collection included the hands of Rodin himself; Victor Hugo; Voltaire; Generals Pershing and Joffre; Sarah Bernhardt; Sam Hill and Loie; and half a dozen royal personages, including the king of Iraq. Other hands, possibly of less

221

permanent interest, included those of Rudolph Valentino, Carol of Rumania, and Magda Lupescu.

She had had an enlargement of Marshall Joffre's hand made at a cost of 4,500 francs, and proposed to build a "museum of hands" at Maryhill, housed in a giant model of a hand fifty feet high, on a concrete base. People " . . . must mount and pay to get through the gate at the bottom to go up and see what Marshall Joffre has written on the hand." Fortunately, Sam showed no interest in giving Loie a big hand. She also had reduced models of several hands made, including Valentino's, which she suggested be palmed off as charms in a "Hippity-Hop" souvenir shop at the museum.

Loie's taste in art was often above reproach, as in her recognition of Rodin's genius. Some of her acquisitions, however, cause the brow to knit, such as a portrait of Cardinal Mercier made with silk thread, rejected by Alma Spreckels; Loie " . . . accepted it with the greatest of joy." In another letter, she wrote Sam about reading that, "A man in New York paid $20,000 for a lock of Beethoven's hair. I have a beautiful lock of Rodin's hair and of Queen Victoria's, and I guess they are both as interesting as Beethoven's — but they are not for sale."

In the last year of her life, Loie frequently wrote Sam about her ideas for making Maryhill a success. She persuaded Sam to send for a large marble statue of Diana by Carrier Belleuse, a teacher of Rodin. The statue, seven feet high, was obtained for the cost of packing and shipping it from France. She wrote to Julius Witmark, the New York music publisher, for contributions of sheet music of famous popular and classical pieces. She had known him as a boy when he was " . . . singing in my concert company and went with me throughout America." For some reason, this collection did not materialize.

There was no doubt correspondence between Loie and Sam, and Queen Marie and Sam, about the queen's visit to the United States in 1926, but unfortunately this has not been preserved. Loie did express her regrets about some of the shenanigans on the trip (Chapter 25).

Beginning in March 1927, Loie wrote Sam half a dozen long letters urging him to undertake construction of an American museum in Paris as an "eternal headquarters of Maryhill," to be combined with a fashionable apartment house on the upper floors in order to help pay expenses. She thought M. Tierman could persuade the Municipal Council to give the land rent free for 50 years. Queen Marie, Madame Joffre, and other well known wealthy people would lease the apartments. She sketched a plan for the building and wrote out estimates for construction and financing. There would be a Loie Fuller Salon, a Good Roads Room, a library, and exhibits of American history, industry, and agriculture. It was Sam's kind of project, and it was probably with reluctance that he wrote in April 1927, "Don't count on me to put the building over. While I think the plan looks good, I am tied up. You forget I had to get $20,000 for the Rudier [Rodin's molder, presumably in payment for at least some of the Rodin sculptures Sam gave to Maryhill Museum]."   Besides, he had had to borrow $25,000 the week before because of the recurrent financial difficulties of his Alabama coal mine.

Two months later he added that he had talked with an architect and hotel operators who had discouraged the project; after all, the number of Americans abroad who would pay $5,000 rent per year was limited. However, he also told Loie he had telephoned the Chase National Bank " . . . that if I could help Rumania, I was at their service." Whether the bank forwarded this welcome news is unknown.

But in spite of her importunate pleas, Loie was really ambivalent about the project, either from fatigue or a suspicion that it would never happen. She wrote Sam, "But dear, we are not forced to do it, nor is my heart set on anything any more! . . . It is my brain acting, not my heart; that is already past being a prop to go on. I see now without enthusiasm, and without that everlasting impetus, 'I must do it,' which has always urged me on! . . . I must dwell on making good that which I did hang on to. . . . "

Loie intended to return to Maryhill in the fall of 1927 to help raise money to finish the museum and to bring with her Joanovitch, painter of European royalty, as the first curator. But in another letter, she confessed that she lacked money for the packing and transportation of things she had bought for the museum. A $200,000 contract for the continuation of her American tour had been canceled and Loie was in debt.

The difficulties of her situation were " . . . augmented by Alma Spreckels never paying me for the 'Victoire' [an heroic war memorial statue which Loie hoped could be shipped to Portland free on a French battleship. She did not think small]. . . . We had to do something, and Gab [Gabrielle Bloch] wrote a scenario from one of the *Tales of Hoffman*, 'Coppelius and the Sandman.'"

Loie had accumulated in her 35 years of experimentation a great many lights, costumes and screens worth two million francs. With these assets, she was depending on the film *Coppelius* to rescue her from financial difficulties. Plump and dowdy-looking in her later years, she was reported to be directing the film from her bed, wearing dark glasses because her eyesight had been damaged by laboratory experiments with lights for her dances years before. She was enthusiastic about the film: "We are experimenting in trick photography in my garage and we have got onto some wonderful things, for instance: man walking in space — walking upside down — walking on the sky; a tornado cyclone, funnel shaped, sweeps twirling and swirling across the screen, taking up inside it everybody and everything; walking absolutely *on*, not in, the water; the spirit leaving the body and going back into it again; monsters that become invisible before your eyes, invisible instantaneously; a tremendous jump over the moon; and eyeglasses that drop luminous eyes!" Alas, she died the following year before the film could be finished.

One gets the impression from her letters to Sam that these proposals for Maryhill were generous and not mercenary. She does not hint that her help for Sam's museum was contingent on his cooperation in building a

Loie Fuller Museum in Paris. In chronic financial difficulties in spite of her large income, in her last letter to Sam on file she wrote, "Ten thousand francs which we danced for on Friday night has not been paid. . . . I am obliged to wire and ask you to cable [the money] to me." She soon wrote to acknowledge Sam's check. Sam sent her another draft for $500 in care of Gaby Bloch in December 1927, in spite of his own financial difficulties.

Were Sam and Loie lovers? In June 1923, when he replied to her ideas for the proposed Maryhill Museum, he wrote, "Your idea grows on me, as does my love for you." A month later he was awaiting a reply for his invitation to visit there. He assured her, "I have finished with Alice Barton." Sam obviously was fond of Loie, who possibly was bisexual. Further their correspondence deponeth not.

At the time of her death in 1928, Janet Flanner describes Loie Fuller as "the most widely known American woman in France." Her death " . . . drew from the French press such tender phrases as 'a magician is dead' and 'a butterfly has folded its wings.'"

So ended a life as remarkable as it was different from Sam Hill's. In her time, her fame surpassed Sam's but the memory of each quickly and undeservedly faded for many years. How strange that these two Americans, so dissimilar except in vision and imagination, should form an alliance which led to the visit of a queen and the founding of a museum in a place of lonely grandeur overlooking the Columbia!

Professor Meany

Among the friends Sam cherished and admired was Professor Edmond S. Meany (1862-1935), in his day the leading historian and teacher of history in the state of Washington. Sam had been a member of the Minnesota Historical Society and remained a history buff for the rest of his life. Meany no doubt inspired Sam's interest in Indian and Northwest history.

In 1899, Meany helped to organize the Columbia Historical Society in Seattle, later incorporated as the "Washington University State Historical Society" on January 1, 1903. Meany, by then professor of history at the University of Washington, was secretary and Judge C. H. Hanford, Judge Thomas Burke, and Sam Hill trustees. Membership was $2 a year. The trustees favored consolidation with the Washington State Historical Society based in Tacoma, but the wish was not reciprocated. The secretary of the Tacoma group wrote a circular letter to the "Newspaper Fraternity of Washington" condemning the " . . . evident attempt by a high-salaried official of the State University to 'crib' our title for his own benefit." Meany was no doubt rueful that the "high-salaried" part of this allegation was stretching the truth.

The objectives of the University group were to promote the study of history at the University of Washington; to commemorate important historical events in the history of the state; to mark historic sites, such as those of the American and British camps on San Juan Island (Sam paid the deficit of an anniversary celebration in 1904); to collect relevant manuscripts and artifacts; and to solicit papers on Northwest history for the *Washington Historical Quarterly*, which began publication in October 1906.

Meany got financial aid from a few prominent Seattleites, including Sam, to keep the society and publication afloat. Sam gave $845, half the printing costs for the first nine issues. (In 1912 publication resumed under the auspices of the University of Washington. The title was changed to *The Pacific Northwest Quarterly* in 1936, a year after Meany's death.)

In August 1903, Sam wrote to Meany, addressing him by his Nez Percé name of "Three Knives": "I have just got back from a pow-wow with Chief Joseph [who has been called "The Red Napoleon" because of his military genius in wars against the white man]. . . . I am very jealous, however, because the Chief did not give me a name. He is thinking over what would be a good name for me, I guess. If he takes too long, I will probably be called Denis." Meany later wrote, "I have not yet recovered from our whirlwind interview of yesterday. If I were Chief Joseph, I would give you a Nez Percé name meaning 'Swift Wing.'"

Chief Joseph died in September 1904. Sam was one of ten guarantors to the publisher of Meany's work on Chief Joseph, so that the first edition of 500 copies could be published. In June 1905, the Historical Society, with Sam's aid, erected a monument to Joseph at Nespelem, Washington. His successor, Yellow Bull, adopted Sam into the tribe and gave him the name, "Wya-Tan-Atoo-Way-Kyk't," meaning "Necklace of Lightning." Sam took a humorous stab at the phonetic pronounciation, giving his name as "Wen-I-Wen-Tuahead." He added, "My idea is to organize a band and proceed against certain people here now with the idea of removing their scalps."

About ten months after Joseph died, a big potlatch and funeral ceremonial were held at Nespelem, Washington. Sam could not be present at the ceremony because of good roads meetings in Portland, but Meany wrote Sam that he had attended with about a hundred other white men. Of these, only three were honored, including Meany and Sam. Meany wrote, "Your present was an old beadwork purse that Chief Joseph had used for years. . . . I am today mailing it to you."

In return, Sam sent Yellow Bull, the Chief's successor, a beautiful blanket in care of the Nez Percé agency at Lapwai, Idaho. Sam considered installing a frieze showing Chief Yellow Bull, his father by adoption, and Sam's own father " . . . writing Indian signs around the ceiling" of the main hall of his chateau at Maryhill. He wrote to his architect about this but for some reason dropped the idea.

Meany wrote Sam about spending the summer of 1905 visiting eighteen Indian reservations and taking over 150 photographs, some of which he sent to Sam. His studies formed part of Edward S. Curtis's classic work, *The North American Indian*. Sam sent Meany four boxes of cigars after this fruitful summer's work, and Meany took the liberty of giving one to a lawyer who would take no pay for settling a claim against Meany when his

Prof. Edmond Meany speaking at the dedication of the altar stone of the Stonehenge Memorial, July 4, 1918. Frank Terrace is at Sam Hill's right. (Maryhill Museum files.)

dog bit a man. Perhaps Meany considered this gesture as newsworthy as "Man bites dog."

Sam's interest in Indians was not confined to the Nez Percé. He wrote to the director of the Bureau of Ethnology of the Smithsonian Institution, "I should like very much to receive any publications relating to the Tineh of Alaska." He had heard that their " . . . language was similar or identical to that spoken by the Apaches in Arizona, and the matter interested me very much." The reply, in case the reader wishes to drop this into dinner party conversation, indicated that these tribes both spoke the Athapascan language.

Sam corresponded with other history enthusiasts on occasion. Ezra Meeker, an Oregon pioneer, wrote Sam in 1910 to ask him to persuade the S.P. & S. Ry. authorities to change the name of the railroad station located near the upper end of the "Long Narrows," of the Columbia River, a few miles west of Maryhill. Meeker complained that the station was called " . . . Spedis, after a worthless Indian," and thought the Indian name, Wish-rum, would be much more desirable. The railroad agreed to the change in name. The heights above Wishram now overlook the large lake formed above The Dalles Dam.

When Meany presided at the exercises on the occasion of the 54th birthday of Seattle in 1905, he asked Sam to give a brief speech, knowing Sam would rise to the occasion, given occasion to rise. Sam gave the presentation speech at the location of the first steam sawmill on Puget Sound, built in 1852. The party went on to Alki Point to dedicate a granite shaft commemorating the landing of a little colony of settlers in 1851.

When Meany's book *The History of the State of Washington* was published in 1909, he sent Sam a copy with this warm inscription: "During more than twenty years of research work in the history of the Northwest I have received assistance and encouragement from many kind friends, but from none of them as much as you. In grateful memory of your many kindly acts extended as to a brother, I wish to present to you the first copy . . . just received from the press."

In thanking him, Sam wrote, "Naturally I shall do all I can to disseminate the book owing to its all too kind inscription. . . . While others appreciate what you are doing for our state and for the University and for the young men with whom you come in contact, there is no one who realizes the value of that work more than your friend, Samuel Hill."

In 1915, at a time when Sam's Home Telephone Company was experiencing heavy weather, he managed to send Meany $250 for binding and copying various historical documents for the University of Washington library. He wrote, "I always come through because I believe in you and believe in your work, but remember, dear boy, that money just now is a very scarce article. . . . The $50 I wanted to send is a present for your daughter on the occasion of her marriage, but I waited until the end of the month until I got the money."

Meany came to Maryhill to speak at the dedication of the altar stone of the Stonehenge Memorial on July 4, 1918 (see photo). He and Sam continued to correspond about historical matters, for example, on Meany's book on the history of Mt. Rainier in Washington. Sales were disappointing and Sam purchased a number of copies to be sent to friends.

In 1925, Sam had established his restaurant and watering hole at Semiahmoo just north of the Peace Portal. He wrote Meany, "I must dig up a legend for Semiahmoo!" He contemplated building a replica of Ann Hathaway's cottage on the grounds of the restaurant, and Meany had a drawing made to help in the plan. However, Sam was pressed financially and had to abandon that idea.

One interesting letter in their correspondence was written by Sam after his visit to Thomas Edison's laboratory in the summer of 1913. Sam made a prophetic suggestion about using motion pictures and the recorded voice together for teaching. "You know I had rather hear you talk than go to a play. . . . Now there you are, a man to revolutionize the teaching of American history. I see the Pilgrim fathers going down to Plymouth. I hear them saying farewell . . . and so on through the War of Independence . . . and the scenes at Independence Hall . . . and then Lincoln and Gettysburg and the slow-moving immigrant train across the prairie and the transcontinental railway is being built and the Indians are attacking the engineers in North Dakota — and history is to be studied at the 'movies' in the classroom . . . and you have the imagination to do it and I am going to talk to Edison about it." Years later, Sam himself put together a silent historical movie, which can only be called a rudimentary documentary, in connection with his Peace Portal (Chapter 21). Like some of Sam's other projects, the outcome was not up to the idea.

Sam made many lasting friendships characterized by mutual respect and admiration, but his association with Meany was special. There was no trace of condescension of patron to beneficiary; rather, one senses in Sam a hint of wistful envy of Meany's purposeful academic career as compared to his own multiple and often hectic pursuits. Their correspondence over the course of thirty years illustrates some of Sam's best qualities: generosity; loyalty; intellectual curiosity; and admiration for the accomplishments, virtues, and values of others.

Other Famous Friends

At least in correspondence, Sam Hill was not an inveterate name dropper, but on the other hand, he was not loath to mentioning the noble or notable among his acquaintance if the occasion arose. Newspaper interviews provided him with opportunities to refer to James J. Hill, King Albert of Belgium, Queen Marie of Rumania, and others, and he was not adverse to glory, earned or reflected. There may be some of us who could resist recounting what King So and So had said at lunch the other day, but what can one do when conversation lags?

Sam met Albert of Belgium in Canada when the prince was the guest of J. J. Hill on Albert's first visit to North America in 1898. Sam later wrote Meany that he had entertained the prince, who came incognito, in Portland and Seattle and would tell him some stories, unfortunately not recorded, of the visit. Albert's biographer writes, "Foremost among his hosts was James J. Hill [sic], the railway magnate, who received him at Seattle in a house built especially for this purpose. The friendships which he made on these occasions were to bear fruit in later years, when those who remembered his visit became the advocates of the Belgian cause and the staunchest supporters of Belgian relief during the War."

Sam wrote to the prince in November 1905: "Fearing I cannot get over this winter and call upon you, I have asked my personal friend, Mr. J. D. Farrell . . . latterly president of the Great Northern Steamship Company, to take this letter to you and to give you my best greetings."

Sam told a reporter that in the summer of 1908, Albert and he " . . . completed arrangements in Brussels for the prince to visit the Alaska-Yukon-Pacific Exposition and also to take a trip to Alaska" in 1909. Although he told the press the house was built especially to entertain the prince, it seems certain that this statement was an afterthought (Chapter 13). Albert wrote in March 1909, thanking Sam for the globe he had sent, and regretting that he could not come to the exposition: "This week I am leaving for the Belgian Congo where I intend to travel for about four months." Never proficient with English adverbs, he signed himself, "Yours affectionate, Albert of Belgium."

Albert's aide, General Jungbluth, assured Sam that if circumstances permitted, Albert would go to the United States later: "Don't go to any extraordinary effort to receive the Prince differently from your own manner of living. They would be desperate if they thought they would disrupt you." He did not go so far as to say that the royal couple would be pleased to take pot luck.

Sam had an hour and a half talk with Albert late in 1909 when he was in Brussels to prepare for an international road building meeting to be held there in July 1910. The prince, who was interested in good roads, sent invitations to American delegates from each state. He succeeded to the throne soon after that.

In a 1910 letter to Jungbluth, Sam refers to correspondence of December 1898, between King Leopold and James J. Hill regarding designs for flat boats for use on the Congo, and the construction of portage railways around three main falls of the river. (Sam naturally did not mention the notoriously cruel and greedy treatment of the natives by King Leopold's agents in what amounted to a vast personal fiefdom, ceded to Belgium as a colony in 1909.) Sam said that he had taken up again with J. J. Hill " . . . the question of steamers on the rivers in the Congo which His Majesty had asked me to look into." He offered to invite John F. Stevens, chief engineer of the Great Northern, who had also worked on the Panana Canal, to go with him to see the king in July 1910, but Albert did not pursue this.

The king wrote Sam in 1913 thanking him for the gift of " . . . that series of volumes describing the Indians of the United States," that is, the classic work of Curtis on the North American Indian.

In March 1916, King Albert appointed Sam Honorary Consul-General for Belgium, representing Oregon, Washington and Idaho. Sam had a lantern slide made of the elaborate document. The appointment was made in recognition of their long acquaintance and Sam's work early in the war as Oregon chairman for Belgian relief.

In May 1916, Sam went to Belgian Army Headquarters by way of London and Paris and met with the king and army commanders to discuss improving the transshipment from Vladivostok of war materiel for Russia via the Trans-Siberian railway (Chapter 20).

In 1918, the king wrote Sam to thank him for a donation for Belgian relief. "I need hardly tell you how much touched I am by the handsome gift of $5,000 you so kindly sent. . . . You may be quite sure that your generosity will be placed to good account in alleviating distress here, as I shall see to this personally." Sam had a slide made of this letter, also.

In March 1919, Sam sailed to Europe with Hervey Lindley for the celebration of the king's birthday. Later that year, Sam received the decoration of Commander of the Order of the Crown from the king in San Francisco on Admiral Rodman's flagship, the *New Mexico*. Sam told a reporter there were about seventy at a round table at dinner, including the governor of California, the mayor of San Francisco, and Mr. and Mrs. Herbert Hoover.

Sam wrote to the king in 1923 to ask if he had any objection to his writing " . . . a short sketch of my trip to pay my respects to you at La Panne, which I did on May 3, 1916" and to " . . . printing the picture which you gave me of the shell dropping near you, your aide, Marechal Joffre, and President Poincaré. I showed the picture to Marechal Joffre when he was here, and he recalled the circumstances very well indeed." Neither the sketch nor the photo has been found. Sam promised the king to deliver a print of his nearly finished movie, "The Sacred Faith of a Scrap of Paper," for screenings for charity.

Sam called on the king in Brussels in June 1923, and wrote Loie that he had been " . . . entertained royally for an hour and forty minutes." Sam was much impressed by the palace gardens and greenhouses. He took the opportunity to ask Albert if he and the queen would pose for Joanovitch for portraits for Maryhill Museum. On Sam's return to the United States, he met Cyrus McCormick on shipboard and showed him other Joanovitch portraits. McCormick was captivated by them, Sam told Loie.

Albert wrote Sam in April 1929, to welcome him on a trip Sam made to France and Belgium that year. The king's last tribute was a floral wreath at Sam's funeral service.

Sam's acquaintance with King Albert led to an introduction to his sister, the Duchess of Vendôme, and to Prince Henri de Croy. He had entertained de Croy in Seattle in 1903, and again in Portland ten years later.

Sam had met Jusserand, French Ambassador to the United States, through James J. Hill. When they came to the Pacific Coast in 1909, Sam turned over his quarters at the Perry Apartments in Seattle to them. They visited Sam's new townsite on the Columbia, and it was at Jusserand's suggestion that the name was changed from Maryland to Maryhill.

Sam probably first met Joffre, whom he greatly admired, at the conference on providing aid to Russia via Vladivostok in May 1916. An account of his travels around the world with Joffre and party is given in Chapter 26. Mme. Joffre accepted Sam's invitation to dedicate a room at Maryhill Museum in Joffre's honor, but this plan was not fulfilled.

Sam told Paul Douglas he had first met Marie, then Crown Princess of Rumania, in 1893, with the help of a letter of introduction from her grandmother, Queen Victoria. Sam was in Europe at the time, selling Great Northern Railway bonds to royalty (Chapter 5). If this is true, it is likely that Sam and Marie corresponded from time to time during the next thirty years. Only a few letters survive, others probably having been lost or stolen: it was not in Sam's nature to discard such treasures.

Sam wrote Marie in 1917 in the rather stilted style he reserved for royalty: "Our friend, Miss Loie Fuller, has told us something of the sufferings which seem almost beyond comprehension . . . which ripened into deeds which no writer of history can fail to record and remember. . . . You have fought the good fight, you have kept the faith. With admiration and respect, I beg to sign myself your obedient servant, Sam Hill." In an undated letter, probably in response to this, the queen wrote, "Dear Mr.

Hill: Will you and your friends not try to come to Bucharest to see our sad situation and see what you can do to help? Please tell this to the king of the Belgians to inspire you to come. You can help and we need help — I shall bless you always. Marie."

She wrote from the Sinaia Palace in November 1921 to thank Sam for the sculpture in white marble of the hand of her daughter Elizabeth, then Crown Princess of Greece. After she became queen, Elizabeth agreed to be founder of a room at Maryhill dedicated to Greece and acknowledged Sam's thanks for gifts already provided. For some reason, the room filled with gifts did not materialize.

Marie had heard that Sam would be counselor to the Japanese at the world conference: "I do not forget that through you and Baron Condo [sic] I can look upon Japan as my friend. . . . You are perhaps the greatest peace-worker in the world today, and we are looking anxiously toward how you and your friends accomplish your part toward it. . . . You must write me all about it." Sam didn't counsel the Japanese, so far as we know; at least he didn't write all about it.

There were other Europeans of high station whom Sam either visited or entertained. Among these were Lord Edward and Lady Grey and party. Lady Grey thanked Sam for giving up his apartment at the Perry to accommodate them in Seattle on their visit in 1909. Five years later Lord Grey made his famous remark about the lights of Europe. Sam saw him again briefly in London after his 1916 visit to Belgian Army Headquarters.

Sam met Cardinal Mercier of Begium in 1921 on the occasion of his blessing of a piece of wood from the *Mayflower* to be placed in the cornerstone of Sam's Peace Arch at Blaine, Washington. He corresponded a number of times with Monsignor Antonini, introducing friends traveling to Rome who wished a Papal audience. Sam delighted, in fact, in writing letters of introduction for friends and acquaintances. Among those addressed were the Belgian minister to China at Peking; Charlemagne Power (lovely name), U.S. Minister Plenipotentiary to Germany; Bellamy Storer, ambassador to Austria; Edward Tuck, a wealthy financier who made his home in Paris; W. Cameron Forbes, commissioner to the Philippines; and Sir Horace Plunkett of Ireland.

Sam met some members of the English peerage through James J. Hill. Sam mentions J. J. in letters to Lord Northcote, Governor of Bombay (1903) and later of Australia (1907). He did the honors for Lord Elphinstone, an early investor in the Manitoba Railroad, on a hunting trip in 1904, and wrote of sending a mounted head* to James J. Hill in St. Paul. Sam had been entertained in England by Lord Strathcona, a big investor in the Great Northern, and wrote to thank him for some birds sent to Sam at Minneapolis; "I directed that half of them be sent to Washington, D.C. [to Sam's wife] and the other portion sent here. The birds were received in prime condition and were perfectly delicious." During World War I, Sam

---

*The species was unspecified; it probably would have been that of Teddy Roosevelt if J. J. had had his preference. As for Sam, he would continue to seek the greater kudos.

was escorted to Stonehenge by Lord Kitchener, who probably did not often act as a tour guide (Chapter 21). Sam wrote to Count Durkheim of Munich in 1908, recalling sadly, "I think with pleasure of the good times we had together, and that you are no longer, probably, a blonde young man, but have grown gray-haired and portly as I have."

In this country, Sam knew many famous people in politics, education, banking, and industry. He wrote Judge Thomas Burke of talking to Theodore Roosevelt about making him "an honorary member of our association," probably the Asiatic Association of Seattle, which Sam had helped to establish in 1902.

Sam told Paul Douglas how he and his father-in-law had conspired to fool J. P. Morgan, who " . . . thought he knew everything . . . [and] boasted that he could identify the hide of every animal that ever lived." Sam and J. J. " . . . went out to Montana and bred a bull moose to a cow. When the resulting offspring was a year old, they had it killed and its hide tanned. They then presented the rug to Morgan and asked him to identify it. Morgan had to confess he could not. Sam then said triumphantly, "Of course you can't, Mr. Morgan. There never before was such a creature!"

Sam met Charles Evans Hughes, then governor of New York, when he visited Seattle in the summer of 1909. He wrote the following year to congratulate him on his appointment to the Supreme Court, and wrote also to Edward White, just appointed chief justice. Clarence Barron wrote of meeting with Sam and Secretary Hughes in 1921 and discussing the question of post-war American loans to Europe. He also related a story Sam had told him about the appendectomy Dr. Charles R. McBirney* had done on William Rockefeller. "When at dinner later McBirney said, 'It has now been determined by doctors that the appendix ought to be cut out before people are fifteen years old,' Wm. Rockefeller said, 'McBirney, you have a better thing than Standard Oil!'"

In 1905, Sam wrote his friend Cooke, then in Pasadena, suggesting that he call on John ("Bet a Million") Gates about " . . . separating any of those millionaires from their hard earned money. . . . He knows me, all right. Between you and me, Gates is easy in a game, altho' most people do not think so." Sam also mentioned meeting a more successful gambler, Hetty Green, in New York in 1907, and dining with Andrew Carnegie at Aix-les-Bains in 1901.

The impressive list of prominent businessmen and political figures at a dinner Sam gave in Tokyo in April, 1920 is given in Chapter 19. He wrote to other well-known people whom he had met at one time or another, including Presidents Wilson, Harding and Hoover; the well-known engineer John F. Stevens; Charles Francis Adams; Admiral Dewey; and Charles Schwab of U.S. Steel, the latter possibly bewildered by the gift of a model of Joffre's hand. Frank Lloyd Wright accepted Sam's invitation to dinner in Tokyo in 1920. On the receipt of some rosebuds Sam sent him, Luther Burbank

---

*Famous for describing "McBirney's point" of maximum tenderness in the right lower quadrant of the abdomen in the diagnosis of acute appendicitis.

complimented him on the " . . . unusually fine odor which I have never found in roses before."

Sam was invited to Edison's laboratory at Orange, New Jersey where he saw movies and heard a recording, inspiring him to write to Professor Meany about using films and records in the teaching of history. Edison was one of the recipients of Sam's famous globes. His letter of thanks, written after the outbreak of the first World War, closes with, "The only thing that troubles my mind now is the possibility that some of the boundary lines will have to be changed as a result of the present conflict." This proved to be the understatement of the year.

Well, all of this may not amount to more than tedious name dropping today. Still, one must admit that such a roster would make an impressive Christmas card list!

In his old age, Sam told Lockley, "After all, there is only one aristocracy and that is the aristocracy of intellect and merit. King Albert of Belgium and Queen Marie of Rumania and many of my other friends can qualify in the aristocracy of integrity and intellect." If pressed, he might have admitted that a golden crown or the traditional silver spoon sometimes helps to focus attention on these admirable qualities.

Sam liked to bask in the limelight of celebrities, but his heart was truly with his old friends, Frank Terrace; C. P. Chamberlain; Charles Babcock, Edmond Meany; R. C. Thomson, and others. As Sam might have put it, confidentially, "An old crony is better than an old phony, any day."

25

Queen Marie's Circus Train

The "nine day's wonder" is a term of old coinage which has enjoyed new currency in the era of rapid communications which began with the telegraph. Instant fame or notoriety was bestowed on many people in America in the 1920's, providing a field day for the press and briefly elbowing more important news out of the spotlight. Some events are forgotten today except by a few oldsters, such as the Judd-Snider murder case; Gertrude Ederle's swimming the English Channel; Roy Riegel's wrong way run in the 1929 Rose Bowl Game; Amy Semple McPherson's brief disappearance in May 1926; the scandals of President Harding's personal life and administration; and so on.

To this number should be added the fifty day visit to the United States of Queen Marie of Rumania in the fall of 1926. It is still recalled vividly by the older residents of "Sam Hill country" who live around Goldendale, Washington. A glamorous and beautiful queen crossing the country with her retinue to visit a remote and desolate chateau on the Columbia River; stories of intrigue and open dissension in her party; rumors of scandalous goings-on, including Marie's neglect of her ailing husband in Bucharest; cynicism about the queen's motives for making the trip; all combined to make an intoxicating brew to serve daily for several weeks to American newspaper readers.

It was not that Marie lacked competition on the front pages and rotogravure sections of the newspapers. The Hall-Mills murder trial; the juicy story of Peaches, age sixteen, and "Daddy" Browning; the Teapot Dome scandal; preparation for the trial of Fall and Doheny; the death of Houdini; and appeals for a new trial for Sacco and Vanzetti all clamored for attention. Her Majesty was no novice at holding her place at center stage, not did she need an acting coach to produce the quotable line or regal smile or gesture. In fact, she could scarcely have received more notice in the press had she walked across the Atlantic and all the way to Maryhill.

The governing body of Rumania was reluctant to sanction her trip because of the expense, but later the objections were withdrawn, perhaps when it realized there was to be virtually a free ride. The liberals, out of power at the time, were against the trip, fearing unfavorable publicity and " . . . the queen's dangerous enthusiasms which can be so easily misinterpreted." Prime Minister Alexander Auerescu, leader of the People's Party, however, thought the expedition would "put Rumania on the map."

Fears of expense were assuaged by the offer of the Baltimore and Ohio Railroad to provide free a train of ten cars. John Carroll, Washington lobbyist for the B & O, Great Northern, and Northern Pacific, later told Barron that Daniel Willard, president of the B & O, had asked Carroll if the U.S. Government had any money to entertain the queen. Carroll replied, "Not a cent." Willard said, "She was our great ally during the war, hence we all owe much to her" and so made the decision to supply the train. Carroll claimed that Sam Hill planned to take the queen's party to Vancouver, B.C. by way of the Canadian Pacific. When the American railroads changed the arrangements, Sam insisted that Carroll be the host for the party.

Other railroads in the United States and Canada were expected to furnish free transportation. The Southern Pacific and Santa Fe Railroads ungallantly wanted pay for their services, so California was dropped from the itinerary just before the tour began. The elimination of Hollywood from the schedule must have given the queen a pang. It was reported that she had been offered a movie contract for $25,000 a day, and also that she wanted to interest a studio in producing a film based on her play, "Lily of Life." After she left Bucharest, however, the Rumanian legation denied her permission even to appear in a movie for charity.

A few cynics had the temerity to suggest that the trip was part of a campaign to launch a Rumanian bond issue or to obtain an American loan.

Rumania was on the Allied side in World War I, but having defaulted on its loans from France and England, did not exactly have an "A" credit rating. It was pointed out that if the queen could raise money in the United States, it would permit her and her family to live in the style to which she had so graciously become accustomed. To quote an editorial in an unnamed newspaper: "The brutal truth is that the United States recently turned down a Rumanian touch, and the queen wanted to see if anything could be done about it — and thus raise the mortgage on her throne. Somehow it would have been a little more clubby if the queen had not said so much about wanting to study American happiness."

The New York *World* observed that the trip had brought together " . . . the world's first ultramodern publicity machine and the world's first ultramodern queen. . . . The lid is off and almost anything can happen. Applesauce flows thick and fast." The connoisseur of applesauce can decide for himself whether or not the queen's prime aims were to learn more about America and its people and to fulfill the dream of her great American friends, Sam Hill and Loie Fuller, by dedicating his great house at Maryhill as a museum of French art.

Marie was the daughter of the Duke of Edinburgh (a son of Queen Victoria), and of Grand Duchess Marie, daughter of Czar Alexander II. Sam told Paul Douglas he had met Marie, then Crown Princess of Rumania, in 1893 on a trip to Europe to sell Great Northern Railway bonds to royalty. It was probably on his return to Rumania in 1919 that he advised Marie of his plan for a museum featuring a Rumanian room, and she promised to dedicate it for him.

Correspondence about this has not been preserved, except that Sam wrote his former secretary just before the queen's trip, "Years ago, I invited Queen Marie to come and open the museum. I tried to get her to put it off until 1927. She preferred going now." He didn't say why he preferred waiting, but the reason was probably financial. "I think I wrote you of my financial condition. . . . I am president of the Deep Water Coal and Iron Company, Jasper, Alabama. I get no salary. . . . I am not going with Her Majesty on the trip. I shall be at Maryhill . . . for two hours when she dedicates the museum. I shall motor over part of the Columbia River Highway . . . [and] go to Blaine and see the Peace Portal and go back to work at Jasper. . . . " Sam must have wished fervently he had clung to this plan instead of accompanying the queen on the northwestern part of her trip. It is not clear why he changed his mind; perhaps Marie and Loie Fuller persuaded him.

Queen Marie had written several books and magazine articles about her life, particularly about the dark days of World War I, when the Rumanian government had had to flee from Bucharest. Her visits to military hospitals, sometimes in the company of Loie Fuller, were recounted, accompanied by photographs of the queen in a spotless nurse's uniform. American newspaper accounts of the tribulations and fortitude of the beautiful fifty year old queen had no doubt prepared the way for winning the hearts of the American public on her triumphant tour. The North American Newspaper Alliance had contracted with her to write a series of articles about her impressions of America. Some six articles were published. Mr. Gray adds, " . . . as they ran 2,000 words each, one suspects she must have had a ghost writer — and there was one such in her party."

The queen first told the press of her trip in May 1926, stating that she hoped to stay three or four months to see " . . . every phase of American life . . . My contact with the poor and lowly of my own country will make me feel as much at home in the humble logger's hut as in Mrs. Vanderbilt's mansion." She never made it to a logger's hut, but she probably saw more mansions, not to mention city halls and memorials, than she had bargained for, if that is the proper phrase. This press release helped set the tone for many another issued just before and during her journey.

Early in October 1926, she left Bucharest for Paris to acquire a suitable wardrobe for the trip. Three well known couturiers were reported to be working night and day to complete her costumes. Every detail of her dress and hairstyle and those of her seventeen year old daughter, Princess Ileana, was faithfully recorded for the American reader.

In Paris the queen told reporters that she wanted to make the trip as a "hundred percent American" from the moment she stepped on the deck of the *S. S. Leviathan*. It was announced that corn-on-the-cob, candied sweet potatoes, and pie would be introduced to the queen on her voyage. She declined to have wines and liquors served to her party aboard the United States liner, although this was permissible by diplomatic privilege, because she wanted to conform to the law of the land, Prohibition, whether aboard ship in in America.

Her 32 year old son, Carol, had abdicated on January 1, 1926 as heir apparent to the throne and his son, Michael, became heir. Carol was living in Neuilly, a suburb of Paris, with his famous red-haired mistress, Magda Lupescu.* Queen Marie's daughter, Queen Marie of Yugoslavia, had paved the way for the reconciliation of her mother and brother. They had a four-hour meeting at the Ritz. *The New York Times'* information was that the queen told Carol " . . . he must resume his position as the heir apparent and return to his wife, Princess Helen [of Greece]. Once Carol regained his right to the throne and joined his wife, his relations with the pretty Rumanian girl would be a matter which would concern no one but the prince himself."** It seems safe to assume that Magda Lupescu did not attend the family conclave.

---

* Their liason was the inspiration for a well-known limerick of the time:
  A young girl named Magda Lupescu
  Came to Rumania's rescue:
  "It's a wonderful thing
  To work under the king —
  Is Democracy better, I esk you?

** Not even his wife?

Carol saw his mother off on the boat train for Cherbourg. Her entourage, then consisting of seventeen persons, left Paris in two private cars attached to the boat train. The fifty trunks containing her "American trousseau" were loaded on the ship on October 12 and she was given a gala send-off. In the corridors near her suite were many crates of gifts for Maryhill Museum.

The queen and her children, Ileana and Nicholas, were the guests of the United States Line, but she paid $5,000 for the passage of her suite to New York, an appropriation of the Rumanian government. Other members of the party were given the "customary twenty-five percent diplomatic discount." Many Americans had arranged to be among the 1100 first class passengers.

Her activities on the *Leviathan* were fully reported: what she wore, what she ate, how she spent her time with commoners in the public rooms and on deck. One bulletin confided that the royal party was learning to chew gum. Even Crag, her spaniel, held his own as an object of the attention of the press.

The American press representatives on board were reminded by the queen's business manager, Madame Simone Lahovary, that they would not be permitted to print interviews with the queen because of her contract with the North American Newspaper Alliance. Advance sums had already been paid, and the Alliance claimed that she should not grant any interviews. The queen already had a contract with Famous Features Syndicate for which she had been writing articles for many months. She was said not to have understood the terms of her original unexpired contract when she signed the new one.

Meanwhile, preparations were being made for her reception at the Hotel Ambassador in New York. Thirty detectives, seven of them women, were hired to safeguard the royal party, which was to occupy a twenty-four room suite on the fourth floor of the hotel on Park at 51st Street. The hotel's solid gold dinner service was readied and a housekeeper with her twelve assistants and chambermaids briefed. Loie Fuller was staying at the Plaza.

Visiting royalty had been a decidedly rare sight in the United States. King Albert and Queen Elizabeth of Belgium had come in 1919, returning the visit of the Woodrow Wilsons to Brussels. The Rumanian foreign office had contacted the U.S. State Department through the American legation in Bucharest. The State Department returned word that President and Mrs. Coolidge would be happy to receive Queen Marie at the White House. She was to stay at the Rumanian legation in Washington.

The *Leviathan* stopped at quarantine on October 18, and was greeted by a twenty-one gun salute and the steamer *Macom*, with Grover Whelan, Mayor Jimmie Walker's welcome man, and newsmen aboard to take her to the Battery. At a press interview she repeated that her principal objective for going to the West Coast was to open Maryhill Museum, variously reported to be in Seattle and in Oregon. She would inaugurate the Rumanian Room of the Museum and was bringing over "lots of Rumanian art" for that reason, because Mr. Hill was an old friend of hers.

On the day of her arrival, Sam was asked by a reporter if he was well acquainted with the queen. "Ha!", said Sam, turning to his secretary. "This fresh cheeked boy asks if I know her!" There was, of course, speculation during and after the queen's tour about Sam's relationship with her. Was she his mistress or only a friend who wanted to do him a good turn by publicizing his proposed museum and the Peace Portal? Her biographer ignores the whole affair.

A Coast Guard cutter with Sam Hill and various American and Rumanian officials also met the *Leviathan*. Although he was the person responsible for her visit, Sam may well have felt lost in the swarm of officials buzzing around the queen. He stayed out of the limelight until Marie's train reached Spokane two weeks later.

Seven hundred fifty of New York's finest and fifteen detectives of the bomb squad stood by on her triumphant procession from the Battery to City Hall through a shower of ticker tape, escorted by soldiers, sailors, and marines. Crowds lined the streets and there was steady applause and an occasional cheer. Their ardor may have been dampened by the heavy rain which had fallen that morning. The queen, announced by a flourish of trumpets by a quartet of women in Grecian costume, made a brief appearance on the balcony of City Hall with Mayor Walker and was applauded by the throng in the plaza. She responded to the mayor's welcome and presentation of the gold medal of the City of New York with a short speech, broadcast by radio. Later, Marie said that the speech was the first one she had ever made in her life, except for one she made to American doughboys in a YMCA hut in France in 1919, in which she pointed out the differences between democracy and Bolshevism.

She caught a cold her first day in New York and wrote a friend, "It was only my royal training which kept me on my feet. . . . American hospitality is rather bewildering, and one must have an iron constitution to be able to get through."

Within an hour, the party had left New York for Washington by special train, protocol requiring a visit to the White House before she began her tour. The queen waved to people greeting her along the way. Among them was a group of Negro track-workers near Baltimore. The queen exclaimed, "Oh, they're delightful! I love those colored boys. They remind me of the gypsies of my own country." A player piano had been installed in the lounge car. Her children, Princess Ileana and Prince Nicholas, spent most of the afternoon listening to such favorites as "Why Do You Roll Those Eyes?" and "Thanks for the Buggy Ride."

Reporters were told that the expenses of the trip from New York to Washington would be paid out of the State Department's fund for entertaining distinguished visitors. It was rumored that Sam Hill would assume the expenses of the rest of her journey.

A squadron of cavalry was on hand at Washington's Union Station to escort the Queen to the Rumanian Legation. She was not received at the

White House until the next afternoon. The queen and the Coolidges exchanged pleasantries about the weather, their children, and the queen's forthcoming trip. Mr. Coolidge was not pleased at being photographed with the queen but managed a wintry smile.

Half an hour later, the President and Mrs. Coolidge returned the call by visiting her at the legation. That evening, there was an official dinner. The *Times* reported that President Coollidge and Prince Nicholas " . . . conversed extensively in the study and frequently both were in laughter." Unfortunately, the cause of Mr. Coolidge's unwonted merriment is lost to history.

In Washington, Frederick Moore, secretary of the committee of the Maryhill Museum delegated by Sam Hill to act as his representative, announced the queen's itinerary for her proposed two months' stay. John H. Carroll, age 73, general counsel for the Baltimore and Ohio Railroad and an honorary colonel, was in charge of the queen's party after she left New York for Canada and the West. Later, Carroll announced that Moore would not be on the queen's train. "Only those will be on the train who are wanted by Her Majesty," he said bluntly. This was a warning to Sam indicating who was in charge and an inkling of the discord to come.

Not everyone was charmed by the queen's arrival. There were protests over political prisoners and persecution of the Jews and other minorities in Rumania. British newspapers took a dim view of American enthusiasm over the queen's visit. The *Evening Standard* sniffed, "We have not yet heard that by some marvel of engineering the Statue of Liberty, which guards New York Harbor, has been made to curtsy as Queen Marie of Rumania passes. But nothing else seems lacking to show how dearly a republic can adore a regular royal queen." The *Daily Express* opined that " . . . judging from the cabled furor, it would seem to be a good thing that the U.S. is a republic. If they had a king and queen over there, they would soon be suffocated by popular adulation."

The queen's special train took her to Philadelphia where she attended a service at the Rumanian Church and was the honored guest at the Sesquicentennial Exposition. Loie Fuller's troupe performed a ballet there based on the story by Marie, "The Queen's Handkerchief." The tickets for boxes ranged up to $50, but scarcely half were occupied. A slight gaffe became evident in the placement of the royal box, from which the queen was visible to the audience but from which she could not see the stage. Her party therefore moved to another location. Another contretemps occurred at her hotel when Prince Nicholas, arriving late, had to go through the kitchens because the dining room was locked and the man with the key could not be found. Later, armed with a New York operator's license, he went for a drive in his new Willys-Knight sports roadster, which he had ordered by wire from the *Leviathan*.

The queen returned to New York and a round of reviews, receptions, dinners, and tours. At a luncheon in the Bankers' Club, she assured her listeners she had come to America only to seek its love, friendship, and understanding.

During her stay in New York, the queen wrote notes of praise for the various states, addressed to their governors. One example, the greeting to Tennessee, should suffice:

> Oh, Tennessee! Down where the cotton grows and Southern music fills the air and rings throughout the world! You have given to us all the mighty fruits of your mighty industries, which, in the great battle against injustice, have been the means of defense beyond all danger. What has not the industry of cotton done in the time of need? And to the people of Tennessee I give my greetings, above all for the greatness of their hearts. I will come.

Marie,
Queen of Rumania

The queen attended a dance performance based on Marie's story, "The Lily of Life," under the direction of Loie Fuller at the Metropolitan Opera House. The former American ambassador to France, A. P. Moore, had seen the company of twenty-five dance at Versailles and had wired the Sesquicentennial Committee in Philadelphia to invite them to America. Arrangements were then made with Loie and the New York Symphony Orchestra for the benefit performance for a "women's memorial" to be built in Washington, D.C. Tickets were offered from $3 to $15 with a few at $25 and box seats at $100.

In an interview, Loie Fuller said that the film "The Lily of Life," featuring her dancers, was first exhibited in Paris in 1921 and attended by Queen Marie. It had been produced on the Riviera, at a reported cost of several million dollars. (Loie, who wrote her own publicity, probably exaggerated the expenditure at least tenfold, according to Margaret Harris.) The names of the angels were not invoked. An attempt made to market the movie in America was not successful, and the print was held by Sam Hill to be preserved at Maryhill Museum. (The film has not been found.)

Paris Soir noted the story was of a princess " . . . who preferred ideal love and a life devoted to arts rather than the tyrranic exigencies of the throne." The paper deplored the indiscretion of the American press in repeating gossip about Loie and the queen. Regarding her arrival in the U.S. at the same time as Queen Marie's, Loie said it was a mere coincidence, because she had come primarily to stage her ballet in Philadelphia.

The benefit performance was not a conspicuous success. Many orchestra seats were empty and speculators outside tried to sell the lowest priced seats for as little as fifty cents. The performance grossed only $17,000, about one third of an earlier estimate. The queen arrived fifteen minutes late and came in through the main Broadway entrance. Meanwhile, the reception committee had been waiting for her at the south entrance. Some consolation to the queen was afforded by the friendly crowd which broke through police lines to greet her when she left the opera house for the train station.

When her party left the Hotel Ambassador, Marie left $2,000 and other presents for the house staff, gratuities which might bring faint smiles even today.

On October 25 the train, the "Royal Rumanian," left New York City for Buffalo, stopping en route at West Point and Niagara Falls to review the cadets and the falls respectively. There were official receptions in Toronto, Montreal, Ottawa, and Winnipeg on the way west.

The royal party included three ladies and one gentlemen in waiting; an aide-de-camp; Professor Nicholas Petresco, a professor of sociology from the University of Bucharest representing the Rumanian government; Ira N. Morris of Chicago, Consul General of Rumania, and his wife; Albert Tierman, Counsellor of State and the French representative of Maryhill Museum; Col. Carroll; Col. W. V. Shipley, traffic director of the train; and Major Stanley Washburn, liaison officer. Washburn had been a news correspondent in Rumania during World War I and had been selected by the queen for this role.

There were persistent rumors that King Ferdinand of Rumania was ill at the time of the queen's departure. On October 30 his physicians issued a bulletin indicating that he had inflammation of the royal sigmoid. The queen repeatedly denied that he was recalling her to Rumania. Such rumors were attributed to "radical sources." Unfavorable criticism of the queen's trip in the foreign press was not reprinted in Bucharest. The public there was said to be proud of Queen Marie's success, and rumors persisted that the prospects for an American loan to Rumania had been enhanced by her visit. The queen celebrated her 51st birthday on the train on October 29, and the day was marked by religious services throughout Rumania.

The Sunday rotogravure sections were now replete with photos of receptions and reviews in cities along her route. Loie Fuller was probably not delighted at a picture of a young Sally Rand in a filmy costume in Los Angeles, doing the "Dance of the Butterfly," the inspiration for which had no doubt been Loie's own dance of that name introduced a quarter of a century earlier.

The train stopped at Minneapolis on October 31. The queen and her children attended a dinner and reception at the home of Louis W. Hill, Sam's brother-in-law and chairman of the board of the Great Northern.

A day or so later in Mandan, North Dakota, a delegation of Sioux Indians met her train and the queen was photographed with a war bonnet of eagle feathers. She was given the title "The Woman Who Was Waited For." Red Tomahawk, the chief who had killed Sitting Bull, greeted her as the queen who had made great sacrifices for her people during the World War. She knelt on a white buffalo robe as the war bonnet was placed on her head. Ellerby, author of *Marie of Rumania*, describes this as the "high point of her trip." She was so moved that she turned to her son and whispered, "Nicky, never forget this, for it is so sincere and so wonderful."

Ellerby was no fan of Sam Hill, whom he describes as a " . . . raving American eccentric . . . a giant aging sheepdog of a man with a cherubic face, a shock of white hair and a penchant for building ramshackle monuments to pipe dreams," among which was the "dilapidated stucco [sic] arch on the U.S.-Canadian border." He describes Sam " . . . with his huge bulk, Santa Claus face, twinkling blue eyes, and curiously soft voice . . . " as arriving at the formal reception in Spokane dressed in a tweed suit, carrying a cowboy hat. The queen was said to refer to Sam as "the white lion," which Sam probably preferred to Santa Claus, although the public seemed to identify him as the latter in connection with the queen's tour.

The train arrived in Spokane on November 2, and Sam Hill, Loie Fuller, and Alma Spreckels came aboard. One reporter described Loie, now sixty-four, as " . . . little and dumpy. . . . She shrouds herself in flowing draperies and her moist eyes look odd through horn rimmed spectacles."

Meanwhile, frantic preparations were being made at Maryhill for the queen's visit. Mayor Zola Brooks of Goldendale had received a wire from Hill telling him that Queen Marie would dedicate the museum on November 3, and that he was to get the place in shape for the occasion. This was no small chore. Henry Gray wrote that he had seen the place not long before the dedication and it was " . . . a picture of dilapidation. . . . There were holes in the concrete walls; many doors and windows were not in place; and the spring supplying water was overgrown with weeds and partly filled with debris." Edgar Hill, a museum trustee, admitted later, "I burned down one barn up there to get it out of sight when Queen Marie was there."

Brooks gamely put a crew to work cleaning and fixing up. He brought a large supply of bunting with which to drape the interior of the building with the Rumanian colors, red, yellow, and blue. Sam had asked Mrs. Cyrus A. Dolph and her daughter to go to Maryhill to supervise the reopening of the Meadowlark Inn, which had not been used for two years. With a party of socialites from Portland, they stayed overnight at the inn and prepared for the reception. They did what they could by draping the concrete walls of the reception room of the castle with pine boughs and bouquets of chrysanthemums and placing American and Rumanian flags behind the throne on a platform which had been hastily constructed.

When Sam alighted from the queen's train at Maryhill early on the frosty morning of November 3, he was asked if he would complete the mansion and improve the grounds, now that the museum was about to be dedicated. Sam replied, "That depends solely upon what cooperation I get from the people of the Northwest. My building will be dedicated today to the purpose for which I built it. I want to finish it — to fulfill all the plans I have had for it. But I shouldn't be expected to build roads through all this part of Washington and Oregon to get to it, should I? Look how difficult it is to get to the town of Maryhill, Washington. Why should I go ahead if the people won't make the museum accessible through highways to this section? Is it quite fair? Isn't it time I was being shown a little cooperation?"

George Mullen, the S. P. & S. Railway chef, had his moment when called upon to prepare "Breakfast a la Imperial" for the queen, consisting of white meat of chicken between toast rounds topped by a poached egg

242

Sam Hill and Queen Marie of Rumania stepping from the queen's special train at Maryhill. (Photo courtesy of Oregon Historical Society.)

wrapped in bacon and covered with a cream sauce. Marie offered him a $10 tip and a job in Rumania, but he declined the latter.

The queen stepped down onto a red carpet at the small depot that morning, and the party was driven up to Meadowlark Inn. Sam greeted the queen there with the same treatment and presented her to his entertainment committee and other guests. They then proceeded to the chateau, Ileana and Nicholas riding in the car of Goldendale's undertaker. They were again welcomed by a red carpet which had been obtained " . . . after a frantic search . . . by removing it from a hotel back stairway in Portland. The same carpet was used at each site, then . . . quickly rolled up and rushed to the next location."

Marie must have been dismayed by the sight of the half-finished

"Museum of Fine Arts," built on what was then a by-road. Three years later, Carroll told a Senate subcommittee investigating lobbies, ". . . we had on our train a million and a half dollars in paintings and statuary to put in the Napoleonic Room when we got there, and we had half a million dollars of the same thing to put in the Rumanian Room. When we got there, there was no Napoleonic Room . . . no Rumanian Room. It was perfectly ridiculous and I never was so embarrassed in my life. I thought, 'What in the world are we going to do?'"

If she was aghast, the queen gave no visible sign when she appeared on the east ramp to show herself to the crowd, which included 400 school children, brought by trucks from the Goldendale area and a caravan of people from Portland.* The queen asked to meet Chief Alex Saluskin and his wife, dressed in full Indian regalia, as the Pathé news cameraman recorded the scene.

The queen released carrier pigeons to deliver messages to ten cities. Among the intended recipients were the mayor of Los Angeles and the editor of the San Francisco *Examiner*. The message stated that she was sorry she could not come to sunny California, but sent best wishes. The parsimony of the Southern Pacific Railroad was not mentioned. One pigeon, "Princess Drift Snow" entrusted with the first stage of the trip to Los Angeles, flew into Portland bleeding from a bullet wound, and presumably was excused from proceeding.

Now came the time when the queen displayed true noblesse oblige. After some long and flowery introductions, she rose to speak:

> As I stand here today in this curious and interesting building, I would like to explain why I came. There is much more than concrete in this structure. There is a dream built into this place — a dream for today and especially for tomorrow. There are great dreamers and there are great workers in the world. When a dreamer is also a worker, he is working for today and for tomorrow as well. For he is building for those who come after us.
>
> Sam Hill is my friend. He is not only a dreamer but he is a worker. Samuel Hill once gave me his hand and said that if there were anything on earth that I needed, I had only to ask. Some may even scoff, for they do not understand. But I have understood. So when Samuel Hill asked me to come overseas to this house built in the wilderness, I came with love and understanding. Samuel Hill knows why I came, and I am not going to give any other explanation. Sometimes the things dreamers do seem incomprehensible to others, and the world wonders why dreamers do not see the way others do.
>
> Some have wondered at the friendship of a queen for a woman whom some would call lowly. That woman is Loie Fuller. Her name has often been slighted. That woman stood by me when my back was to the wall. That woman gave me her life in my hour of need. She went all over America getting aid for my people. This has almost been forgotten by the rest of you, but I could no longer be silent. In this democracy, there should be no gap between the high and the lowly. As woman to woman, I wish that there would be no doubt in any heart that that woman gave me hope. Samuel Hill knows this.

---

*Carrying the crown for the queen was seven-year-old Richard Turner, who has long been a friend and neighbor of the author.

A *New York Times* reporter described the queen as standing proudly in front of the scarlet-draped throne in the "garishly decorated room." Describing the some fifty boxes of gifts she had brought from Rumania, she said, "They are simple gifts, made by simple hands; embroideries and handiwork in wood and metals." She herself had made some of the furniture and had written manuscripts for the museum.

She ended by extending her hand to Sam Hill, who was standing off to one side, saying, "Mr. Hill, I would like very much to shake your hand." He walked toward her, grasped her hand and kissed it. There was loud applause, and reportedly, not a dry eye. The party then moved toward the automobiles on the ramps leading to the building. One reporter added, "One of Samuel Hill's friends climbed to an eminence above the crowd of 2,000 who had heard the Queen's address from the amplifiers, and proclaimed, 'Samuel Hill, the friend of the people of Washington and Oregon!'"

Loie Fuller had stayed on the train, apparently feeling that her presence at the ceremony would embarrass the queen and Sam Hill. When she was told of Queen Marie's profession of friendship and gratitude, she sobbed, "I never dreamed she would do anything like that!"

In an interview, Loie said that the idea for a museum for international art had ocurred to her after Sam had told her about his house. She suggested discussing the plan for a museum with a number of Sam's friends. At the meeting (she did not specify the place or date), she told the story of Pericles, who had wanted to beautify Athens with the work of artisans. The people laughed at him, she said, so he borrowed the money to accomplish his dream. She pointed out that " . . . those works of art are now in ruins, but they pay the city today 5,000 percent on the investment and have given eternal life to the city." She predicted that people would come in increasing numbers to see the museum, "the only one of its kind in the world."

When she had returned to her railway car, Marie was reported by one of her entourage as saying, "This was the most touching experience I have ever had except where there was suffering."

The queen's speech had saved the occasion from being a ridiculous anticlimax. But another bit of comedy was to come, delighting the reporters. The party returned to the train and crossed the railroad bridge at Celilo Falls. The queen is said to have had the train stopped in the middle of the bridge so she might have lunch while enjoying the view of the river from both sides of the car. They were met by Oregon's Governor Pierce and a procession of some thirty Lincoln automobiles. They drove west to Portland by the Columbia River Highway, glorious in its fall colors, stopping at several towns and at Vista House on their way to Portland. At Vista House, the queen retired to the ladies' room while the crowd waited. Frank Sterett, photographer for *The Oregonian,* liked to recall that before she emerged, he announced, "Listen folks! A royal flush!"

Sam rode with the queen, the governor, and Major Washburn in a car driven by Marie's Rumanian chauffeur. Her children followed with Mayor and Mrs. George Baker of Portland, A detective accompanied the royal party to protect the queen's car. It was difficult for him to run forward from his own car at every stop, so he asked Governor Pierce if he would take a place in a car farther back, so the detective could sit in the queen's car. The governor agreed and changed places. The car door was shut and they started off. Then the detective heard Sam Hill tell Major Washburn that he had insulted the Governor of Oregon and had slammed the door in the governor's face. Washburn denied this, whereupon Sam told him that he was giving the orders and that if the Major did not obey them he would "crush him."

As yet unaware of the argument, the people of Portland prepared to welcome her Royal Highness. She stopped for an unscheduled visit to the Shrine Hospital for Crippled Children. The parade route through the city streets was decorated with American and Rumanian flags. A newly formed Rumanian society welcomed the queen at the Multnomah Hotel.

That evening, the queen and her party appeared at the horse show of the Pacific International Livestock Exhibition. Portland society in formal dress filled the boxes and the hoi polloi the stands. Sam and Washburn were in the royal box, and it was said that Sam sought out Washburn and repeated his accusation and threat. "When Washburn objected to Sam's intemperate language, Sam Hill was heard to say, 'Shut up! Keep still or I will slap you in the face!'" When Carroll spoke up in Washburn's behalf, Hill turned on him, " . . . and you shut up," he thundered, "or I'll put you off the train!" Carroll and Washburn left the box, leaving Sam the field, if not the honor.

Next morning, there was a seven a.m. stop at the new city of Long-view, Washington, not on the original schedule, so the queen could visit the world's largest sawmill. It seems that R. A. Long, president of the Long-Bell mill, an important customer of the Northern Pacific, insisted on the stop. She was welcomed by a brass band " . . . playing an approximation of the Rumanian national anthem."

The train thus arrived in Seattle two hours late. Sam took the queen's party on a motor tour of Seattle, to tea at the Yacht Club, and then to his Seattle home. The Sunset Club of Seattle, with many socially prominent members, had invited the queen to be their guest at lunch. She declined because of a previous engagement to lunch with Sam in his Seattle house. Sam suggested to the secretary that the queen might " . . . look in at the club for a few minutes for a brief reception," but the directors decided they had been snubbed and turned down the invitation.

In Seattle, Colonel Carroll told the press he was in command of the train by authority of the railways and with Marie's approval. Washburn would remain on the train. He expressed regret at the quarrel and intimated that the queen's speech at Maryhill might have turned Sam's head. Mrs. Spreckels, who was to have been Sam's official hostess to the queen in Seattle, sensibly changed her mind and left the train in Portland. Marie was reported to be greatly disturbed by the strife. The private car which had been added to the train in Spokane for Hill, Loie Fuller, and Mrs. Spreckels was now dropped "because of the excessive weight of the train," and Major Washburn gave Sam's party the private car he had been occupying.

The *Minneapolis Times* had a special insight into the Hill-Washburn feud because of political history important to the two former Minnesotans. Stanley Washburn's father, General W. D. Washburn, was president of the Minneapolis, St. Louis, & Sault Ste. Marie Railroad, a rival of J. J. Hill's Manitoba road. The general, a Republican, was elected to Congress in 1882. Young Sam Hill was the state Republican chairman. After winning, the general termed it " . . . the worst-managed campaign I ever saw." He was elected to the U.S. Senate in 1889 in spite of the opposition of the Hill interests. In 1894, Knute Nelson became governor, and Sam helped to promote his candidacy to the U.S. Senate. Nelson was elected the following year, ending Washburn's political career. Neither his son nor Sam forgot this.

While Queen Marie was in Seattle. an enterprising ex-convict convinced a theater manager to turn over his playhouse for a benefit for Rumanian orphans. He wired Sam Hill an invitation for the queen to attend and Sam replied, "Her Majesty graciously accepts your invitation." The scallywag escorted Sam, the queen, and her party to a box where they remained for twenty minutes. He hastened to the box office where he collected half of the profits, $900, returned a rented tuxedo, and departed for California.

The train moved north to Vancouver, B.C. to an official reception on November 5. Sam had wanted to have the party return to Seattle by boat, but Colonel Carroll arranged a compromise by which the train stopped at Blaine, Washington, in order to have the queen rededicate Sam's Peace Portal. The party would then proceed to Seattle by automobile. The queen was reported to be conferring with both factions and trying to avert further clashes.

Sam did not attend the ceremonies at Vancouver, but drove up to his bungalow at Semiahmoo to prepare for the royal visit. When the queen and her children arrived at the house, located a few hundred yards from the Peace Arch, Sam welcomed them and escorted them to the kitchen in the basement, where the queen herself prepared waffles for her family and a few guests. The press noted she was not superstitious: a black cat crossed her path on entering and breakfast was served by a cross-eyed Chinese (Mah Ying, Sam's servant).

The *N.Y. Times'* reporter referred to the Peace Portal as one of Sam's " . . strange public works, built as it was on no road." Marie and her children sat on chairs on the weather-beaten, moss-grown planks of the permanent dedication platform, under the red, white and blue lights illuminating the arch, perhaps wondering why rededication was necessary: Washington and British Columbia officials and General Joffre had already done the honors.

Discord in the party diminished when it was announced on November

6 that Sam would leave the train rather than going on the eastward journey. Loie Fuller persuaded the queen to invite Sam to accompany her back to Washington, D.C., but this announcement " . . . again threw the party into a frenzy, most of them violently opposing Mr. Hill's presence on the train." The queen withdrew the invitation, but Sam did not hold this against her. After her departure, he told reporters at Seattle, "She is a wonderful woman. There is no one like her."

Loie wrote Sam later, decrying the queen's lack of " . . . strength of character or moral courage," to do anything but deny she had requested Sam to leave the train. Loie added, "She was held between two friends, you and Washburn. . . . She wants to be friends to all and someone is sacrificed for it! . . . so the fault is not hers, it is mine."

The queen diplomatically, or perhaps despairingly, invited Sam and Carroll to lunch with her in the train, after which she "spent the afternoon reclining."

That evening, Sam hosted a farewell dinner at his home for the royal party including Carroll, Washburn, Washington's governor, and the mayor of Seattle. Three traffic officers held back the crowds from the iron entrance gates. The atmosphere inside, one suspects, was chillier than outside.

Carroll afterwards made a statement that Sam's official duties as host for the royal party in the Northwest had ended. Carroll gave orders, later rescinded, that Loie Fuller could not go through the train to call on the queen. May Birkhead, Loie's press agent, "near nervous collapse," was reported to have driven to Sam's house for a late conference which was the occasion for Carroll's ukase. Sam was not to be allowed to board if he reconsidered his decision. He did, however, come to the train after dinner to bid the queen and her children goodbye.

The train now proceeded east to Spokane and Glacier National Park, where the Blackfeet Indians adopted the queen into the tribe. Ileana and Nicholas, outfitted in Indian costumes, obligingly imitated a war dance for newsmen.

Professor Nicholas Petresco, the representative of the Rumanian prime minister, got into the act as the train passed through Wyoming. He called a press conference to say that from now on all news releases would be channeled through him. He professed uneasiness over the informality permitted news correspondents in their conferences with the queen on the train. There is no indication that this pronouncement had any effect whatever.

Peace had finally settled on the train by the time it reached Denver, where the queen received the warmest greeting of her trip. Loie Fuller, her companion, Gabrielle Bloch, and May Birkhead, her secretary, had been put on a special car provided by Col. Carroll and sent off to New York, from whence they sailed to Europe with Loie's troupe on November 29. Carroll announced they were going of their own free will because of engagements in New York requiring Loie Fuller's presence. He thereupon excused himself from the day's official ceremonies in Denver and locked himself in his compartment for a rest.

The Ford Motor Company had furnished Lincoln cars for the royal family on the trip at a reported cost of $250,000. A Ford representative, Mr. J. B. Ayers, had kept up with the train when it left New York, going by train and automobile until the party reached Ottawa. He then was permitted to board the train because of the difficulty he would otherwise have had traveling west to carry out his arrangements. Carroll asked Ayers to leave the train in Seattle because of a statement, attributed to Ayers but denied by him, that Henry Ford was paying the incidental expenses of the entire royal party, amounting to nearly half a million dollars. This rumor was also promptly denied by the queen, who reportedly was upset by it. Mr. Ford's private secretary issued a statement that Ayers was unknown to company officials. If so, one wonders how he got all those Lincolns! Whatever Mr. Ayers' real status was, Carroll graciously announced that the party would continue to use his cars and Ayers would go ahead of the party to arrange the service. At Denver, Mr. Ayers, probably with some satisfaction, foiled an attempt of the fire department to let Prince Nicholas ride on a fire truck, producing a contract he had with the Rumanian legation specifying that only Lincolns were to be used for transporting the royal party.

The queen went on to new triumphs in Chicago and the East. Sam was invited to sit at the queen's table by Mrs. Rockefeller McCormick, who gave a luncheon for the queen. Sam had told Carroll he was in Chicago on business and would not call on the queen. He did not stay after lunch, but departed alone for New York. Paul Douglas recalls that Sam phoned him on this stopover, and " . . . sounded like a wounded King Lear, bereft of his daughter." But Sam was confident of the outcome, saying, "Our ties are so close that we will surely be reunited."

While in Chicago, Marie visited a synagogue where Rumanian Jews gave her an ovation. A few protesters distributing handbills attacking the queen were arrested and detained for several hours. She assured her listeners that the royal way in which she had been received would give great satisfaction to the king. Meanwhile, Ferdinand was opening Parliament at Bucharest, and was cheered by the deputies when he spoke of her visit to America and the resulting rapprochement with its people. The king's pale sunken face and weak voice were noted by the press.

Through Major Washburn, Marie denied that she had ever discussed the possibility of a loan to Rumania. "The only financial aid she is taking back to Rumania is five dollars which an old woman [in Philadelphia] gave her for the poor," he said.

In mid-November, the queen decided to cut short her tour and return to Rumania because of a report that the king had cancer. In a farewell speech in Chicago, she pleaded with her listeners not to believe that she had come for anything but to see America and to thank its citizens for what they had done for her country during and after the war. She hoped that Americans would not " . . . shut their hearts away from the Old World, for the Old

Queen Marie's dinner at the Multnomah Hotel, Portland, on November 3, 1926. Sam Hill is at the queen's right, Portland's Mayor Baker on her left. (Photo courtesy of *The Oregonian*.)

World and the New must live together and help each other and understand each other. So goodbye, America, dear, beautiful America!"

The rest of her stay was marred by several incidents. Princess Ileana was involved in a minor accident while driving in Indiana. There were protest meetings of Rumanians in Detroit and Hungarians in Cleveland. The Southern Baptist's convention announced that Marie had rejected an audience to hear their protest of persecution of Baptists in Rumania. Another mishap occurred near Louisville when the car containing some militia officers accompanying the party had a puncture. They halted the next automobile, containing two correspondents and a woman guest on the queen's train. One Willard Johnson, a Ford employee now mysteriously in charge of the Lincolns, appeared and said the occupants would have to give up their car. The dispossessed passengers waited for half an hour in the snow until the puncture was repaired, and later aired their troubles to the press.

By this time, a certain ennui had crept into news accounts. *Vanity Fair* nominated the queen for oblivion. Although she was accused by some of being a champion freeloader, it must be said that she turned down all offers of paid endorsements. Many a politician could envy her studied composure while in the public eye.

The queen's farewell dinner was held on the train on the way through Maryland to New York. With pardonable hyperbole, she said, "I want to thank you, Col. Carroll, for this very happy trip which we have had." She presented gifts to Carroll, Washburn and others.

Washburn had a less pleasant surprise in store. He told Barron, "When I returned to Washington, I was fired by President Connelly [of the Northern Pacific] as though I had been a bootblack. I was told to close up my accounts and be through January 1."

Bookings had been made on the liner *Majestic* leaving New York on December 11, but news of Ferdinand's deteriorating condition induced the queen to sail on the *Berengaria* on November 24. Just before her departure, she accepted the practical gift of an armored sedan from the Willys-Overland Corporation. The donors had thoughtfully arranged for a demonstration of its imperviousness to bullets by firing a Thompson machine gun at the side of the car while the queen stood by.

When interviewed at the Ritz in Paris after her tour, she told the reporter, "Sam Hill was just like a big Newfoundland in whom everybody could have confidence. Sometimes his ideas came so rapidly and he talks so fast that his very great friends, King Albert and the queen of the Belgians, scarcely understand him."

At times, it is also hard for us to understand Sam. He did not leave an account of Marie's visit and its effect on him, but he must have especially regretted the squabbles with Washburn and Carroll and the embarrassment to the queen. He would certainly have come off better with the public had he managed to emulate her poise and imperturbability. Sam had often shown his skill at obtaining favorable notice in the press when he was in control of the interview. But this time, he was caught up in the great American publicity machine, which could turn out jibes and snide innuendos as readily as it could bestow fulsome praise.

After the queen's return to Rumania, it was reported that the tour and the Rumanian representatives here had displeased her, but in a cable to Mrs. I. N. Morris, she indignantly denied she had said this. Mrs. Morris wrote a book, *On Tour with Queen Marie*, the profits of which were designated for the Rumanian Red Cross. This recounted the running feud between Mr. Morris and Carroll. Mrs. Morris' first impression of Sam was that he " . . . looked like a hero who had stepped out of a book of legend. . . . One could not help loving his great enthusiasm and devotion to the queen." Later, she found him " . . . doing his utmost to disarrange all the plans of the train."

The queen had made a farewell broadcast to the Amerian people from New York, asking pardon for disappointing the people of the cities she had been unable to visit. She hoped she would live " . . . in the hearts of those I have learned to love. . . . This time America has seen me; the next time I intend to see America." But there was not to be another time. She withdrew from public life after Ferdinand died in 1927. She died of pernicious anemia in the Sinaia Palace in Rumania in July 1938.

So ended the American tour of a unique personage, a tour unlike any before or since. The journey had begun with an impressive bang, but ended, if not with a whimper, in anticlimax. Her progress may have been intended to be like the triumphal march in *Aida* before the adoring throng, but there were overtones of comic opera. The queen had put Rumania on the map, all right, but the images of royalty and Old Europe did not project as she had intended. The Queen had perhaps learned more about America than she had wished and America had learned about her.

The parking area near Maryhill Museum at its dedication on November 3, 1926. (Maryhill Museum files.)

Part VII

CODA

Other Ventures, Other Visions

In the years following the first World War, Sam's career was extraordinary in that he was engaged in a bewildering number and variety of plans and projects, ranging from the impractical, extravagant, or frankly harebrained through the shrewd and far-sighted to the unselfish and noble. Some have been described in previous chapters: completion of the Peace Arch in 1921 and the Stonehenge memorial in 1930; his trips to Japan in 1920 and 1922 on behalf of good roads; his continued efforts to promote highway construction in this country, particularly the Pacific Highway; Loie Fuller's endeavors to have him construct a combined art museum and apartment house in Paris; and his role in Queen Marie's visit to dedicate his future museum in 1926. These would have sufficed to earn him the reputation, bestowed, if not enjoyed, of being an eccentric, erratic, egotistical day-dreamer.

But there were other proposals and enterprises engaging his compulsively restless spirit in the 1920's. Some of these, fortunately, did not materialize, probably as often because of the lack of resources to push them to fruition single-handedly than to a sober decision about their impracticability.

One has to stop and ask: is this the shrewd, hardheaded lawyer, trust officer, and railroad executive we knew earlier? What made him assume the role of an emotional, belligerent crusader in his gas and telephone company wars? Did some midlife crisis simply release the irrepressible romantic from a mold which had constrained him but could not hold him? Had he been an absolute monarch, and not the "Prince of Castle Nowhere," he might have been called "Sam the Good" in his prime and in later life, "Sam the Mad" by his bewildered and admiring subjects. More of the madness in his methods later.

The various plans, proposals, and projects which follow are presented in no particular order. The background and outcome of some of them are not well documented, either because of scanty reports in the press or loss of relevant correspondence.

"Ye Olde English Restaurants, Ltd."

Sam could not resist the combination of an attractive business deal and helping his fellow man, in this case, the American tourist, who, parched as a result of the 18th Amendment and Volstead Act of 1919, was eager to help Canada's trade balance, even at the risk of upsetting his own. Sam had

Sam's restaurant buildings at Semiahmoo, 1979, about to be demolished. (Author's photo.)

known the country around Blaine, Washington and the southern part of British Columbia for many years, having put Blaine on the map with his Peace Portal. What was more logical than to set up a watering hole just over the Canadian side of the border, within a stone's throw of the Canadian customs and immigration station? Sam called the area "Semiahmoo," meaning "half moon," but did not explain how it came to be so named.

According to Ed Hanna, Sam formed the company, "Ye Olde English Restaurants, Ltd.," and built a hotel there in 1923, with his cousin Edgar Hill as manager. Edgar had been a banker and part-owner of a paper mill in Carthage, Indiana.

Sam built a large house* near the border station, and it was here that Queen Marie prepared a breakfast of waffles on her way to dedicate the Peace Arch. A house for the manager was moved onto the property in 1925, and the following year construction of two restaurant buildings was begun. These buildings, forty feet apart, contained a central hallway with small dining rooms on either side of the hall. In 1924-25, another 161 acres were purchased from several neighbors, setting Sam back $35 an acre. Clearing land for the golf course began in 1926. Since the " . . . fairways were 100 feet wide and the rough was a jungle of broken fern, stinging nettles, blackberry vines and snakes, it was not uncommon to lose twenty or thirty balls per round." The first nine holes opened to play in 1927 and the second a year later. Greens fees were fifty cents a day. About that time, Mr. Howard Merrill became resident manager in exchange for a half interest in the complex.

Sam told Lockley in 1928, "Right now I am spending several hundred thousand dollars at the international border between Washington and British Columbia. I have visited every well known summer resort and famous hotel and restaurant to get ideas for building a tourist resort and a

---

*Torn down in 1948.

256

in 1921. One of the partners wrote Sam offering him the opportunity to be the American representative in a deal to sell American locomotives to Poland. The Baldwin Locomotive Company had expressed some interest. "Whilst the Baldwin Group would not be willing to do the business entirely, they might be willing to discuss a share of the finance of business. . . . I would, however, point out that whilst the minimum requirements are 1,000 locomotives, the Poles believe in the motto that 'half a loaf is better than no bread at all' and for that reason they are anxious to secure any number of locomotives from, say, fifty upwards . . . We trust that even if it is not possible to finance the locomotive deal, we may be permitted to forward details of other attractive propositions." Whilst the author searched the correspondence, he did not find that Sam bit on this or other "attractive propositions" from this group.

In the same year *The Oregonian* had a front page headline, "Samuel Hill Will Reclaim Desert Land," The project involved rehabilitation of the Central Oregon Irrigation District by taking over its rights to reclaim arid land in the high plateau in an area between Bend, Redmond, and Prineville. Sam told a reporter, "The company reclaimed about 50,000 acres in this locality, but its costs of construction so overran its estimates that it found itself selling lands at less than it cost to put the water on them." The district's rights to reclaim another 27,000 acres would soon lapse if steps were not taken to complete the system. He added, "My interest in Central Oregon lands has been of long-standing; I made three trips to Europe to purchase the holdings of Lazard Frères and Company; but for the death of the head of the house, I would undoubtedly have consummated that purchase."

Sam was referring to a proposal he made late in 1909 in a long memo to Lazard Frères, offering to organize a syndicate of bankers and engineers to purchase the former vast holdings of the Willamette Valley and Cascade Mountain and Wagon Road Company. This deal, described in Chapter 14, fell through. Apparently Sam did not pursue the Central Oregon irrigation project; at least no holdings of stock in the company are mentioned in the list of the assets of his estate.

In the 1921 newspaper interview, Sam compared, as he had often done before, the area and population of Oregon with that of Germany. He claimed Oregon could eventually support 33 million people. Sixty years later, the contemplation of the influx of such numbers must depress everyone except the developers among Oregon's present inhabitants.

E. W. Frazar, a long time resident of the business community in Yokohama, wrote Sam in December 1922, in response to a letter from Sam " . . . giving particulars of the big sawmill and lumber proposition now occupying your attention. . . . " His brother's death and a trip east kept Sam from replying until February 1923. He wrote, "So sure am I of the success of this proposition that I am wiling to take a one-tenth interest in the $7,000,000 deal." Nothing came of this, probably due, at least in part, to Sam's not having that kind of idle capital.

Late in his life, some of Sam's proposals lacked conviction. In 1923, during a very cold February at Maryhill, he wrote to the U.S. Department of Agriculture, "It is my intention to see what we can do here in the way of propagation of interesting plants and especially those which produce food. By this time next year, I hope to have a school established here which will carry out my plans to a greater degree."

One of Sam's quite practical visions was that of state planning, based on an inventory of resources, such as water power, transportation, soils, and timber. In a talk to the Washington State Chamber of Commerce in July 1928, he told the audience that the time had come when they should " . . . take account and marshall the assets of [their] state. . . . We are trustees . . . [and] should conserve the heritage of those who come after us." He suggested that a committee be appointed to make the first industrial survey of Oregon and Washington. Wise words, accepted eventually and piecemeal.

In 1913, Sam had made the grand gesture of taking members of the Oregon Legislature and the press to Maryhill by special train to see his experimental roads. For the 10th anniversary of that visit, February 11, 1923, he planned an even more ambitious affair, inviting the governors and legislators of both Oregon and Washington to be his guests. The Oregon contingent was to come from Portland by auto caravan over the Columbia River Highway, led by John Yeon and Julius Meier.

Sam announced, "I have three distinct objects in doing this, or possibly four. First, to let the two bodies see Celilo Falls, which, with the adjacent water power, is the largest undeveloped proposition, as far as I know, in the United States . . . I hope the legislature will . . . submit recommendations to the governing bodies of the two states at the next sessions of the legislatures which will show how best to develop and utilize this power.

"Second, I wish to call to their attention the railroad situation in the Northwest." Sam referred to the late J. J. Hill's efforts to merge the Great Northern, Northern Pacific, and Burlington railroads. (He had written to President Harding and the governors of the Pacific Northwest states the previous year urging the amalgamation.) Sam asserted that " . . . the attempt to separate these properties I regard as a crime." Northwest timber, he said, " . . . is not a seasonal crop but furnishes traffic every day in the year with the railways supplying the treeless country."

Sam also wanted to promote investigation of construction of a bridge over the Columbia at Biggs Rapids to link the highways in Central Oregon and Washington. He mentioned the possible military usefulness of such a bridge to supplant the ferry, which on some days carried as many as 200 cars. He ended by renewing his pledge to establish a museum when its accessibility to tourists had been improved, a museum " . . . which will rival anything proposed on the north Pacific Coast."

The visit to Maryhill was canceled, however. The Washington Legislature had had a late night session the night before, February 10, and sent word to Sam that it could not participate. There was "much snow in the gorge and a gale blowing" so that it was deemed unwise for the Oregonians to come. About thirty senators and representatives were in Portland, prepared to make the trip, when the announcement of the cancellation was made.

It was just as well they did not come, and that Sam did not repeat the offer. The desolate, cold, unfinished chateau would scarcely have been a congenial place for Sam's famous hospitality, however spirited the individual internal heating he would no doubt have provided. To accommodate those staying overnight at the Meadowlark Inn, Sam had had a Portland department store send bed linens, towels, and rolls of paper to cover tables. The store included ". . . 300 cookies, baked especially for you today." Sam had rented 12 dozen sets of silverware and folding chairs.

Merger of the railroads was much on Sam's mind that year, and of more immediate importance than a future hydroelectric dam (completed in 1957), the bridge at Biggs (opened to traffic in the fall of 1962) and a museum for the public (opened in May 1940). Sam's mind was accustomed to operating in the future as well as in the present, and he found it difficult to be patient with those who could not look ahead with confidence, as he did.

In 1927, Sam wrote to Loie Fuller about his interest in a company called Radium Limited, U.S.A., which " . . . handles radium emanation water . . . I myself have taken this water . . . for over a month, and I am sure that it is no sense a fake. It has been approved and recommended by the Mayo Clinic . . . and by the American Medical Association. . . . " He asked Loie if she could obtain " . . . a letter from Mme. Curie which would be of very great assistance, and, I think, under the circumstances, justified." No glowing testimonial from Mme. Curie is to be found in the files.

In 1929, Sam invested in the "Aerocrete Corporation of American," with an office in the Vanderbilt Avenue Building in New York City. It was later acquired by the Akoa Corporation of America, but Sam's estate did not realize anything from it. It was a bad time for a business venture, and the company probably was a casualty of the Great Depression.

How does one characterize Sam's last decade? It is not like the unraveling of a fabric, because that implies the presence of a continuous thread which can be wound up again and rewoven. It is more like a disintegration of some elaborate fabrication of an artist, combining the practical, the visionary, the decorative, the irrelevant, and the foolish, held together by some ineffable wish for self-realization and immortality. How does one put together the hard work (the coal mine); will-o'-the-wisps (Solomon's Temples); the acute urge to write (the biographies); the ingenious organization of a large tourist restaurant and golf course (Semiahmoo); the compulsion to travel (to Japan and elsewhere); the need for identification with the famous (Queen Marie and Joffre); the devotion to a cause (good roads); the paranoid precautions against an enemy (the Soviets); and the demand to be remembered (the Peace Arch and Stonehenge Memorial)?

There are significant clues. When one reviews Sam's correspondence arranged chronologically, he cannot help but be struck by the comparison of the relative scarcity of letters and telegrams written by Sam from about 1913 on with the profusion of those of February 1923, when he undertook a great burst of letter writing about a variety of subjects. He was obviously "racing his motor," but what is the explanation? One possibility is that in the "febrile February" of 1923 Sam had made a resolution to pursue vigorously a number of projects which he had had in mind for years but had been putting off.

The author's conclusion is that Sam experienced the manic phase of a manic depressive state, probably precipitated by the death of his brother Richard early in 1923. Older textbooks of psychiatry refer to various factors likely to bring on such a condition: death of a close friend or relative; loss of money, employment, or social esteem; disappointments in love or pursuit of a goal; or exposure to danger. Characteristically, in the manic phase there is elation, talkativeness or a flight of ideas, and often temporary swings to depression. Rather commonly, a patient may be hypomanic, remaining well oriented and "even impressing the public with his initiative and drive." There may be "transient hallucinations or delusions . . . [but] there is no mental deterioration or basic lack of power to think, reason, and judge." Nor did Sam quite lose his sense of humor. In thanking a man for a check in February, he wrote, "I have opened today about 400 letters. This is the only one that contained a check. A great many of them asked for money, however, so I answer your letter first."

A psychoanalytic view is that the manic-depressive syndrome arises from the mother's rejection of her child, and leads to alternating feelings of guilt and displays of affection. The subject (or "dysmutual," in the jargon) then lives " . . . with a feeling of basic rejection and lack of worth. . . . " Manic moods are " . . . desperate reactions to unbearable feelings of depression. . . . " When paranoia appears, it is as a protection against depression, and the world is perceived as a "hateful place." We know, at least, of Sam's paranoia about the Soviets being out to kill him and the elaborate precautions he employed against intruders in his Seattle house (Chapter 13).

How long this phase lasted, we don't know. Some of Sam's involvements, such as the Seattle gas war, the Maryhill venture and other financial speculations, his restless urge to travel, his construction of great houses, lead one to conclude that he was hypomanic for nearly two decades before the full-blown syndrome became manifest in 1923. There is no record that others commented on it or that Sam developed insight into the problem. He wrote his former secretary, the mother of one of his illegitimate children, in 1926, "I am over my great strain." Perhaps he was referring to this trying and bewildering period.

If he was a driven man in this decade, he could still steer amongst the tasks he set for himself. Most of us at some time or other have had the desperate awareness of so much to do and so little time. Had he poured out his heart about private demons, and if, indeed, a heart can be emptied in that way, we might know the answers.

27

Honors, Legends, and Old Age

Honors and old age go gracefully together and legends sometimes follow. Most of us are lucky, if that is the word, to achieve old age, much less honors, beyond possibly a gold watch or an award as den mother of the year. If legends make a person legendary, Sam qualifies, at least as a near-legendary figure. Acquiring a legend or two is difficult for your average mortal: retold errors or misconceptions about one's life are much commoner. Sam probably abetted the legend process by initiating a few himself. Let us start with some errors about Sam Hill before listing his hits and runs and retiring the metaphor.

The most pervasive fallacy is that the phrase, "What the Sam Hill" originated with our Sam. The author was made aware of this whenever he imparted the news of writing this biography and heard the inevitable response, "What the Sam Hill are you doing that for?"

The consensus among experts, including H. L. Mencken, seems to be that "'Sam Hill' is a euphemism for hell," but its origins are obscure. The source of the saying was discussed in several letters written to the *New York Times* in 1925. One correspondent speculated that the expression arose from the song about a murderer about to be hanged, "My name, it is Sam Hall." Another cited its first appearance in print in the Elmira (N.Y.) *Republican* in 1839, to wit, "What in Sam Hill is that fellow ballin' about?", and he noted the Puritan reluctance to use phrases with "the devil" in them. He surmised that Samael, the name of the snake which tempted Eve, was an acceptable substitution. Corrupt "Samael" and "Hell," if that's possible, and get "Sam Hill."

When J. J. Hill was outraged at something or other, Seattle newspapers are said to have carried the headline, "Jim Hill Mad as Sam Hill." Some think that the expression derived from Solomon, used an oath, and Hill as a euphemism for hell. With admirable prescience, one authority promised in 1960 that " . . . within another forty years the term will be completely dialectic and archaic."

A more attractive account of the origin of the phrase was given in another of the letters to the *New York Times*. Samuel Hill (1678-1752), born in

Guilford, Connecticut was reelected judge so regularly by the assembly that the presiding officer would simply announce that they were again assembled to nominate and reelect Sam Hill to the next general court. This gave rise to the expression, "He runs like Sam Hill" as applying to an unusually successful candidate for office. By an odd coincidence, Judge Samuel Hill was born in Guilford, Connecticut and our Sam Hill near Guilford County, North Carolina.

Another letter writer, who must have had an extraordinary memory, told of hearing, nearly eighty years earlier, a workman singing:

> Old Sam Hill
> He built a mill
> Upon a sandy plain,
> Where there was no water
> In a mile and a quarter
> Unless there came a rain.

Our Sam might have considered this uncomfortably close to the cause of his troubles in his Maryhill development. As Paul Douglas says, " . . . if the expression had not been derived from his actions, he had modeled his acts to live up to the expression." But what the Sam Hill! Let's get on to something else.

Another common error has been to identify Sam as the son, rather than the son-in-law, of J. J. Hill. Stewart Holbrook marveled at hearing a stranger told that Maryhill "castle" was a monument to his beloved mother, erected by Sam Hill, a son of Jim Hill. The same error about Sam's parentage was committed by at least a dozen reporters and by the biographers of King Albert, Chief Joseph, and others. The mistake arose, no doubt, from a Hill marrying a Hill. A writer resolved to "lift up mine eyes unto the hills" would have done better to look up the Hills first.

An exotic variation of Sam's family name was heard from an old timer living near Maryhill. At the time of Queen Marie's visit in 1926, he had heard that Sam actually was a Rumanian with a long name which he was required to change to Hill before J. J. would give him the hand of this daughter. One obituary of Edgar N. Hill, a cousin of Sam's, names him as Sam's brother, and "builder of the International Peace Arch at Blaine."

The probably apocryphal story about the collapse of Sam's deal to buy the farm from the teetotaling Jewetts at White Salmon, when he offered to drink a toast to celebrate it, is told in Chapter 22. Ellen M. Ewing wrote a three-part series in *The Oregonian* (June and July 1940), containing a number of items about Sam which gets the blue ribbon for questionable authenticity. Many of these yarns were later repeated in newspaper accounts of Sam's career.

Sam knew Albert of Belgium (1875-1934) before and after he became king. Mrs. Ewing's story of their meeting is as neat as it is apocryphal, placing Sam at the University of Munich about 1881, greeting his new roommate in their modest quarters. Later, his friend invited Sam to spend the November holidays with him at his home in Brussels. There they went

The old boy in a jovial mood — Seattle house. Undated photograph, probably about 1925. (Maryhill Museum files.)

straight to the palace of King Leopold II and the "French student" was revealed to Sam's astonished eyes as the heir apparent to the Belgian throne. Albert would have been six years old at the time, and even his admirers do not claim that he was at the university as an infant prodigy.

Another O. Henry-type story, which conceivably may be true, has Sam watching the tennis matches at Nice. He " . . . spotted a stately elderly gentleman to whom he took an immediate liking." They struck up a conversation in French and Sam proffered his card, identifying him as Honorary Consul-General of Belgium for Oregon, Washington, and Idaho. The stranger commented that this must be an important post. When Sam asked for his card, " . . . the bright blue eyes twinkled. I never carry a card. I am only the King of Sweden."

There is also the story of Sam with a " . . . troupe of jiujitsu artists he had brought over from Japan . . . " being turned away from the White House by Teddy Roosevelt who " . . . emitted a forceful 'No!' Indignant, Sam Hill installed his muscle artists in Boston's Quaker School House and promptly forgot about them, but not the presidential snub. For years afterward he wold recount this story with the frowning denunciation, 'I never liked Roosevelt after that.' "

A possible overstatement occurs in Mrs. Ewing's report of his 1916 visit to Russia: "Sam Hill hurried to St. Petersburg and spent eight months checking over every one of the 7,000 miles of Russian railroad" (and muttering, perhaps, "Blessed be the ties that bind it"). She has Sam looking over the Trans-Siberian before, instead of after, his conference with Allied leaders in Belgium. After the conference, he is supposed to have returned to the United States, grown a beard, and disguised himself as "Mr. Montgomery." This disguise was so impenetrable that when he came to Seattle, ready for the trip to Japan, "Frank Terrace looked through and beyond him without the faintest dream of recognition." From Yokohama to Vladivostok, she has him signed on as a beardless cabin boy. On the ferry crossing Lake Baikal,* a German agent asked Sam, "Have you seen him? I take it you are the other detective." The German then took out a picture of a clean-shaven Sam Hill and offered to divide the reward of 2,000 pounds in gold for the capture of the American spy.

Here, the line between legend and fact becomes indistinct: in 1921, Sam himself told Barron that an agent had been offered 40,000 pounds to kill him, and Sam had offered to split the booty with the agent before disappearing.

Mrs. Ewing has Sam taking advantage of his status as honorary Northwest Belgian Consul to import " . . . the finest wines and liquor to his Seattle house, storing the overflow at Maryhill" but being thwarted in carrying out the plan by Mabel W. Willebrandt, Special Assistant to the U.S. Attorney General. On arising each morning thereafter, Sam is supposed to have hissed, "I hope to live to spit on her grave!" On another occasion, she says J. J. Hill entrusted to Sam the key to his private stock at his St. Paul home. "Accompanied by several associates, Sam Hill decided to sample. When James J. Hill received his key there was not a corked bottle remaining in the vault." One suspects that Mrs. Ewing's informants had a lively and wicked imagination.

Thelma Kimmel has contributed her bit by repeating some of these stories and noting the claim of one Thomas Yalaup, son of the "Chief of the Rock Creek Indians in the Maryhill area," to being Sam's valet.

C. T. Conover of Seattle says Sam was a Great Northern station agent when J. J. " . . . in making a trip over the line, was impressed by the attractive, well-cared-for appearance of Sam's station. . . . A few days later, Sam was summoned to Hill's office in St. Paul . . . " and told that J. J.

---

*The railroad route around Lake Baikal was completed over ten years earlier, so why the ferry story?

272

would finance his law education provided he first went through Harvard. After that, Conover repeats the Albert-at-Munich story.

There are other stories more difficult to refute or confirm. Sam was given credit for much worthy effort for Belgian and Rumanian war relief, the name of Herbert Hoover usually being linked with Sam's in this connection. The author's sketchy findings in this regard are set forth in Chapter 20.

There is no lack of stories about Maryhill "Castle", either. The favorite is that Sam planned it as a military fortress. The Seattle *Times* had it that the " . . . castle [was] fashioned after the fortresses along the line of defense at Liege. . . . The curious questioned, and under pressure, Hill confided that he had constructed it as a place of refuge for King Albert if ever he should be forced from the throne by communistic forces. . . . Hill once said that he had built the citadel on the Columbia to be a last bastion against anarchy 'when the great social revolution should occur.' The citadel is well stocked with rifles and ammunition, and some even go so far as to cite the presence of machine guns and light field pieces."

It was not like Sam to lead a reporter impishly down the garden path. The reporter was probably unaware of Sam's paranoia about the Communist danger. The crumb of truth is that there was, indeed, a large artillery shell stored under the east ramp of the building: a dud, said to be the first shell fired into Belgium, and presented to Sam by Albert. Rolled down the cliff at the proper moment, it would surprise, if not actually rout, any would-be invader.

The turn-arounds at the upper end of the east and west entrance ramps were said to be intended for gun emplacements. Just how an invader would get nearly 200 miles up the Columbia to reach the embattled defenders at Maryhill, or why they should wish to, is not spelled out. Another wild rumor has Sam intending to found a monarchy and use Maryhill as its capitol.

During Queen Marie's visit, there was the inevitable scurrilous gossip that the queen was Sam's mistress. Mona Bell Hill (Chapter 28), who did qualify, once told her son that as she and Sam were walking along the beach one day, he said to her, "Mona, I don't know what to do. I'm in love with the queen." This does not settle the question, but the reader is free to speculate.

Compound errors did not cease with the opening of the museum. A 1954 article stated that, "The U.S. Engineers had seventeen acres of the Hill property upon which the chateau set which they did not need. On April 10, 1942, the government deeded the property to the state. . . . A park caretaker lives in the chateau on the hill where the Hills formerly lived."

The list must stop somewhere. The author is well aware he may be initiating or perpetuating other mistakes for which he will be sternly brought to task.

One can surmise that Sam's accomplishments in promoting good roads and public acknowledgement of his contributions sustained him in his many disappointments. There were governmental honors, too, and if one counts these as blue chips, Sam had a small but respectable stack when he cashed in. He prized these awards and had projection slides made of them as a big share of his life's winnings. Perhaps he had too often lost more important stakes to hold decorations in high esteem. Though heaped upon him, honors did not submerge his character.

His 1916 trip to Vladivostok with the objective of expediting rail shipments from Allies to the Russian front led to his being decorated as an officer of the Legion of Honor and given a medal of thanks by the French goverment.

King Albert of Belgium made him a Commander of the Crown and Honorary Belgian Consul General for Oregon, Washington, and Idaho for his role in the Russian venture and his contributions in money to Belgian relief, respectively. Queen Marie made him a member of the Queen's Body Guard, and in 1928 gave him the "Order of the Crown of Rumania in the Degree of the Grand Cross." Whether this was awarded for his part in the queen's American tour or for other services to queen and country is not clear. His devotion to promoting good roads in Japan was rewarded by the Order of the Sacred Treasure, third class.

He was made honorary life president of the Washington Good Roads Association; honorary president of the British Columbia Good Roads League; vice-president of the Columbia River Highway Association; president of the American Road Builders' Association; and president of the Pacific Highway Association.

In 1922, the United States Senate and Canadian Parliament each passed resolutions of thanks for his donation of the Peace Arch at Blaine. Senator Robert Owen wrote Sam " . . . By the way, it was without precedent for the Senate to pass such a resolution, as far as I know."

A number of other offices and honors have been mentioned in previous chapters, including his being made honorary chief of the Nez Percé tribe, and president of the Harvard Clubs of Minnesota, Seattle, and London. He was an honorary member of the Great Northern Veterans Association and of the Oregon State Medical Society. In connection with his interest in earthquakes and ocean currents, he was at one time the only American member of the Geographic Society of Germany.

Sam received only one honorary degree, an LL.D. In the 50th report of the Harvard Class of 1879, this is listed as having been conferred by Penn College, Oskaloosa, Iowa in 1912, (the name was later changed to William Penn College). The college, however, lists Sam as having received the degree in 1925, along with Herbert Hoover. The award cites Sam's " . . . ample scholarship . . . his service in the interest of good roads, not only in this country but in other countries, [and] because of good roads legislation that he has been influential in securing, which . . . has become a model for similar legislation in many states in the Union." It may be that Sam had done the college a good turn long before, while he was president of the Minneapolis Trust Company. He wrote to his successor as president of

274

the company, "I hope by this time that you have passed on the Penn College bonds matter."

Be that as it may, the wonder is that he was not honored by other colleges, such as the University of Washington, to which he contributed funds to establish chairs in studies of the Russian language and highway engineering. Sam would never have admitted that he coveted an honorary degree from Harvard, but considering his accomplishments and what he did for his Alma Mater, it would not have been undeserved.

How did Sam spend his last years? The previous chapter has outlined his often hectic and eccentric activities in business and in the public eye. He did not fulfill his ambitious plans to write at that time, but in June 1930, did dictate accounts of two railroad strikes which occurred in 1894. In the 1920's, he lived at the Arlington Club in Portland for the most part, visiting his Seattle house, the restaurant at Semiahmoo, and Goldendale and Maryhill from time to time. We don't know how much time he spent at the house at Bonneville, Oregon, which he had built for Mona Bell.

On his visits to Maryhilll, Sam would stop at the Babcock house, often for a day or two at a time, to see the family. Charles Babcock developed carcinoma of the tongue in the last years of his life. Though weak and in pain, he attended the queen's dedication of the Museum in November 1926. Edgar Babcock says that Sam had met Madame Curie in France and arranged with her to have radium sent to St. Vincent's Hospital, Portland, for treatment which Charles Babcock could not otherwise have afforded.

The senior Babcock died in 1927, four days after surgery. He and Sam had an agreement that the survivor would preach the other's funeral sermon. This Sam did at the Babcock house. Sam had planned for two niches for the ashes of Babcock and himself in a mausoleum constructed below Stonehenge. Babcock would have none of it. Not only did he not believe in cremation, but he told Sam with mock indignation, "I'd rather be with the Indians [in the Maryhill cemetery] than to be looking at you for all eternity!"

Sam made business trips as late as 1929 and 1930 to New York because of an interest in the Aerocrete Corporation of America. He wrote to a friend in the dark days of 1929, "The town is pretty badly upset. A man goes into a hotel to rent a room and asks for the top floor and the clerk says, 'Do you want a room to sleep in or do you want one to jump from?' . . . What with dodging the automobiles on the corners and looking up so as to dodge men jumping from the windows, one appreciates a residence at Maryhill or Goldendale more."

The traveling itch persisted, but his enthusiasm for tourism for the Northwest had waned. Early in 1930 he wrote the editor of the *Oregon Journal* to thank him for a complimentary article, and added, "I ran down to Havana and left a cough I had down there after a two day stay. But Coronado Beach is still on my mind. A Chinese wall around part of British Columbia, Washington, Oregon, and California, and a man at the gates taking tickets, would be a fine picture."

One wonders if Sam in his old age sighed "the lack of many a thing . . . " he sought. There must have been regrets aplenty, most of all for his unhappy family life: his failed marriage and the estrangement from his son, James. What he might have done with his wealth and energy instead of engaging in the Maryhill venture, the futile purchase of Stockbridge, the discouraging battle with the Bell Company in Portland, and the pursuit of various will-o'-the-wisps must be left to the imagination. As Freud might have said, but didn't, "The fault lies not in ourselves but in our scars."

On February 6, 1931, Governor Meier informed Sam that the Oregon Senate and House had passed "Concurrent Resolution Number 13" inviting him to address them on the evening of February 9. Just eighteen years before, in a joint resolution also numbered 13, they had thanked Sam for the train excursion to Maryhill to inspect the experimental roads and see his slides. He had " . . . made every provision for the comfort, entertainment and enjoyment of his guests, making it one of the most delightful and enjoyable days ever experienced by those present."

It was while enroute to this appointment that Sam was taken acutely ill. The press was told that he had "intestinal influenza," a handy waste basket diagnosis, still in popular use. A later account said that his illness had become apparent about two months earlier at Victoria, B.C.: "Contrary to the advice of physicians, he made a trip to New York. . . . " After his return, and on his way from Portland to Salem, " . . . he was feeling very badly Sunday night when he reached his room at the Arlington Club, but was insistent that he would go on to Salem Monday to deliver what he considered an important message, after which he planned to go to Olympia to address the Washington legislature on the same subject, namely, the regulation of trucks to protect the condition of the highways. [In one of his last letters, Sam wrote Ralph Budd from the Cosmos Club, Washington, D.C., that he had called the President [Hoover] " . . . to discuss the truck and bus damage. The President is with us. . . . "] On Monday, February 9, his condition was such that his friends persuaded him to go to St. Vincent's Hospital, Portland, for treatment." It seems fitting that Sam, impatient as always in spreading the gospel of good roads, should be afflicted while heading for the podium for the last time.

His physician was Dr. William H. Skene, who called into consultation Dr. Thomas Joyce, Portland's most prominent surgeon. A student nurse of that time recalls working on a ward adjacent to Sam's large private room with his special nurses in attendance: "The bathtub was filled to overflowing with the most beautiful flowers. . . . [He was] a handsome man with snow white hair, reminding one of Lloyd George or Samuel Clemens."

Sam had improved somewhat after about ten days in the hospital and abdominal surgery, but his condition then deteriorated and his son James was sent for. There was no mention of his wife, who had been in seclusion for years. James arrived by air on February 25. Sam was cheered enough to say, "I have won the fight." The *New York Times* reported that James was at the bedside, along with Sam's cousin, Edgar Hill, and W. F. Turner, president of the S.P. & S. Railway, when the end came on the evening of February 26, 1931.

The hospital chart was destroyed years ago, but the death certificate, completed after an autopsy, indicated that death was due to an abscess of the lesser peritoneal cavity which had ruptured into the stomach, producing "fatal terminal hemorrhages." The cause of the abscess was not stated, but it may have complicated acute pancreatitis, a perforated duodenal ulcer, or some other lesion of the intestine. The certificate gave his age at death at 73 years, 9 months, and 13 days and his occupation as "laywer and capitalist." The answer to "date deceased last worked at this occupation?" was "February 1931."

Sam's body was taken to a Portland mortuary where it lay in state for friends to say farewell. James accompanied the body on the train trip to Seattle, and to Sam's house where friends and officials paid their respects, and then to a mortuary for the funeral. A minister of the Friends Meeting officiated and Frank Terrace gave the eulogy: "His monuments are of cement, stretching over the miles of roads he pleaded for." Half a dozen of the "Old Guard" of good roads days were honorary pall bearers. There were flowers from British Columbia, the governors of Oregon and Washington, and the Japanese, Belgian, and several other consulates. The Washington Good Roads Association sent a model of the Peace Arch in flowers and the A.A.A. its floral initials.

A number of his friends and admirers wanted to construct a suitable memorial to his lifelong work for good roads while Sam was still alive. A memorial to be placed on the Columbia River Highway at the "Rowena Loops," a dramatic series of long hairpin turns near Hood River, was proposed as early as 1926 by civic groups in The Dalles, Oregon. In May 1929, Rufus Holman suggested to the Multnomah County commissioners that a committee be established to collect funds and construct a suitable roadside memorial. Retired Major General Charles Martin, Holman, Mrs. C. A. Dolph, and others were named to the committee. The memorial, a fifty ton granite boulder at Chanticleer Point, was not dedicated until more than a year after Sam's death, on the anniversary of his birthday, May 13, 1932. On one side is a bronze bas-relief of a bust of Sam, facing toward Maryhill. Three other plaques depict the early history of the Gorge and its people: the Indians; Lewis and Clark; and the pioneers. The sculptor. Alonzo V. Lewis, was a descendant of Capt. Meriwether Lewis.

At the dedication of the monument, Governor Julius Meier said of Sam, "He lifted Oregon out of the mud, put an end to the isolation of our communities, and changed the whole mode of life of our people." Frank Terrace and Sam Lancaster spoke at the ceremony. Sam's family was represented only by his cousin, Edgar Hill.

An *Oregonian* reporter had once asked Sam where he wanted to be buried. He had the answer ready: "Standing on the bluff in front of my place at Maryhill and looking down on the canyon of the Columbia, you will see a mass of jagged rocks, nature's great upheaval. Here on the bluff in

Sam Hill's monument below Stonehenge Memorial. (Author's photo.)

time to come, I hope there will be over my ashes a bronze tablet bearing this inscription: 'Samuel Hill: amid nature's great unrest, he sought rest.'"

In accordance with Sam's wishes, his body was cremated and the ashes placed in the crypt at Maryhill, built a little distance below Stonehenge. Sam had ordered work started on the tomb years before his death. He was not satisfied with it, and it was rebuilt during the winter of 1928-29 by the workmen who were finishing the Stonehenge Memorial. The original crypt had two large oak doors in front, one of which had a bronze plaque giving the dates of birth and death of Sam's friend, Eben F. Wells. On the other door the plate carried the epitaph Sam himself had written.

As an ironic touch, the mausoleum, intended for a man who built for the ages, deteriorated in the next twenty-five years and was replaced in 1955 by a granite monument bearing his epitaph and covering his ashes. Other more notable monuments can be seen from this site: the Sam Hill Memorial Bridge, opened in the fall of 1962; the Stonehenge Memorial; and Maryhill Museum, the "Castle" to the domain of which he had at least returned.

278

Sam Hill Memorial Bridge leading to Biggs, Oregon. Maryhill State Park and the town of Maryhill in the foreground. 1979. (Author's photo.)

28

Legacy with Bar Sinister

Cervantes put it cynically: "There is a strange charm in the thoughts of a good legacy . . . which wondrously alleviates the sorrow that men would otherwise feel for the death of friends." With Sam's legacy, the charm was muted by the law's delay of over fifteen years until the final settlement and by the hostility of his widow and son, James, who, goodness knows, did not need the money. For a long time, his last testament seemed a Hill will that would blow nobody good.

The document, signed on November 29, 1930, about three months before his death, seems straightforward enough. He provided for funeral expenses and completion of the crypt, located on the bluff below the Stonehenge memorial.

No bequest was made to Sam's wife, who had been "amply provided for" by reason of gifts from her father. If, however, a reverse of fortunes should occur, the will provided that she was to receive $1,000 per month; " . . . that sum is mentioned because I have since our marrige provided her with that amount."

Sam's Seattle house, previously conveyed to his U.S. Trust Company there, was to be part of his estate. One-half of the estate was to go to Maryhill Museum and one-half to the U.S. Trust Company, as his executor. In 1923, the U.S. Trust Company had executed a deed transferring owner-ship of the unfinished chateau and 32 acres surrounding it to Maryhill Museum. The trustees of the company were Edgar Hill, president; Warren Berry, vice-president; and James S. Blain, secretary. Attorney Zola Brooks was to be elected to the next vacancy on the board of the U.S. Trust Company. The executors were each to be paid $5,000 a year for not more than three years.

The trust company was to provide for his daughter's maintenance and "Mary's cottage" at Maryhill was to be kept available for her. His son was to receive a life income of $12,000 a year. At James's death, any remaining share would go to the museum. Sam included an "implied reminder" to James of his " . . . obligation to help every worthy cause within his reach and means." James may have considered this admonition a gratuitous reproach for selfishness.

A house on the grounds of Ye Olde English Restaurant Company, Ltd., just north of the Peace Arch, was to be kept for Sam's cousin, Edgar Hill, during his lifetime. (In 1928, Sam had, by letter, conveyed a $25,000 interest in the company to Edgar, a sum said to have been paid in considera-tion of Edgar's marriage of convenience that year to Mona Bell, so her son would be legitimized and named Sam B. Hill.) Sam's Chinese servant, Mah Ying, got the use of a small house near Edgar's.

A Minneapolis newspaper reported the estate to be half a million dollars, a horseback estimate of a legacy which proved to be saddled with troubles. Although he was a lawyer, Sam does not get an "A" in devising and bequeathing. The will does not mention that he had been the sole stockholder of the Minneapolis Athenaeum Company, with assets with a book value of $300,000. The Stonehenge Memorial, which stood on Mary-hill ranch land set aside as "Well's Park," was not referred to, either. Perhaps Sam felt that the monument was indestructible and needed no provision for landscaping and maintenance. He had made an oral promise to Miss Clara Carter and Miss Lucy Wetherby, his housekeepers in Seattle, that they would have the use of the Meadowlark Inn during their lifetimes. Other property stood in the name of "Sam Hill, Inc.," but these assets were not listed in the will, either.

The will's provisions must have seemed scanty fare to James and his mother, however welcome they might have been to your average heir. It is not known whether or not they were aware that Sam had set up three trust funds for the three mothers of his illegitimate children. In any case, this bit of news, the exclusion of Sam's wife, and the skimpy bequest to James, as compared with that to Maryhill Museum, were not to be accepted gratefully. Sam's wife engaged E. L. Skeel, a Seattle attorney, to file a petition with the probate court of King County, Seattle, to establish community property. James had Skeel introduce a petition questioning the validity of the bequest to the museum. Skeel was appointed guardian ad litem (i.e., for the purpose of law) for Mary Mendenhall, who was judged incompetent.

Let us skip to five years later, by which time, after many discussions with their clients, Skeel and Zola Brooks agreed to a settlement. Mary Hill and James would drop their petitions in return for a half share of the liquid assets for James and Mary Mendenhall, plus Sam's share of certain timberlands in Lewis County. The matter of timber interests was complicated. Sam owned a 30% share and had advanced Edgar Hill $15,000 to pay for Edgar's 30% interest. He had advanced lesser amounts to R. Auzias de Turenne and to Frank Terrace, each of whom held 20%. After adjustments for advancements the net proceeds of the timberland sale were to be divided between James and Mary Mendenhall on the one hand, and the museum on the other. The museum was to receive all of Maryhill Ranch and the Olde English Restaurant properties. Mah Ying's claim was settled for $1,000 and Edgar Hill's for $20,000. The Washington State inheritance tax was $77,664 and the U.S. estate tax $1,896. Skeel would receive 10% of the children's share of the liquid assets and 15% of the proceeds of the timberlands.

By 1936, it was understood that there would be no necessity to maintain Mary's cottage for her because she would be cared for elsewhere. Half of the children's share was divided between them and the other half used to establish a trust fund at Seattle First National Bank, which paid James and Mary Mendenhall a lifetime income. Skeel estimated that the children's shares would total about $200,000, about two-thirds of what he expected originally. Sam's stocks, mostly in Great Northern Railway certificates and shares, held in the name of the U.S. Trust Company, had depreciated greatly in value.

Sam's interest in the Alabama coal mine proved to be a liability. There was a suit against his estate, settled for $2,000 in 1934. Edgar Hill wrote Brooks, "We felt we could win any suit they had against us but it would cost us at least $5,000 to fight it."

In the settlement of the estate, there was a claim by a Dr. Kohlander, unexplained in the correspondence, for whom Sam had set up a trust, affording her the interest on $50,000 in telephone company bonds. Attorney Garvin noted that Sam had promised " . . . if the Aerocrete deal did not work out he would return the bonds and in the meantime would pay her an amount equal to the interest on the bonds." This claim was settled for $6,750.

Still another claim on the U.S. Trust Co. for $57,000 was made by the First National Bank and Trust Co. of Minneapolis, as trustee for the estate of Sam's brother Richard. Sam had, for some reason, given a guarantee to his brother's estate for this amount. The bank won a judgment of $3,036 plus interest, but altogether the suit cost the museum about $20,000. Garvin, representing Sam's estate, argued the case before the Minnesota Supreme Court in June 1935. He wrote, "The contract makes it clear that Sam took on himself [half] the obligation which his brother had incurred."

There was also the matter of distribution of the personal property in the Seattle house to settle. Skeel and Brooks agreed that James would get the grandfather's clock and the Curtis pictures and books on North American Indians. The silver, china, and linen were to be sold and the proceeds divided between James and the museum. The rest of the furniture and furnishings went to the museum, including a rickshaw, carriage, and an old Studebaker. There was an old Locomobile stored in the garage at Maryhill which Brooks thought he could sell for $25.* To facilitate the distribution, Skeel was to be made a director of the U.S. Trust Company. Garvin wrote Brooks in 1935, "While I was in the East I had a nice visit with James Hill in New York. He was entirely satisfied with the settlement."

The last word in probate court about Sam's estate was not uttered until September 1946, when the court acknowledged that the U.S. Trust Company as executor had liquidated and distributed all the assets of the estate, so that its stock could be surrendered and canceled. By this time, the residual assets amounted to only $21,100, half of which went to the museum, one quarter to James in cash, and one quarter in trust for him at the Seattle bank. Mary Mendendall had died in the meantime, in 1941. Sam would have been aghast at the 15 year time lapse, the skimpy proceeds, and the miscarriage of his plan for a large endowment for Maryhill Museum.

What of the three trusts Sam had set up for his other children and their mothers? More important, what do we know of these women and their children and their relationships with Sam?

One part of these questions can be answered briefly: nothing, except the name of one mother and the address of her son who lives in British Columbia. (He signed for a registered letter from the author requesting information, but did not reply.) Two other women who bore Sam's children had remarkably different personalities. The effects on their lives of raising their offspring and of receiving legacies from Sam reveal their differences dramatically.

Annie Laurie Whelan was born in Stillwater, Minnesota in February 1880. She was one of eight children, six of them girls. Since there was no school in Stillwater, their father employed a competent teacher and transformed a small farm building into a schoolhouse. Their father died suddenly

---

*Old car buffs, eat your hearts out!

Mrs. A. W. Ehrens and Elizabeth, about 1918. (Photo courtesy of Elizabeth Wade.)

in an accident and the family immediately faced serious financial difficulties.

The family knew the J. J. Hills in St. Paul, and it is likely that Sam, in order to help out, offered Annie (or A. L. Whelan, as she always signed herself in business letters written for Sam) a secretarial job. She worked at the Seattle Gas Company in April 1902, and also for Sam's land company at Maryhill and for the Home Telephone Company in Portland until 1914, leaving when she became pregnant.

Her daughter, Elizabeth, was born in New York on December 27, 1914. Elizabeth gathered that her mother had met a Henry Ehrens through Sam and had married him. Ehrens, a German Swiss, was recalled for military duty early in World War I and did not return. Elizabeth, at the age of six weeks, was taken to Chicago where her grandmother lived. Mrs. Ehrens soon moved with her daughter to nearby Moline, Illinois. After obtaining a divorce in Reno in 1917, she used the name "A. W. Ehrens," the A. W. standing for Anne Whelan. Mrs. Ehrens moved to California in 1918 where she lived until her death on January 1, 1942.

Mrs. Ehrens was always very reticent about Elizabeth's paternity; in later years, this piqued her daughter's interest. Her mother wrote her in 1934, "For heaven's sakes, stop digging up what I have buried!" She destroyed her seventeen-year correspondence with Sam except for seven letters. In a 1913 letter, Sam notified her that he had sold her interest in the Wren place at Maryhill for $2,000 in Home Telephone Company bonds. In April 1914, he advised her that she would receive the income from $50,000 of these bonds, which some might have termed "guilt-edged." The bonds proved to be a slender reed. Potter, the phone company auditor, wrote her in May 1916, "Confidentially, it has been nip and tuck with us to get money enough to pay our bond interest at this time," but he arranged for the interest to be paid to her account. In October, however, the company could not pay the bond interest, so Sam advanced the amount to her personally.

After the phone company went into receivership in June 1917, Sam made Mrs. Ehrens the beneficiary of his six life insurance policies, which had a face value of $25,900. In an undated letter with deletions, she told Sam of her financial worries for herself and daughter, and that to accept the beneficiary status " . . . as a permanent arrangement is impossible." She added, "As always, I trust you in these matters. . . . I know the collapse of the telephone company is a drain on you, but this time, won't you arrange my matters safely for all time?"

When the Portland Home Telephone Company was sold to Pacific Telephone on March 1, 1919, the bond holders received seventy cents on the dollar, most of it in the 5% bonds of the Home Telephone Compay of Spokane, maturing in 1936. Sam instructed Potter to reinstate Mrs. Ehrens' income by holding the Spokane bonds for her in trust, and to send her a declaration of trust.

Sam sent her a note in 1920, dictated to Potter, about his gloomy financial picture: "Last year it seemed as if the whole world were going to smash, and for that reason life insurance policies were adjusted so that if everything else failed, there might be one anchor to windward. The situation today throughout the world has improved somewhat, but it looks now as if there were dark clouds ahead. No investment is sure. Railroad stocks may be wiped out entirely; coal mines, owing to high wages, have paid no dividends; the milk business [The Carnation Co. in Seattle] during the first six months will show a loss of about a quarter of a million dollars. The telephone bonds seem to be a reasonably good investment at this time."

Three years later, Sam wrote advising her to deposit her bonds at the Chemical National Bank of New York. He added this mysterious note: "The lady came here for money — a loan (?) — and left with it, and as to the man referred to in my letter, he is down and out, having, I fear, gone to drinking again, but he may recover." Perhaps the "lady" was the mother of one of Sam's other children and he had told Mrs. Ehrens of her existence.

In a letter to Mrs. Ehrens in October 1928, Sam wrote that he had reduced his working hours as president of the Alabama coal mine from nineteen (in 1926) to " . . . about 16 hours per day. . . . Poor Mr. Potter is a county charge in the hospital in Portland." It was not in character for Sam to neglect coming to Potter's assistance. Two months before that letter, Sam B. Hill was born, and Sam's attentions, and probably much of his ready money, were directed to providing for Mona Bell Hill and her son.

After Sam's death in 1931, the proceeds of his insurance policies were paid to Mrs. Ehrens. When her bonds, in trust at the Seattle First National Bank, matured in 1936, the money was reinvested for the benefit of her and Elizabeth.

Elizabeth attended schools in southern California and was graduated from Stanford in 1936. She worked as an architectural draftsman, an unusual career for a woman at the time, until she married an architect in 1940. They have three sons. Elizabeth continues to be a student of art history and an art collector.

She kindly furnished the author copies of her mother's letters. About these, Elizabeth wrote, "Her interesting and cheerful letters to her daughter show the warm and witty, gentle and generous side of her nature, although to the world she had presented a remote and melancholy mien. Her dignity of bearing never faltered. Pleasure in her daughter's academic achievement became the single solace in an otherwise sad and lonely life, and to that end she dedicated all her time and means." Though Elizabeth always admired her mother's solicitude for her and her courage in her prolonged last illness (Parkinson's disease), it was not until 1979 that she learned the reason for her mother's restraint and withdrawal. Annie Laurie Whelan's life was sadly blighted by the moral judgments and attitudes of her generation. One gets the impression of a Hester Prynne, atoning for a sin of passion or pity with a life of devotion to her daughter, Elizabeth.

It was not until the author wrote to Elizabeth Wade in May 1979, inquiring about correspondence and photos of Sam, that she had an inkling that Sam was her real father. She was most appreciative, rather than embarrassed, in discovering her paternity, and became very interested in pursuing information about her father. The author and his wife had the privilege of escorting Mr. and Mrs. Wade and two of their sons to Maryhill Museum in May, 1980. The emotional impact of seeing pictures and memorabilia of her father for the first time can be imagined. She and her family also met Mrs. Lois Plotts, who can recall Sam at Maryhill. These experiences and subsequent correspondence alone would have made the writing of this biography worthwhile!

The personalities of Annie Laurie Whelan and Mona Bell were as opposite as one can imagine. Miss Whelan was reticent and withdrawn, devoted to her daughter, Elizabeth. In her youth, Mona Bell, as Sam B. Hill, Jr. describes her, was outgoing, adventuresome, even reckless — not cut out for the role of conscientious mother.

Edith Mona Bell was born in January 1890 in East Great Forks, Minnesota. Her father was an alcoholic and her mother was obliged to support the family by operating a small grocery store. Mona, as she preferred to be called, left home at eighteen and got a job as a bareback rider in William Cody's Wild West Show. She became bored with this, and, dressed as a man, competed in bronco riding in a number of local rodeos. It was at one of these, when she was about nineteen, that she told two cowboys of her intention to get "prettied up" for a photograph to send to her mother for Mother's Day. They ungallantly laughed at the idea that she could make herself pretty and feminine, whereupon Mona challenged them to pay the expenses of renting a dress and having the photo taken if she could convince them she could to it. The cowboys at first were reluctant to believe the transformation, but when convinced, paid up.

Mona studied journalism at the University of North Dakota for a year, then went to work as the society reporter for the newspaper in nearby Grand Forks, North Dakota. About 1910, when Sam Hill came through town to talk about good roads, she covered the story. Sam offered her a ride home. She not only caught his eye but literally swept him off his feet. He was astonished when, on the spot, the small girl lifted his large bulk off the floor. He was so impressed that he asked her the date of her birthday,.and thereafter did not fail to send her a card or present on the date. After this encounter, they met occasionally through the years until establishing a close relationship in the late 1920's.

From about 1910 on. Mona Bell worked in New York for a firm specializing in streetcar advertising, and then for a dozen newspapers in Midwestern cities. Later, she was a society reporter for a San Francisco paper, but coveted an assignment as a crime reporter. One Abe Ruff, a suspected grafter, was being held incommunicado by the police, and she determined to obtain an interview with him. Through unspecified means, she succeeded. Her editor at first was incredulous when she brought him the interview and told him he could use it if he made her a crime reporter. She got the assignment becoming, perhaps, the first woman in this country to achieve this distinction.

Prior to the time Gertrude Ederle swam the English Channel in August 1926, there were others in training to earn fame by accomplishing this feat. Mona Bell, besmeared with grease, intrepidly swam the colder and rougher currents of the Straits of Juan de Fuca near Seattle.

Mona Bell at 19. This portrait won her a bet. (Photo courtesy of Sam B. Hill.)

Except for Sam, she had no lasting relationships with men. Sam B. Hill is convinced that his father stood as a father figure to Mona Bell and that Sam was the only man she loved. The photos of Sam and of their son were the only ones she continued to display in her home. Her first marriage was to a dentist and the second to a doctor whom she called "the butcher." In her eyes, he had earned the sobriquet by performing a Caesarean section on her instead of calling in an obstetrician. The baby, a girl, did not survive.

Sometime in the 1920's, Sam bought about thirty-five acres of wooded land lying on either side of the Columbia River Highway, about forty miles east of Portland. On this property, commanding a fine view of the river, he built a twenty-two room house for Mona Bell, probably in 1928. Being a garden enthusiast, she had the grounds planted with a great variety of flowers and shrubs, some of which Sam had purchased in Japan and which were new to the U.S.

Sam B. Hill was born in August 1928, in Multnomah County Hospital, Portland. The baby was legitimized through an arranged nominal marriage of Mona Bell with Sam's cousin, Edgar Hill, so that Sam could bestow his name on a son who, Sam probably hoped, would prove more worthy of it than James, now completely estranged from his father.

During Sam's last illness, Mona Bell tried to see him at St. Vincent's

Sam B. Hill, about age 10. (Photo courtesy of Sam B. Hill.)

Hospital, Portland, but was refused admission to his room. Undaunted by the hospital rules, she first dressed as a nurse, but was caught and ejected. Disguised as a janitress, however, she succeeded in gaining access to Sam. There is an unconfirmed story that she appeared because of wanting to persuade Sam to provide her with a larger financial settlement. Mona Bell, however, told her son that she never had such an intention.

In 1933, two years after Sam's death, the U.S. Army Corps of Engineers began to construct Bonneville Dam adjacent to Mona Bell Hill's property, and took over her house and land through condemnation in February 1934. The government offered her only $25,600 in settlement, and a court fight ensued. Mona Bell's realtors placed the figure at $100,000 or over. Oregon's governor, Julius Meier, an old friend of Sam's, testified to support Mona Bell's claim. The jury awarded her $75,000 and interest. The government appealed and the final award was $72,500 plus interest.

Sam B. Hill was six when he and his mother had to leave the house at Bonneville. They moved first to Hollywood and then to Mona Bell's birthplace in Minnesota. Sam was sent to a dozen primary and secondary schools, including two military academies, Culver in Southern California and Breck in St. Paul.

Not long after the court settlement, Mona Bell set off on a two year round-the-world voyage. She visited Osa Johnson, who had made photographic safaris in Africa with her husband. Mona resolved to organize her own expedition to the Congo and spent six months in Africa, covering some 7,500 miles. One can imagine the impression made by a woman, fearlessly or foolishly going on safari without the protection of a white hunter or knowlege of the language.

She told her son of an encounter with a Congolese tribe which her own bearers were afraid to approach. Carrying her movie camera, she walked alone into their village. She took down her hair and bared her breasts to show the warriors she was female. After taking movies, she offered by signs to exchange her bloomers for the beaded G-string worn by one of the women. The exchange was effected in the nearby undergrowth, to the amusement of the tribe. She continued her world-wide travels through 1939, collecting art objects and curios from many countries.

Sam B. Hill first knew the identity of his father when he was about fifteen, but his mother did not confirm this in so many words until he was over forty. He earned a B.A. in psychology and sociology at the University of Minnesota and a Master of Social Work at the University of California at Berkeley. After serving as a probation officer for Los Angeles County for ten years, he entered private practice with his wife as a counselor and psychotherapist. They have three children.

Francis Bacon may have been exhibiting his male ego in his wry saying, "He that hath wife and children hath given hostages to fortune; for they are impediments to great enterprise, either of virtue or mischief." Who can say what course Sam's life would have taken had he married happily and pledged his hostages willingly? James and his mother were released by their own choice, and there was then only Mary Mendenhall, a prisoner of her mental illness. How did he value the other hostages he gave later in life, his mistresses and the three children he fathered? He probably did not regard them as "impediments to great enterprises": the ransom he readily paid was for his own release from guilt through providing them with financial security. Conjecture is fruitless, since we know so little about Sam's relationship with two of the women, and nothing at all of the affair with the third. Nor do we know how they felt about him.

Sam undoubtedly had more than his share of ego, and regarded himself, with reason, as something special among men. Anyone with Sam's desire to be remembered by monuments might find it difficult to leave this world without siring descendants to pass on his unique qualities. Let us turn to another of his living monuments, Maryhill Museum, the "castle" of the title, and to its awakening to the fulfillment of Sam's dream.

Epilogue

The Castle Wakes

Sam Hill's monument, just down the hill from the Stonehenge Memorial, bears his epitaph, "Amid nature's great unrest he sought rest." Since his death, there must have been times when his spirit has been restless, indeed. The "castle" slept until 1938, before his dream of converting it into an art museum began to come true. During his lifetime the delay was due primarily to Sam's resolve not to complete and furnish the building until the State of Washington had finished a highway on the north bank of the Columbia which would afford easier access to Maryhill.

Soon after his death in 1931, the highway was completed but another cause for delay developed, the prolonged legal battle over his will. As Clifford Dolph, the museum's first director, wrote, "By the time the courts and lawyers finished with the litigation . . . a pitifully small amount remained." Sam probably had anticipated leaving to Maryhill a million dollars in stocks and bonds alone, but during the Great Depression, dividends stopped and the price of the bonds plummeted. As late in 1947, the market value of these was under $92,000. The museum trustees could expect no help from Sam's estranged wife and son, but had to depend on revenue from the cattle ranch and peach orchard near the museum and the small income from Sam's endowment.

The museum had been incorporated in July 1923, and the articles signed by Sam Hill as president; Edgar N. Hill; and Charles Babcock, who died in 1927 and was replaced by Zola Brooks. The Board was self-perpetuating and the first trustees, including Loie Fuller, were appointed by Sam. Edgar Hill, Sam's cousin, became president when Sam died. The other trustees were Mrs. Hazel Dolph Clark, wife of E. W. Clark, a Philadelphia banker, who had been appointed to succeed Loie Fuller; Robert Tierman of Paris, who resigned in 1935 and was replaced by Alma Spreckels; and Raymond Auzius de Turenne of Seattle, Belgian consul for the Northwest, elected in Sam's place in March 1932 and made vice-president. Attorney Zola B. Brooks of Goldendale was appointed by Sam as a director of the U.S. Trust Company and trustee of the museum. He was the son of Judge Nelson Brooks, who had been Sam's lawyer in the days of the "Promised Land." Zola Brooks was directed to draft a new set of by-laws in March 1932, at the first board meeting after Sam's death.

Because the other trustees lived in Seattle, Philadelphia, and Paris, it fell to Brooks to deal with ranch and estate matters and with the Washington Highway Depatment, which was finally building a road through Maryhill Ranch. He had to obtain court orders to get advances for such items as repairs to the museum roof and work on the roads around Stonehenge.

The trustees had a big job on their hands in completing and remodeling the unfinished chateau (which was not even supplied with electricity until 1938), and in organizing the many crates of art objects in storage at the museum and in warehouses, and even at the Brooks' home in Goldendale. The board did not get around to starting an inventory of its art objects until the fall of 1934.

Leverett Richards, an *Oregonian* reporter, was shown through the building in 1936 by Zola Brooks. The interior was as unprepossessing as it had been in 1929 (Chapter 23). Throughout the cavernous structure, steel studs extended from concrete floor to concrete ceiling, covered with metal lath. The original five miles of plumbing had not been properly drained during cold weather, and needed to be replaced by copper pipes, but the boiler could be operated. The elevator shafts were empty. From the great reception room, one could see to the south the Columbia River and the Oregon hills. On the north side of the room was a fireplace twenty-four feet long that lacked a mantle. The museum exhibits were in crates. Richards saw only one exhibit, too heavy to be moved, located under the west ramp of the building. It was the 3,000 pound shell, the first German shell to be fired in World War I, given to Sam by King Albert of Belgium.*

Brooks told Richards that his audit of the books showed that the construction costs of the building had been about $120,000 to date; another $50,000 would be required to finish it. The cost of remodeling and plastering the interior would be about $25,000; for new plumbing and finishing the basement floor, $5,000; and covering the rough concrete exterior of the building with sand-colored stucco another $8,500. Oak floors were to be put down throughout the building. Work on the remodeling finally began in 1938.

The board lacked funds to hire a professional director and adequate staff. Mr. J. M. Dolph, a brother of Hazel Dolph Clark, had an adopted son, Clifford Dolph, whom he brought to see Edgar Hill in 1938, when someone was needed to make showcases and tables and get the exhibits in order. Soon Dolph was hired by the trustees as director of the museum.

Clifford Dolph and his wife were the sole staff of the museum for the next few years. The season for visitors was from May to November. During the rest of the year, Dolph made the display cabinets, set up exhibits, installed book shelves, and took care of the correspondence and accounts. Hardworking, loyal, intelligent, and pragmatic, he was a fortunate choice for the new museum.

Emerson's epigram, "An institution is the lengthened shadow of one man" was probably not an intentional expression of male chauvinism. For Maryhill Museum, the shadows were those of the two persons who accomplished the most in transforming Sam's chateau into a museum: Clifford Dolph and Alma Spreckels.

Alma Emma Charlotte Corday le Normand de Bretteville Spreckels

---

*For the man who has everything, one's gift may prove to be a dud.

The Sam Hill plaque by Alonzo Lewis at the east entrance of Maryhill Museum. (Maryhill Museum files.)

was born in 1882. One of her ancestors was head of the French Army after the fall of Napoleon. Another was Charlotte Corday, who was guillotined for stabbing Marat in his bath during the French Revolution. She undoubtedly inherited some of the characteristics of both ancestors. Her family was aristrocratic but not rich. She got a job as a stenographer at age fourteen and later took night classes at the Mark Hopkins Institute of Art. In 1908, she married Adolph Spreckels who had made a fortune in sugar and shipping. The Spreckels built the California Palace of the Legion of Honor, and Alma donated her large collection of Rodin sculptures and sent many other works of art there. After she became a trustee of Maryhill Museum in 1935, she became its principal benefactor.

She had met Sam Hill in 1915 through John C. Lewis, a Portland wholesale grocer. She presented Sam to Loie Fuller at the Pan-Pacific Exposition that year. Alma also introduced Sam to Paul Verdier, owner of San Francisco's "City of Paris" department store, and to a number of other prominent people in the city. She entertained Sam when he brought Marshal Joffre and party to her mansion on his 1922 trip around the world. In 1926, Alma was to have been Sam's hostess in Seattle for Queen Marie, but she prudently withdrew when she saw a debacle in the making.

In February 1937, she wrote Zola Brooks, offering to loan her collection of Byzantine furniture, including Queen Marie's throne; the Queen's cloth of gold robe which she had worn at the coronations of the tsar and the king of England; her gold crown, gold goblets, photographs and paintings of royalty; a white porcelain dinner service; and other objects. She had acquired the lot for the bargain price of $12,000. These were only the first of a great many things she loaned or gave to Maryhill Museum. Early gifts included sixty-eight French World War I posters, and a mantle for the fireplace in the great hall from the William R. Hearst collection. After World War II, she sent a large collection of mannequin dolls, outfitted by the foremost couturiers of Paris.

Brooks wrote her to accept the acquisitions on behalf of the board and added that metal bars had been placed on the windows so that her gifts would be safe. Queen Marie's furniture and other artifacts remained in packing cases until 1938. When Sam's estate was settled, furniture, rugs, and other objects were sent from his Seattle house.

Trustee Hazel Clark now began to help set up exhibits. She had pungent words to say to Zola Brooks about all those portraits and memorabilia of vanished or vanishing royalty: "Having put a great deal of money in the past in the Maryhill Museum dedication, I feel, as a trustee, a right to voice my sentiment. . . . Both you and Clifford [Dolph] are not too eager to have the first floor of our fine museum look like a scene from a Balkan comic opera."

Alma Spreckels was always acutely aware of the fiduciary responsibilities of trustees. She was upset because she did not receive complete financial reports and lists of gifts to the museum, and so sent in a letter of resignation in June 1941. She was persuaded to stay on by Edgar Hill, but resigned again in 1946 out of dissatisfaction with what she considered unbusinesslike conduct of museum affairs. She reluctantly agreed, however, to stay on as honorary chairman of the board.

Mrs. Spreckels came to Maryhill for the museum's opening on May 13, 1940, Sam's birthday, and stayed with some other guests at the Meadowlark Inn. In its news report, *Time* called it, "The world's most isolated art museum." With some 49,000 visitors, its first season was a success when it closed for the winter in early November 1940.

When Edgar Hill died he was succeeded by D. B. Hill, another cousin of Sam's. Warren Berry, vice-president of the Seattle First National Bank, and D. A. Shelor, editor of the *Washington Motorist*, both friends of Sam's, were appointed to fill vacancies on the board in June 1946.

There is voluminous correspondence between Alma Spreckels and Clifford Dolph at Maryhill. In 1948 and 1949 the flow from San Francisco became a flood. Dolph gamely and politely replied several times a month. Her letters were nearly all handwritten; a few were typed by her secretary. There were days when she sent Dolph two or three letters and thirty-seven letters arrived in August 1948, alone! If Sam exhibited a manic state with acute graphomania early in 1923, Alma more than matched it.

She returned to certain themes many times. Among these were criticizing the conduct of museum and ranch affairs and the lack of reports and audits; pointing out the need for recruiting prominent business people and political figures to be trustees or honorary trustees; and actively soliciting gifts from potential donors (for example, from Mme. Gulbenkian — whose husband, the enormously rich oil baron, endowed an art museum in Lisbon but unfortunately did not become interested in Maryhill — and other wealthy friends of Alma's); starting a museum shop and tea room; appointing an art committee so that the museum would not be stuck with third rate acquisitions; and improving the appearance of the museum and its galleries.

One of her pet peeves was the presence of the carpets from Sam's Seattle house. "No museum has carpets," she sternly reminded Dolph many times, and finally succeeded in having them taken out. She had given the museum a portrait of herself by Richard Hall, and Dolph had postcards made of it. For some reason, Alma sent Dolph many requests to send these postcards and photographs of her various gifts to scores of wealthy friends and relatives. It is not clear why she did not have her secretary do this: the expense of postage could scarcely have been a consideration.

Dolph no doubt considered her many loans and donations ample recompense for responding to a fraction of her importunate letters. She sent Riviere and Malvina Hoffman bronzes and Gallé glass with explicit directions for their display. During 1948 and 1949, three van loads of art objects and furniture from her home and the California Palace were sent to Maryhill. She visited the museum with Paul Verdier in August 1948 and he left a watercolor of Loie Fuller. Alma's most valuable loan was Whistler's "Gold Scab" which she had bought from A. L. Gump of San Francisco. It was at Maryhill for several years and was loaned to other museums before she had it returned to the California Palace of the Legion of Honor.

Alma spoke her mind to the Maryhill trustees on many occasions. The spate of letters subsided after 1950, but she kept a watchful, benevolent,and maternal eye on the museum. Her long relationship with Clifford Dolph was a special one, with respect and genuine fondness on both sides. At her death in August 1968, her will transferred ownership of a formidable list of art objects and antiques to the Museum. Although her efforts for her first love, the California Palace, far outweighed those for Maryhill, Sam Hill's museum, for which she was angel and Argus, always held a special place in her thoughts.

The history of the Museum since 1940 deserves a book by itself, but except in the unlikely event of popular demand, this epilogue must suffice.

Not all the Museum's troubles occurred in its early years. The most notable was a prolonged and well-publicized hassle during 1967-77, centering on the responsibilities of the trustees and the new director, Robert Campbell. He was appointed after Clifford Dolph resigned in 1974 and was let go in 1976. Lawsuits and countersuits ensued, quietly ended after an agreement was reached and approved by the attorney general of the state of Washington. A reorganized board of trustees has supervised changes in procedures and handsome improvements in the display of the collections.

At this writing, the museum has not yet surmounted its difficulties with financing and staffing. There is a possibility that Washington State may be asked to take over its operation.

Today, one can imagine Sam Hill proudly escorting the three most important women in its history through his museum. Queen Marie would be pleased with the Grand Salon, filled with memories of the days of faded glory in Rumania. Alma Spreckels would no doubt be gratified with the exhibition of the many things she contributed, but would probably have a dozen suggestions before the tour was completed. Loie Fuller would be delighted with the display of the Rodin collection, which she did so much to acquire, not to mention the memorabilia of her own life. And Sam himself would come near bursting with pride over the fulfillment of his dream.

We have watched Sam "strut and fret his hour upon the stage. . . . " a bit part in the history of his time, perhaps, but played, if imperfectly, with passion and devotion. We can do no less than to preserve his intention and his memory at Maryhill, and in so doing, pay tribute to his indomitable spirit!

Sam Hill memorial on Columbia River Highway west of Crown Point. (Author's photo.)

Bibliography

Adams, J. Trudeau, *The March of Democracy*, Vol. 2, Charles Scribners and Son, 1932.

Auman, Wm. P,: *North Carolina's Inner Civil War: Randloph Conty*, (Thesis, University of North Carolina, 1978).

Barron, Clarence, *They Told Barron*, Harper and Bro., 1930, *More They Told Barron*, Harper and Bro., 1931.

Blow, Ben, *California Highways*, H. S. Crocker Co, San Francisco, 1920.

Bolitho, Hector, *A Biographer's Notebok*, The McMillan Co., 1950.

Commaerts, Emile, *Albert of Belgium*, The McMillan Co., 1935.

Cavanaugh and McGedrick, *Fundamental Psychiatry*, Bruce Publ. Co., 1953.

Conover, C. T., *Mirrors of Seattle*, Low-Hanford Press, Seattle, 1923.

Curie, Eve, *Madame Curie*, translated by Vincent Sheehan, Doubleday and Co., 1973.

Drawson, Maynard C., *Treasures of the Oregon Country*, Vol. 4, dba DEE Publishing Co., Salem, Ore., 1977.

de Caso, Jacques and Sanders, Patricia B., *Rodin's Sculpture — A Critical Study of the Spreckels Collection, California Palace of the Legion of Honor*, Charles E. Tuttle Co., 1977.

Douglas, Paul H., *In the Fullness of Time — The Memoirs of Paul H. Douglas*, Harcourt Brace Jovanovich, 1972.

Ellerby, Edmond S., *Marie of Romania*, St. Martin's Press, 1972.

Fie, Chester A., *Chief Joseph*, Wilson Erickson Co., Seattle, 1936.

Flanner, Janet, *Paris Was Yesterday*, Viking Press, 1972.

Fremont, John C., *Memoirs of My Life*, Belford Clark and Co., N.Y., 1887.

Fuller, Loie, *Fifteen Years of a Dancer's Life*, Maynard and Co., Boston, 1913; republished by Dance Horizons, N.Y.

Harris, Margaret Hale, text of *Loie Fuller, Magician of Light*, exhibition catalog of the Virginia Museum, Richmond, 1979.

Hill, James J., *Highways of Progress*, Doubleday Page and Co., N.Y., 1910.

Hinshaw, Seth B. and Mary E.: *Carolina Quakers — First Tercentenary, 1672-1972*.

Holbrook, Stewart A., *The Age of the Moguls*, Doubleday and Co., 1953.
The Columbia, Rivers of America Series, Rinehart and Co., 1956.

Holcombe, Maj. R. E. and Bingham, Wm. H., *Compendium of History and Biography of Minneapolis and Hennepin County, Minnesota*, Henry Taylor and Co., Chicago, 1914.

Hudson, Horace H., *A Half Century of Minneapolis*, The Hudson Publishing Co., Minneapolis, 1908.

Josephson, Matthew, *The Robber Barons*, Harcourt Brace and Co., 1934.

Lang, Margaret, *Where Nature Dwells*, White Rock, 1966.

Lancaster, Samuel, *The Columbia, America's Greatest Highway through the Cascade Mountains to the Sea*, The Killiam Co., Portland, Ore., 1915.

Lockley, Fred, *History of the Columbia River Valley from The Dalles to the Sea*, S. J. Claril Publishing Co., Chicago, 1928.

Martin, Albro, *James J. Hill and the Opening of the Northwest*, Oxford University Press, 1976.

May, Pete, Editor *100 Golden Years — 1872-1972*, Centennial Corp., Goldendale, Wash., 1972.

Meany, Edmond, S., *History of the State of Washington*, McMillan Co., 1909

Miller, Williams, *A New History of the United States*, Dell Publishing Co., 1968.

Nesbit, Robert C. *He Built Seattle*, University of Washington Press, Seattle, 1961.

Plotts, Lois Davis, *Maryhill, Sam Hill, and Me*, 4120 Olive St., Vancouver, Wash., 98660.

Popple, Charles S., *Development of Two Bank Groups in the Central Northwest*, Harvard University Press, 1944.

Pyle, Joseph G., *The Life of James J. Hill*, Vols. I and II, Gloucester, Mass., 1968.

Ruby, Robert H. and Brown, John A., *Ferry Boats of the Columbia River*, Superior Publishing Co., Seattle, 1974.

Rose, Albert C., *Historic American Roads*, Crown Publishers, Inc., 1976.

Turner, William, *To the Great Ocean*, Little Brown, 1965.

Wolman, B. B., Assistant Ed. Vol. 6, *International Encyclopedia of Psychiatry, Psychoogy, Psychoanalysis, and Neurology*, Aesculapius Publishers, 1977.

Wood, Charles and Dorothy, *The Spokane, Portland and Seattle Railway*, Superior Publishing Co., Seattle, 1974.

Index